THE CANADIAN REPORTER

THE CANADIAN REPORTER

News Writing and Reporting

SECOND EDITION

CATHERINE McKERCHER
Carleton University

CARMAN CUMMING
Professor Emeritus
Carleton University

Harcourt Canada

Toronto Montreal Fort Worth New York Orlando
Philadelphia San Diego London Sydney Tokyo

Canadian Cataloguing in Publication Data
McKercher, Catherine
        The Canadian reporter : news writing and reporting

2nd ed.
Authors reversed on first ed.
Includes bibliographical references and index.
ISBN 0-7747-3562-7

1. Reporters and reporting — Canada. 2. Journalism — Canada. I. Cumming, Carman. II. Title.

PN4781.C85 1998   071'.1   C97-932007-0

Senior Acquisitions Editor: Heather McWhinney
Senior Developmental Editor: Laura Paterson Pratt
Supervising Editor: Semareh Al-Hillal
Assistant Production Co-ordinator: Shalini Babbar

Copy Editor: First Folio Resource Group, Inc.
Cover and Interior Design: Matthews Communications Design
Typesetting and Assembly: First Folio Resource Group, Inc.
Printing and Binding: Transcontinental Printing Inc.

Cover Photographs: Ian Scott (middle) and Brian Gavriloff/Edmonton Journal (all others)
Part Openers and Chapter Openers Photograph: Brian Gavriloff/Edmonton Journal

This book was printed in Canada.

2 3 4 5 6   03 02 01 00 99

FOREWORD

Why do people go into journalism?

One fairly obvious reason is that the job is, almost by definition, *interesting*. Journalists go to interesting places and meet interesting people. Whether they're covering sports, the arts, politics or business they tend to be where things are happening: where people are reaching decisions, making changes or fighting small and large battles. Journalists covering a bizarre court case, a prominent sports event, a rock concert or an election campaign may sense that there are thousands of people in their city who would like to be at the event they're covering, but are tied to their offices or stores. Journalists, because of their trade, can *be there*.

What are the other attractions of the job? For some, journalism holds the promise of power or influence — a chance to change the world. It also offers the possibility of quick fame, or at least a public identity. Young journalists often find it heady when people recognize their faces because they're on the TV news, or know their names because they're on the front page or in the radio newscast. On a more substantial level, reporters may draw simple esthetic rewards from their writing or from creating a TV or radio documentary.

All these attractions compensate for the drawbacks of journalism — and drawbacks there certainly are. A journalist's life is stressful, the hours are bad and the financial rewards uncertain. The status rewards are significant but unstable. Society does not always look kindly on journalism. And unlike law or medicine, for example, journalism, at least the reporting end, does not tend to favor long experience. It is a game for young people. Many older journalists go on to become editors or public relations people, which takes them away from the more interesting edges of the craft. Others may become executives. The burnout rate is high.

To balance these drawbacks, novice journalists tend to think of the excitement and status. The more enduring personal rewards of journalism, however, probably come in less obvious areas. Above all, they lie in the opportunity it gives for *learning*. There must be few jobs in which the challenges are so varied and the process of learning so central. Consider: journalists are constantly seeking to find things out. They deal with people who normally know more about their topic than they do. They have to stretch their minds to brief themselves before interviews. They have to stretch their minds to understand what they're being told. And they *must* understand. It's never open to journalists to let information pass over their heads. They must insist on clarification.

Thus the essential ingredients of learning are all present. Reporters have both the need to learn and the opportunity to learn through contact with knowledgeable sources. But a crucial stage of learning is still to come: after they have asked the questions and heard the answers, their job is to organize and retell material in simpler terms, in a way that's likely to reinforce the learning.

Journalists seldom emphasize the learning aspect of their work. The reasons may have to do with group self-image — now changing fast, but still retaining a healthy distrust of pomposity. The old-time mystique of journalism was of course hard-bitten, cynical, bohemian — and very masculine. Journalists delighted in practical jokes, prided themselves on their irreverence, drank before noon. The few women who penetrated the ranks were regarded with suspicion at best. In modern times this image has been transformed, and not just by the gender revolution. Journalists now are seen as more serious people who admit to reading books — even writing them — and have a strong consciousness that what they do has an impact on their world. But journalists still think of their trade as something distinct. They think of themselves as outsiders who ask the rude questions that deflate balloons of hypocrisy. They see themselves as curious and irreverent and not too respectful of authority. Their self-image is close to that of the child who pointed out that the emperor had no clothes on. Although they often move in packs, journalists are strongly motivated to act independently.

The journalist's job is thus endlessly demanding and mindstretching. Journalists must build on a personal store of knowledge, using information to get information. They must be flexible, facing different people and different circumstances each day. They must be resourceful, devising solutions to new problems and challenges.

Can all of these skills and attributes be taught? Possibly not — but they can be developed, by anyone who has the intelligence and energy to undertake the task. It is with the idea of helping in that development that we have written this book.

A NOTE ON PRONOUNS

In reading this text you'll note that the authors have wrestled with one of the most common problems facing English-language writers, the lack of a neutral third-person pronoun.

In the past, common practice was to use "he" as the generic pronoun. Though grammatically acceptable, this practice is troubling because it tends to make women readers feel excluded.

Some modern authors deal with the problem by rewording to avoid the singular pronoun or by avoiding pronouns altogether. This works well in some cases, but in others it sacrifices clarity. For that reason we have chosen, in cases where a singular pronoun is desirable, to vary the gender — using "he" in roughly half the examples and "she" in the rest.

We feel this approach works well. We hope you agree.

PREFACE

In the five years since we brought out the first edition of *The Canadian Reporter*, much has changed in Canadian journalism.

When we began work on this project around 1990, few reporters had any notion that the Internet would become such a key tool for research, as well as a forum for publication of their work. Then, it was difficult to find a reporter who had an e-mail address; today, it's almost impossible to find one who doesn't. We have all had to master a whole new set of terms — search engine, Web site, net browser and so on — to equip us for collecting information electronically. And we've had to teach ourselves not just how to gather electronic information, but how to evaluate it.

If reporters' tools have changed, so have their workplaces. In the newspaper business, concentration of ownership has progressed to the point where a single company, Conrad Black's Hollinger International, controls most of the daily newspapers in the country. In broadcasting, years of cost-cutting have bled the CBC to a shadow of its former self. Private television, meanwhile, has been growing sleeker and more specialized. On radio, the news–talk format has brought a rude energy to the discourse of democracy.

The practice of journalism has shifted too, though perhaps more subtly. We may be seeing less investigative work and more personality journalism than we saw earlier this decade. At the same time, journalists are taking a more aggressive approach to crime and court reporting. In beat reporting, we are seeing more emphasis on issues and less emphasis on events. We are also seeing more diversity on the news pages as editors and reporters adapt to the changing character of the Canadian population.

In this second edition of *The Canadian Reporter*, we try to take into account some of these changes. We have included new material on using the Internet in reporting. We have made substantial revisions to chapters on research, writing and crime reporting, and we've produced a new chapter tracking the rhythms of a single day in a big-city newsroom.

This edition also reflects one final change: a reversal of the authors' names. While both editions have been produced by a partnership of the writers, the responsibility of direction has shifted to Catherine McKercher following the retirement of Carman Cumming.

Features of the Text

The shaping of this text is based on a belief shared by most journalism instructors: that all news media demand common skills and knowledge in many areas, including language, research sources, interviewing, story ideas and ethics. On another level, each medium has its own demands. While stressing the common elements, this text tries to identify differences in the way each medium approaches fundamentals, but it makes no attempt to cover the special aspects of *presentation* in, for instance, newspaper makeup or videotape editing.

The text draws (as does all journalism education) on a variety of disciplines: grammar, ethics, political science, law and library science, to name only a few. The aim is to apply material from these various fields to the journalist's special task.

Structure of the Text

Most reporting texts begin with discussion of the nature of the news business or of news writing, especially in newspapers. This text breaks with tradition by beginning with an intensive look at the fundamental approaches all novice journalists must learn, in such areas as simplicity, judgment, accuracy and respect for evidential rules. These approaches apply not only in every medium of journalism and in every specialty, but in every *stage* — from the reporter's first phone call to the last writing or editing touch.

Part Two and Part Three turn to detailed analysis of skills: the development of story ideas (an area sometimes overlooked), the use of research sources, interviewing and writing.

Part Four offers more intensive reportage on the news business generally, especially newspapers (the medium in which most journalists start out), and on the demands of particular beats. It begins with a chapter on a day in the life of a newsroom, then moves on to detailed chapters on general assignment reporting, police and court reporting, coverage of municipal governments and senior governments, coverage of sports and entertainment, and reporting on business and labor. It concludes with a chapter on freelance writing. While the discussion in this section relates mainly to newspaper reporting, we hope that in most cases (on courts, for instance, or business or entertainment) the material will be of use as well to beginning broadcast and magazine journalists.

Finally, Part Five addresses the difficult question of journalistic ethics, again attempting to cover patterns that apply in all news media. It discusses the nature and origins of ethics in western journalism, and emphasizes the development of a personal approach to ethical decision making. It offers as well a number of short ethics cases for classroom analysis, along with a tentative ethics code for discussion, and an extended reading list of articles on recent problems in ethics.

Throughout, the text relies heavily on examples and cases drawn from Canadian journalism and Canadian journalists. The sidebars, in which many of these are found, deal with everything from research strategies to the reporting of polls to organization of the major article. They include craft advice from a number of outstanding journalists such as Robert Fulford, Joey Slinger, Jan Wong, Edward Greenspon, Andrew Nikiforuk, Jim Romahn and Charlotte Gray.

Instructional Package

The text includes a number of features designed as learning aids, including an extended appendix on the most common language problems editors encounter and another on basic aspects of libel. It offers as well a glossary of terms and extensive examples drawn from Canadian newspapers and magazines.

ACKNOWLEDGMENTS

While the authors take responsibility for the final product, we are in debt to a host of colleagues and working journalists who have helped us with the project. They include: Ray Aboud, Ira Band, Eric Beauchesne, Bob Bergen, Claire Bickley, Stephen Bindman, John Blackstone, Agnes Bongers, Stephen Brunt, Carrie Buchanan, Don Campbell, Stephanie Chamberlain, Beppi Crosariol, Ian Darragh, Celia Donnelly, Tim Doyle, John Eberlee, Dale Eisler, Erin Ellis, Christine Endicott, Robert Fulford, Jock Ferguson, Carol Goar, Alison Gordon, Charlotte Gray, Steve Green, Edward Greenspon, David Hedley, Eva Hoare, Jeff Holubitsky, John Ibbitson, Mary Janigan, Bob Johnstone, Lynn McAuley, Gerry McAuliffe, Shawn McCarthy, Don MacGillivray, Angela Mangiacasale, Don Martin, Cathryn Motherwell, Andrew Nikiforuk, Kimberley Noble, Laura Byrne Paquet, Wayne Parrish, Steve Proctor, David Prosser, Dahlia Reich, Bob Remington, Gail Robertson, Kevin Rollason, Jim Romahn, Gillian Sadinsky, Harvey Schachter, Joey Slinger, Rosemary Speirs, David Lewis Stein, Larry Still, Ruth Teichroeb, Michelle Walsh, Judy Waytiuk, Paul Wiecek, Jan Wong, Dave Wreford, Max Wyman, and Geoffrey York.

We also thank Murdoch Davis, Sheila Pratt and the newsroom of the *Edmonton Journal* for letting us observe a day in their life.

We are grateful to Don Gibb and John Miller of Ryerson, and Mack Laing of the University of Western Ontario, for their contributions. Steve Simon of the photojournalism program at Loyalist College in Belleville was enormously helpful in rounding up photographs by Loyalist students, some of which appear in this edition. And we thank William Callaghan of Lawrence College, who shared his students' impressions with us. At Carleton, there are a number of people we'd like to thank, including Roger Bird, Sandy Forbes, Barbara Freeman, Alan Frizzell, Wilfred Kesterton, Lionel Lumb, Mary McGuire, Nancy Peden, Klaus Pohle, Dan Pottier and Bob Rupert, all of whom offered support, ideas, encouragement and, occasionally, editing help. We also thank Peter Johansen, who, as director of the School of Journalism and Communication, provided us with student researchers. Chris Armstrong, Kate Keating, Jon Ohayon, Barbara Plett, Uyen Vu and Klaudet White helped out with the research for the book. Jon Ohayon was particularly helpful in "field-testing" the first edition and offering suggestions for the second. Jen Ross devoted long hours and boundless energy to helping with the day-in-the-life chapter. We couldn't have done it without her.

We acknowledge the help of Carleton's Graduate Studies and Research Faculty in funding original research that found its way into the volume.

On behalf of Harcourt Brace & Company, we would like to thank the following people for their thoughtful and careful review of the manuscript at various stages: Lindsay Crysler, Peter Desbarats, Russell Elman, Doug Firby, Helen Hanna, Adrian Kennedy, Judith Knelman, Sat Kumar, Loren Lind, John Lott, Robert Martin, Eugene Meese, Walter Nagel, David Spencer and Peter Walls.

We are grateful to all the editors at Harcourt Brace & Company who have had a hand in the first and second editions of the text, including Dianne Horton, Semareh Al-Hillal, Dan Brooks, Chris Carson and Laura Paterson Pratt. They have offered support and thoughtful comments at every stage in the project.

We especially want to thank Betty Cumming and Vincent Mosco for their help and encouragement.

Finally, we offer a word of explanation: in this book we condemn loose writing, inaccuracy, incompleteness, unfounded assumptions and a host of other reporting sins. In doing so, we realize we ourselves should be as pure as saints. We know we are not — and therefore we plead in advance for forgiveness of our lapses.

A Note From the Publisher

Thank you for selecting *The Canadian Reporter*, by Catherine McKercher and Carman Cumming. The authors and publisher have devoted considerable time to the careful development of this book. We appreciate your recognition of this effort and accomplishment.

We want to hear what you think about *The Canadian Reporter*. Please take a few minutes to fill in the stamped reader reply card at the back of the book. Your comments and suggestions will be valuable to us as we prepare new editions and other books.

CONTENTS

INTRODUCTION

Active
Journalism

THE ADJECTIVES THAT DEFINE "GOOD" reporting in our time include these: informed, knowledgeable, independent, in-depth, interpretative, investigative — and, occasionally, *active*. The adjectives that sum up bad reporting include shallow, ill-informed and passive, the last term implying that someone other than the journalist decides what to report or how to shape it.

This text tries to address not just the basic mechanics of how to *do* reporting (how to cover a fire, a city council or a demonstration) but also *how to do journalism worthy of the first set of adjectives above*. In other words, the text aspires to produce reporting that is knowledgeable, intense, independent and active. Napoleon said every soldier should carry a marshal's baton in his knapsack. The aim of the text is more modest, but it is based on these two convictions: first, that reporters working on even the most basic tasks should have the full range of reporting tools at hand, and second, that they should constantly look beyond the immediate demand. Every court reporter should think not just about covering trials and convictions but also about how the judge was chosen, or whether a new pattern is showing up in drug possession cases, or whether several restaurant arson cases add up to a trend. Every business reporter should be thinking not just of annual reports and share transfers but also of less obvious patterns — the effect of pension pools on investment, for instance, or the defection of Western Canada from

Toronto's economic control. Rookie reporters have to make sure the basic tasks are done, and done well, before they venture into more challenging territory. But for their own sake and their employer's, as well as for their audience, they must be constantly broadening their view.

For shorthand purposes the authors of this book have chosen the term "active" to cover some of these broader qualities. We might also have called this "investigative" reporting, but the term is at once too ambitious and too ambiguous. It is too ambitious because, when done properly, investigative reporting takes much more time and effort and expertise than beginning reporters can command. It is too ambiguous because it is often used to describe hostile but shallow reporting. Among some Canadian journalists, too, a feeling has developed that investigative journalism is something more often talked about than done. Journalist Geoffrey Stevens once wrote that the way to identify Canadians at an international airport was to put up two signs in a corridor, one labelled *free love* and the other labelled *conference on free love*. Canadians, he said, would choose the conference. A similar point might be made about investigative journalism, that it is more honored in the conference room than in the field.

For all these reasons, we chose the less ambitious term "active" reporting, hoping that those who adopt it may graduate in time to investigative reporting. In large measure the kind of reporting we advocate is simply a product of reading, a curious mind, energy and broad cultural experience. But in every area of reportage there are patterns that novices need to learn, natural skills they need to hone. For instance, library resources and computer databanks become every day more extensive and more complex. Any reporter who wants to escape shallowness *must* be comfortable with those resources. Similarly, interviewing or writing techniques may depend mainly on individual talent, but some approaches work better than others — approaches to development of story ideas, for instance, or to story organization. A considerable body of professional knowledge exists that can help a novice reporter move beyond the merely routine.

Some (not all) of these patterns are learned better in college or university than on the job. The aim of academic training for journalists lies, of course, in combining the best of the journalism tradition, which works to draw new information from people's minds, and the best of the academic approach, which finds and analyses rich stores of already collected information (see Adam 1988). Both stress discipline and creativity, two aims that are by no means incompatible. The best architects or engineers, the most aggressive and creative and imaginative, must also have firm control of the basics. Schools of architecture must teach students to build a garage properly, while at the same time giving them the capacity to grow, to be the kind of architects who will eventually build cathedrals.

THE CRITICAL MIND

This aim — the desire to encourage reporting that is active, creative, knowledgeable and disciplined — informs the organization of the text. But it is shaped as well to help in developing what might be called *critical thinking*. That does not mean a simple pattern of nay-saying, of cynical negativism. Rather it means a capacity to analyse new developments in the light of knowledge already gained and a predisposition to challenge rather than to accept information passively.

For the best journalists, this critical view extends to a capacity to look within journalism to see its key weaknesses: its tendency to embrace conventional wisdom, its vulnerability to the influence of sources, its structural distortions, its tensions between commercial and public interests. Criticisms of this kind seldom appear explicitly in the text, but the craft advice relates directly to the need to be aware of — and resist — patterns like these:

1. **The tendency in journalism toward faddishness, or pack values.** It is the nature of the business that, as Anthony Westell (1976, 62) writes, competition induces conformity. The urge to "match" the opposition, the fear of being beaten, tends to keep reporters operating as a group. As well, every press corps and newsroom has socializing pressures that tend toward conformity. Reporters do compete actively, but in the nature of their work they also see a great deal of other reporters, in the press club or at news events. They hear more trade talk — about new ideas, or conventional wisdom, or rising and falling reputations — than some other professionals who work in relative isolation. In that setting it is hard to chart an independent path. The reporters who manage to do so generally base their independence on knowledge.

2. **Journalists' vulnerability to manipulation by sources.** In an age of television and image politics, and of public relations sophistication in government, it is difficult for reporters to stay away from the media events created to fit their appetites, or from the media relations officers who pass out a carefully filtered supply of information. And it is not just companies and government departments that pose this challenge: associations, churches, sports teams and universities have joined in, for reasons that make a lot of sense to the

organizations. From hard experience, they know it can be trouble-some to have their staff making conflicting comments when controversy strikes. From hard experience, they know some of their members may perform badly for media, especially television. Few people are trained in how to select and shape "news bites" or how to defuse or redirect public criticism, and hence the increasing reliance on a new profession of media relations people who seem, at times, almost to outnumber the journalists. It is always possible for reporters to get past this public relations funnel, but it can't be done by someone with only a few minutes to spare and no particu-lar knowledge of the area.

3. **The media tendency toward stylized, formulaic writing.** This pat-tern can apply to the inverted pyramid print lead (the traditional starting point in most reporting texts), or to the hackneyed television report that winds up with the conventional stand-up homily: "the future remains to be seen…" Again, the most knowledgeable reporter is the one most likely to have the scope to escape formula writing.

4. **Reporters' perceived lack of independence within the news orga-nization.** Journalists by tradition and inclination resist allowing anyone else — editor, publisher or pressure group — to dictate how a story will be treated. But the business hierarchy that controls news flow naturally makes for some degree of conformity. Top exec-utives typically don't tell reporters to slant their stories, but they do hire those reporters, and they prefer people whose views and demeanor are congenial to them. Again, reporters can best escape these effects through *knowledge* that brings them the respect of their peers and of their editors.

Personal Rewards

Finally, this text builds on the assumption that active, intense, knowl-edgeable reporting produces not only better journalism but also *more pro-fessionally satisfying* journalism. It is true that general assignment reporters who jump from area to area, covering an arts controversy in the morning and a business story in the afternoon, may enjoy the variety. But in most cases reporters who are thoroughly engaged in their own area, whether it's sports, entertainment, politics or the environment, find the process more educational and more satisfying. They are more likely to achieve the rewards discussed earlier: of gaining public recognition; of accomplishing reform; of experiencing self-education, adventure or esthetic satisfaction.

In recent years newspapers have widened the range of specialties to include such areas as computers, cars, singles, the environment and native affairs, along with the more conventional areas — education, religion, medicine, theatre, music, books, sports, politics, science, the workplace. The active approach is useful in all of these areas, but it applies as well to general assignment reporters, especially to those who *hope* to develop a specialty.

It is true, of course, that practicalities of journalism often dictate grab-it-and-write-it tactics. But that makes it all the more important that journalism students go into the trade with a conception of broader and deeper possibilities. The aim is to make the most of every opportunity, within the always-present limitations.

PART
one

FUNDAMENTALS

Training in reporting can start in many ways. It can start with the writing of news stories — the who/where/what of leads, for instance. It can start with development of story ideas, a process that comes before the writing stage. It can start with exploration of research sources from which the story ideas often spring.

Instead of picking one of these options, we have chosen to begin with a number of basic patterns in journalistic work. These are patterns that apply to all journalistic media, print and broadcast. They are also patterns that apply equally to what happens in the field and what happens at the keyboard. These patterns are part of the necessary mental equipment of a journalist's career, from the start to the finish.

CHAPTER 1

Fundamentals
of
Reporting

EVERY ART OR CRAFT OR PROFESSION HAS fundamental moves that newcomers must learn. In teachers college or acting school, instructors drill students on the importance of speaking toward the audience. In nursing school, students learn the importance of sterilizing instruments and making repeated accuracy checks as they administer drugs. Singing coaches repeatedly urge their charges to breathe from the diaphragm. In each case the need is fairly obvious, but students must learn the moves by conditioning until they become second nature.

Journalism has a number of fundamentals of the same kind. In newsrooms, most have long since come to be taken for granted, but for newcomers they demand basic changes of approach. They cover not just routines like selecting an appropriate story form and avoiding loaded questions, but basic steps on how to go about drawing a "story" from a mass of information. In most cases these fundamentals sound obvious as soon as an instructor states them, but they still need analysis, particularly to define how students can develop them. They relate to the following:

- simplicity
- synthesis
- judgment
- abstraction levels
- evidential rules

- accuracy
- completeness

SIMPLICITY

Most newcomers to journalism realize that the craft demands simplicity and clarity in writing, but the concept is much easier to endorse than to achieve. Part of the problem is that at least some teachers reward pompous, obscure writing. In university, students learn special languages and delight in displaying them. The result is forced writing like this passage in a student newspaper, commenting on disorder at an annual college football classic:

> Without going into specifics, there is a "kneejerk" reactional movement calling for the abrogation of the ... game. As a representative of the students, I am advocating its continuance for the simple reason that terminating the game through a moratorium is an absolutely impotent panacea. The crux of the issue is not the game, and any attempt to label it as such should be construed as indifference to pursuing a veritable solution.

> — *THE CHARLATAN, OCT. 29, 1987*

WRITING IN STYLE

When editors speak of "style" they're often invoking a special meaning — the particular standards or usage of the publication or program. In this context, "style" covers a variety of things, ranging from spelling (honour or honor?) and terminology (miles or kilometres?) to capitalization and abbreviations (PEI or P.E.I.?).

Style considerations raise frequent and furious debate in all newsrooms — including those of radio and TV stations, where the debate may be on pronunciations (SHED-ule or SKED-ule?). Often the debate is on more contentious points, in areas where social change puts pressure on language.

It took years, for instance, for "Ms." to become acceptable style. More years of debate have gone into the question of whether reporters should use "inclusive" terms (chairperson? chair?). Another area of contention is the appropriate language for a variety of groups: people with AIDS rather than AIDS victims, for example, or people who use a wheelchair rather than handicapped or disabled people.

But virtually all journalists accept that an agreed style there must be; it's not desirable to have a variety of spellings in one publication or a variety of pronunciations in one broadcast. In Canada, The Canadian
(continued)

Press's *CP Stylebook* (1995) is the reference most commonly followed, although many publications and broadcast outlets have their own style books.

For newcomers, learning style often seems an annoying task. Does it really matter, they ask, whether the name of the Canadian Wheat Board is capitalized? To this, the veterans reply, first, that you're going to have to learn style some time so it may as well be at the start; second, that with practice, it will soon become second nature; and third, that style errors are one of the quickest ways of annoying your supervising editor.

More important, perhaps, correct style is part of an overall professional approach. The reporter who is careful on style points is more likely to be careful as well on more important things, like facts.

This passage is typical of a certain kind of writing approach, perhaps flowing from teaching that encouraged a pretentious style. In journalism, the first task is to strip out these pomposities and develop the plain style advocated by George Orwell (1968), among others — a style that is simple and direct, designed to convey messages rather than to impress with "sound" and erudition. The discipline of stating thoughts plainly is useful not just for readers but for writers as well, forcing them to define clearly what they *mean*. As one of the characters observes in Robertson Davies' novel *The Manticore*, it is "much harder to get away with nonsense in the Plain Style than in the looser manner" (1972, 58).

How do you achieve this style? Consider an analogy: just as typographers use various typefaces (the typeface in wedding announcements, for instance, is quite different from that used in stock market tables), so all of us have in our minds various language *codes* or *types*. We have one language type appropriate for academic seminars, perhaps, and quite another for use while chatting with friends in the pub. In the pub chat, most people would not say, "It may be appropriate to contemplate a further libation in advance of our repast." They would say instead something like, "Let's have another drink before dinner."

The point is that using the plain style means reaching first for conversational language codes. This may seem obvious, but it's an important fundamental for anyone in the early stages of a writing career. It means that whenever you hesitate, wondering how to write a passage, you should shift ground and ask instead: what do I want to say? What do I want to transfer to my reader's mind?

This does not mean the writer must abandon a rich vocabulary. It does not mean writing exclusively for Grade 8 level. But it does mean abandoning the luxury of heavy, pedantic writing. It means writing of "doctors," not "medical practitioners," of "social patterns," not "societal paradigms." It means writing "before" rather than "prior to" or "in advance of." It means, as Orwell (1968, 134) puts it, not saying "In my opinion it is not an unjustifiable assumption that" when you mean "I think." The plain style in writing is not quite the same as conversation, which includes a great deal of repetition and body language. But a good test is to ask whether you would be likely to use a particular word or phrase in conversation. If you wouldn't say "prior to dinner" in conversation, it's best not to say it in writing.

One of the advantages of the plain style is that it improves the flow of your writing. If you are concentrating on what to say rather than how to say it, your thoughts are likely to connect more logically. Gaps in the flow will be more obvious. If you are concentrating on content, you are more likely to have firmly in mind the thought delivered two paragraphs back — and the one you plan to deliver two paragraphs later. You're also more likely to write in simple or compound sentences rather than in labored, complex sentences. You are less likely to run into diction or syntax problems. You are more likely (again quoting Orwell) to "let the meaning choose the word, and not the other way about" (138).

Some media sources or critics will, of course, complain that simplification means loss of precision, and sometimes they are right. In general, though, there is merit in William Zinsser's brilliant argument for simplicity. The secret of good writing, Zinsser says, is to clear out the clutter, to strip every sentence down to its cleanest components:

> Every word that serves no function, every long word that could be a short word, every adverb which carries the same meaning that is already in the verb, every passive construction that leaves the reader unsure of who is doing what — these are the thousand and one adulterants that weaken the strength of a sentence (1990, 7–8).

SYNTHESIS

This fundamental has to do with understanding the *whole* of your subject in a way that allows you to create a *unified image* in your mind and in your story. That means you must fully internalize your material — absorb it, make it your own — rather than writing in bits and pieces of your sources' language. Again, the point may seem obvious, but it is critically important. Novices write mainly by piling up source materials — interview notes, handouts or whatever — beside their keyboards, and then moving phrases or even paragraphs from the source material to the screen.

Accomplished writers use just as much source material, but they absorb it, digest it and then write largely in their own words. Anyone who doubts this should compare amateur writing with professional writing in leading newspapers or magazines. The latter will contain a much higher ratio of writer's language to source language. Journalists, as Walter Lippmann writes, "must have mastered the subject so completely that it becomes very simple in the statement" (quoted in Steel 1980, 201–202).

FULFORD'S GUIDELINES

BY ROBERT FULFORD

Robert Fulford has for many years been a leading Canadian editor, critic, commentator, educator and reporter. Asked to offer advice for beginning reporters, he responded with these points — many of which help to explain his own success as a journalist.

Some suggestions for a young reporter:

- Recognize that in almost anything you do there is a chance to be original and thoughtful. Don't lightly dismiss that possibility, no matter how trivial and routine the job may seem.

- Much of your time will be spent covering the obvious stories, those that everyone automatically covers. But never forget that the really good stories you write will be those you identify and discover for yourself.

- Don't be afraid to ask questions of your elders, even if you're afraid the questions are stupid. More experienced journalists will likely be flattered, and glad to help.

- Before interviewing anyone, find out in the library as much as you can about him or her. That seems obvious, but in fact it will probably put you ahead of most of the competition.

- Avoid the "inverted pyramid" story structure like the plague. It kills good writing by eliminating the possibility of surprise.

- You are the latest in a long line of men and women who have followed your craft, many of them admirable and historically important figures. Samuel Johnson, Charles Dickens, Rebecca West, Ernest Hemingway, H. L. Mencken, Mary McCarthy, and George Orwell were all, at one time or another, reporters. Search out their journalism in the library, study it, and try to understand what made it valuable.

- Get out of the library the three volumes of autobiography written by Hector Charlesworth in the 1920s and 1930s. He was a great journalist who could write

(continued)

about anything from a murder to a symphony performance, and he founded public broadcasting in Canada. Reading him will give a historical dimension to your understanding of Canadian journalism.

- Read two other books by great Canadian journalists, *The Man From Oxbow: The Best of Ralph Allen* (1967) and *Blair Fraser Reports: Selections 1944–1968* (1969). Allen and Fraser were exemplary figures, and reading them is an education in journalism.

- Read one extremely good newspaper every day.

- Remember that all good journalists in print or broadcasting (whatever their age, sex, race, national origin) have one thing in common: they read far more than most people do.

- Early in your working life, find a subject that matters to you and make yourself an expert in it. You may write on dozens of subjects, but your work will be better if you can write on one (or eventually two, or three, or four) with authority. There is another benefit: it is only by learning a great deal about one thing that we understand how little we know about everything else.

- Be grateful you are a reporter. There are few jobs more interesting.

- Don't let it slip your mind that people have died for your right to do what you do.

Mastering the subject means that the tone or "voice" of the article is more likely to be consistent. More important, the fully synthesized work is likely to reflect the research more accurately. That statement may be controversial. Novice writers often think they are being most fair to sources when they quote them directly. That is often true: a compelling quote can capture the essence of the source's thought and style. But the reverse also happens, and the reason this is so is central to understanding the importance of synthesis as a fundamental.

Again, an analogy may help. Consider the task of a landscape artist, confronted with a scene in which there are literally millions of things — pieces of data — to perceive. It is not enough for the artist to select one accurate piece of data from a tree trunk, another from a cloud, another from a rock, and squash them together on the canvas. The artist must apprehend the whole scene and reproduce it, creating a synthesis of the whole. This synthesis, of course, is not the original — it is a mental creation that represents the original. As semanticist Alfred Korzybski put it: "the map is not the territory" (Hayakawa and Hayakawa 1990, 20).

In a volatile world, reporters make the first judgment about *what happened.* But what they "see" may depend on many things, including their values and where they are located physically. This photograph was taken in Toronto in 1992. Is it a picture of police attacking protesters, or protesters attacking police? If the picture had been taken from behind the first row of protesters rather than from behind the police line, would it tell a different story? *(Toronto Sun)*

Similarly, a journalist who has spent all day covering a conference or court case has taken in millions of pieces of data. It is never enough to take a phrase here, a phrase there, and cobble them together in a news story. The reporter must apprehend the whole and produce a mental synthesis that is not the same as the original, but does justice to it. Precise detail and apt quotes set in context contribute to the synthesis, while accurate quotes torn out of context are a sign of amateur journalism and a horror to people quoted.

Good synthesis also gives a quality of *density* to a story. Of a "thin" story, people say that the writer seems to have gathered 20 facts and used 19. "Dense" stories, by contrast, read as though the writers know a great deal more than they're using, and have selected and connected with care.

JUDGMENT

The most important thing journalists do is not just report what they see and hear, but make judgments about what ought to be reported. At various times and in various news systems, those judgments differ greatly; but in any system only a very small part of what happens in society actually becomes *news*. The values by which such choices are made are largely hidden from the audience. Some of these judgments are based simply on commercial considerations, while others reflect a civic obligation to report the public acts of legislatures, courts, schools, hospitals, businesses and cultural groups. Some of the values that decisions are based on are personal, some institutional and some cultural, leading to constant debate about whether journalists can be independent or whether they are simply creatures of the news system.

Questions about news judgments thus pose endless problems; but despite this, it is possible to identify two fundamental points about the process of making judgments:

- Journalists do indeed have at least some scope to make judgments about what to report — possibly more than newcomers expect.

- Their judgments must be simple and natural, cutting through complexity to the journalist's own conviction about what ought to be told.

The first point deserves stress because newcomers to the craft may think there is a "right" way to make a judgment, to select a story or a lead, and that the purpose of journalism training is to discover that right way. Over time they find that they themselves must make the choices of what they deem to be significant, interesting or new (S/I/N). They choose from elements that are always much more varied and complicated than the eventual news story will be, and discard a great deal. As they cross the line that separates consumers of news from creators of it, they may well reflect that until now reality has been packaged for them — and that now they themselves have become the packagers.

Given this concern, new journalists trying to understand the judgment process can explore the media's approach from a number of starting points. They can analyse decision making in news industries, noting that some media give more attention to what's interesting (sex, scandal, bizarre behavior), than to what is, arguably, significant (a change in the law or employment rate). They can examine the idea that what is new varies by medium: magazine writers tend to go for the pattern that is new this month, while newspaper or radio reporters go for the event that is new today or in the past hour. They can analyse the factors that make a pattern or development "newsworthy," such as the impact of the news on audience members or the fame of the newsmaker. They can probe deeper and analyse the way news selection meshes with marketing by nurturing audience myths, fantasies or fears, or the way it supports or challenges the controlling sectors of society.

But when all of this has been considered, it may help journalists to return decision making to a simple and natural level based firmly on their individual understanding of the world, on their own views about what deserves to be told. This approach recognizes that any society has an orthodoxy, a conventional wisdom that no one entirely escapes. Journalists are useful only if they can identify that orthodoxy and go beyond it, bringing individuality and conviction to news judgments.

The same natural approach is important in the shaping of the message. This statement is based on the belief that the act of passing on news in face-to-face contact is a spontaneous one, familiar to all of us. The choosing and shaping of the message always reflects not just an informed decision on what is worth telling, but also a *judgment on what the receiver already knows*, and an *expectation of response*. When you pass on a piece of news to a neighbor ("I hear they're going to build a shopping centre down on the corner"), you assume the receiver hasn't heard the news yet, and you expect a reaction: "isn't that appalling," or "Isn't that fortunate." Next day, there is a natural evolution in the way you pass on additional news: "I hear there's going to be a department store in that new shopping centre." Again there is an assumption about what is already known, and what may cause the hearer to react.

For many reasons — including a tendency to analyse news values to death — the naturalness of this kind of face-to-face news-telling is often lost when people start to write the message. So when you confront the unexpected complexity of news judgments, try to cut through to the natural choice. If, for instance, you've been covering a day-long science conference, you can ask yourself what you've learned during the day that you would pass on in dinner conversation to a person interested in science. If you can't imagine sharing the message with one other person, it's highly unlikely you'll be able to put together a story that will interest a larger audience. Another technique is to think of what you would say about the conference if you had only three or four sentences to sum it up in a radio report. A third is to imagine what you would say to your editors if you called in to urge them to save a space on page 1, or in the newscast, for the story. All of these devices imply a kind of *projection* — an act of putting yourself into the hearers' or readers' mind to anticipate how they might react. That projection is natural in face-to-face communication, and crucial in interviewing and writing, as we shall see in later chapters. It is also a part of all news judgment. Projection depends on sound knowledge of the area you're reporting on, but it is also linked to a basic curiosity about the human condition, an empathy that allows you to identify what interests other people. These qualities nurture natural decision making.

The importance of individual judgment must be qualified by the recognition that both cultural conditioning and media competition produce not individuality but conformity. Three experienced reporters covering a conference for the same market may all select the same speech, or the same lead, because their experience tells them what is likely to be competitive. At the science conference, for example, all journalists present may recognize that a certain scientist is better known than others or perhaps more controversial. Or they will know that developments on a particular issue are more likely to be understood and debated than others. If Stephen Jay Gould is speaking on evolution in Conference Room A, it's highly unlikely the scientist in Conference Room B will get any attention, whatever the message. Such collective decision making protects the reporters, but is not necessarily *good* reporting, since it excludes people and issues that are less recognizable to editors or readers. The best journalists are those who spot as significant the pattern that neither their editors nor their readers have yet noticed.

Discussions of this kind still leave open the question of whether journalists, scanning the immense variety of patterns and events in society, can look to guidelines on what ought to be chosen. What exactly *is* news? What *should* be news? Can any authority dictate what can or can not be described as news? On a fairly abstract level, Stuart Adam (1993, 24) sees news as "a shift in the state of things" in the world beyond our senses, pointing out the reporter's role as scanner of the environment charged with letting the rest of the world know what is alarming, reassuring or useful. Peter Desbarats (1996, 128–33) discusses some of the patterns and pressures of news selection, citing studies that show journalists tend to select material that is relatively simple, that can be personalized or dramatized, and that is consonant with their expectations. When it comes to defining what *ought* to be selected, however, it is difficult to go beyond the general statement (expressed in slightly varying language by various writers) that news is the information people need to enable them to respond intelligently to their environment.

This definition places responsibility squarely on the journalist, who must, in the end, figure out what society needs to know. So the practical question remains: how is the judgment to be made? Journalism texts often discuss news judgment on two levels: the "who-what-where" approach and the "news values" approach. The first demands that a lead cover the basic "5 Ws" — who, what, where, when, why and, of course, *how*. Typically, the writer selects for the first paragraph the elements deemed to deserve immediate attention first, and then adds the others in the next two or three paragraphs. This device gives no guidance on how the main element is chosen, so it is of limited value. But in the press of writing it's easy to overlook one of these elements, so it's worthwhile, after the story has been written, to make sure they're all in place.

The "news values" approach invokes a number of criteria for evaluating news, such as proximity (Did the story happen locally?), prominence (Are the people well known?), impact (Is it going to cost readers money?) and visual impact (Are good photos, sound or TV footage to be had?). These criteria may be worth some thought, but can be reduced to a few simple questions: will this affect my readers' lives? Is it something they're likely to talk about? Will they react at all?

More formalized criteria are not only of limited use, but may actually be destructive, producing news that is narrow and conventional. More useful for journalism and society is the kind of reporter not bound by any such conventions, a reporter who reads and explores widely and finds a world filled with patterns and happenings begging to be reported. In a sense this suggests a paradox: reporters who are tuned in to audience concerns, yet independent in their news judgment. These are, however, the qualities of the best journalists. They often show up in what is called a "sense of story" — a conviction that some pattern or problem deserves to be explored. That sense of story brings with it a kind of excitement, or at least a confidence that the story is worth writing. Reporters who research and write with this kind of conviction find the task both easier and more rewarding.

Natural judgments, while they may or may not stand the test of time, reflect the best capacity and understanding of the journalist at the time the decision was made. These decisions balance an understanding of what the editor wants, what the audience wants, and what the source wants against a personal conviction of what ought to be told. Understanding the dynamics involved in natural judgments may also help in coping with frustration that arises from another paradox: journalism, when done well, *looks* easy. The choice of story, or story lead, once it is on the front page, seems inevitable. Only the journalist who produced it knows how many other directions it might have taken.

ABSTRACTION LEVELS

In all communication, we make statements that can be located on a sort of abstraction scale ranging from the concrete to the highly abstract. Consider, for instance, the following two statements:

> Jones won the association presidency with 35 of the 60 votes cast, Martin placing second with 18.

> Polls across North America show that more and more people are rejecting materialism and seeking new paths to spirituality.

The first statement is concrete, factual, verifiable. A jury of 12 neutral people, looking at the statement, would probably agree that it conveys the information clearly, unambiguously and "factually." By contrast, the second statement, even though it claims to be based on evidence ("polls show") is actually a broad generalization. What polls show these patterns? How many people were polled and how were they selected? And what *is* materialism, anyway? What poll responses would demonstrate rejection of it? The neutral jury would probably not accept the statement uncritically, since it piles abstractions on abstractions.

The suggestion here is that you can classify statements as fact, inference, judgment or opinion in a pattern like this:

Abstract	Opinion
↑	Judgment
	Inference
Concrete	Fact

Complex debates arise regarding these definitions (concerning what constitutes a fact, for instance), but in commonplace terms it is easy to identify the various abstraction levels. If, for instance, a student gets up and throws a tomato that hits the instructor in the face, you can report factually that student A stood up and threw a tomato that hit the instructor in the face. All hearers are likely to agree on the factual character of such terms as "tomato," "instructor" and "face." If you report, though, that the student threw a tomato *at* the instructor, or that a *discontented* student threw a tomato, you are going beyond what you perceived and making assumptions about the thrower's intention or state of mind. You are thus making an inference. If you say that the student threw a tomato at the instructor, *with great accuracy*, you move up into the realm of judgment. If you report that the student pitched the tomato, *wisely and courageously*, you have reached the level of opinion.

These levels need to be kept in mind, because novice reporters tend to write at high levels of abstraction. More experienced reporters keep their work farther down the scale. While some level of inference is inevitable in any communication, the fundamental that reporters must learn is to drive down abstraction levels, to write what they perceived, not what they thought about what they perceived. The weaknesses of high-abstraction reporting are often more clear in the long perspective. A classic case is the Vancouver *Sun* headline of June 29, 1914, which reported

> Archduke's death removes danger of European conflict.

On a more mundane level, one of our students many years ago submitted a story that began this way:

> Women's birth control problems may be over if research on a vaccine for women brings the hoped-for results.

Although not "wrong," that lead made a high-level inference ("problems may be over"). In more concrete terms, the student could have summarized her available information this way:

> A birth control vaccine developed in India is to undergo extensive testing with support of Canadian aid funds.

The danger of the high-abstraction lead is obvious when you consider that this story was written years ago — and women's birth control "problems" are far from over. Experienced reporters are more inclined to keep down the abstraction levels, if only to protect themselves from instant challenge or later ridicule.

EVIDENTIAL RULES

Every apprentice reporter undergoes the pain of getting stories back from editors with the marginal question (phrased in various ways), "How do you know this?" or "What's your authority for this?" or "Who says so?"

All these questions reflect the difficulty in learning another fundamental of reporting: respect for evidential rules. In the legal system, a complex body of law defines acceptable evidence, confining witnesses to matters that they state on their own knowledge and applying tests like these:

- Is the statement verifiable?
- Are any unfounded assumptions built into it?
- Is it internally consistent?
- Does the source have a vested interest?

THE ISSUE OF OBJECTIVITY

Objective: *external to the mind; actually existing; real...*(Oxford Encyclopedic English Dictionary, 1003).

Should journalists be "objective"?

If the term is taken at face value, meaning to make the effort to understand the reality outside our minds instead of working from subjective images already in storage there, it seems obvious that it is an admirable journalistic goal.

It is true, of course, that full objectivity is impossible to achieve. What we perceive is shaped by our cultural conditioning, by our language, by (in the case of journalists) institutional practices and values that come to be taken for granted. Yet it would seem axiomatic that journalists should try to understand these limitations and strive for objectivity.

The term has, however, become bogged down in confusion and controversy. In part that is because of the way journalists have used it. Historically, the term "objective" described the neutral, balanced, "just-the-facts" news that evolved after western journalism left behind the personal and partisan eras.

That new factual style was congenial to the monopoly newspapers, the wire services and the networks that had to speak to everyone in the community, not just those of one viewpoint. It was thus mainly a marketing approach, designed to avoid alienating anyone.

In this style, equal time was given to each party or to each side in a controversy. It didn't matter whether one side was right and the other wrong, or whether "reality" was something different from either version. Just reporting both sides was sufficient. While the pattern was called "objective," it was more usefully described by scholars such as Carlton McNaught as "specious objectivity" (1940, 75–77).

In modern times, many journalists have spurned it as well, rejecting the hypocrisy that equates neutral presentation with objectivity. Some critics (again thinking of presentation rather than research) insist that since perfect objectivity is impossible, it is better to recognize this and report from a frank point of view. Others argue, though, that it is desirable to strive for objectivity in *research*, even though perfection is impossible. They say that the constraints under which journalists work are no different from those facing scholars, scientists or judges; that objectivity is desirable for all these people and is not at all inconsistent with offering a point of view in *presentation*. Judges, for instance, often state strong points of view in their rulings, even though they have been rigorously objective in looking at the evidence. Reflecting that view, journalism as a whole has
(continued)

moved in the direction of allowing reporters, specialists in particular, to show their viewpoints.

That trend does not, however, remove the central question: if improved objectivity in research is possible and practical and desirable, how does a reporter achieve it?

This question has no simple answer. In part it is a matter of trying to identify biases or preconceptions, of setting aside a desire to promote particular causes and focusing instead on *finding out*. In part it is learning to understand how our language codes both affect and restrict perceptions, of trying to be *objective about our own subjectivity* (Justman 1983). It is a matter of intensity in research, of staying with the problem until the findings themselves begin to dictate what will be reported. Historian Barbara Tuchman might have been writing of journalists as well as historians when she said, "If the historian will submit himself *to* his material instead of trying to impose himself *on* the material, then the material will ultimately speak to him and supply the answers" (1982, 23). Historian Donald Creighton might have been speaking of journalists as well as historians when he wrote, "Every historian must have a point-of-view; but it will be valuable to his readers precisely to the extent to which it escapes from the parochial and transitory" (1948, 6).

So objectivity is partly a matter of intensity, depending on reporters'

levels of knowledge and depth of research, along with their willingness to find what is there, instead of making the outside world conform to what they already know. Few journalists attain the wisdom that will allow a future generation to judge them fully objective, but that does not mean they should abandon the attempt.

Several other journalistic patterns are commonly linked with objectivity, including

- fairness, in which major points of view on a current issue are given serious treatment and aired in more-or-less equal time;

- neutral, unloaded language, especially in stories by reporters without expert credentials;

- professional detachment in manner, in which reporters at news conferences, interviews or public meetings are careful not to seem partisan; and

- detachment from causes, in which reporters in their private lives are urged (or required) not to identify themselves publicly with controversial views, since readers might assume the reporter or publication is biased.

Some of these — the idea of fairness, for example — are deeply ingrained in the professional practice of journalism. Others are mostly practical matters, bearing on the public image of journalists and the news organs that employ them.

(continued)

Most owners or managers have policies on the points, meant to protect their circulation or their audience share. The policies may not be unreasonable, in a profit-based media system. They may even be socially desirable, especially for major media that have a duty to serve as a forum for a diverse audience. They should not, however, be seen as identical to objectivity.

In journalism the problem is less precise but no less important. Reporters soon come to realize that public discussion contains a great deal of half-truth or outright error, that people often state as fact things they don't know for certain to be fact. So, like lawyers (but more politely) reporters must constantly examine the evidential base for statements. If a source says, for instance, that "three-quarters of our municipal budget goes to education," it's never enough for the reporter to quote it and reply to any challenges with the answer "That's what the source said." On the contrary, the reporter must seek the *source's* evidential base. Without rudeness, it's possible to say: "that's an interesting statistic; can you point me to the actual figures?" Such challenges often disclose that the source doesn't have evidence for the statement, or that the evidence shows the source's summary statement is wrong.

In respecting evidential rules, reporters must constantly consider what statements a source is qualified to make, what other sources are more qualified or whether documentary sources are more reliable than live ones. If you're interviewing a Canadian farmer on acid rain, for instance, he may be an excellent source on the question of how his maple trees have degenerated. But if he says 60 per cent of Canada's acid rain damage is caused by Americans, the statement is of little value unless you can find its base. You could, appropriately, say that the farmer points to a study by biologist P. K. Smith indicating 60 per cent of acid rain comes from the United States. (More thorough reporting would demand a check of other studies, or of Smith's evidential base.)

In a variety of cases, then, reporters must phrase subtle questions that test the source's reliability. ("How close to the crash were you?" or "Could you tell me more about how you arrived at this conclusion in your study?") Sometimes they find to their dismay that sources are basing their statements on erroneous or half-understood news reports — setting up, in effect, a recycling of tainted information. More often the sources sprinkle conversation with unfounded assumptions. They may assume that because John Smith was born in Australia he must be an Australian citizen. They may assume that because Smith attended

Dalhousie University he must have graduated from it. They may assume that because Smith once supported free trade he still does. These false assumptions may not matter much in casual conversations, but they become a problem when they break into print. Reporters must therefore guard constantly against accepting them uncritically.

One aspect of the problem is the danger (and temptation) of quoting sources who may seem knowledgeable but who go at least slightly beyond their areas of competence: the teacher who defines school board policy, for instance, or the opposition critic who explains government legislation. In those situations the reporter must be rigorous in going to the source who *is* competent to speak.

Of course, no one expects the reporter to challenge every minor point a source makes or to cite authority for every minor detail. The best guide may be to imagine an intelligent reader absorbing your story. If you think this reader may question the authority for a statement, or wonder where it originated or how the source backs up the generalization, you

At the Oka confrontation of 1990, Alex Norris of the Montreal *Gazette* taps out instant history on his laptop computer. Reporters' first definitions of events are crucial; outsiders seldom realize the complexity of the choices. (Shaney Komulainen)

should cite the source and signal how you tested the statement. If reporters fail to challenge doubtful statements, they may find that they themselves are challenged when they get back to the newsroom. So it's best to learn from the start to build respect for evidential rules into your approach, developing a cast of mind that doubts and challenges, rather than one that accepts things uncritically. If you are lucky, you will have an editor who takes little on faith and makes sure you develop the same attitudes.

ACCURACY

Everyone wants to be accurate and means to be accurate. No pharmacist means to give the wrong pills to a customer. No airline worker means to put the wrong amount of fuel into a plane's tank. No reporter means to get a name or other fact wrong. But good intentions are not enough: in each case they work on, reporters must develop mechanisms to ensure accuracy. It's vital to realize how easy it is to get things wrong. Journalism instructors know that the accuracy levels among new students are low and that they must somehow inculcate the ideas that accuracy is important and that it demands a system of double-checks. Just as nurses must go through a three-stage check before administering a drug, journalists must check and double-check to ensure accuracy. That means, among other things, constantly checking on terminology or on shades of meaning. (Did the source say mortgage rates *ought* to come down, or *are likely* to come down?) It means taking legible notes even on material you *think* you'll remember, and noting a full source when you take information from a book or article. In an age when all journalists constantly tuck various bits of information away in their computers, it's vital to distinguish clearly between your own notes and lines or paragraphs taken from another source.

On a more basic level, accuracy means never assuming a name is spelled as it sounds. (A name that sounds like "André," for instance, may be spelled "Andrejs.") It also means knowing that it's easy to *hear* wrong, so the reporter must double-check, reading back the name or even showing the source a notebook with the name spelled out. It also makes sense (editors will try to catch you out on this one) to check sources' names in the general phone book or in specialized phone books. In part, this cross-checking process depends on knowing the references. More will be said on this subject in Chapter 3, "Research Sources," but the basic tools include the city directory, the *Canadian Parliamentary Guide*, the calendar of the local university, the staff phone directory for city hall, the atlas, the almanac, the postal guide — even the dictionaries that often include

INFORMATION BANKING

When it comes to storing information, many of us are like squirrels, stuffing pieces of information in files and boxes and ragged notebooks, then later wondering where we have left them. Anyone intent on practising full-time journalism can profit from a systematic approach to what might be called Information Banking — the saving of various kinds of information that will provide a payoff later. While each reporter's needs will vary, it is useful to create and keep up computer files of the following information categories:

Futures: Journalists make notes on coming events. If the committee on a new library is due to report in September, the journalist may make a calendar note for an Aug. 15 check to see how the report is progressing, and another for Sept. 1, and then Sept. 15, to see if the committee has completed its work.

Summaries: Months after a complex decision is made by city council or a hockey league, reporters writing summary copy find it difficult to remember precisely what was said. So they file tight summaries that they can retrieve quickly when they need a one-line or one-paragraph reference.

Story ideas: As we say elsewhere, many good story ideas never get done, because they're thought of in passing and never put on the list.

Quotes: While the non-journalist who hears or reads a trenchant quotation or anecdote may chuckle or nod appreciatively, many of the best journalists will take time to tuck the item away, knowing there'll come a day when it will be useful to drop into a story — or perhaps even inspire a column idea.

Facts: What was Canada's gross national product last year? What was its divorce rate? How many automobiles did it produce? How many tonnes of wheat? The best journalists, in discussion or writing, seem to have facts of this kind at their fingertips. That may be because they *literally* have them at their fingertips, in a computer file.

Sources: Just as they carefully store facts, so the best journalists keep close track of sources, recording not just the sources' names and numbers, but, as well, short notes on their backgrounds, biases and connections. In calling a particular executive assistant, for instance, it may be useful to know that she was raised in Saskatchewan, has a degree from Harvard Business School, and acts in Little Theatre.

One important side benefit of information banking is that by recording the material you refine it. Setting down a tight summary of a new policy helps you remember what it's about. Jotting down story ideas helps you think of how a story might be researched. Recording a name on your source list reinforces recollection of that person.

(continued)

The same principle applies to any kind of journal, whether it's a record of your academic life — new ideas encountered, books read, patterns observed — or descriptions of scenes and people from your personal life. The act of writing up your journal reinforces your memory.

The term "information banking" is an apt description for this kind of storage because it implies an investment of time for later reward. And, as in banking, there is little to be gained by wishing *now* that you had made the investment at some earlier time.

famous names like Adolf (not Adolph) Hitler or Sir John A. Macdonald (not MacDonald).

More broadly, accuracy demands sophisticated understanding of how error arises in communication. Chapter 4, "Interviewing," covers some ways of dealing with this problem. None of these tools will be of use, though, unless the journalist recognizes the importance of accuracy and follows standard methods of double-checking. Understanding the importance of accuracy in turn depends on a recognition that good-quality reporting *matters*. Editors become profoundly unhappy if they are forced to print even three or four corrections to the thousands of facts reported in yesterday's paper. They are aware that each error harms the paper's credibility and thereby makes it less useful and less effective.

COMPLETENESS

At first glance, the need for reporters to write complete stories must seem the most obvious of clichés. The point deserves emphasis because the habit of completeness is a developed one; it does not come naturally. Over time, reporters acquire the habit of pulling back often to look critically at the material they've collected or written, and to ask questions like these:

- Is it all there?
- Am I leaving questions unanswered?
- Are there important viewpoints on this issue that I've overlooked?
- Have I used the best sources, or only the usual ones?
- Is this the fullest version of the situation I can reasonably obtain, or should I hold the story over for another day's work?

These — not by coincidence — are among the first questions a copy editor asks in evaluating a story, so in a sense reporters learn to protect

FUNDAMENTALS

A checklist of reminders on fundamentals of news writing:

✔ Simplify. In your writing, draw mainly on the language you use in conversation, not on what you've been used to putting down in writing. Say "buy" rather than "purchase," "sell" rather than "market," "home" rather than "residence."

✔ Synthesize. Internalize the material and tell it in your own words. Don't tack together bits and pieces of your notes.

✔ Make a judgment about what's significant or interesting. Consider whether it's a natural judgment — that is, whether you can imagine passing the information on to even one other person. Shape your story accordingly.

✔ Keep down the level of abstraction. Tell what you perceived, not what you thought about what you perceived. Prefer concrete detail to generalizations, and facts to inferences.

✔ Respect evidential rules. On material open to challenge, cite authority. And find out from sources (politely) what *their* authority is.

✔ Develop ways to ensure accuracy. It's not enough to want to be accurate: you must build into your approach ways of making sure you are.

✔ Work on the habit of completeness. Before you turn in a story, ask yourself whether there's anything missing.

✔ Write every story with conviction, with a "sense of story." Write it the way you think it should be written, not the way you think the editor wants it. If your approach is criticized and the criticism makes sense, build it into your approach for next time — but write again next time with the same sense of conviction.

themselves by asking the questions first. A novice reporter about to turn in a story may find it useful to take a moment to play this mind game: imagine that you have just become a copy editor and that you're looking at your story for the first time. What other information does the story need? Another test is to imagine how the story will look to the people most interested in it. Might they find it unbalanced, incomplete? The importance of these fundamentals — simplicity, synthesis, judgment, abstraction levels, evidential rules, accuracy, completeness — is likely to become more clear with experience. All reporters become more accurate in time, if only to escape censure. Most reporters over time become more careful about evidential rules and more deliberate in judgment, as they look back with chagrin on stories they wrote that failed to stand up to the tests of time or public challenge. Novice reporters can develop respect for the same fundamentals by reading old newspapers and analysing their limitations. The exercise is often troubling, especially in defining how journalists are caught up in the conventional wisdom of their times, but it provides a salutary reminder of the hazards of the craft.

Respect for these fundamentals does not, of course, guarantee that a reporter will produce ultimate truth. At best, it allows a reporter to provide a quality of information that can be relied on to a certain extent in public decision making. But even that limited goal is one worth pursuing.

RECOMMENDED READING

Justman, Stewart. (1983). "Orwell's plain style." *University of Toronto Quarterly* 53(2), Winter 1983–84: 195–203.

Orwell, George. (1968). "Politics and the English language." In Sonia Orwell and Ian Angus, eds., *The Collected Essays, Journalism & Letters of George Orwell,* Volume 4 (127–140). London: Secker & Warburg.

Zinsser, William. (1990). *On Writing Well.* 4th edition. New York: Harper & Row.

PART
two

COLLECTING THE NEWS

Reporters are usually portrayed as doing two kinds of work: digging out information and then writing or telling the story. The reality is more complex, usually falling into these stages: getting the idea; digging out background; collecting live information; organizing the material; and writing the story.

People often undervalue the first two stages. This text gives them full-chapter treatment, as part of an effort to deal with problems and possibilities in each stage in the writing process.

Keep in mind, though, that the five stages are interdependent. Running into difficulty in any of the later stages may signal to a reporter a need to back up one or more stages to plug the hole.

CHAPTER 2

Story Ideas

T HE PROCESS OF JOURNALISM BEGINS WITH AN idea: a hunch, a question, a niggling thought at the back of the mind that some person or pattern or problem deserves to be explored and written about.

The process of identifying those ideas and translating them into journalism may seem to be more or less automatic. In fact, it is an important area of craft that journalists must develop.

This is one skill where instruction, training and practice can markedly improve your performance. In some other areas, effort seems to achieve little in the absence of native talent. But when it comes to generating stories, students can improve their performance dramatically by learning new approaches.

Clearly, a capacity to generate stories is vital. Most editors expect their reporters to come up with a steady flow of ideas. More important, it makes for both effective reporting and satisfying reporting. It may be fair to say there are two kinds of journalists: those who develop their own ideas and those who take assignments. The craft is probably more satisfying for the first group. They buy independence from sources, from editors — and from conventional wisdom. So the process of generating ideas cannot be taken for granted.

The essentials of an active approach to story ideas at first glance seem deceptively simple. The main guidelines go like this:

1. Invest time in developing story ideas systematically and imaginatively. Time spent on this task is time well spent. (Some students seem to think they're wasting time if they aren't interviewing or writing. They're wrong.)

2. Always work with a number of ideas, not just one, so that you can compare and evaluate, and so that you can stay flexible.

3. Frame ideas to show what you want to *find out* — not what you want to say — and cover not just the question or set of questions to be asked, but also possible sources and a possible audience. The formula can thus be represented as

$$Q - S - A$$

That means you're combining a *question* that needs to be asked, a *source* that may be willing to answer and an *audience* that may be interested in hearing the answer.

4. Emphasize ideas that seek developments, not just opinion.

5. Base your ideas on knowledge and show your sources that you're informed and have information to trade.

Let's now look at each of these points in turn.

INVESTING TIME

It may seem obvious that you can develop your story ideas systematically, but in fact, few beginning reporters, left to their own devices, will do so. They're much more likely to fasten on some area that interests them and charge ahead with it, whether it's been done before, whether they've defined a question that needs answering or whether the early research indicates that a good story is developing. Often the idea simply duplicates what was already done this morning on the CBC or in the *Globe and Mail*.

So, assuming you can develop story ideas systematically, how do you do it? At least six ways are worth remembering.

The Straight "Follow"

This is the bread-and-butter approach, in which you go to the files, journals or committee transcripts in an area of interest and look for issues that haven't been covered or have dropped out of sight and deserve to be revived. You find that a task force was set up six months ago. What has it done? A proposal was made last year. Has it been accepted? A program was announced two years ago. Has it been implemented? If not, why not? If so, have any problems developed in the original design? In any area, a few hours' work in the files will produce dozens of such potential ideas.

The Two-Stage Approach

Go to people knowledgeable in your area of interest and ask them what's going on that hasn't been reported. This is an easy and useful ploy that most students are reluctant to use, apparently because they don't want to seem to be beginners. In practice, it's productive not only in generating story ideas, but also in establishing contacts. Most sources are not hostile to someone who comes to them and says, "I'm just starting to work in this specialty and I'd be grateful for advice on what I should read, where the best files are and what issues need to be reported." That approach is more likely to get you through doors than an attempt to bluff your way into a substantial interview before you're backgrounded.

A Genuinely Creative Process

Let any stimuli (the objects in front of you, the casual conversation of friends) touch off fresh questions. For instance, imagine you're writing about hockey and thinking of ideas while staring at a computer screen. You might ask yourself: how have computers changed hockey? Are the records getting more complicated? Are trainers using computers to hone conditioning or nutrition programs? Can coaches or managers call up computer records of a particular player to look at discipline or weight patterns? None of these questions may produce a story, but they're the kinds of questions that can be found by deliberate brainstorming, alone or in a group. (For more about group brainstorming, see Osborn 1963, 151–158.)

Other creative connections come accidentally, when least expected. The important thing is to appreciate their value and follow up. Edward Greenspon of the *Globe and Mail* suggests that ideas often come when the imagination goes to work on material stored earlier in the mind. He finds that the creative associations that lead to stories usually come to him when he's in the shower or falling asleep. "So my advice is, learn to relax."

Observation

Some of the best story ideas emerge when you simply go and look. If you're writing about ballet, for instance, you should try to get access to rehearsals or to the classes. Ask to be allowed backstage. If you're writing about the elderly, it's never sufficient to talk to the social workers and bureaucrats. You must also go to the seniors' residences and use your eyes, while also getting to know some of the residents. More broadly, journalists constantly come up with story ideas in what they see around them in everyday life: in crumbling pavement downtown, in a theatre lineup, in algae collecting on a local river, in a garage sale, in a store closing. Other people may note such things and wonder about at least some of them. Only able journalists will consistently translate such material into story ideas.

Listening

Any experienced journalist can pull story ideas out of a social evening, a radio debate or a parent-teacher meeting. Dahlia Reich, then with the *London Free Press*, recalls one instance when she was working out at the YWCA and fell into conversation with a judge's wife who remarked that her husband was going to Vancouver for a seminar on sexual harassment. She followed up and found that the seminar was part of a much larger effort — at the time unreported — to sensitize judges to women's issues.

Watching for Spinoff Possibilities

Any active day of reporting will give a journalist who is alert to the possibilities a number of story ideas for tomorrow. Reich recalls covering the opening of a new women's shelter and discovering that the security system had cost $60,000. She worked up a full story on the security problems of such buildings. Another time she was assigned to an inquest into the death of an immigrant worker crushed by a tree he was felling. She used it as a starting point for a feature on whether immigrant workers were adequately trained for dangerous jobs.

TESTING IDEAS

The concept of working with a number of ideas simultaneously may seem obvious. Again, most newcomers won't adopt it unless they're required to do so. Their tendency is to work on the best story idea now before them, rather than building a bank of ideas. If the story goes nowhere, they're likely to report to their editor that they can't get a story today because a key source is out of town. This is a bit like saying they must go hungry because McDonald's is closed for renovations. When it happens, it's an indication that the reporter has fixated on one idea, rather than working with a number of story ideas simultaneously and making probes until one story develops.

Journalism students are not exempt from the common trap of wanting instant gratification. Once they think of a story idea, they're frustrated if they can't do it in the next 10 minutes. Most sources don't work in those rhythms, so reporters must learn to be flexible. It's the norm to be blocked on several story ideas before you find one that unfolds as it should.

When they're required to dig out a list of ideas, students find that their work becomes significantly more efficient. They're no longer caught wondering if they have anything at all to work on. They are able to choose from among a number of ideas.

And while the world is full of story ideas, some are better than others. It's possible to evaluate them only in comparison with other ideas. So as you look at your list, evaluate your ideas according to variables such as these:

- Is the idea light and featurish, or is it designed to draw out developments — something clearly new?

- What's the scope or breadth of the idea? Is it a short, sharp question that will produce a story in the next hour, or is it something so broad it will take a week of research?

- Are sources readily available?

- Is your knowledge level adequate?

- Are you competitive? There's not much point in doing a story you know is going to be covered by other reporters before you can get your story into print or on the air.

- Does the story idea have broad appeal? Are there elements of mystery or human interest to draw people in?

FRAMING QUESTIONS

Phrasing story ideas as questions rather than statements helps to overcome another chronic problem of novices. Many new reporters don't focus on finding out something new; they want to write about something they already know about and perhaps feel strongly about. They want to do a story on the Brazilian rain forest, for instance, and when their editor asks why, they will reply that it's an important issue that deserves attention. The editor's next question, of course, is, "What do you hope to find out?" Jaded editors may go on to observe that a reporter's job is usually considered to be one of collecting new information, rather than regurgitating what's already known.

The tendency to write what you already know is entirely understandable, given that many people go into journalism with the hope of changing things. Thus, they think of making an argument, pressing a cause. They realize gradually that the journalist's central task is to draw out new information. Their reformist tendencies may still emerge — in the attention they give to underreported areas, for example — but they move toward finding out rather than simply preaching.

Phrasing a story idea as a question also helps in narrowing the research thrust, and this is almost always necessary. Reporters just starting to work on foreign affairs, for instance, want to cover the whole gamut of Middle East politics in a single story. Those starting to write on social issues may want to consume the whole topic of public housing at a gulp. The set of narrow questions thus helps in developing a practical line of research, one that can be evaluated by asking: are sources readily available to answer this question? If I get an answer, will it probably provide a story? Is it an effective question with which to get a foot in the door?

The question or set of questions, if you keep it firmly in mind, forms a research *guideline* that keeps you on track (see Copple 1964). This means that if you ask the question and get a useful response, the shape of the story will begin to emerge. A good deal more research may be necessary, but it is likely to be tightly focused. (The inefficient alternative approach is to take a story topic, research widely, and then consider what you have to write about.)

More fundamentally, the focus on questions is important because it reflects one of the most typical characteristics of the best journalists: the habit of constantly asking questions of the world about them. For the able journalist, it seems, posing questions is more or less a state of mind. When they're reading papers, listening to news, attending church or hiking in the country, journalists constantly encounter things they wonder about. The non-journalist may (for instance) read a story about the resignation of the CBC president and store it away as a piece of information that deserves retention. The best reporters will read the same story and instantly ask a number of questions. Who will succeed the president? Does it mean any change of style or policy for the CBC? Does the change suggest any in-fighting within the corporation? Some of these questions will be unanswerable. Some may become story ideas, and some of these in turn may become actual stories. But the most crucial, and difficult, step lies in developing the kind of mind that questions constantly.

Beginning reporters must deliberately nurture this instinct to question — while they're reading, listening to lectures or riding on the bus. Some of the questions will be straightforward "follows": who will the new CBC president be? Some are creative, forging fresh mental connections. A reporter covering native affairs may see the story on the CBC president's resignation and think of questions with only a tenuous link: what's the future of the CBC in northern broadcasting? Are any native representatives serving on the CBC board? Has the corporation made any special efforts to hire native people in response to employment equity legislation?

No matter how the questions arise, it is essential to write them down. Many of the best story ideas are never done, because they're not recorded and are therefore forgotten. Others may be abandoned because the reporters don't have the confidence to follow them up, test them and firm them up.

GOING FOR DEVELOPMENTS

The guideline stating that reporters should go for developments rather than opinion is a standard rule for most kinds of journalism, but is especially important in print. In broadcasting, it may be possible to get interesting material from an exchange of ideas or a well-articulated viewpoint. For print stories, it's better to ask what people are doing, or have done, or plan to do. While all stories combine fact and opinion, guidelines based on specific actions or plans are almost always stronger than those based only on opinion.

WORKING FROM KNOWLEDGE

Another standard and vital rule of reporting is that you get information with information. That is why your story ideas should always be demonstrably based on knowledge. Anyone can go to a doctor and ask, "What do you think of the ethical dilemmas doctors face?" Only an informed reporter can go to a specific doctor and say, "I've been reading your report for the Medical Research Council's ethics committee on in-vitro fertilization, and I'd like to follow up on it, to find out whether your recommendations were adopted and how the profession has responded." It doesn't take much imagination to speculate on the kinds of response likely in each of these cases and the kinds of information each will produce.

All these concepts are so important in learning active reporting that a couple of reinforcing examples are in order.

SHARPENING THE IDEA

Example 1: A student proposed to do a story on native incarceration. When her editor asked what research she planned, she replied that she intended to speak with native groups and native affairs bureaucrats

Story ideas can come from many sources, including things reporters *see* that intrigue them. Here, *Edmonton Journal* reporter Jim Farrell finds out how roof thatcher Peter Caron goes about his job, at the Ukranian Cultural Heritage Village near Edmonton. (Ian Scott)

about the inordinate numbers of native people in prison, and ask why this isn't being corrected.

The editor argued that this guideline was open to criticism on the grounds that

- it is too broad; it's not calculated to elicit new information;

- it calls for opinion;

- it is slightly hostile, and therefore not the most effective initial approach to sources; and

- it is not based on knowledge (that is, any well-informed person knows that there are inordinate numbers of native people in prison, so the reporter gets no particular edge from knowing it).

After more background research, the student came up with this narrower guideline:

> Several months ago the corrections department accepted a recommendation that native spiritual leaders be allowed to take part in prison rehabilitation efforts, since standard programs were having no effect on native prisoners. Has this idea been put into effect? If so, with what results? If not, is it still in the works?

This is a better guideline because it's narrow, it calls for research into developments rather than opinion and it's based on knowledge. That last point makes it hard for sources to shut off the reporter. It's easy to imagine a response that would provide a story ("Yes, the program is in effect and working well," or "No — the implementation has been delayed because …"). In either case, or in the event of several other possible replies, the reporter will get a very quick indication of whether a story is to be had. At that critical point, she can decide to go ahead with the effort or abandon it. If she decides to go ahead, her remaining research is likely to be well directed. It will be clear what else she needs to flesh out the central theme. The actual story will already be taking form, as the reporter imagines how it will look on the front page, in the magazine, or on the TV news show. She will then find it easy to see what else is needed to complete it. This approach is more efficient than one in which the reporter chooses a broad topic, and researches various aspects, then decides what part of the research will be used to create a story. That way, too much material ends up on the cutting-room floor.

The guideline may change as the project develops and the reporter encounters more important problems or questions. In the case of the native prisoner rehabilitation story, the research thrust may even return at some point to the reporter's original concern: why there are inordinate numbers of native prisoners. But the story will not depend on source opinion about this well-recognized problem.

TIGHTENING THE FOCUS

Example 2: A student journalist proposed doing an in-depth story on child abuse. Asked how he would do it, he said he planned to interview psychologists, psychiatrists, social workers, teachers, police officers and hospital staff on the incidence of child abuse and steps taken to counter it. The editor turned down the idea on the grounds that it was far too broad and demanded at least the scope of a book. Also, it was not based on knowledge and was not phrased as a question.

Further file research defined a narrower idea, based on a two-year-old story about a doctor at Children's Hospital who had developed and started to use a system for recording suspect child injuries. The guideline then became the simple question of whether the system was working out well.

To test the difference between these two approaches, imagine yourself as a beginning reporter assigned to the child-abuse story. In the first case, there are a thousand ways the sources can put you off. They'll ask you if you've read the definitive three-volume work on the subject by Bloggs and Crippen — and if you haven't, they'll suggest that you do so before you start to interview. They'll tell you Professor Schlugg is the person you really want to see. They'll dazzle you with jargon, or tell you it may well be possible to grant you an interview next month, if you'll get back to them after their big spring convention.

In the second case, by contrast, it's almost impossible to imagine the doctor *not* answering. She'll be at least slightly flattered that you know of her work, at least tentatively respectful of your knowledge.

STORY IDEAS

A checklist of reminders on story ideas:

✔ Invest time in developing story ideas, systematically and imaginatively.

✔ Work with a number of ideas, not just one, so you can compare and evaluate, and so you have plenty of ideas to fall back on.

✔ Phrase ideas in terms of what you want to find out (the guideline), not what you want to say.

✔ Keep in mind not just the question, but also possible sources and possible audience.

✔ Go for developments, not just opinion.

✔ Make sure your ideas are based on knowledge.

She'll also realize that she is the logical person to deal with the query. It won't be easy to pass you on.

For all these reasons, the chances of getting a practical project going increase sharply. The guideline may still fade out, of course. The doctor may tell you her system is working well — and, in fact, was reported on in detail last month in a local paper. This is the most embarrassing possibility, and it's one you must take into account in the wording of your first approach. ("I'm working in the area of child abuse and was interested to read the story two years ago about your system of registering injuries. I haven't seen any later coverage of it, so I was wondering how it had worked out. …")

Again, a response from the doctor that the system is working well, or that it has been replaced or abandoned, promises at least the crucial edge of a story. Much more may have to be done. (Are other hospitals using the same system? At what point does the hospital seek co-operation from what other agencies? When and how is the decision made to intervene?) But the remaining research is narrow and efficient. It will be easy to see what else is needed to round out the story. And at each of the later stages you'll be operating from knowledge. You will have information to trade and a specific entree. ("I've been talking to Dr. Hameed at Children's Hospital about her injury-registering system for child abuse, and she mentioned that she's been working with your branch on intervention decisions. …")

In sum, then, the beginning of a professional approach to active reporting means posing constant questions as you read background, talk to people in your area or explore the area physically. It means reading a great deal more than most people do, and reading the things that others aren't reading, such as specialized or foreign magazines. It means reading with a pen and notebook at hand, so you can jot down ideas when they emerge. All of this means making an effort now for a benefit later. It's like spending some time studying the map before you head into the wilderness.

RECOMMENDED READING

Drobot, Eve, and Hal Tennant, eds. (1990). *Words for Sale*. Chapter 2: "How to Get Started." Toronto: The Periodical Writers Association of Canada and Macmillan of Canada.

CHAPTER 3

Research
Sources

THE MOST OBVIOUS WAYS REPORTERS GET their information are through interviews and observation. Another vital way of gathering information, and perhaps the most difficult to learn, is through the use of documents. The difficulty arises in part because technology is changing so fast, creating an enormous increase in our ability to store, find and transmit information. But researching documents is not just a matter of understanding the Internet or CD-ROMs; it is also a matter of learning what kinds of documents yield what kinds of information.

In the short term, the new technology may actually make it more difficult for journalists to find the best documents, as old systems fold and are replaced by an array of databases of varying quality and cost. This may tempt reporters to fall back on the lazy approach of reading a few news clips, and then phoning an expert or a spokesperson. In the long run, reporters who know how to find and use documentary sources — online or on paper — will have an immense advantage. Almost any area of reporting (fisheries, adoption, child care, pensions, and a thousand other topics) offers vast amounts of valuable and "nearly new" material that reporters are free to use. The information comes in the form of reports, studies, articles and hearing transcripts that flow from think tanks, companies, universities and, especially, government. The shelf life of this material is often short and the quality uncertain, but this makes it all the more important for reporters to learn to evaluate it.

Consider, for instance, the range of document sources underlying this lead:

THE GREAT MAMMOGRAM DEBATE

If you're baffled by recent conflicting statements on whether women under 50 should have annual breast X-rays, imagine the dilemma faced by doctors who must counsel patients based on the evidence at hand.

While the American Cancer Society has come out in favor of annual mammograms for women in their 40s, the U.S. National Cancer Institute looked at the same evidence and recommended against them, while many doctors say they can't decide. Through it all, Canada's health authorities, including the Canadian Cancer Society, have stuck to a long-standing view that there isn't enough proven benefit to recommend regular mammography for women aged 40 to 49.

At last week's World Conference on Breast Cancer held in Kingston, researchers said that with current techniques of screening, there is no right answer. ...

Meanwhile, the *New England Journal of Medicine* has declared the situation a "toss-up," and said doing nothing offers just as many benefits and risks as using radiation to look for early signs of the disease. ... Documents that came out in the U.S. debate about testing on younger women illustrate how a process that isn't perfect can actually cause more problems than it solves. ...

— WALLACE IMMEN, *GLOBE AND MAIL*, JULY 23, 1997

The variety of documents in a subject area such as breast cancer suggests that journalists starting to use the systems should first choose just one sector for exploration. Only reporters with some specialized background will understand (for instance) the stature in the health community of the *New England Journal of Medicine*, or the political bias of various think-tanks. This kind of specialized knowledge comes only with time and study. It may be of some comfort to journalism students that learning to use this kind of material is one area where their university or college training should give them a clear edge, not just in reporting but in journalism-related jobs like research, public relations or government information. While many people are now comfortable surfing the Net, few can track their way through legislative committees, medical journals or company annual reports.

GOVERNMENT INFORMATION

While most students are familiar with standard indexes, abstracts and compact disc collections in their school libraries, they may be less familiar with the vast amount of material that comes from government at all levels. This information is suspect to some extent — but all information contained in documents is suspect, not just because it may be outdated or may contain errors but because it is usually gathered and written to advance a particular point of view. Much government information, especially in agencies

Reporter Helen Plischke confronts a circle of electronic equipment in the "cop room" off the newsroom of the *Edmonton Journal*. Besides the regular computer and telephone equipment, the array includes three police scanners, a two-way radio to keep in touch with photographers and the city desk, and the Hot Line used by police to call all media simultaneously with information. (Ian Scott)

detached from political wars, is fully as reliable as that from corporations, news media or think-tanks. Federal, provincial and municipal bureaucracies, in fact, can be seen as giant structures collecting and organizing information, both on paper and in the minds of their experts. A great part of this material is readily available to journalists, who are free to find out more about it, reorganize it, simplify it and then publish it.

A few years ago, access to this information was more or less restricted to reporters in the national or provincial capitals. Increasingly, in the age of the Internet, fax and compact disc (not to mention good old-fashioned telephones and mail), that is no longer so. Reporters in Truro or Moose Jaw can check a variety of print or electronic directories and write or call to obtain material that is itself publishable, and also points to story ideas and interview leads. Technology is eroding the big cities' monopolies on knowledge.

It's easy to be intimidated by the task of identifying these sources and exploiting them, especially because they are changing and expanding so quickly. In time you'll learn that the effort pays. It often turns out to be more valuable than the equivalent effort in live research. But the first steps are difficult, and you should look on the effort as something that offers rewards mostly in later research, after the processes have become more familiar to you.

The prime rule is that you must never back off from the complexity. Never throw up your hands in despair, thinking the systems are too complicated to use. Ask for help and keep going, in the confidence that every move ahead will make the process easier next time. A second guideline is that live and secondary sources often interact. That is, reporters may ask a live source for guidance on finding the best and newest documentary material on a topic. Or they may use an expert's article as the base for an interview, expanding on some parts of it or updating as necessary. A third rule is that all research produces accidental reward — the three other studies you stumbled on while searching for a particular article, or the totally unrelated article that caught your eye and suggested a story idea.

DEFENDING THE WORD

BY ANDREW NIKIFORUK

While most journalists welcome computers as an aid in research, writing and distribution of news, veteran reporter Andrew Nikiforuk argues that the flood of facts they generate undermines a critical part of the journalist's task. The following was excerpted from The News *(Summer, 1990):*

The invention of the computer and the subsequent Malthusian multiplication of facts not only forced many of us to write faster but created a fearful paradox: it is now possible to know more facts and understand fewer and fewer ideas. As a consequence "writers" can now make a living by simply collecting and peddling pieces of meaningless data. The computer has transformed journalists into trivia processors, and many newspapers into dazzling puzzles of information.

Paralyzed by too much information and dependent on machines that feed our data addictions faster than a draw of crack, many writers have forgotten a lot of basics. Whether they are writing about budgets or widgets, the central mission of a writer is to defend the word, restore meaning, present ideas, interpret facts and tell the truth. ...

Instead of being information junkies, we must become the defenders and presenters of whole ideas. We must interpret facts, examine consequences, make historical connections, and generally find the sense in all the numbing nonsense that floods us as "information."

FRAMING SEARCH STRATEGIES

Librarians stress the importance of *search strategies*, to define what you want and how best to get it. For reporters the concept is useful in either live or document searches. In both, the process has at least two parts in which you define areas of interest and then use various techniques to narrow your search.

In live research, you first need to figure out what *kinds* of organizations or individuals can help you on a particular topic. For a story on park spraying, for instance, you might think of environmental groups first, then the environmental department at the city or provincial government, university biology departments, or the federal or provincial agriculture department. At the same time, you might consider which sources can point you to other sources — which person you know is in a good position to list the top local experts on herbicides, for instance. Could a university public relations officer point you to the right expert in the biology department? Could a local environment group tell you which city officers are most closely connected with the issue?

An RCMP official briefs reporters on a murder investigation. Scrums of this kind demand short, sharp questions, designed to cut through the confusion and misunderstanding that are often built into such encounters. (Mario Bartel)

The document search goes through parallel stages. You might first define what document collections would be useful. On the park-spraying story, for instance, you might want to look at the magazines of environmental organizations, academic studies from biology departments or government reports from agriculture departments. Again, too, you will also work in stages as you narrow the search. You might look first at an index listing of magazine articles or abstracts summarizing those articles, before choosing the ones that are newest and best shaped for your topic and your level of understanding. (For more about search strategies, see Ward and Hansen 1997.)

In general, document sources can be divided into those that lead to specific information and those useful for *scanning*. The former usually work through indexes, menus or lists, pointing on to second-stage work. The latter allow you to brief yourself broadly on a topic. For instance, using the first approach, you might turn to an index source to find out what has been written on genetic manipulation of cattle. Using the second approach, you might scan reports of the Royal Commission on Reproductive Technology to get an overview of trends in genetic manipulation. Specialized magazines and legislative committee transcripts are also useful for scanning — for thorough briefing on a topic.

The chapters in Part Four ("How Journalists Work") discuss some of the sources linked with particular beats. This chapter is meant to offer a practical short list of some of the best general sources available, with some advice on how to use them.

SEARCH STRATEGIES

At times as a reporter your search strategy is the essence of simplicity: you have a question you want answered, and you cast about in your mind to figure who might answer it.

Other times, on a major article or documentary, the process will be much more complicated, and it will help to look at possibilities more systematically.

For instance, assume you're thinking of a major article on immigration violations. You've been told of an increase in people entering the country illegally and being exploited in low-paid jobs. You want to know if this is a major problem and how public agencies are responding.

You now have the start of a tentative research *guideline*, but what's the next step? You could simply call the federal immigration department and ask to speak to someone who knows about illegal immigration. But the chances are you wouldn't learn much without some basic information already in hand.

(continued)

It may help at this point to draw up a list of the kinds of secondary and live sources you might use, keeping in mind that your research path will go back and forth from one level to the other. The kinds of sources might include the following.

Secondary Sources

- *Indexes* that point to articles already done on the topic, such as the *Canadian Index* or the *Canadian Periodical Index*

- *Abstracts* of studies or government reports, from tools such as the *Canadian Research Index* or *Academic Abstracts* (You'll find from various sources, for instance, that six western universities are conducting a major study of immigrant integration.)

- *Reports, press releases* or *media summaries* from the library of Citizenship and Immigration Canada

- *Transcripts of legislative committees* — for example, the Commons committee on citizenship and immigration (available online, and searchable by keyword)

- *News stories* from databases, such as *InfoGlobe Online* and *Infomart Dialog*

- *Summaries of document holdings* in Citizenship and Immigration Canada (These can be identified through a keyword search of *Info Source*.)

- *Books* (Along with your own library listings, check a tool such as the *Bibliography of Canadian Politics and Society* on CD-ROM or the Internet.)

- *Governmental phone listings* for departmental branches, such as those covering public affairs, media relations or workforce analysis at Citizenship and Immigration Canada

Live Sources

- *Government agencies*, such as the federal Immigration and Refugee Board

- *Social services*, such as the Catholic Immigration Centre or a municipal immigration services organization

- *Ethnic organizations*, such as the Caribbean Committee or the Somali Centre

- *Professionals*, such as immigration lawyers

- *Academics* who have studied immigration problems (check the local university information office)

- *Political parties' research staff*, or opposition MPs with special responsibility for immigration

- *Union bodies*, such as the Canadian Labor Congress, which may be concerned about health and safety issues, or the exploitation of illegal immigrants

- *Lobby groups*, such as the Canadian Civil Liberties Association

- *Police*, especially the RCMP

- *Church bodies*, such as the Canadian Council of Churches

- *Advisory groups*, such as the Canadian Ethnocultural Council

(continued)

- *Regional offices* of Citizenship and Immigration Canada (see *Info Source* directory)
- *Informal sources*, especially in areas where illegal immigrants may be employed, such as night janitor work

Once you have drawn up this list, your next step may be to decide how best to brief yourself in a general way. Your first step may be to call some of the available sources to ask advice on recent studies or legislative hearings or suggestions on the best-informed experts on the subject. Only when you've got command of the best and most recent material will you be able to start serious, knowledgeable interviewing.

Your research strategy may thus be conceptualized in this form:

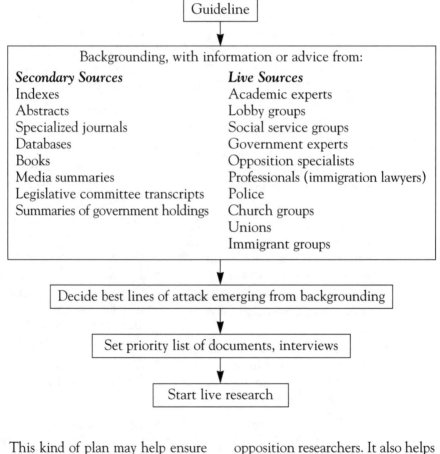

This kind of plan may help ensure you don't overlook some potentially useful sector, for instance, the labor unions or academic and opposition researchers. It also helps you set deliberate priorities, rather than simply going for the first sources that come to mind.

Sources in the Newsroom

Most newsrooms have libraries, some still known as "morgues." Their quality varies immensely, but most have topic files on past stories (often on computer), obituary profiles on leading local residents and such reference works as the following.

City Directory This is not the familiar phone directory, but a more complex directory that lists residents by street and occupation, as well as alphabetically. The directory has a number of uses, and every new reporter must become familiar with it. You can, for instance, use the city directory to

- find neighbors (if there's a fire or hostage-taking at 22 Harvard Avenue, you can quickly find who lives next door at number 20, or across the street at number 21, in a search for witnesses);

- trace people whose telephones are unlisted; and

- trace (by consulting past directories) marriage or employment histories.

Sources: The Directory of Contacts for Editors, Reporters and Researchers This is a regularly updated national volume containing an indexed countrywide listing of journalistic sources — in effect, a contact list giving the public relations officers for businesses, lobby groups, associations and other service-sector organizations. It's a useful guide to experts in almost any field, but the organizations listed have all asked to be included, and this is a limitation.

The Canadian Almanac & Directory **and equivalents** These almanacs, some of them online, list associations, publications and a variety of other information. They are useful for checking names of towns, universities, associations, judges and a host of other things.

Handbooks of Quotations *Bartlett's Familiar Quotations* and *Colombo's Canadian Quotations* are typical of the kind of indexed reference in which you can find quotations covering everything from *ambition* and *angels* to *superstition* and *tobacco*.

The Canadian Parliamentary Guide This source not only gives biographical summaries of current MPs and senators, but also has details on past elections, a listing of members of the Parliamentary Press Gallery and other information. *The Canadian Parliamentary Handbook* is a similar resource available both online and in print.

Directory of Associations in Canada More comprehensive than the almanac list of associations, this directory includes information about contact people and publications and has an extensive keyword/subject index.

The *Matthews Media Directory, Matthews CATV Directory* and *Canadian Advertising Rates and Data* These are the most up-to-date listings of media executives across the country.

LOCAL GOVERNMENT SOURCES

In addition to internal telephone books, many city governments publish a broad range of directories and reports helpful to reporters. In the Ottawa area, for example, the regional government produces *Master Contact List of Community Organizations* with names and contacts for hundreds of community groups. Local governments also publish directories of available services, and books and pamphlets on how things work — how to apply for social services, for example, or how the budget dollar is raised and spent.

Since local governments rely on property taxation, they are also the best source for information about land ownership and use within a municipality. Tax assessment rolls, compiled by the province to assess land taxes, are available at the town or city hall. They indicate the names of the owner or owners of the land, the exact dimensions of the lot and the assessment — the number used as the basis for calculating property tax. You can also use these assessment rolls in tandem with the provincial land registry files to do research on the history of ownership of a piece of land.

Municipal halls are also the place to look for school support lists, voters' lists for local elections, building permit records and so on. This information can be useful in *pattern* stories or in stories about individuals.

FEDERAL AND PROVINCIAL DOCUMENTS

For many journalists, not just those in federal or provincial capitals, an important resource is the set of regularly updated government phone listings, as a source of experts in a variety of areas. Human Resources Development Canada, as an example, offers listings for the National Adoption Desk, Old Age Security Programs, the Youth Affairs Group, the Occupational Safety and Health Branch. Health Canada has listings for the Office of Tobacco Control, the Bureau of Chemical Hazards, the Bureau of Nutritional Services, the Laboratory Centre for Disease Control, the Bureau of HIV/AIDS and STD, among scores of equally useful offices. Clearly, the federal phone listings are not of interest only to political journalists or to Ottawa journalists.

Anyone who doesn't have access to government phone listings (online or in print form) can get advice on which department handles a particular topic by calling Reference Canada or an equivalent provincial office, such as

- Communication Quebec,
- New Brunswick Inquiries,
- Provincial Inquiry Centre, P.E.I.,
- Citizens' Inquiry Service, Manitoba,
- Access Ontario or
- Inquiries B.C.

(Some of these agencies cover both federal and provincial sources.)

As with any directory, government phone listings can be used for a variety of purposes. In courses on investigative reporting at Carleton University, John Sawatsky and T. Joseph Scanlon have advocated comparing new and old phone listings to determine, for instance, who has recently joined or left a particular agency. A person who has just retired or been shifted to another job may be an excellent source. The same may be true of the person who has just arrived, and therefore is not committed to defending the actions of predecessors. Comparison of phone listings can also help in spotting organization changes — the creation or disappearance of a branch, the expansion of staff in a particular agency. (Ironically, such comparisons may become harder to do as governments move from phone books to online listings, and print versions become more difficult and expensive to obtain.)

***Info Source*: Sources of Federal Government Information** *Info Source*, available in print form, on CD-ROM and online, is the key to locating material under the Access to Information Act and the Privacy Act. More important for reporters are the descriptions it offers of documents grouped under various subjects. These descriptions give an indication of the responsibilities of various sectors, and suggest areas reporters may want to explore.

Below are two descriptions from the 1996–97 *Info Source*, the first from the Solicitor General of Canada and the second from Health Canada:

Institutional Corrections

Description: Information on incarceration and on topics arising as a result of sentence to a prison term, including information on specific programs, research and statistics. *Topics:* Long-term incarceration; classification and typologies; inmates' rights; health care; correctional investigator; dissociation; grievance procedures; riots; hostage taking; suicides; independent chairpersons; life skills; trade and professional education; treatment program; living units; remission; rehabilitation. *Program Record Number:* SGC COR 045

HIV/AIDS and STDs

Description: This bureau conducts national surveillance and research of the epidemiology and laboratory sciences related to HIV/AIDS & STD; directed at identification and quantification of risks, assessment of proposed prevention strategies and the evaluation of existing surveillance, prevention and control activities. Investigation of HIV and STD disease outbreaks are carried out as well as development of recommendations for their control. The bureau guarantees the quality of HIV testing in Canada, introduces new HIV testing technology and develops guidelines/recommendations for HIV and STD control in Canada through the coordination of a network of scientific experts, public health officials and advisory committees/working groups. *Program Record Number*: HCan 003 131

Until a few years ago, *Info Source* was accompanied by a useful index of topics showing which departments or branches dealt with each. That index has now been abandoned, but those who use *Info Source* online can get the same benefit with a keyword search, which will take them, for instance, to the record groups that cover pesticides, pensions or parks.

By itself, of course, the record group listing does not help much, since it doesn't even guarantee the records described are accessible. But it may suggest lines of attack, pointing to documents that are already in the public domain. It may, for instance, provide terms for a keyword search through government documents in the *Canadian Research Index*, or through academic/scientific reports in a database like *Academic Abstracts*, which has citations and abstracts of articles from 775 periodicals in various disciplines, or through hearings and reports of the relevant committees. *Info Source* can also provide the basis for a call to the relevant information office, where a journalist can ask for advice on the latest and best studies relating to STDs or prison grievance procedures.

One other point: *Info Source*, as noted earlier, is the basic document for formal applications under the Access to Information Act. These applications usually mean some cost and delay, and are normally not made until a reporter has a clear line on documents that have not been released. Some reporters have made the access act one of their key reporting tools, but in general it is most useful for specialists who have a good deal of independent knowledge of an area, who have already worked through the information routinely available and who have the time to wait for several weeks or even months for responses. (For more on this, see the discussion by Jim Romahn on pp. 279–282.)

Departmental Libraries All federal departments and most agencies have libraries or reading rooms in Ottawa and in some regional centres as well. Most of them are accessible to journalists, and most are extremely useful for specialists, because they contain documents from the recent past — the up-to-date reports or transcripts produced in the last weeks or months. Many provincial departments also have libraries, often containing federal information as well. Some university libraries have extensive government documents sections, but none has the full range held by specialized government libraries. For instance, most departmental libraries have press clipping collections and departmental announcements, as well as transcripts of the proceedings of relevant committees (more information on these sources follows). In some cases departments have more than one library: Health Canada, for instance, has no fewer than four in Ottawa, covering areas such as environmental health and disease control, as well as a scattering of branch libraries in other cities. The departmental chapters in *Info Source* set out each library's holdings. (The information in these chapters is often outdated, as government constantly reorganizes, but it provides a starting point for live inquiries.) National libraries whose material is available online and whose role might not be readily evident include the following:

- The Canada Institute for Scientific and Technical Information (usually shortened to CISTI, pronounced "Sisti"). This library is operated by the National Research Council and is a massive source of information on science, technology, and medicine. It can be reached from anywhere in the country online or at the general number, 1-800-688-1222 and provides copies or loans from its collection, as well as referrals to experts and database searches.

- The Sport Information Resource Centre (SIRC). Located in the same Ottawa complex as the national headquarters of various sports bodies, it contains a great variety of information about everything from sport medicine to financial support for athletes. Its *SPORT-Discus* database, listing publication references from hundreds of sources, is available online and through most major libraries on CD-ROM. Researchers normally use the database to get a list of references, such as article or report titles, and then seek out the documents in their own libraries or get them from SIRC through a service called SPORTExpress.

In addition to searching specific databases, reporters can use the World Wide Web to find sites that are points of entry to a variety of databases. Some of these sites represent years of effort by individuals or organizations to catalogue Web resources that reporters might find useful. One example is the *Database of Canadian Databases*, put together by the Ryerson Institute for Computer-Assisted Reporting in Canada.

Other such sites are more limited but still useful to the reporter, such as the Government of Canada Web Site, or the *Government Information Finder Technology (GIFT)*.

Legislative Committees One of the most useful and productive information resources is the committee transcripts of Parliament and the legislatures. Records of debates in the Commons, Senate or legislatures — known informally as *Hansard* — can also be useful, especially because they are indexed by topic on a daily basis, and also on a periodic cumulative basis. That is, you can look up the most recent index (online or in print form) and find out when gun control was discussed or when a particular MP spoke and then refer to the volumes containing the actual debates. Those references are useful in pinpointing which legislators are interested in your topic, but they are often fragmentary — including perhaps a question and quick reply, containing more rhetoric than information.

By contrast, the transcripts of parliamentary committees typically contain rich veins of information. The committees can call before them the best available experts and can demand detailed, factual information on every conceivable topic. The experts usually organize and present the material with care, while the legislators examine it critically. For these reasons, the transcripts contain a blend of information, which is much more useful to the reporter than what could be obtained from a long interview. The information is, of course, always dated to some extent, depending on when the committee met. But it often provides an excellent base for live research. Any reporter launching a major research effort for a series, documentary or magazine article ought to check to see whether there has been a recent study of the topic by a legislative committee. If such a study exists, it's likely to be a mother lode of information — both its transcripts and other documents, possibly including commissioned research studies or the committee's own reports. For instance, an online search of documents from the Special Senate Committee on Euthanasia and Assisted Suicide will yield not just hearing transcripts, written submissions and the final report (*Of Life and Death*, 1995), but also substantial appendices covering topics such as palliative care in Canada, or assisted suicide in The Netherlands. Such documents can be searched by keyword, and useful sections can be e-mailed to your own computer. Reporters looking for story ideas will also find a limitless supply in committee reports. In fact, these documents probably represent the most commonly overlooked reporting treasury in the country. They're available in many university libraries as well as in the specialized departmental libraries.

Media Reviews Most federal departments spend a good deal of money putting out daily collections of what the media say about them. The collections, sometimes available in regional offices, may include broadcast transcripts as well as newspaper and magazine articles. So if you're interested in, say, pay equity, it makes sense to find out whether Status of Women Canada or the labor ministry has a media review with pay equity indexed. If so, you can quickly read what's been published and broadcast on the subject in the last week, month or year. This step helps in defining what's already been done, so you can direct your research to questions still unanswered. It also provides factual information and leads on points that need to be updated, plus possible sources, live or secondary. Because the material is all media reportage, it's not as useful for quoting as government documents. But it is easy to scan and absorb, in contrast to some of the more authoritative governmental or research studies. Often it's a good starting point, leading on to more precise research in the heavier documents.

Statistics Canada At first thought, many people might see "StatsCan" as a repository for rather dry and dull stuff. In fact, it has emerged in recent years as a good storehouse for pattern information, not just in economic areas but in fields as varied as sports and crime. Unfortunately, it has also become more costly and complex to access, meaning that (unless you're willing to pay) it is sometimes easier to find a description of an interesting study than the actual study results. While working reporters can usually circumvent such costs by asking that material be sent to them by fax or e-mail, thus avoiding online costs, journalism students are not as lucky. (It's true that the agency has an arrangement with universities to provide material at a special collective rate, but such material is barred from re-sale.)

Despite these problems, Statistics Canada is an extremely useful source for journalists working in a society that thirsts for seemingly objective measurements. In recent years, to cite just one instance, the agency has launched a massive "longitudinal" Survey of Children and Youth that will follow a sample of children over many years and gather an immense variety of data, including math and vocabulary test results, health characteristics, family and custody history, dwelling and neighborhood characteristics, and parenting style in the family (supportive or critical). Its early results have shown, among other things, that children born prematurely are more likely to show slower motor and social development, and that hyperactivity is the biggest risk factor in delayed math skills. More controversially, it also reported that a child growing up with a single mother, whether or not she has a low income, is 1.5 to 2 times as likely to show emotional and behavioral problems, or academic and social difficulties. The study thus illustrates the problems that appear when the agency moves beyond "provable" figures, such as how much coal was mined last year, or how many marriages ended in divorce. Critics

In publications like *Canadian Social Trends*, Statistics Canada uses graphs, charts and photographs to put a human face on its statistics. (*Canadian Social Trends*, Autumn 1996, Cat. no. 11-008-XPE. Reproduced with the permission of the Minister of Supply and Services Canada, 1993.)

are quick to ask what can be defined as an "emotional problem," or what constitutes a "supportive parenting style." StatsCan defends such labels by pointing out that it often does studies of this kind in collaboration with other agencies that have expertise in the area. But the potential for controversy remains and tends to extend to journalists who report on such material. The agency typically includes explanatory notes when it releases data, for example, warning that its often-quoted "Low Income Cut-off" (LICO) figures should not be interpreted as a poverty index.

Most StatsCan measurements are less controversial, for example, those showing that 112,000 new motor vehicles were sold in April of 1997, or that traffic deaths tend to be high on Saturdays in January and February. The agency's main commercial database, called CANSIM, has about 600,000 such statistical measures, open to anyone willing to pay a general subscription fee plus a few dollars for each specific search. However, much of the material is distributed free, through regular announcements and through publications like *Canadian Social Trends*, *Canadian Economic Observer* and *Perspectives on Labor and Income*. While transferring many of its publications to electronic form, the agency says it plans to continue the print form of these "flagship publications."

For online searches, the best starting point is the StatsCan Web site (http://www.statcan.ca). The following is a typical entry:

Immigrants in Canada, selected highlights
Occasional, Paper.
The publication presents a comprehensive portrait of immigration since 1852 and of Canada's immigrant population today. It examines the immigrant population's demographics, education, place of birth, labor force activity, income and citizenship, as well as selected family and household characteristics.

Basic information of this kind is free to anyone, under the "Canadian Dimensions" category, but the best material is found only in the commercial CANSIM database. The agency is also developing an expanded database called CANSIM II (to open around the year 2000), featuring not just raw data but also links to what it calls "metadata," information about underlying concepts, collection methodology, data limitations, etc. This kind of context may help, though it will never cure, the problem of varying interpretations, increasingly of a kind that are driven by interest groups. For instance, from one set of measurements released in 1997, two reporters produced these contrasting leads, neither demonstrably wrong:

AGING SOCIETY SHAPES NATION

Old age is creeping up on Canadians, a trend that has implications for everything from pensions to the structure of the health-care system.
    Data released yesterday from the 1996 census show people aged 65 and over

made up 12.2 per cent of the population in 1996 compared with 11.6 per cent in 1991 and just 8.1 per cent in 1971. ...

— OTTAWA CITIZEN, JULY 30, 1997

GREYING OF CANADA OVERSOLD NOTION

New census figures indicate that the pace of growth in Canada's population of senior citizens has slowed markedly, and demographers say it is bound to continue slowing for more than a decade until the baby boomers begin to hit retirement age.

In fact, panic over the so-called greying of the population and the supposed burdens it will inflict on Canada is at least 15 years early, demographers say, despite the flurry of policy changes being made in the name of aging.

"There's scapegoating going on," said Susan McDaniel, a demographer at the University of Alberta and one of Canada's foremost experts on the aging population. "There are these myths of the aging population scarfing up health care resources."

— GLOBE AND MAIL, JULY 30, 1997

The contrast between these stories shows clearly the challenge reporters face in putting statistics in context. It also shows the importance of critical analysis and the value of competing media. And it suggests the way statisticians and the press sometimes combine to affect both public opinion and public policy.

Private indexes   *The Canadian Research Index*, for instance, provides abstracts and actual copies of a great range of government documents, mostly federal and provincial but also including some municipal material. It covers more than 140,000 documents published since 1982, and allows you to search online or on CD-ROM for titles by keyword or keyword combination (for instance, fish and British Columbia). If a title looks useful, you can then call up the abstract, which gives a bit more detail. A typical abstract looks like this:

A Review of the Young Offenders Act and the youth justice system in Canada: report
Federal-Provincial-Territorial Task Force on Youth Justice (Canada). Ottawa: The Task Force, 1996. v, 651 p. French ed. (*Examine de la Loi sur les jeunes...*): 97-01929/8.
MICROLOG 97-01899 (7 fiche)
Presents the work of a task force that undertook a comprehensive review of the Young Offenders Act and its application by profiling the youth justice system in Canada, identifying problems, and making appropriate recommendations. Six broad priority areas were examined: inter-relationships and co-ordination with other agencies and community resources; matters related to diversion, pre-trial detention, community-based sanctions, and custodial processes; legislative and program issues; administration and sharing of costs; matters related to due process of law; and information-related matters including publication of young

offenders' identities and information sharing. The justice system's treatment of special types of offenders such as Aboriginals and females is also addressed. CA CI JU ND PR SA SS

To obtain the actual report, a researcher can follow various channels: microfiche in many libraries, online databases or departmental libraries.

Library of Parliament Publications At the request of parliamentarians or on its own initiative, the parliamentary research branch of the Library of Parliament regularly produces factual background papers on a variety of current issues. These are distributed to some other libraries. If a recent one has been done on your topic, it's likely to be extremely useful.

CHALLENGING THE POLLS

Public opinion polls are sometimes called a basic tool of "precision journalism," because they explore systematically some patterns that reporters (or politicians or scholars) usually define only on the basis of gut reactions.

On that level they are indeed useful. Newspapers are increasingly using them, along with detailed content analysis of public records, to measure attitudes and patterns. The results often provide a useful challenge to conventional beliefs.

Sometimes, however, polls themselves are open to challenge.

A 1991 Angus Reid poll on medicare done for Southam News asked respondents:

Tell me whether you support charging a $5 user fee for every visit to a hospital emergency room, in order to discourage people from abusing the system.

As critics soon pointed out, the phrase "in order to discourage people from abusing the system" loaded the question and brought a predictable reply: 71 per cent of respondents were described as in

favor of user fees (Ottawa *Citizen*, May 16, 1991).

The case suggests that journalists using poll results should look carefully at how the questions were asked, to detect possible loading. Minor changes in wording may produce radically different results. (See Wilhoit and Weaver 1990, 7–9.)

As well, they should consider these matters:

- *The sponsor of the survey.* Was it commissioned by an association or group with a particular ideological position? Is the polling company associated with a particular political party?

- *The size of the sample.* Social scientists generally agree that a properly drawn national sample of 1,200 to 1,500 respondents will produce a response that corresponds with a high degree of accuracy to the views of the whole country. Beyond that level, the benefits of further polling flatten out quickly. But watch out for results drawn from only (*continued*) part of the sample: a national poll of 1,400 Canadians may show a valid pattern in their views about capital punishment, but if responses are reported from provinces or particular groups, they will be much less reliable.

- *The way the sample was chosen.* Pollsters have elaborate mechanisms for drawing a "random" sample of the population to be polled. The aim is to provide a faithful reflection of the whole group, taking account of region, language, sex, age and so forth. Pollsters normally use what is called "stratified" sampling to ensure they choose numbers of respondents proportionate to the total number of men and women, anglophones and francophones, and so on (although actual respondents within each of these strata are chosen randomly). "Sampling error" is the extent to which the results are presumed, under laws of probability, to vary from what you would get if you interviewed the total population under study. It is usually expressed in a line in the news story saying something like this: "In 19 of 20 cases, these results would differ by no more than four per cent each way from the result that would be obtained by interviewing the total population."

  (Journalists sometimes grossly misuse the term "random sample," referring to a "random" poll when they've interviewed half-a-dozen people in a shopping mall.)

- *How the poll was administered.* All types of interviews have built-in limitations. Phone interviews can include a broader sample of respondents than face-to-face interviews, but the response rate is much lower. In face-to-face interviews, respondents may reply in what they see as a "respectable" way — claiming, for instance, to spend more time reading the editorial pages than the comics. They may also react to the pollster if there is a racial, cultural or gender similarity or difference. Self-administered mail polls have very low response rates and may be skewed, or distorted, because those people who take time to fill out a questionnaire (or who are sufficiently literate to do so) are unrepresentative.

- *When the poll was taken.* Did it come before or after a major news development that might change public views?

- *What response rate was recorded.* A low response rate may mean that those who refused to respond have a different opinion from those who did. (Demers and Nichols [1987, 50], in their useful guide to survey research, say most pollsters find a response rate of 50 per cent satisfactory, and 60 per cent good.)

(continued)

- *Whether full results of the questioning were released.* For instance, were the "undecideds" dropped? Did the poll discover anything that's not being reported?

Finally, journalists should keep in mind that polls don't predict — they merely sample opinion at a particular time. This is especially true, in recent years, of voter preference polls taken between elections, which have not been a good indicator of behavior. Journalists must therefore be cautious about using the results of one poll to define a trend.

OTHER SOURCES

InfoGlobe Online, Infomart Dialog These are examples of online information services available in most newsrooms and major libraries, as well as through the Internet, that allow reporters to search for stories from a particular newspaper on a particular topic. For instance, it's possible to call up on *InfoGlobe Online* every *Globe and Mail* story in the last two decades that mentions flooding and insurance, or to call up from *Infomart Dialog* every *Edmonton Journal* story on welfare and the Reform party. (To hold down research costs, it's possible to get a listing of headlines and look for actual stories on microfilm.) As well, the two services offer gateways to many thousands of Canadian and foreign publications and information services. *InfoGlobe Online*, based on Thomson newspapers, offers the full text of the *Globe and Mail* since 1977, along with the text of some 17 other Thomson dailies for briefer periods. It also provides, along with Canadian stocks and mutual fund quotations, access to a number of other services, legal and financial databases, *The Canadian Periodical Index* and a number of Canadian magazines. *Infomart Dialog*, originally covering the *Toronto Star* and Southam papers, has added other papers, along with an expanding list of news wire and corporate databases, such as The Canadian Press news wire, the *Financial Post Corporate Survey* and the Can/Law series of databases.

Many Canadian reporters also draw on the U.S.-based Lexis-Nexis service. This service includes an enormous legal database of interest mainly to specialists. Of broader use are searchable, full-text files of hundreds of non-Canadian newspapers, including the *New York Times* and *Boston Globe*, as well as business periodicals, magazines, newsletters and so on.

Canadian Index, Canadian Periodical Index Updated monthly, these are the most useful indexes for Canadian reporters to determine what has been written on their area. The *Canadian Index* (embracing the former *Canadian News Index*, *Canadian Newspaper Index* and *Canadian Business Index*) indexes more than 600 Canadian and American newspapers and periodicals. A typical entry in *Canadian Index* looks like this:

Journalism
  See also Media coverage: Newspapers and
    newspaper industry; Periodicals; Television
    broadcasting – News
  [Rebel daughter: an autobiography] Anderson,
    Doris **Book Review** • *HERIZONS* 11(1)
    Wint'97 p31
  The media's meaty meal: stung by the Food
    Lion case, the press has a chance to redeem
    itself by redefining news [Food Lion vs ABC
    News case] - After *NEWSWEEK* 129(5) F
    3'97 p31
  Perils of gotcha journalism [Undercover report-
    ing can backfire] • *US NEWS & WORLD
    REPORT* 122(4) F 3'97 p11
  Shortsighted journalists forgo reality for rhetoric
    [Kevin Taft's Shredding the Public Interest] -
    Salutin *G&M* F 14'97 pC1
  Jews have come long way in field of journalism
    • *CDN JEWISH NEWS* 37(42) F 20'97 p41
            Awards
  Globe reporter honoured [Amnesty
    International-Canada's media award for
    national print journalism] *G&M* F 27'97 pA2
            History
  Alms for oblivion *HARPER'S* 294(1762) Mr'97
    p9-11
          Study and teaching
  See Journalism education

(Excerpt from *Canadian Index*, February 1997.)

An electronic version, called the *Canadian Business and Current Affairs Index*, is also available. Similarly, the *Canadian Periodical Index* indexes more than 400 titles, and is offered online.

Specialized and Academic Journals In any area from computers to religion, specialized journals offer detailed information, often narrowly focused but very high grade. They include everything from *Canadian Yachting* and *Canadian Funeral News* to the *Canadian Journal of Education*. They offer information that needs to be translated, and perhaps amplified, for broader audiences. The best source for identifying these sources is *The Canadian Writer's Market*, available in most libraries.

Specialized Abstracts Anyone doing a series on developmental handicaps, divorce or dreams would find leads in *Psychological Abstracts*, which gives quick summaries of recent studies. Other disciplines have similar tools, some too technical for the non-specialist, others extremely useful to reporters. Again, some libraries have computerized indexes that will allow you to summon an instant listing of studies in your area. Increasingly, too, these abstracts are available on CD-ROM, which means you can search much more quickly than you could with printed volumes. You can also avoid online search charges and can download to your own disks.

Research and Lobby Groups Think-tanks like the C.D. Howe Institute, lobby groups like the Canadian Cable Television Association and consumer groups like the Consumers' Association of Canada are all sources of specialized information.

Specialists in Post-secondary Departments   Most university and college information offices have a databank listing experts on campus in various areas. They may be interview sources, of course, and as well they can be helpful in pointing you to the best published work.

RESEARCH SOURCES

A checklist of reminders on research sources:

✔ Start your digging process with a search strategy, defining what kind of information you want and how best to get it.

✔ Keep in mind that all documentary information may be outdated, and may be written from a particular viewpoint.

✔ When asking help of librarians, give them the clearest possible picture of your needs.

✔ Remember that live and secondary research interacts: a live source may be the best guide to the newest and best documentary background.

✔ Don't feel cut off from government information if you're not working in a capital city. Find the ways you can tap into it from a distance.

✔ In the early stages of any journalism course or job, take time to get familiar with the research tools available in your own morgue or library.

✔ As you learn to use research tools, remember the principle that their usefulness grows as you become more familiar with them.

✔ Keep in mind the "serendipity factor" — that all research produces accidental rewards.

FINDING THE REWARDS

The collections and sources listed in this chapter are just examples, in a rapidly changing area, of the resources you can find in libraries. As you explore them, keep in mind these three principles of library research:

1. The first time you use any research tool, the ratio of rewards to effort will be very small. On the second or third try the rewards will increase markedly.

2. Librarians can help best if you let them know, succinctly, just what your needs are.

3. All research produces what might be called the serendipity factor: the unexpected discovery that goes beyond what you were looking for. So almost any research effort pays off, though it may not be in the form you expected.

FINDING GEMS ON THE INTERNET

BY MARY MCGUIRE

Mary McGuire teaches journalism at Carleton University and is co-author of The Internet Handbook for Writers, Researchers and Journalists.

The Internet has affected everything journalists do on the job. It has changed the way they find things out, check them out and then tell others about them. It has done that by offering journalists a new and vast source for leads, background information and interview subjects, as well as an entirely new way to publish or distribute their product. It is a tool they must learn to use with skill.

For journalists doing research, the Internet can be invaluable, untrustworthy and overwhelming, all at the same time. It can provide access to government documents faster than you could arrange to get them by courier. It can help you to track breaking news stories in more

detail than they appear on live television. It can give you easy access to experts and ordinary people around the world. It can even allow you to listen to live radio broadcasts from countries rarely visited by foreign correspondents.

For people in the business of collecting information, the Internet is a treasure chest. But its gems are hidden among a lot of junk. Learning how to find what is most valuable, on deadline, is critical. In addition, the Internet is always changing and if you find a useful resource online today, there's no guarantee it will be there next week.

Journalists who want to take advantage of the Internet to find
(continued)

sources, story ideas and background information must learn about four things:

- techniques and strategies for using search engines and other search tools to find information quickly
- resources beyond the World Wide Web in mailing lists and newsgroups
- guidelines that help determine the credibility of information on the Internet
- rules about how and when to use information from the Internet in published stories

Many staff reporters now have Internet access on the job. Freelancers will probably find it's worth the monthly charge for an Internet service provider. If you're thinking about hooking up to the Internet, shop around. The fees and time you are allowed to be online can vary widely among service providers.

Search Strategies and Techniques

The Internet is not like the computer on Star Trek. You can't just say: 'computer, who are the 10 biggest crooks that donated money to the sleazebag politician in my city?' and wait a few seconds for the answer. The Internet will not make stupid reporters smart. But it will make smart reporters smarter. The Internet is a vast, largely unorganized, ever-changing library (in fact, many of the world's best libraries are actually on the Internet). And — like any library — you have to do the hard work to find the nugget of information you want. The books don't walk off the shelves into your hands.
— JULIAN SHER, MEDIA MAGAZINE, WINTER 1995

Much of the information reporters need is out there — somewhere — online. But the Internet wasn't set up by librarians who organize things in a logical way and provide central indexes to make them easy to find. Nor was it organized by journalists who need information immediately to meet tight deadlines. Just as learning to ask the right question of the right source will determine the success of your story, so will learning to use the right online search tools well.

The first thing most journalists do when they begin research on a story is to look for stories other journalists have written on the subject. If you work for an organization with a news librarian or have access to a database such as *Infomart* or *InfoGlobe*, it's easy to conduct such searches. If you want to use the Internet, however, you need to develop a strategy.

You may think the easiest thing to do is use a search engine to conduct a keyword search on your topic. But such a search will just flood your computer screen with an endless list of references, most of which will be useless and almost none of which will be past newspaper or magazine articles. It is far better to go to the Web site of one of the many news organizations that archive past editions or stories and search by keyword. The *Washington Post* and the *Christian Science Monitor*, for example, have some of the best archives available free online. Other newspapers allow you to search their
(continued)

archives without charge, but charge a fee for retrieving the full text of the article. The *Globe and Mail* and the CBC's National and Newsworld sites are among Canadian news organizations that provide at least limited access to past articles and newscast transcripts.

If you want more resources, there are three other places on the Internet to begin your search: starting pages, subject trees and search engines.

Starting pages are Web pages designed to provide a useful set of links to general reference information. All you have to do is scan the list for links that might be useful. No searching skills are required. Starting pages such as My Virtual Reference Desk are the online equivalent of a library reference desk, with almanacs, encyclopedias, newspapers and reference guides.

One of the most useful starting pages for Canadian journalists was created by Julian Sher, an award-winning investigative reporter and television producer with the CBC's *fifth estate*. Called JournalismNet, Sher's page includes an extensive list of links to valuable resources for journalists, including online newspapers, online telephone and e-mail directories, news archives, Canadian government Web sites and articles with tips and tricks for journalists who want to make better use of the Web. It also includes links to a vast number of Canadian and American databases on the Net. Many Canadian journalists make this page their first stop when they log on to the Internet. Web site addresses are always changing, but as this book was being written Sher's was http://www.journalismnet.com/

Subject trees are the online equivalent of library subject catalogues — you can browse for links related to your topic. The most popular subject tree on the Internet, Yahoo, has a subject tree for Canadian information called Yahoo Canada. When you first go to Yahoo, you will find a general index of broad subjects such as Arts, Computers, Health, Media and Reference. Each heading has subheadings you can follow until you get to the specific information you want. It is also easy to search all of Yahoo or only a specific category by keyword.

But while subject trees are a great place to start, they are not comprehensive. They are put together by human beings and it is not humanly possible to index all the pages on the Web. Subject trees help you find the haystack. You will need other tools — search engines — to find the needle.

Search engines are the most sophisticated tool you can use to search the Net for information. They use computer programs that scour the Net constantly, compiling indexes of all (or parts of) the Web pages they find. When you call on them, they will search their indexes for keywords or phrases you choose, and provide you with a list of "hits" — Web pages that contain those words. But just as no two private

(continued)

investigators operate exactly the same way, no two search engines follow the same pattern. So it is always best to use more than one search engine in any search.

Phrasing your request well is also crucial. If you send a search engine out on a simple search for a keyword or phrase, it will most likely return with very long lists of matches or possible hits. It would take hours to check each one to determine whether it contains not just the keyword, but useful information. For journalists working on deadline, thousands of hits are almost as useless as no hits at all. You need to develop a few strategies and learn a few tricks to get more manageable results.

The best strategies depend on which search engine you are using. Each contains a help menu outlining tips and tricks for conducting advanced searches and getting the most out of that search engine. Journalists, like most people, hate reading help menus, but time spent learning will be time saved sifting through a lot of useless hits.

The most popular search engines are AltaVista, Excite, HotBot, Infoseek, Lycos and Open Text. Each has its strengths and weaknesses and it is best to try each of them and get comfortable using advanced search techniques on a least a couple of them.

AltaVista is probably the most powerful; it allows you to refine your searches in more detailed ways than most of the other search engines. One of its basic features is that it allows you to search for phrases, not just words. Let's say you are working on a story about hard-rock mining. From the AltaVista home page, you could type in hard rock mining in the search box and click on the button labelled Submit. Seconds later, you would get a list of thousands of hits. Many would be pages about hard-rock music. Others would be about Hard Rock Cafés. Some might be about hard-rock mining, but they would be difficult to find. If, however, you simply put quotation marks around the phrase "hard rock mining" in your search request, the only hits that AltaVista will display are those with the words appearing together. Don't assume, however, that you can use quotation marks in the same way with other search engines. Different search engines have different rules. Read the help menu.

There are also more sophisticated ways to refine your searches with AltaVista. If you are doing a story about children's television in Canada, you may want to use what librarians call Boolean operators. They are the words AND, OR, NOT and NEAR. For example you can search for "children's television" AND Canada. Each of the hits will include the phrase "children's television" and somewhere else on the page the word Canada.

But keep in mind that search engines are dumb, too. If you ask AltaVista to search for Canada, it will not find Canadian. If, however, you use a wild card (in AltaVista the wild card is an aster-

(continued)

isk) and search for Canad*, it will find all references to Canada, Canadian and Canadians. Again, the rules for refining searches and using wild cards vary from search engine to search engine.

Search engines are dumb in other ways, too. Many of them are case sensitive. This means that if you search for the word French with a capital F, it won't find references where french is spelled with a lower-case f.

Other search engines look not for keywords, but for concepts. In other words, they try to find not just the precise word or phrase you gave them, but things that might be related to that phrase. If you use them to look for job postings for journalists they might also find you jobs for reporters. Excite is the most popular concept search engine.

Excite, Infoseek and other search engines have also added directories to their home pages to save you the trouble of using a subject tree, like Yahoo, as well as a search engine. And, if you don't want to be bothered going back and forth between different search engines and subject trees, there are even a few meta-search sites. Again, they have their idiosyncrasies, but they are essentially one-stop searching sites. They allow you to use several of your favorite search engines and subject trees at once.

Beyond the Web

Some of the most valuable online resources for journalists exist beyond the World Wide Web. Online dis-

cussion groups are great places to find interesting people sharing opinions, both informed and uninformed. You can use discussion groups to pick up tips, locate experts and make other contacts. There are also online groups where you can network with journalists, researchers or experts on your beat.

Of the two kinds of electronic discussion groups, listservs or mailing lists are far more valuable to journalists than Usenet newsgroups. The latter are often the online equivalent of the radio phone-in show: anyone can call and offer an opinion, no matter how uninformed, and anyone else can listen in.

Listservs are less public and the participants are more likely to have first-hand experience with the group's topic. People must subscribe to participate in these groups. All messages posted by participants arrive in the mailboxes of all subscribers.

For researchers and journalists these groups can be very helpful. For example, if you are doing a story comparing school policies on children who are allergic to peanuts, you could subscribe to a mailing list for allergy sufferers and monitor the discussion of people who regularly share advice and compare strategies. You could even post a query for information and would probably get a lot of helpful replies and leads. For beat reporters, especially those on science or health beats, mailing lists are a terrific resource because

(continued)

researchers regularly participate in the discussion on such lists.

Fact or Fiction

Evaluating the information you find on the Web and in newsgroups and mailing lists can be one of the biggest challenges facing journalists. When it comes to Web sites, it is best to view them with the same skepticism you would bring to an infomercial. Just as you wouldn't publish unidentified material that landed in a brown envelope on your desk without verifying it, you should not publish any information you find on the Internet without checking it out. There are some guidelines for determining what is reliable:

- Check the authority of the person or institution that published the material. Look for a phone number or address to use to verify that the information is legitimate.

- Check the accuracy of the material with other sources.

- Check how current the material is. If the site does not indicate when the material was last updated, don't assume it is fresh.

- Beware of hackers. Remember, Web pages can be deliberately altered by hackers. And many have been.

To Cite or Not to Cite

Journalists need guidelines about how to quote people's comments from e-mail messages and newsgroup postings, as well as how to cite facts and figures obtained from Web sites and home pages. In the past, reporters often quoted directly from e-mail messages without identifying how the quote was obtained. They argued that journalists rarely specify whether quotes are obtained by telephone or in person and they didn't want to treat e-mail differently.

But as news organizations develop policies on this and other Internet issues, few of them allow the lack of e-mail citations to continue. The problem is that it is impossible to tell who really wrote an online message because people share accounts and because it is easy to use pseudonyms online. Many news organizations now insist that reporters treat e-mail messages or discussion group postings as leads only, with all direct quotes being obtained the old-fashioned way. Some allow the use of quotations from e-mail messages, but with qualifiers such as "...said someone who identified herself as Jane Doe in a message posted to the Internet newsgroup misc.kids." Such qualifiers make stories less than graceful.

Even with qualifiers, however, journalists argue over whether they have the right to publish what they find in newsgroup postings. Many argue that such postings cannot be considered private because millions of people around the world read them. But news organizations that have developed policies tend to take a more conservative approach. Many say people should not find

(continued)

themselves quoted in a news story unless they have been asked for and given their permission.

The Associated Press, often a trendsetter on journalistic style, issued guidelines in 1996 about the use of online resources. It warned all its employees to behave themselves online as they would at a public meeting and never to take sides on matters of public debate.

What you write, even in private e-mail but especially in posts to lists and Usenet newsgroups, could be forwarded to millions of people, and no doubt will be saved somewhere by somebody. ... In short, if you wouldn't want your online activity to be shown on CNN or in Times Square, don't do it on the Internet or America Online.

The same guidelines, however, warn AP journalists not to consider any e-mail or postings written by others as public information.

Respect the privacy of individuals, who may not be aware that their comments in electronic forums could be distributed by journalists. Do not quote private individuals or public figures from online communications unless you verify the identity of the author and assure yourself that the author meant to speak publicly.
— Quoted in McGuire et al., 1997, 223–225

New Job Opportunities

The Internet offers more than just information resources for young journalists; it also offers a wide range of job opportunities. Many news organizations — newspapers, magazines, radio and television stations — offer online versions of their product. Some online newspapers are simply electronic versions of the daily paper. But increasingly, news organizations are adapting to the new medium and offering something different online. For example, news stories in the online edition may include links to background information, searchable archives and other resources to help readers understand stories better. More and more newsrooms are hiring people with a combination of journalistic and Web design skills to work exclusively on their online publications.

A Final Word

The Internet is not and never will be a substitute for research in the library, or for contact with expert sources and witnesses by phone and in person. But it is a valuable addition to the range of research tools journalists use. The Internet can give easier access to more sources and more information than has ever been possible before. It can provide leads to story ideas, paths to good interviews and even new job prospects. Whether it makes you a better journalist, though, depends on how well you learn to use it.

Further Reading

McGuire, Mary, Linda Stilborne, Melinda McAdams and Laurel Hyatt. (1997). *The Internet Handbook for Writers, Researchers and Journalists.* Toronto: Trifolium Books Inc.

Reddick, Randy and Elliot King. (1997). *The Online Journalist; Using the Internet for Research and Reporting.* 2nd edition. Forth Worth: Harcourt Brace & Co.

RECOMMENDED READING

Demers, David Pearce, and Suzanne Nichols. (1987). *Precision Journalism: A Practical Guide*. Newbury Park, CA: Sage Publications.

Horowitz, Lois. (1984). *Knowing Where to Look: The Ultimate Guide to Research*. Cincinnati: Writer's Digest Books.

Neff, Glenda Tennant. (1991). *The Writer's Essential Desk Reference*. Cincinnati: Writer's Digest Books.

Overbury, Stephen. (1989). *Finding Canadian Facts Fast*. Revised edition. Toronto: McGraw-Hill Ryerson.

Ward, Jean, and Kathleen A. Hansen. (1997). *Search Strategies in Mass Communication*. 3rd edition. New York and London: Longman.

Wilhoit, G. Cleveland, and David H. Weaver. (1990). *Newsroom Guide to Polls & Surveys*. Bloomington: Indiana University Press.

CHAPTER 4

Interviewing

NTERVIEWING IS ONE OF THE DISTINCTIVE things that journalists do. All disciplines — science, the arts, economics — have experts more skilled than journalists at taking information from books, reports and databanks, and reshaping it. The journalist's special task is to get into people's minds, to find out what hasn't yet been written down. And while other professionals may interview (police or social workers come to mind), the journalist's task is distinctive in that it must be done without "official" leverage.

Yet despite the importance of interviewing, and the fact that there *are* people who can do it well, the teaching and learning of interviewing technique are frustratingly difficult. Mastery of some journalistic tools can be acquired routinely, but interviewing depends crucially on a student's level of knowledge and on interpersonal skills. If these are not well developed, instruction in technique is not likely to help a great deal. If they *are* well advanced, then analysis of technique may improve a journalist's performance.

One of the best means of making improvements may be through examining the work of the best interviewers, to discover what makes them good. Consider, for instance, the work of radio broadcaster Peter Gzowski, who brings to his work not only broad and eclectic knowledge, but an intense *curiosity* — or at least the appearance of curiosity — whether he's interviewing a nuclear physicist or a quilt-maker. Does he trick himself into this, or is he simply showing a God-given thirst for knowledge? From the listener's point of view, the question may be academic: certainly he *appears* to be engaged, and seems to find the interviewing process intensely rewarding. As a result, it often becomes rewarding for the subjects as well. And for the audience.

The suggestion here is that it's useful to think about interviewing in terms of rewards, both for the sources and the journalists. If those rewards are kept in view, they provide clues on how to do the task — or on patterns to avoid.

REWARDS FOR SOURCES

For the source, the rewards are complex. Many people think that a media interview will put their case or their cause before the public effectively. There's also a personal status reward in getting on the 6 o'clock news or in being quoted in the newspaper. But beyond those obvious rewards there are more subtle benefits. Most people *like* to talk about their work (or their hobbies, interests or pet peeves). Interviewing often focuses on the very topic that makes a person expert, and which therefore is closest to that person's self-image. The source may not always have access to a sympathetic audience. If a person's area of expertise is a narrow one, there may be few friends or family members still ready to listen. Conversation in modern times tends to be competitive: people have to be witty and dynamic to get their share of attention. So it may be gratifying for sources to have the close and sympathetic attention of a reporter.

It's true that some people prefer to avoid reporters, because they're afraid their causes will *not* get just treatment, because they're nervous about appearing on camera, or because they fear the reporter won't be knowledgeable enough to be an intelligent listener or will get it wrong. But often reporters are surprised, not by how difficult it is to get sources to open up, but by their *willingness* to talk — about their hopes, their pasts, their love lives, their crises. Some people find it impossible to resist the temptation to spill their inmost concerns to a nice, nodding reporter who seems to be so genuinely interested in their plans or problems. Joan Didion once wrote: "my only advantage as a reporter is that I am so physically small, so temperamentally unobtrusive and so neurotically inarticulate that people tend to forget my presence runs counter to their best interests" (1968, Preface).

While the question of "best interests" may be moot, Didion's overall point is a compelling one: people will indeed open up to a quiet, sympathetic listener. As they do, complex psychological exchanges take place. We all need to know how the world is responding to us, so we may welcome feedback from a reporter. We all watch television and therefore know that Important People have reporters hanging on their words. In crisis times we need to talk, to unload fears and frustrations. In social encounters we play power games, taking gratification from being able to demonstrate our superiority. All these tendencies can work to a reporter's advantage. The line between empathetic human responses and crass manipulation in this area is dangerously thin.

REWARDS FOR REPORTERS

If it's important to think of the possible rewards of interviewing for sources, the same is true for rewards for the interviewer. For new reporters, the interviewing process may seem one of unmixed frustration, a matter of constant difficulty in getting through to sources, getting them to talk and getting them to be specific. In the midst of those challenges, it's possible to forget that a good interview — if, in fact, you manage to break through to "third-level" rapport with an interesting person — can be exceedingly rewarding.

This "third-level" designation suggests that interviews can be divided into various categories. The first level is the quick, over-the-microphone question: "have you any comment on …?" In this kind of interview the reporter is mainly a recorder, needing little background knowledge. The second level is a more substantial "Tell me about your project" interview, a type that demands something more of the reporter in preparation and response. The third level is much more complex and varied, but demands, first of all, a good deal of knowledge on the reporter's part — either specific information or general expertise. It may also include some of these attributes:

- a measure of mutual respect, developed either by previous meetings or by knowledge of the other's work;

- information trading on a complex level. Sometimes this is as subtle as a nod or a look of puzzlement that helps one participant understand the other's reaction. Sometimes it is a matter of bartering information gleaned from other sources;

- a kind of synergy, an analysis of information in a way that enables both participants to gain greater insight than either could have gained in isolation;

- a high level of intensity of a kind that goes beyond generalizations to specific cases, to detailed anecdotes, alternative explanations or refined context; or

Most people draw their image of the journalistic interview from television — with all this implies of color, drama and conflict. Print interviews, however, are usually low-key detailed, factual. They may also take place in unusual settings — as in this interview of a food relief worker in Ethiopia by Rob Mills of the Halifax *Chronicle-Herald.* (Len Wagg)

- a sense that the interview has an importance transcending the personal satisfaction of the participants.

    For reporters, such interviews may be one of the most gratifying aspects of their work. Sometimes, though, when the experience itself has been stressful, this sense of reward develops only in retrospect. This is not just the reward of name-dropping, of letting your friends know which political or entertainment star you lunched with last week. The accumulation of interview experience can be seen as the richest part of a journalist's life. And third-level interviewing is rewarding as well to the sources, sometimes bringing from their minds information they hardly knew they had.

ADDING TECHNIQUE TO KNOWLEDGE

If this kind of interviewing is rewarding, the next obvious question is, How do novice journalists make sure their interviewing moves to that level?

Clearly, new reporters should not expect to transform themselves overnight into confident, poised, knowledgeable people who will impress sources and make them want to respond. All that takes time and consistent effort. Nothing substitutes for thorough knowledge.

But if the reporter is knowledgeable, then demeanor, or technique — natural or artificial — may come into play. All experienced reporters understand that general manner, voice tone and a host of other nebulous factors will affect their interviewing success. If they seem bored, hostile or fearful, the interview is certain to be affected. Webb and Salancik (1966, 9–10), in a classic summary of social science research on interviewing, observe that in the first seconds of an interview, a "titanic" exchange of information takes place — on whether the other person will be agreeable or tough, ingratiating or hostile or doubting. This factor is as important on the phone as in person, where tone of voice or inflection can affect the outcome. Rightly or wrongly, people at the end of a phone read a great deal into voices, making judgments about character, strength and status. A reporter who speaks in a hesitant or apologetic way is likely to be brushed aside. Another who is too forceful and demanding may be cut off. A confident, relaxed tone is needed — but it is not easy to produce if the *person* is not relaxed and confident. Journalist June Callwood writes sensitively on this point, observing that the factor of voice tone is almost beyond human control because it depends so much on the bedrock of ego strength formed in childhood. "People judge one another swiftly on the basis of vocal timbre and pace: thin, wispy voices are associated with lack of importance; breathy voices sound unstable; nasal voices lack forcefulness; hoarse voices sound anxious; firm, deep voices impart an air of authority" (1989).

The same wild-card factor shows up in the "presence" a reporter brings to a face-to-face interview. This is partly luck-of-the-draw physical attractiveness, but it also includes aspects of demeanor that deserve thought. Often people do not realize the non-verbal signals they are sending out that reflect their agreeableness, their hostility, their fear, their boredom, their shallowness or their confidence. Some experts suggest this means reporters *must* "play a role" — that the worst possible advice is to "be yourself." But if the "self" is confident and knowledgeable, it can't be a mistake to "be yourself." If you are not confident and knowledgeable, it's more important to change the essentials than to create a disguise. Experts often advise reporters to be neither sycophantic nor aggressively hostile, to signal to sources that they're adopting a stance of interested, professional neutrality. That is usually good advice — but again, the stance should reflect the reporter's core values, not just a convenient persona. Some reporting texts discuss in detail the dangers of limp handshakes or of sloppy dress. Those dangers are probably obvious to most adults, although they may be unaware of subtler kinds of body language.

CHOOSING YOUR QUESTIONS

Interview questions fall into a number of types, including the following examples:

Open: "Tell me about your program." *(Invites sources to roam freely, set their own priorities.)*

Closed: "I notice you attended Harvard Law School. Did you graduate from that program?" *(Pins source down to a yes or no.)*

Narrowing: "I understand the point, but I'd welcome an example. Can you think of a particular instance that illustrates the problem?" *(Moves source from abstract to concrete level.)*

Reflective: "I've often wondered what it's like in that very last moment before a ballet dancer goes on stage …" *(Invites source to share perceptions.)*

Leading: "Are you concerned about the way the government is pushing industry out of the country?" *(Prods sources to say what you want them to say — and is generally a bad technique.)*

Indirect: "I'm sure you're aware that some analysts have called your program shoddy and fraudulent. How do you respond to those critics?" *(Puts blame for hard question on someone else.)*

Idiot: "I'm sorry — I'm not sure I have this straight, so I need to ask you again …" *(The question you'd rather not ask because you're afraid it makes you look like an idiot — but which you must ask, if you don't understand.)*

Double-barrelled: "Are you hoping for a profit next year, and have you any plans for a new approach to your unions?" *(Considered hazardous since it allows source to choose which part of the question to answer.)*

Followup: "That's an interesting point; does it mean that …?" *(A good way to make sure you aren't leaving loose ends.)*

Synthesizing: "Okay, let me pull back a bit then, and ask you to sum up the effect of these patterns.…" *(A device to get source to sum up rambling thoughts in succinct form.)*

Review: "I think I have the overall picture, but let me run over the main points and make sure. …" *(Allows feedback for correction or co-orientation.)*

THE HAZARDS

While interviews may be enriching, they are also, as anyone of experience knows, *fallible*. Much of the literature on interviewing concentrates on the hazards of misunderstanding, of selective perception and retention, of mishearing, of language that means different things to source and reporter. Of all the ways reporters get information, the "most perilous and unreliable" is the interview, Webb and Salancik say, adding, "None of us, as journalists or social scientists, trust the report of a single interview" (1966, 1, 3).

That last statement should be taken more as an admonition than an accurate reflection of reality, but it is true that experienced reporters come to realize the fallibility of interviews. They learn that they must doubt and question what sources say (as noted in the section on evidential rules in Chapter 1). They develop their own mechanisms for testing what they're told. For novices, a "Three Cs" formula for interview checking is worth remembering: corroboration, consistency and co-orientation.

Corroboration

Whenever possible, statements of one source should be corroborated by another, especially by a document source. Remember that memory plays tricks and that people make honest mistakes. They tend to say in conversation what they wouldn't write down without checking. Even the most honest among us tend to select those parts of a story that reflect best on us or our cause. And lots of people lie.

Consistency

Most extended interviews will show at least marginal inconsistencies. There is a human tendency on the part of hearers to *rationalize* the inconsistency, to smooth it over and to create an explanation that covers the inconsistent statements. This is dangerous for a reporter. Like a good detective, the reporter must home in on the inconsistency to discover what it means. For instance: the organizer of a disarmament protest speaks of the remarkable unity of all peace groups taking part, but later says something that implies a philosophic disagreement with one group. As soon as this inconsistency appears, a bell should go off in the reporter's mind, a reminder to make sure the significance of the gap is explored.

Co-orientation

This useful term, borrowed from social science, identifies one of the central hazards of interviewing. It is based on recognition that the process of conveying images or ideas from one mind to another is *always* imperfect.

Different understandings of language and different frames of reference mean that any word or set of words is understood differently by any two people. That is especially true of material at high levels of abstraction. If a source says (for instance) that a national *movement is* taking shape to protest *abuse patterns*, the thought can evoke quite different images. So it is always necessary for a reporter to *feed back for correction*. What sort of movement? you ask. A national organization? A letter-writing campaign to MPs? What kind of abuse patterns? Physical abuse? Sexual abuse? Abuse of women or children? Abuse of substances? This kind of feedback and correction helps to bring the images in the reporter's mind and the source's mind into a closer fit — to *co-orient* them. But the images will never be identical.

NEWS VERSUS ENTERTAINMENT

One of the modern hazards for news reporters, especially in print, is the impact of certain kinds of television interviews in establishing what people expect of reporters. Everyone is familiar with the overly cosy interviews of daytime TV, or the confrontational style of shows like *60 Minutes*. But few people have seen the more low-key, information interviews conducted by print reporters or by broadcast reporters working on story research or pre-interview preparation. As a result, people coming into journalism, and many of their sources, may draw their conception of the journalistic interview from entertainment broadcasting. The latter often depends on dramatic tension between source and interviewer, a tension that arises from witty repartee, from warm rapport or from sharp disagreement. Any of these can create "good television" or "good radio," in which both personalities become part of a dramatic (perhaps even rehearsed) encounter. In news interviewing, by contrast, the interviewer is much less prominent. The image of silent sponge suggested by Joan Didion's earlier comment is very much a description of news interviewing, not of on-air broadcast technique.

As well, news interviews seek a different kind of material. In many broadcast interviews, especially those shaped for entertainment rather than information, an interesting, well-articulated point of view may be sufficient. The news interview depends more on facts and developments. The entertainment interviewer asks: "what do you think?" or "What do you feel?" The news interviewer asks: "what did you do?" or "What are you planning to do?" News interviewers traditionally avoid loaded questions; entertainment interviewers sometimes deliberately build them to stimulate a response.

These are generalizations, of course, but they suggest a major caution, at least for those going into print reporting. Keep in mind that sources may draw their conception of proper interview behavior from what they've seen on TV. Keep in mind as well that rhetorical flourishes may sound grand on your tape ("We find this violation of our rights intolerable") but weak on paper, unless you can go on to say what is *happening*.

Print interview material is typically built on painstaking questions designed to flesh out a plan or an account. There is a great deal of double-checking, and of feedback for co-orientation, corroboration with available colleagues or documents and pausing while a note is completed. In general, print interviews make poor broadcast material. The reverse is often true as well: the tight time limitations and the demand for drama mean broadcast journalists often leave loose ends, or deal in generalizations and opinions.

This is not to suggest that the print interviewer's personality is unimportant. Its impact, however, is much more subdued. In broadcasting, the interviewer's personality must be front and centre, very much a part of the action. In print, the interviewer's role is deliberately kept subordinate. As John Hohenberg put it, in his classic line (directed, of course, at print people), "No talking reporter ever held a decent interview" (1973, 367). Print reporters are rarely hostile or argumentative, and then usually only as a calculated effort to get better information.

All these thoughts must be qualified by the realization that interviews vary within the print and broadcast categories. In broadcasting, there is a vast distance between the quick outside-the-meeting scrum; the thoughtful half-hour interview show, done in-studio; and the off-air news interview. The scrum demands paparazzi skills seldom spoken of in journalism schools, especially leather lungs and leather sensitivities. The in-studio encounter demands high levels of knowledge and self-possession. The off-air news interview demands skills and efforts very like those of a print reporter, including background preparation, a clear guideline, corroboration and review.

FIGHTING SOURCE CONTROL

Each of these interview types also implies different kinds of source manipulation in different settings. Ironically, given the appearance of reporter aggressiveness that goes with it, the scrum assault is the interview type most open to source control. All political leaders are now schooled to deal with the scrum by coming to it primed with a key message, a "sound bite" that they want to get on national news. Then, no matter what questions the reporters ask, they keep coming back to the key point. Quite quickly, the journalists tire of repetition and shut off the cameras or tape recorders (or the source disappears — perhaps up the escape stairs or into a helicopter).

While journalists easily recognize the ploy and work to counter it, the politician's key message will often get through to the TV or radio news.

By contrast, the in-studio interview gives the reporter a good deal more control, and not just because of time, although that factor is indeed crucial. In the studio, the interviewer faces less competition from colleagues. And there is a *milieu* factor, too: in the studio, politicians or business people are out of their element, dependent to some extent on the interviewer as guide and protector in the unfamiliar world of lights and cameras and cables and makeup. This interviewer control can be transferred from the mechanics of the interview to its content. The sources are relatively vulnerable, no longer able to rely on the status elements they have in their own offices, behind a large desk, perhaps flanked by subordinates. Social scientists suggest that such *perceived status relationships* are crucial in interviewing, and they are undoubtedly right. The reporter in-studio has a much higher status "platform" than the reporter sitting at the corner of the source's desk, in the chair usually reserved for supplicants and stenographers.

If these considerations are important for reporters (perhaps especially for those in broadcasting) it is because they need to be aware of how their subjects are playing the game. They need to understand the kind of training politicians (and some business people) are getting, in areas such as the following:

- *message control*, in which the politician identifies and rehearses the key message, and repeats it, no matter what;

- *tone control*, in which the politician is taught to understand that she is not speaking to the annoying reporter, but *past the reporter* (whose questions may not even show up on-screen) to the person in front of the home TV set. The implication is that the source's tone must NOT be geared to what's appropriate for a badgering reporter, but to what's appropriate for a thoughtful viewer;

- *setting control*, in which the politician tries to be filmed at the factory gate, the farm or the supermarket, preferably with a loyal, attractive aide at his elbow, or in which the business person or scientist appears with symbols of authority (books, lab equipment, maps, flow charts) in the background; and

- *status control*, in which the source conveys to the reporter what future benefit may accrue from favorable reportage, given the source's (usually) stronger power position. Of course, such an attempt to manipulate is always subtle, since anything explicit would react against the source. It may take the form of compliment that implies possible benefit. For instance: "that was a good piece you did last night. I'm glad there's finally somebody at *The News* who understands what we're doing." (Translation: "if you're good to us, we'll keep on feeding you information.")

Given this kind of game-playing, the challenge for the reporter is to circumvent these first lines of defence, to get sources away from the adversarial framework and mentality and persuade them to talk on a different level. The most important move in either a print or broadcast interview may be to signal that the aim is to go well beyond a conventional sound bite, or a staged event, or a game — to show that you have a serious interest in the sources and their work, and that that interest justifies a substantial response. That may mean getting the source to neutral territory — for example, a lunch table — and away from competitive status trappings and interruptions.

One advantage for print reporters is that they have more latitude to get to people who are reluctant to appear on TV, and who are therefore less conditioned to play media control games. These are more likely to be people expert in their own area, qualified to answer the fact-based questions preferred by print reporters, and with less inclination to score points in the process. Television reporters, by contrast, are more often limited to a narrow range of sources, usually elected officials, show business people, public relations officers or people with causes. All these people are willing to undergo the hazard and agony of television interviews because they have a good deal to gain, or because they don't dare *not* do them. In dealing with these sources, though, broadcast reporters usually have greater leverage than do print reporters.

GENERAL GUIDELINES

Given all these hazards, how can novice reporters improve their interviewing? These are a few possible ways.

Prepare

It's a cliché of the trade, but it's also the most important single factor in successful interviewing. You *must* base your questions on hard information if you are to get any respect or response from the source. Interviewing is essentially information trading. As Samuel Johnson once noted, those who would bring home knowledge must carry knowledge with them. That means that if you interview politicians, you *must* check *Hansard* or news files to find what causes they have been supporting. If you interview academics, you must check references, usually available in the university information office, on what they have published, what courses they teach, what publications they have recently produced. If you interview business people, you must check the files (or an online information retrieval system such as *InfoGlobe* or *Infomart*) to find what has recently been printed about them or their companies. Some experts say it's possible to intimidate sources by displaying too much information. This may be true, but the opposite problem is more serious. On stories of any complexity, you should spend several hours in preparation for every hour of interviewing. In areas like science, finance and foreign affairs, you may need to do much more. It is not unusual for journalists to have in hand most of the material they need for their story before they go into an interview; at the interview itself they will want to take the final step, to work from the background material toward the key question or set of questions that can be answered only from the source's mind.

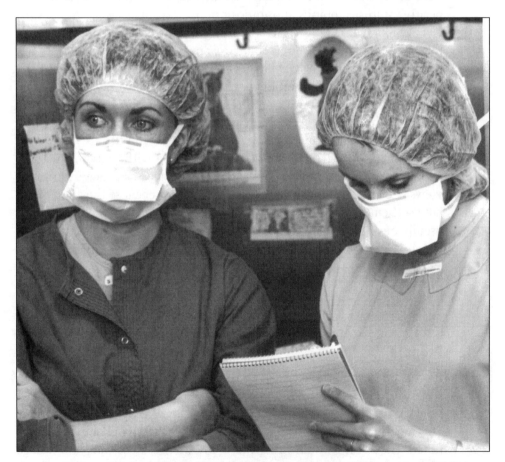

Feature reporter Leslie Smith of the *Chronicle-Herald* makes notes on a child's journey through an operation at Izaak Walton Children's Hospital in Halifax. Some reporters find interviews stressful, and yet see the cumulative experience from many interviews as the richest part of their professional experience. (Len Wagg)

Preparation also means having at least a rough guide to the way you want to shape the interview. It means rehearsing mentally the way you may deal with various eventualities. In general, of course, it's wise to plan for broad questions first ("So, tell me how the project started …") and the more narrow fleshing-out questions later. It may be wise at times to delay hard questions until late in the interview — although in most cases it probably is best to let the source know, courteously and head on, if there is difficult ground to cover. Telephone interviews, in particular, probably demand a clear set of prepared questions, at least as a fallback, since it's easy for a reluctant source to cut off a phone interview.

THE POWER OF OBSERVATION

Interviews are not all about talking, says Edward Greenspon of the *Globe and Mail*. "You can learn a lot about people by what they have in their offices, how they dress, how they treat their subordinates."

Greenspon likes to prepare for interviews by watching the subject in unscripted situations. Getting ready to interview a businessman who had a reputation of never leaving anything to chance, Greenspon went to hear him make a pitch to investors. Afterward, when people came up to the podium to congratulate the man, Greenspon moved closer to eavesdrop. He noticed, stuck to the podium, a yellow adhesive sticker that provided the anecdote he needed. It contained a happy face and a handwritten note: "smile, for $100 million plus."

Another time Greenspon was researching the rather dry topic of auto industry productivity. "One of the people I went to interview was the manager of Volkswagen's main plant in Wolfsburg, Germany. (It also happens to be the largest plant in the world.) His office was on the top floor of one of the factory buildings. I sat down and the room shuddered. About five seconds later, it shuddered again. He apologized. It seems we were above the room where metal parts were stamped out on huge industrial presses. It was like this day and night."

Greenspon's story began:

Every five seconds or so, a tremor of Richter-scale proportions rumbles through the office of Helmut Amtenbrink, manager of the world's largest car plant.

Mr. Amtenbrink, who supervises the production of 4,000 cars a day from his perch five floors above the flagship factory of Volkswagen AG, explains that his workers are operating 300 metal presses downstairs.

"That's how I always know they are working," he deadpans as another wave ripples through the room.

As Volkswagen marks its 50th anniversary this year, the test for the company is not, however, a matter of knowing its workers are on the job. They almost always are.

Rather, the challenge is coping with the high cost this labor harmony extracts. …

— *GLOBE AND MAIL*, OCT. 8, 1988

Go, Don't Phone or E-mail

It's best to do interviews face to face, to help in the difficult task of *reading* the source. That means making judgments (imperfect but necessary) on a number of things: on whether the source is simply mouthing institutional platitudes or seriously attempting to answer your questions; on whether the source is simply providing answers she thinks you want; on whether the differences between you and the source — of personality, class, race or gender — are affecting the interview content. In-person interviews conducted on the source's home turf also offer important visual information about the person and her environment, material you can put to good use in writing the story. You may also collect material at the edges of the interview, from the source's colleagues or family, or the source herself at the end of the interview. (Jan Wong of the *Globe and Mail* comments: "when you close your notebook, or shut off your tape recorder at the end of the interview, by all means keep your ears open. That's when the subject suddenly relaxes, feels the worst is over and often opens up and gives you the best quotes. As long as the subject doesn't say, 'this is off the record,' it's fair game. Run to the elevator and write it down immediately.")

Time constraints, transportation problems or geographical distance often require reporters to interview by phone. Phone interviewing has both benefits and costs. On the up side, working by phone means you can collect a lot of material relatively quickly and efficiently. In addition, the interviewer can watch for a rich set of audio cues — Is the speaker nervous or relaxed? Defensive of helpful? Bored or engaged? Does he sound confident about what he's saying, or is he making it up as he goes along? On the down side, it's more difficult to establish rapport or credibility with the source over the phone, and it may be more difficult to take notes or to concentrate. In addition, the phone robs you of visual details you would pick up on during an in-person interview. For all these reasons, it's best to keep phone interviews short, and to work out clear ideas about what kinds of interviews you can safely do by phone and which ones you feel must be done in person.

In the last few years, some journalists have experimented with doing "interviews" by electronic mail. These are not, strictly speaking, interviews at all, but exchanges of correspondence. As such, they have some advantages: if you're shy or worried about stumbling over questions, you may feel you can get your questions across better in writing. In addition, each party in an e-mail exchange can reply at her convenience: there's no need to synchronize schedules, or to adapt your work routine to someone else's hours. However, the drawbacks of such e-mail "interviews" almost always outweigh the benefits. The key difficulty — and it is insurmountable — is that you lose any sense of the source *as a person*. You reduce fascinating, creative individuals to typescript on a computer screen. Because both parties in an e-mail conversation may write and rewrite their responses before sending them, these exchanges offer neither spontaneity nor serendipity. They tend to lack passion or humor. It's no surprise that material collected by e-mail is rarely as quotable as material collected in other ways.

E-mail and the telephone can be invaluable for arranging interviews, checking facts or confirming quotes. But as we stress in the next chapter, the most important things about writing happen in the field, not in the office. The more in-person interviews you do, the better your interviewing technique will become. And you will gain expertise not only in collecting quotations, but in amassing the rich stores of detail, context and color that make stories come alive.

Project

Just as able writers project themselves into the reader's mind, so the best interviewers seem able to project themselves into the source's mind, to imagine what the source's fears or hopes may be and to shape questions accordingly. This kind of empathy is hard to create artificially, but it is a useful exercise for reporters to try consistently to imagine themselves in the source's shoes. Even in a routine factual interview the process can be beneficial. Conducting a telephone interview with the survivor of an air crash, for instance, the reporter may try to imagine what the subject went through. (What was it like when the plane took off? How was the weather? How full was the aircraft? What was the first hint of trouble? How did other passengers react? What did the crew do? What happened when the plane hit the ground?) The act of imagining the sequence will help the reporter ask the natural questions.

The same kind of empathy comes into play in, say, interviewing an older person about what it was like in wartime. The interviewer must be capable of imagining the fears, the shortages, the separations from family and friends, in order to draw out the subject. On an even more routine level, the same kind of projection can help in interviewing a school board member about her plans for school closings. It may help to consider what this board member hopes to achieve, who her opponents may be, how long she has been working on the project, what her alternatives are, what it will mean if her plan is defeated. By getting into the subject's shoes, the reporter will not only be more likely to come up with the right questions, but also to show curiosity (of the kind discussed earlier in the chapter). It may be useful, too, to imagine in advance the kinds of responses you may get to your main questions. This will steer you away from the wrong question (a question on possible policy changes, for instance, to a spokesperson) and will also enable you to plan the fallback question, if the source dodges your first one.

Listen

Again, it is a cliché to say that most people are poor listeners and that reporters must deliberately develop the skill. Inexperienced reporters will tend to nod and pretend to be listening when they're actually thinking of the subject's office decor or (more likely) of their own next question. As a result, they will tend to run through a list of prepared questions, rather than shaping their questions from the last reply. Even a cursory study of the taped interview of a novice reporter will show many instances of failure to follow up. And a scattered collection of answers inevitably will produce a more fragmented story than an interview in which a theme or set of themes has developed naturally, as in a good conversation, with one thought building from another.

Poor listening is also responsible for a complaint made frequently by those who deal with the press: reporters too often interrupt, cutting them off before they get a chance to complete a thought. "That reporter didn't really want to hear what I had to say," the sources will complain. "He just wanted me to confirm what he already knew."

While the problem of listening is obvious, the solution is not so clear. One approach is to school yourself to pause after each reply, to think about what you've heard and consider whether a followup *ought* to be asked, before you go back to your list of questions. All interviewing books emphasize that such pauses are useful. They not only allow the reporter to think of the best followup, but they also give the source a chance to add a crucial thought. They may also — since people tend to want to fill the silence — prompt the source to say something he is thinking, but hadn't really planned to *say*. (This technique applies in television as well, where some of the best interviewers develop what might be called the "thoughtful" two-second pause.)

The pause may also help you counter the most insidious of all problems for novice interviewers: the temptation to act as though you understand when you don't. To counter that problem you must force yourself to ask the "idiot question" — the question you don't want to ask because it may make you look foolish, but which you don't dare not ask. The most disastrous approach possible for reporters is to nod and nod, hoping things will come clear eventually and that they'll be able to work it all out as they write. This approach is also an encouragement to a pattern shown by most expert sources, of speaking in arcane jargon until they're brought down (gently) to plain language, with a line like: "I'm going to have to summarize this process in my story, and I wonder if you can help me work out a simple explanation of how the experiment was set up. Would it be fair to say …?"

Focus

Another aid to listening is to concentrate on the focus of the interview, the central guideline — the reason you are doing the interview. One way of doing this is to imagine how your story is shaping up, to imagine what the headline or the lead may be. If that story shape emerges clearly in your mind, you are more likely to ask the questions that will round it out and to assess replies in the light of how they complete the design. (If the source comes up with an answer substantially different from what you expect, of course, new interviewing paths open up.)

In most cases it's useful to convey the focus or guideline to sources, both at the start of the interview and later, if it changes. This allows the source either to help you fulfil the guideline or to challenge you if she thinks you're heading the wrong way. You can say, for instance, "When I started this project I thought the story would be on your institute's research plans, but now I'm inclined to think I should concentrate on the province's refusal to fund your new building. …"

If the source objects to the thrust of your interview, it's wise to define that challenge clearly and give it careful consideration. Sources may indeed have good cause to object. And if their reasoning seems flawed, you will need to make your own case as effectively as possible. Any such disputes are better dealt with immediately and face to face, rather than next day after the story has been printed, when your editor becomes an unwilling part of a three-cornered fuss. If the dispute can't be resolved, it's better for all concerned, including the editor, to know of it before publication.

This line of advice is likely to be resisted by some journalists who think that it's best to keep the source in the dark about the thrust of a story. That may be valid sometimes, when there's a clear danger of source manipulation or when there's a danger of giving a story away. But in most cases the task has little to do with trapping sources, and much to do with enlisting their co-operation, and understanding as fully as possible what they're saying.

Objections in principle can also be raised to the idea of going into an interview with an explicit guideline and of firming up an explicit story line within the interview. The concern is that this approach will encourage you to find what you expect to find and ignore everything else — a very serious danger. While this is indeed a hazard of all journalism, the explicit guideline, or story line, has advantages. It permits analysis and testing by the reporter, by sources and by editors. In effect it is like the scientific hypothesis, set up to be tested.

(A classic case of failure to adjust the guideline came from a very young reporter who went to the local airport to do a story on noise pollution. He returned to report thus to his editor: "there's no story there, because they have this new device on the planes that cuts noise levels by 30 per cent.")

Thus, it is crucially important to evaluate while you're listening, so that you can define the next question and at the same time assess the material. This technique requires a good deal of concentration, but practice will increase your capacity for concentration. Social science research shows that the average person can think four times faster than the average speaker can speak — 600 words a minute as compared with 150 words a minute (Nichols 1948). You can use that time differential to your advantage, thinking on more than one level at once as you listen to the source, plan your next question and at the same time think of the overall shape of the story. An aphorism of the trade is that if you *can't* see the shape of the story by the end of the interview, then you probably haven't got one.

Review

In print interviews, a good deal of review is necessary. It's also a useful technique if you encounter that uneasy feeling that you've run out of questions while the story seems incomplete. The best solution to this difficulty is to glance over your notes and say something like "I think I have the overall picture but I'd like to double-check a couple of things. You say that your plan is to…" In the review process, you'll probably spot holes in your story. And at the same time you'll fulfil the important task of offering feedback for co-orientation. Review questions are especially important in phone interviewing, where it's easy for the source to cut you off. Every reporter knows, and hates, the feeling of discovering, a minute after hanging up the phone, that a minor but necessary question went unasked — and that the source is no longer available.

Confirm

In most technical interviews, it may be useful to arrange a later call for clarification and confirmation, even if you don't consider it strictly necessary. It helps to reassure the source that you're reliable and it provides an extra guard against misunderstanding. It allows you to check for later developments, or to bounce off the source the latest information you've got in a multi-source story. The conventional last question: "is there anything else we should have covered?" is also useful, if only to signal to sources that you're not blocking out their agenda.

Take Careful Notes

Finally, be sure you have a good record of the interview. Some reporters take too many notes, not knowing what will be important when they come to write them up. A clear guideline and evaluation of material during the interview will help you keep down the quantity of notes, while improving their quality. In general, that means taking notes only on what you fully understand at the time. The most dreadful interview result is a reporter sitting at the keyboard, going over notes and wondering what they mean. If you've been interviewing the mayor, for instance, and you have a note that says "New works building … $6M … next year," and you don't know whether the mayor *hopes* to build such a building, or *plans* to do so, you have a recipe for trouble. It's especially difficult to come back to such notes a day or two later; hence the sound newsroom maxim: "write before you sleep."

Take the time to make a neat and complete note, one that will be comprehensible tomorrow and two years hence. You may need to refer to your notes for court testimony. You may want to show them to your

---

KEEPING TRACK

Jan Wong, as Beijing correspondent for the Globe and Mail, *developed her own trick for keeping track of her interview guide during the interview itself:*

One rule of journalism is *Answer All the Questions*. This is really mundane, but it took me 11 years as a reporter to figure out how to remember to do so. Now I've got half the press corps in Beijing copying my nerdy technique:

Use little yellow sticky papers to note interview questions down beforehand. Also, use a blank one to jot down thoughts or new questions while the interview is in progress. And cross out questions as they are answered.

As you flip the pages of your notebook, keep moving the yellow sticky papers. You'll find that when you walk out of the interview, particularly a confrontational one or a fast-moving one, you've actually asked everything you meant to ask.

editor when a source changes a story. You may want to refer to them when you're writing a long article next year, or when you're writing memoirs 50 years hence. Historically, the leading journalists were people who kept careful *journals* — records of what they encountered, whom they talked to, what they saw, what they read — all carefully and perceptively recorded. In modern times reporters have become poor note-takers, scrawling fragmentary bits of information that are quickly discarded after the story is written. Reporters who train themselves to take proper notes (or to transfer their back-of-the-envelope notes quickly into a computer system) find that the effort pays off. The novelist John O'Hara once commented that his reporting career was useful to him mainly because it taught him to "get it right the first time." O'Hara's thought has meaning on several levels, and one of them applies to note-taking. If a good interview is personally enriching — and it is — then it is worth while taking and keeping a good record of it.

If you're using a tape recorder, test it beforehand and make sure it's operating during the interview. But don't rely entirely on it; take notes at the same time. This is both a backup and a practical aid to writing efficiency. Few reporters have the luxury of time that's needed to fully transcribe each interview. They work mainly from notes, and turn to the tape only for strong quotes or detail. Long, tedious quotes, laboriously transcribed, slow down the story. Recording devices also tend to make sources (and reporters) pedantic, but that's a hazard worth risking, especially if you're interviewing on a highly technical subject.

FIXING, UM, THE QUOTATIONS, EH?

Notebook in hand and tape recorder on the table, a reporter spends an hour interviewing a local environmental activist on housing policy. By the end of the interview, the reporter has a good handle on the activist's position, and some good quotations for the story. But when the reporter plays back the tape to check quotations, it's full of sentences like this: "well, uh, well, uh, land use is, uh, is the issue, the key issue, for the future. I mean, how can we, as a society, go on building, you know, sprawling suburbs. ..."

Spoken face to face, the quotation makes sense. Heard on tape, it's at least comprehensible. Transcribed into print, it is gibberish. The reporter is in a quandary: quotations add authority, substance and life to a story. But quotations also promise the reader these are the *exact* words of the speaker.

What is the reporter to do?

News style guides offer useful

(continued)

advice. "In general, we quote people verbatim and in standard English," says The Canadian Press's *CP Stylebook* (1995, 16). "We correct slips of grammar that are obvious slips and that would be needlessly embarrassing. We remove verbal mannerisms such as *ah*'s, routine vulgarities and meaningless repetitions. Otherwise we do not revise quotations."

The Globe and Mail Style Book (1996, 293) offers similar advice. It says direct quotations are "our first choice," but it's better to paraphrase than to use long-winded or confusing quotations. The words inside the quotation marks should be the exact words of the speaker, so don't tamper with verb tenses or pronouns.

Both style books tell reporters to use an ellipsis (three spaced periods) to indicate that material has been deleted from a direct quotation. And they allow for writers to retain slang or regional words and phrases, though these should be spelled in proper English.

But within the rules of style guides, reporters at Canadian dailies have some latitude — and a wide range of opinions — over whether and how much to "edit" quotations they choose for their stories. A 1991 survey found that reporters take into account three main factors: relations with the source, relations with the reader and the demands of good storytelling.

"If the speaker's grammar is so poor that it actually detracts from his content and message, minimal cleanup is okay," said one Ontario reporter, who asked that her name not be used. "I interviewed a highly qualified francophone woman who was taking a senior policy-making job in the Quebec government. The interview was done in English. Her intelligence and energy were clear in the interview but her English grammar a little weak. To let her quotes stand uncorrected would mean leaving the reader with the impression she was unintelligent, which was patently untrue."

Zuhair Kashmeri, formerly of the *Globe and Mail*, recalls making a decision to do exactly the opposite. "I remember interviewing a visitor from India and leaving his quotes intact. The reason: he was charged with drug smuggling, based on a police interview conducted in English, when he could hardly speak the language. He was acquitted. And leaving his broken English responses was the perfect technique of highlighting his plight and the careless police behavior that cost him a year in jail."

Burt Dowsett of the *London Free Press* says reporters owe it to sources to treat their ideas with respect. "Most people, even educated people, are not as exact in their speaking as they are in their writing. When someone consents to give a reporter an interview, I think the reporter owes the person the courtesy of correcting embarrassing grammatical mistakes. I can't think of any interview subject who would object to this. But do it whenever possible by taking the sentence in question out of quotes."

(continued)

Some reporters may apply a more stringent set of rules to politicians and public figures than to ordinary people.

Says Ron DeRuyter of the *Kitchener-Waterloo Record*, "If a source is barely articulate, particularly if it is a source in a position of accountability and authority — e.g., a mayor — readers should know how he or she really talks."

Many reporters admit they wrestle with the quotation question. They worry about whether cleaned-up quotations present a truer picture of the speaker's words. They worry about whether seemingly minor alterations may in fact change the tone of the quotation. They worry about making their sources appear better than they are or worse than they are, and about where to draw the line between the demand for clarity and the demand for accuracy.

For most reporters, the bottom line is the idea that quotations are real words from a real source.

Roger Taylor of the Halifax *Chronicle-Herald* puts it this way: "to extensively 'correct a quote' is the same as making one up. It cuts into the credibility of the journalist and the journalism profession."

Source: Distilled from a 1991 research project by Catherine McKercher and Klaudet White.

Routine Problems

A number of specific interviewing problems that can be helped by knowledge of technique include the following:

Off-record

The question of not-for-attribution, or off-record, information is often a difficult one for reporters. On one level, it's a problem of terminology. On another, it's a problem of widely varying practices. The terminology problems arise if (for instance) people not used to dealing with reporters say information is off the record when they really mean they don't want to be quoted or they're not sure of the information. So at times you will have to clarify what the source *means*, and then if necessary argue for reconsideration. If the source wants to give you off-record material, ask whether it can't be used on a background basis — meaning without any attribution — or perhaps without any indication even of the institution it came from. If the source offers information on background, without attribution, make a case that it should be attributed ("It will be a lot more authoritative, of course, if you'll put your name to it — especially since our policy is to avoid opinion from unnamed sources").

One tedious problem that often arises is a source request *after the fact* to treat something as not for attribution, or off the record. Most reporters assume, and most politicians realize, that statements made to reporters are on the record, unless a prior agreement has been made. However, it often happens (especially to newer reporters, more vulnerable to source pressure) that a source will make a trenchant comment, then think better of it and say blandly, "That's off the record, though." The reporter's proper response at that point varies with the circumstances. If the statement is a crucial one, the reporter is entitled to make a stand, to insist that the statement be considered as on the record because there was no prior agreement to the contrary. In practical terms, it's seldom worth making a crisis out of it. It is useful, though, to signal to the sources that you are not going to accept their after-the-fact rulings. You can say something like: "I'm seeing a number of people on this, so I'd prefer to keep it on the record. I don't want to end up with a lot of material I can't use."

Student reporters, of course, have a special problem in that sources may not treat them as "real" reporters. That means it is important to keep the process as professional as possible. Make each project realistic, aiming if you can at least for a school or community paper, and let sources know what publication you're targeting. Similarly, new reporters at a newspaper or broadcast outlet should check with their editors in advance to discover local practice, and the station's or newspaper's policy. While reporters usually have a degree of personal latitude in such matters, some news organizations have strict policies. Some discourage after-the-fact requests by printing the off-record comment, adding a statement like "Mr. Ramirez then asked that the remark be kept off the record."

Specialist reporters also have difficulty with sources who come to know them well and begin to expect that they can talk routinely on a background basis. This is especially true of public servants who deal regularly with the press. In one Ottawa case, a public servant who chatted with a reporter on the steps of the Parliament Buildings was furious to find his statements, and name, in print. He wrote to the editor to say that everyone in Ottawa knew public servants' statements to reporters were off the record unless otherwise specified. The reporter wrote a rebuttal, saying everyone in Ottawa knew that the practice was the exact opposite — that everything was *on* the record unless otherwise specified.

Practically speaking, both disputants were wrong. Many relationships exist in politics, from city hall to the United Nations, in which public servants speak freely to reporters they know, understanding that their names won't be used, even though no specific advance agreement is fixed. Sometimes these sources expect that newcomers will understand the practices. They may be naive to do so, given the variance in practice, but the new reporter also has an obligation to guard against ambiguity.

"NOT HER REAL NAME"

A prime interviewing challenge for reporters lies in drawing from sources' minds detailed anecdotes or examples. Inevitably, that means running into the dilemma of wanting to use case histories but finding that use of real names may expose subjects to pity or attack. The result is a pattern most editors dislike, the "not-her-real-name" syndrome.

Practice on this varies, from outright bans to reluctant toleration. In the wake of several well-publicized fabrication scandals, many editors now insist on full authentication of each case. Others are less strict. Either way, you should try to make the source of the anecdote as clear as possible in your story.

That is, if you can't give the subject's name, give the name of, say, the doctor or social worker who described her case, or who put you in touch with the subject. Readers will then understand that if they want to authenticate the story, they can go to the connecting source.

If such authentication is not possible, include in your story or in a note to your editor the fullest possible details on how the anecdote developed. The editor can then decide whether to run the item.

But above all resist any temptation to embellish. The benefits are at best slight. The potential damage to your self-respect and your reputation is immense.

Prior Checks

Another similar problem comes from the source who insists on seeing the finished story before publication. Again, practice varies. Most newspapers have a policy forbidding reporters to take stories back to sources. The reasons for this policy are obvious: few sources can resist the temptation to recast what they've said, to add heavy detail that will sink the story. And the simple logistics of waiting for source approval are intolerable at a daily newspaper. Curiously, though, some magazines go the other way, *insisting* that stories be seen by sources as a guarantee of accuracy. For a novice freelance writer there is some advantage in taking material back to source, especially if it is highly technical. At that stage in your career, you can't afford letters to the editor complaining that your story was wrong or muddled. Furthermore, the kinds of feedback you get from the source may be a useful guide to later practice.

Either way, it's important to know in advance how you're going to respond to a source's request to see the story. If you don't want to show it to your source (and most reporters don't) you should be prepared to say something like this: "I'm afraid I can't, because the material comes from several sources. But I'd be happy to call you when I've written the story to double-check all the material I'm attributing to you."

Elusive Sources

Every reporter recalls with chagrin interview sources who played games, who answered questions in a way that was narrowly truthful while concealing larger truths, who persistently changed the subject to get away from the reporter's guideline, who descended into a bog of technical jargon to avoid giving anything away. There is no single or easy solution for such problems. Experienced reporters know that sources will sometimes lie and often deceive. As a result, they will sometimes ask the same question in a different way, to guard against the "narrowly truthful" response. They will be careful not to ask two-part or "double-barrelled" questions, which allow the source to ignore whichever part of the question is harder to handle. They will be careful to keep their questions neutral and "unloaded," and to guard against letting themselves be drawn into debate. (Some politicians enjoy the classic game of reversing roles, asking of critical reporters what *they* would do about a particular problem. Any reporter unwise enough to be drawn into debate can expect to suffer for the misjudgment.)

The single best defence in these cases is a firm return to guideline — to the reason the interview is being done. Often the source's dodginess is a conscious or unconscious attempt to avoid the central issue.

In this, as in most other cases, it is useful to *level* with sources, to show them clearly that you haven't come to debate or play games but to learn about what they're doing and thinking. With luck, a touch of bluntness may even help get you past that most dangerous of interviewing traps, the artificial exchange of clichés, and on the way toward a degree of rapport and understanding.

INTERVIEWING

A checklist of reminders on interviewing:

✔ Prepare. The more you know before you go, the better off you are. You get information with information.

✔ Let yourself become *engaged* — interested in the source's work/ideas/argument. If you can't be engaged, you must at least appear to be interested.

✔ Listen. (John Hohenberg: "no talking reporter ever held a decent interview.")

✔ Project. Put yourself in the source's shoes and ask what she has experienced, what she hopes to accomplish, who her opponents are and so on. (*Listening* and *projecting* help you become engaged).

(continued)

✔ Have in mind a *guideline* — the reason you're doing the interview — and (usually) communicate it to your source. But be flexible and be prepared to change the guideline.

✔ Make your sources *bring down the abstraction level*. Probe for examples, anecdotes, cases — not just generalizations. Ask for developments, not just opinion.

✔ Don't pretend to understand if you don't. Ask the "idiot question." Try to make the source adjust from technical to ordinary language.

✔ Train yourself to *evaluate* the material as it's coming in, so you can define a tentative theme and shape your interviewing accordingly.

✔ Keep in mind that the interview is a fallible way of exchanging information, because oral information is not as reliable as written material and because misunderstanding occurs in all communication. Remember the Three Cs: corroboration, consistency, co-orientation.

✔ Understand that your *demeanor* — your body language, dress, tone — will make a considerable difference in the process. Practise a stance that's neither sycophantic nor hostile.

✔ Be cautious in using loaded, leading, double-barrelled and closed questions.

✔ Guard against letting the source reverse the process and question you. Don't get drawn into an argument.

✔ Take notes only on what you understand at the time. (John O'Hara: "get it right the first time.")

✔ Be courteously tough if you have to. If you're going to have a confrontation, have it before the story appears.

✔ Make sure there's no ambiguity about remarks made off the record, for background only, and so on.

✔ Use silence to advantage.

✔ Review. Check and check again. Call back to make sure of difficult material.

RECOMMENDED READING

Biagi, Shirley. (1992). *Interviews That Work: A Practical Guide for Journalists.* Belmont, CA: Wadsworth Publishing Company.

Brady, John. (1977). *The Craft of Interviewing.* New York: Vintage Books.

McLaughlin, Paul. (1990). *How to Interview: The Art of the Media Interview.* Vancouver and Toronto: International Self-Counsel Press.

Metzler, Ken. (1977). *Creative Interviewing.* Englewood Cliffs, NJ: Prentice-Hall.

Webb, Eugene J., and Terry R. Salancik. (1966). "The interview, or The only wheel in town." In Bruce H. Westley, ed., *Journalism Monographs*, No. 2, November.

PART three

WRITING THE NEWS

The subject of writing is broad enough to demand a lifetime of study. The two chapters in this section deal with just two small dimensions of this huge topic. The first looks at some general writing patterns and techniques that are often overlooked by novice journalists. The second deals with story forms that are specific to print journalism.

As well, the section reprints from the *Toronto Star* a splendid Joey Slinger column, "How to Write," which gets at the heart of the matter in a way that is more effective than anything we can devise.

CHAPTER 5

Writing Technique

AN EPISODE FROM THE EARLY TEACHING agonies of one journalism instructor illustrates something basic about the writing process. The incident went like this: a student on a feature assignment had spent a day with a class for students with physical disabilities. Her story was clean and detailed but also bland, abstract — boring. Her instructor, looking for ways to make it more vivid, paused at a line that said the teacher of the class was careful not to undermine the independence of her charges.

"There," he said. "That's the kind of abstraction that bothers me. Can you bring it down? Can you tell *how* she made sure she didn't undermine the kids' independence?"

The reporter thought, and said: "she was careful not to do things for the students that they should do for themselves."

"That's a bit more concrete," the instructor said, "but can you give me *one instance* that illustrates the generalization?"

The student then described in detail a revealing vignette: she told of one boy, aged 10 or so and wearing a heavy back brace under his blazer, working on a math problem at the chalkboard. When he reached the bottom of the board, not being able to bend, he had to get down on his knees. When he finished, he glanced up at the teacher to see if she was going to help him stand up. The teacher met his glance but made no move to help, even though she was close by. The boy gripped the chalk ledge and proceeded to pull himself up.

SHOW — DON'T TELL

This small anecdote symbolizes something critically important in all teaching — but also in writing. The abstract statement that the teacher "was careful not to undermine the independence" of her students would have passed instantly through the reader's brain. The anecdote fixed the message indelibly.

The incident also serves to illustrate a number of other points about writing. On the most basic level it signals a shift from expository to narrative writing, echoing the constant plea of writing coaches: "show — don't tell." It demonstrates as well that the most important part of writing takes place in the field, not at the keyboard. While e-mail and the telephone are useful tools for collecting story material, nothing can match the benefit of being there, of observing and taking careful notes. The story shows, too, that writing, consciously or unconsciously, is always selective: we hear and observe an immense amount that contributes to any story, and select what will make our point. On a deeper level, the anecdote prompts questions about the way we go about the act of writing, about how we translate reality into *story* through the use of suspense, creative connections, characterization and visual detail.

Much of the business of writing is, of course, governed (as is any other activity) by subconscious or taken-for-granted mental processes. For instance, anyone who has read a great deal will probably write instinctively with a certain rhythm, or with a sense of what can be held in a sentence. Because of this capacity, some writers prefer not to worry too much about technique. They argue that the way to write is simply to decide what you want to say and then (in Evelyn Waugh's memorable line) "put the words down and push them a bit."

Those critics are a minority. More commonly, writers share a fascination for technique, for discussing and dissecting approaches they like or dislike, and for "modelling" by using the devices they find in the work of their own favorite writers. Most of their readers, by contrast, read only for enjoyment or information, without thinking too hard about how a story is put together. Writers, and especially novice writers, must take a more analytical approach. How, they should ask, did this writer go about his research? How many people did he interview and with what intentions? How was he able to come up with these bits of description, or these anecdotes? What makes the story work? Where might the original story idea have come from? Like an architecture student in Rome, or a nursing student visiting a hospital, journalism students should look at writing with new analytical eyes. As columnist Joey Slinger puts it (see pp. 112–113), learning to write means learning to read all over again, for technique.

This process also requires some command of the language of analysis. The opening anecdote in this chapter, for instance, can be used to set labels on a number of patterns, simple and complex. Most obviously, it illustrates the importance of visuals, or concrete examples. But it also shows, on a modest level, the components of *story*: an element of suspense, a quality of rising and falling tension, of problem and resolution. The boy writing on the chalk board illustrates the importance of precise detail — the small elements like the blazer and back brace that give a sense of "presence," a sense of *being there*.

TAPPING INTO CREATIVITY

If we look closely, we can also see in the student's anecdote a quality central to all good writing — that is, *creativity*, in the sense of creating connections or patterns that have not been made before. Journalism scholar Stuart Adam (1993) calls this the act of imagination, by which journalists (like artists) frame images and form consciousness. Applying words like creativity and imagination to journalism does not mean, of course, that journalists make things up. Rather, it refers to the way in which they create word pictures in their own minds, and in turn in the minds of their readers. That quality of creativity governs everything else in writing: the devising of metaphor, the association of ideas, the deft use of suspense or irony. Barbara Tuchman has written that in history and biography, creativity does not mean to invent material — "it means to give the product artistic shape" (1982, 80). So it is with journalists. True, a journalist who is fascinated by literary technique faces the temptation to make life imitate art. But the ultimate obsession for journalists is *to get as close as possible to capturing what has actually happened*. Life itself is full of interest, full of drama. The task of arranging material so that it transmits the drama to readers can be intensely creative. In the case of the chalkboard incident, the student writer made a creative link between the small happening she witnessed and her understanding of teaching theory. Once made, that link may seem simple, something to be taken for granted, but the making of it is critical.

So what *is* creativity, and how can it be tapped? In *The Act of Creation* (1964), Arthur Koestler argues that all creativity is a matter of bringing together sets of ideas (Koestler calls them "matrices of thought" or "associative contexts") that haven't been linked before. For instance, terms like "single parent" or "Bay Street" touch off complex sets of mental connections. "Single parent" may produce connected images of day care or work/parenting tensions. "Bay Street" may evoke images of profits, corporate domination, immense buildings or throat-slashing competition. Creativity lies in making mental connections that bring such "matrices" together in original ways. In humor, Koestler says (and this simplifies his thought a great deal) the matrices are incompatible, and fall apart in surprising and delightful ways. When, for instance, baseball player John Olerud describes his personality as "just south of comatose," he intersects (unconsciously, perhaps) three associative contexts that can't be easily held together in our minds: illness, geography and personality. The linkage falls apart and, for reasons that aren't entirely clear, we laugh.

By contrast, all great metaphors represent a *synthesis* of image to create a new one that *can* be held in mind. When Shakespeare writes of "the slings and arrows of outrageous fortune," he instantly melds the image of battle with the frustrations of daily life. Koestler argues that creativity in other areas, from scientific discovery to artistic creation, also comes from putting together ideas or images that haven't been linked before. He cites, for instance, Archimedes in the tub, suddenly intersecting the homely image of his body in the water with the complex problem of buoyancy he had been pondering.

On a more mundane level, non-fiction writers are constantly making creative connections. Don Nichol made a very basic but telling creative connection when he wrote this lead:

> *Little Lamb, who made thee?*
> *Dost thou know who made thee?*
> These simple lines from William Blake's *Songs of Innocence* will never mean the same after this week's birth announcement of Dolly, the world's most famous ewe, now seven months old — the first mammal to be created through cloning.
>
> — Don Nichol, Ottawa Citizen, Feb. 28, 1997

Evan Solomon took the same circumstances and made mental connections in a different direction:

> Dolly. Funny how significant things are assigned such banal names. Fat Man and Little Boy for the atomic bomb, Dolly for the cloned sheep. These three benign titles signify the most profound events of the 20th century: the human ability to destroy life and now our ability to create it. The foolish names seem to calm my sense of panic and alarm. After all, how dangerous can something called Little Boy be? How threatening is a ewe named Dolly?
>
> — Evan Solomon, *shift magazine*, May 1997

Journalistic Imagination

Those creative acts are relatively simple, requiring a single mental connection. Environment writer Tom Spears builds a much more complex creative interlocking of ideas in this lead:

Tom Thomson and the Group of Seven made the pines of Algonquin Park's rocky shoreline timeless. Just how timeless, scientists are now finding out as they trace the birth of a white pine log they dragged from one Algonquin lake to the year 930 AD.

The pine was a seedling when the Vikings swept over Europe, and it was already old when William the Conqueror invaded England in 1066. It died in 1147, just as the Second Crusade was heading toward Jerusalem.

The white pine toppled from its rocky perch into Swan Lake, a two-kilo-metre-wide stretch of black water where the cold temperatures and low oxygen content of the water preserved the wood from decay.

It floated for hundreds of years, washing along the shoreline and accumulating soil that nourished smaller plants that grew out of its trunk. Insects laid eggs on the log, while turtles and otters sunned themselves on it. It may still have been floating when Columbus reached America.

When lake water finally penetrated its wood, the log sank by the shore, sheltering small fish such as brook trout.

Last year, a team of scientists used detective techniques to date the tree, the oldest ever found in the park ...

— Tom Spears, Ottawa Citizen, Jan. 26, 1997

This approach is on several levels an act of creativity, a work of imagination, as Adam would define it. On one level it creates suspense, the writer pulling us forward on the long journey of the log. On another it intersects sound and action ("sank by the shore, sheltering small fish ..."). More profoundly, it intersects knowledge about art (Thomson and the Group of Seven), history (the Crusades) and ecology (the interdependence of the various species). Those connections could only come from a well stocked mind fascinated by the subject matter.

The writer does not *invent* this material, but the moulding of it is creative. And the creativity lies not just in the connections within his own mind but also with those assumed to be in readers' minds — about Canadian art, for instance, or about wilderness appreciation. In a sense, the writer makes the log a complex metaphor representing the connections between nature and humans, between deep past and present. Like all metaphors, it connects webs of thought in the writer's mind with similar webs in the reader's mind. Through the story and our own imaginative response to it, a complex piece of the world becomes part of our culture, as well as part of our environment. The Algonquin log may have rested unknown in its lake for hundreds of years, as a piece of nature. But only when the scientists chose to study it, and when Spears extended their work by making it into a cultural artifact, does it take a place of some importance in our world. The same is true of Tom Thomson's pine trees.

Working journalists might well feel that this type of approach goes too far in making everyday journalism (as opposed to so-called literary journalism) into an art. But as Spears's story shows, creativity can lift the ordinary to a new level. Spears could have written a routine lead such as this: "scientists studying the ecology of Algonquin Park have identified a tree that they believe to be the oldest ever found in the area."

MAKING IT WORK

All these rather abstract ideas have a number of practical implications. One is that writers must have confidence in their own pattern-making. While their minds are seized with one topic, they must probe about in their memories for parallels or contrasting images that will make a creative connection, rather than thinking on a one-dimensional plane. Another is that choice of language can also be made more fresh and compelling by creative leaps. Boring speakers, and boring writers, use tired images they have often heard and seen: the reins of power, taking another tack, trail of destruction, hearty applause, warm welcome. Reporters must work to avoid such clichés or break them outright as Archie McDonald of the Vancouver *Sun* did when he wrote that athletes' steroid tests had become a "tempest in a pee cup" ("Ben's 10.6 Just Makes Us Doubt Him All Over Again," Ottawa *Citizen*, June 24, 1992). Similarly, one-dimensional reporting of what a person or a report *said* is likely to be made more interesting if the speaker's thoughts are intersected with other scenes, other comments.

But how is such freshness actually achieved? Many of us assume that any creativity we bring to writing is almost an accidental gift. Koestler sees it as a deliberate process, one that can be induced. He suggests that when writers are well engaged in a topic, they can discover fresh dimensions by "thinking aside," by deliberately pulling other "associative contexts" to the front of their minds. A writer preoccupied with a series on nutrition, for instance, may find it useful to leave the computer and go off to a country fair or a baseball game. The nutrition material will keep percolating in the back of the mind while the writer encounters fresh images: the onion smells of the midway, for instance, or the taste of a stadium hot dog. The writer assessing the importance of "Dolly" the cloned sheep can reach in a number of directions — toward multinational corporations, law-making or art.

Creativity, then, means a capacity to look with fresh eyes, to see fresh patterns. People of genius, Koestler observes, typically have never lost the habit of asking foolish questions. They show patterns of skepticism toward conventional answers, a refusal to take anything for granted, a freshness of vision that picks up on trivial clues. "Taken together, these create an acuity of perception, a gift for seeing the banal objects of everyday experience in a sharp individual light — as painters and poets do, each in his

Different media have different angles on collecting the news. The still photographer freezes a single moment in a sequence of events. The video photographer captures the longer sequence, but from a single perspective. The print reporter explores many dimensions, perhaps including the background of the subject, the reaction of the crowd, or even the quality of the snow. (David Lucas/Loyalist College)

own way; to observe details and notice trivia which escape the attention of others." (Koestler 1964, 705–706)

The best journalists show the same qualities. The best *teams* of journalists constantly interact in creative ways, sparking ideas off each other for new story ideas or new approaches. It seems clear, though, that creative connections come only after a good deal of conscious effort — and are of use only if deliberate work follows the creative burst.

HOW TO WRITE

By Joey Slinger

This much-quoted Toronto Star *article is reprinted from* No Axe Too Small to Grind: The Best of Joey Slinger, *winner of the 1986 Leacock Award for Humor.*

This is being written in a great rush because I have to get out of here and go talk to journalism students about being a journalist. One thing I can tell them is that you'll never be much of a journalist if you always write in a great rush. The other thing I can tell them is that being a journalist you'll never get rich. And that's about it. It will be a short talk.

But that's all right. Then the students can get out of the classroom early and drink beer or make love or read Mark Twain's *Life on the Mississippi* or get on with their nervous breakdowns or do anything else under God's green sky that reminds them that living is living and that journalism — well, journalism isn't the kissing, it's only the telling.

That said, if journalism is still what they care to do, they might as well do it well. So I will pass on some useful tricks.

By doing the following, anybody can improve anything they write 100 per cent — whether it's a letter, a club report, a shopping list, a memorandum, the lead editorial in The Star, the great Canadian novel, or *The Last Spike* by Pierre Berton. Anything. I guarantee it. You won't believe it can be so simple.

1. Learn to read all over again. Learn to read for technique. When Mark Twain describes thunder, how does he make it sound like thunder? How does Woody Allen make us laugh? What sort of detail does Jane Austen give us to make Emma sound too precious by half?

2. Practise. Nobody practices writing. Everybody thinks, "I speak the language, I should be able to write it." I can hum a tune, but would I sit at the Steinway at a concert in Massey Hall without practicing hours a day for years? Nope. So why should I expect to come cold to a sheet of paper and whip off something lyrical

(continued)

and moving. I shouldn't expect to. It is hard work, writing.

3. Rewrite. Don't ever show anybody the first draft of anything. A second draft is always better. A third better still.

4. Read your stuff out loud to yourself. In your mind you always know what you intended to say and how you intended to say it. Your eye is accustomed to feeding written stuff to your mind. They are like an old married couple who can leave a lot out and still know what the other is talking about. But you write most times for other people, often strangers, who don't know your codes and shorthand, who aren't insiders like your mind and eye. Let your ear be editor.

   When you read aloud, your ear will tell you, "That phrase sounds awkward," "I've lost track of what this sentence is about," "People don't talk like this," "This rhythm is herky-jerky." Your ear can be more objective than your eye. If you feel silly reading out loud, lock yourself in the bathroom and do it there.

5. This one is the most fun, and the most amazing. It is called "letting your subconscious do the writing for you and saving yourself a lot of work." I stumbled on it by trial and error, mostly by error. I later read a number of accounts of scientific discoveries and discovered it to be real and useful and respec-

table method. It is all laid out in an essay by Isaac Asimov called "The Eureka Phenomenon." All you have to do is concentrate intensely on the material you want to write about, then go away and think about something else for a while and then come back and watch your stuff spin out of your typewriter like gold from straw.

"Eureka," of course, refers to Archimedes saying, "I can't figure this out," and going and having a bath. Asimov: "if you let go, then the thinking process comes under automatic involuntary control and is more apt to take new pathways and make erratic associations you would not think of consciously. The solution will then come when you *think* you are *not* thinking. … I suspect that voluntary thought may possibly prepare the ground (if even that), but that the final touch, the real inspiration, comes when thinking is under involuntary control."

Asimov likes a mindless action movie to switch his mind from the subject at hand. I get a cup of tea, read the sports pages.

6. Keep it short.

There. Now you know everything I know. When I finish with the students, I will go for a walk, maybe drink beer, maybe make love.

Source John H. Slinger (1985), *No Axe Too Small to Grind: The Best of Joey Slinger* (149–151). Toronto: McClelland & Stewart.

CREATIVE APPLICATIONS

The list of writing techniques that demand creativity is endless, but these are some of the more vital ones:

Suspense Consider these two leads, the first from a novel, the second from a newspaper feature:

> The truth is, if old Major Dover hadn't dropped dead at Taunton races Jim wouldn't have come to Thursgood's at all.
>
> — JOHN LE CARRÉ, *TINKER TAILOR SOLDIER SPY* (LONDON: HODDER AND STOUGHTON, 1974), 9.

> There was another death two weekends ago in the Inuit community of Povungnituk, but this one was not quite a suicide.
>
> — JANET BAGNELL, MONTREAL GAZETTE, AUG. 1, 1992

Any serious student of fiction knows that suspense is a crucial quality, the magic element that draws readers forward from paragraph to paragraph and chapter to chapter. But few newcomers to journalism seem to realize how critical it can be in non-fiction. In the best journalism, it shows up in two forms, *natural* and *artificial*. The first refers simply to what isn't known yet. A hockey goalie has been injured: who will replace him? How long will he be out? A proposal has been made to the board of education to shut down two schools. Which schools? When will they close? How much will be saved? If answers to these questions can't be had, the reporter may be left with good potential for natural suspense. Yet many journalists are reluctant to report what isn't known. They seem unable to admit that there's anything they don't know. And often what isn't known is as dramatic as what *is* known.

This "natural" suspense contrasts with the artificial suspense of the storyteller, who knows how the story will turn out but doesn't give it away instantly. Consider the suspense element in this more extended version of the brief lead given above, in which each paragraph practically compels the reader to go on, to find out more about the shape of the problem:

LIFE AND DEATH IN POVUNGNITUK

There was another death two weekends ago in the Inuit community of Povungnituk, but this one was not quite a suicide.

A 25-year-old man went into convulsions after inhaling a lethal mixture of solvents and died without regaining consciousness.

Built on the northeastern shore of Hudson Bay, Povungnituk is a village of 1,100 people whose wooden bungalows perch incongruously on the barren tundra.

In the past two years, there have been 12 suicides in Povungnituk. One a month since January.

They have all been young, between the ages of 14 and 26, and they were mostly boys. They shot or hanged themselves.

Month after month, the community buried another child, then pretended that nothing is wrong, said Harry Tulugak, the community's mayor.
"Our young people are dying off like flies, but everyone is still trying to cover up the enormous problems within our families.

"We are seeing the breakdown of family values. There's incest, physical abuse, alcoholism." ...

— Janet Bagnell, Montreal Gazette, Aug. 1, 1992

That lead, and the following one from *Report on Business Magazine*, are classic instances of artificial suspense, designed mainly to intrigue readers and draw them on:

THE LITTLE ENGINE THAT COULDN'T

Gerald McKendry is sitting in the television room of his big lakefront house collecting unemployment benefits and explaining what happened to his dream of building plastic engines in Kingston, Ont. ...

— John Saunders, *Report on Business Magazine*, Nov. 1989, 85–91

Again, it's easy to see that the reader is pulled forward, enticed to an explanation of why McKendry is living well despite the collapse of his dream. (For more on that story, see pp. 125–127.)

These leads are almost identical in shape and purpose to classic suspense leads in fiction, starting not with the overall problem but with a small slice of it, a tiny incident that will intrigue and lead the reader toward the main point.

Dramatic Irony If suspense is one of the most obvious tools for keeping listeners leaning forward, a more subtle one is *irony*. Anyone familiar with literary writing knows dramatic irony comes from the tension of secrets held and withheld, of things that are not what they seem to be, of reality tilted slightly on its side.

In simplest terms, irony implies something more than what the statement says on its face. In a drama, for instance, the hero's comment can have special meaning because he and the audience know, while other characters don't, that a body is hidden in the closet. In other writing, simple irony may lie in saying the exact opposite of what is meant, as in a statement like "Attila's gentleness with prisoners was legendary." That statement invokes incongruity in a way that is close to Koestler's definition of humor: the two images of Attila, cruel and gentle, can't be held in mind simultaneously. The same pattern emerges when Tony Atherton writes in a review of Disney's *The Hunchback of Notre Dame* that Esmeralda's gypsy costume was "apparently fitted with one of those early medieval push-up bras" (Ottawa *Citizen*, March 14, 1997). He slides together the medieval and modern images in a way that creates incongruity and amusement.

On a more subtle level, visual arts critic John Bentley Mays maintains a kind of irony, as well as an extended metaphor, throughout this
lead, by insisting his information is unimportant when he clearly
believes otherwise:

SIFTING THROUGH TREASURES...

Because they are the slowest vehicles on the mass communications freeway,
newspapers are forever getting honked at. We're under pressure to be as newsy
as TV, fast as radio, trendy as the tabs. Not that this squeeze is such a terrible
thing: it keeps us and our readers moving, and often ahead of the traffic. But in
the process, we risk short-changing readers on facts about many a marvellous
but decidedly non-newsy thing going on in the country.

There's no way, for instance, to pump up into a hot news item the fact that
David Harris, 42, the studious curator of photography at Montreal's Canadian
Centre for Architecture, went to New York a couple of weeks ago and picked
up a snap at auction for just under $15,000 (U.S.).

The item becomes even less newsworthy when you learn that the image is
merely this year's latest (and probably not last) addition to the CCA's heap of
some 50,000 other photos, which is already — says Harris, without a blink —
"the pre-eminent collection of architectural photographs in the world ..."

— JOHN BENTLEY MAYS, GLOBE AND MAIL, OCT. 30, 1993

Mays uses irony to pique reader interest, by insisting that what he has to
tell isn't very interesting. In other cases a journalist, like a playwright, may
share with viewers some knowledge that's kept from a character on stage.
In the lead of Roy MacGregor's profile of Don Cherry, for instance, (see
pp. 118–120) the writer invites readers to see as amusing or ridiculous some
scenes that participants saw as serious or even tense. In still other cases the
writer may for a time keep knowledge from the reader, as in this instance:

SLAVE LAKE, ALTA. — Ashley Ladouceur is having her first career crisis.

She's an accomplished dog musher and is sure to be in the hunt for gold when
she races today at the Arctic Winter Games. At her home in Fort McMurray,
Alta., there are dozens of medals, trophies and plaques that attest to her abilities,
honed over many years of sliding across frozen lakes and over unforgiving trails.

She loves being a musher, but occasionally dreams of less strenuous pursuits
in a more hospitable climate — namely, moving into a big house in Beverly
Hills and making movies with Tom Cruise.

Hollywood's leading ladies do not need to fear just yet. After all, Ashley is
just 10 years old.

— SCOTT FESCHUK, GLOBE AND MAIL, MARCH 8, 1994

Detail One of the most common concerns of writing coaches is detail
— "precise" detail or "symbolic" detail that allows the writer to show
rather than tell. Variants on the saying "the art is in the detail" are a
staple of all writing handbooks. Spears's story on the Algonquin log, for

instance, could have told us that the log over the years sheltered various kinds of wildlife. Instead the writer picked precise detail: "insects laid eggs on the log, while turtles and otters sunned themselves on it." Similarly, Michael Webster used an accumulation of small symbolic detail (set up with a touch of suspense, and linked to an action sequence) as he introduced a portrait of dairy farming:

> The most noticeable thing about Bill Moreland is his hands. The rest of him is unremarkable: medium height, medium build, glasses, clean-shaven features that are pleasant but, well, unremarkable. He is 42 years old, and the first hints of grey to come can be seen in his hair. Still, his face is largely unlined, and his trim, fit body could belong to a man 10 years younger. His hands, though, appear to have been cut off someone else's arms and stuck into Bill's sleeves. They are red and swollen; scarred, dry and cracked. His fingernails are thick and horny, white instead of pink, more flat than curved. They look as if they belong to a man in his 60s. They are the hands of a farmer.
>
> This morning, as every morning, Bill opens the aluminum door to the milk house at ten to five and fumbles for the light switch. He lifts his hat — a red baseball cap advertising a brand of corn — rubs his hair and yawns loudly, blinking in the sudden light. He has been awake for less than five minutes, just long enough to get dressed and walk out to the barn. It will be three hours before he eats breakfast, and he has not even had a cup of coffee …"
>
> — MICHAEL WEBSTER, HARROWSMITH, SEPT./OCT. 1989; EXCERPTED FROM HOME FARM: ONE FAMILY'S LIFE ON THE LAND

The lead perfectly exemplifies the "Show — don't tell" rule. Webster could have *told* us that Bill Moreland works hard, or has a demanding job; instead, he offers detail that lets us quickly reach that conclusion on our own. But such detail doesn't come easily. "The greatest thing a human soul ever does in this world is to SEE something and tell what he SAW in a plain way," John Ruskin wrote. "Hundreds of people can talk for one who can think, but thousands can think for one who can see. To see clearly is poetry, prophecy, and religion — all in one" (quoted in Allan Gurganus, "The Practical Heart," *Harper's*, July 1993).

Ironically, the importance of visual detail may need special stress in an age that is rich in the visual images of magazines, television and movies. Given that wealth, it appears we of the television age — in contrast to our letter-writing ancestors — have let ourselves become careless about the visual element in our writing. We may even have lost some capacity to experience reality directly, expecting that someone else will already have framed it for us.

Whatever the cause, it's clear that many of today's students have difficulty in describing what they see. Typically, they have well-developed skills in absorbing information from print or the spoken word and re-synthesizing it. But they have little experience in using their eyes to see and describe people, scenes and action, or in using their minds to create visual analogies and metaphors. Surprisingly often, it's possible to go through long student-written features and find not a single item of description, either from the writer's own eyes or from the eyes of sources.

Because of this gap, writing coaches are quick to praise writers who show "an eye for detail." The best writers clearly have the same quick instincts good photographers show when they spot a situation that will make a decent picture. One able photographer underlined the point while talking about the working style of a veteran colleague. "The difference between us," he said, "is that I often find myself thinking, 'That *would have been* a good shot.'"

So it is with writers. Some of them spot the image or happening that will deftly illustrate a point. Some don't. Some are brilliant at extracting anecdotes or visual detail from sources' minds. Some aren't. Some are quick to spot the right element of symbolic detail or dialogue — the bit of business or language that sums up the whole situation and creates presence. Some are just smart enough to realize too late that they should have made notes on a striking bit of action or background. (Notes are always needed. Those who think they'll remember, probably won't.)

DON CHERRY: THE PRIME MINISTER OF SATURDAY NIGHT

BY ROY MACGREGOR

Roy MacGregor has earned a reputation as one of Canada's finest profile writers. The following lead, taken from a story that appeared in the Ottawa Citizen, shows how he maintains that reputation. What makes the intro work? What writing techniques has MacGregor employed to attract, keep and amuse the reader? How does he paint a life-size portrait of the larger-than-life Don Cherry? How does he manage to capture the essence of what he saw, heard and felt without telling the reader his own opinions about it?

It is — at least on Saturday nights throughout the winter and every night for most of each spring — the most recognizable, popular, controversial, beloved and yes, often despised political voice in the country. It has come to Ottawa in the midst of a snow storm, come to Ottawa to speak out and to speak loudly.

"Just *shut* your god-*damn* mouth for a minute!" Don Cherry barks from the far side of the toilet stall.

(continued)

"*Shut* up and let *me* talk — okay?"

"Okay," the young man by the urinals says.

The young man surely never meant it to go this far. He came in to Don Cherry's brand-new Nepean bar, had a couple, saw Cherry heading off to the washroom and figured it was as good a chance as he'd ever have to tell his buddies he'd spent the afternoon raising a few glasses with Cherry and talking about hockey — more specifically, about Eric Lindros and his refusal to play for the team that drafted him, the Quebec Nordiques.

Cherry, after all, was talking hockey with everyone. For nearly three hours he had been sitting in a far corner of the restaurant and it was clear to anyone who wandered in that the last thing the host of *Hockey Night in Canada*'s "Coach's Corner" wished to be was inconspicuous. He had on one of those suits Nathan Detroit last wore in *Guys 'n Dolls*. He had his Wilfrid Laurier collar done up tight enough to choke and yet nothing, not the collar, food, autograph seekers or even the endless cups of coffee, could stop the endless flow of opinion that erupts from the active volcano of Don Cherry's mouth.

"*There they go!*" Cherry would bark and above him, across from him, around him, television screens would fill with the video fists of Bob Probert and Keith Crowder. Every half hour or so the same punchout, the same raw result — and yet each time the bar would stop dead and stare and shout as if the fight were live, the outcome unknown.

"Who's the toughest, Don?"

"Pretty hard to beat Probert."

"Who's your favorite player, Don?"

"Gotta go with Neely, eh?"

"Who's the best you ever saw, Don?"

"Right there," Cherry points to the screen, where Bobby Orr skates by every half hour or so with a grace not seen since the early 1970s. "There's the best. I was behind the bench when he scored that goal, you know, and I got tingles down my back then and I still get tingles every time I see it. Never been anyone like Orr."

But now, with the coffee forcing a break in the action, the prodding has accompanied him to the washroom and Don Cherry, who is nothing if not accommodating to his fans, can take no more.

"You think Lindros should be forced to play in Quebec?" the voice barks from behind the stall door.

"Yeah, I do," the young man says.

"Well, I don't. And I happen to think he's a hell of a fine young man, too."

The man is flustered. "I — "

"*Shut* up. I heard you out, now you listen to me. Eric Lindros is a friend of mine, okay? Where do they get off calling him a *snot* and a *punk* and a racist and a bigot? Who the hell do those politicians think they are saying he should be

(continued)

dropped from the Olympic team? If someone ever said those kinds of things about a *Queebec* kid they'd take him to court. Now whaddya think about that?"

"Okay, eh? I just thought I'd ask."

Moments later, Cherry is back at his coffee, stirring angrily as he recounts the story of the washroom encounter. "I tell you, the closer I get to the Quebec border, the worse it gets."

This being an inward-looking country with but two mad obses-sions, hockey and politics, it had to happen that some day someone would come along to harness them together and, in doing so, create a brand-new power base. Don Cherry has become the Prime Minister of Saturday Night, a voice now so popular that hockey has become the only television sport where the audience goes *up* during intermissions. ...

Source: Roy MacGregor, "Don Cherry: The Prime Minister of Saturday Night," Ottawa *Citizen*, Mar. 14, 1992.

BUILDING THE THEME

If the ultimate use of creativity is to give a work "artistic shape" then a crucial act of imagination lies in seeing the components of a story as a coherent whole. One of the most common writing flaws encountered by all editors is lack of order — disjointed writing that starts on one theme, disappears down a side track, takes a second turn and leaves the reader hopelessly lost. The task of avoiding such confusion is often represented as one of order and discipline, but it is also a matter of imagination, of comprehending the whole, making logical connections and drawing out a dominant theme.

And regardless of whether the definition is explicit, every piece of writing requires a theme — *a reason why the article should be written and read.* The Algonquin log story, for instance, builds to a theme of the interaction of forests and lakes in supporting life. The Inuit suicide lead builds to a theme of social breakdown in the community. Sometimes such patterns are obvious, but beginning writers may find it useful to define the theme and sub-themes explicitly as they get into a major piece of writing. They can even post by their keyboards a "theme state-ment" listing main theme and sub-themes, as an over-all guide to shap-ing the story. Then, as they write and find other sub-themes emerging, they can amend the theme statement. The implication here is that theme definition must not be thought of simply as a proposition stated once and then forgotten. Instead, the theme is a spinal column that

An exhausted firefighter rests after battling a chemical explosion at an industrial warehouse in Burnaby, B.C. The dramatic tension in the picture lies in the small detail, especially the slumping posture and the hand rubbing an eye. In writing, too, it is the precise, understated detail that often tells the story best. (Mario Bartel)

gives structure to the whole story. As each new section is introduced, the writer can indicate how it advances the theme. At the end there will usually be a subtle reprise of the theme.

Brilliant writers probably have less need to craft theme statements in advance, since they don't sit down to write until the story has taken shape in their minds. Most of us, however, tend to write our first paragraph and then cast about to consider what should be in the second. We need to define our theme so we can avoid (or exploit) the natural tendency to "write our way to coherence," in the words of journalist-academic Roger Bird. When we fall into that pattern, we must learn to identify it and revise the story so as to impose the coherence that has eventually emerged.

In the end, content must dictate structure, so if in late writing stages you find that you are working on material that wasn't forecast in the theme statement, you will probably want to review and reconstruct. That may mean working up and following a basic outline — at least a point-form guide or a chart showing themes and sub-themes. As with technique analysis, writers disagree furiously about the usefulness of outlines. (Jacques Barzun, for instance, calls them "useless, fettering, imbecile" [1971, 11].) But when the work is finally finished the writer must have a firm understanding of the structure and must be satisfied that the structure works, fitting the content. Anyone who finishes a piece of writing without knowing its underlying structure is either a genius or a very bad writer.

One way of testing theme structure is to look closely at transitions — the bridges or linking sentences, or summary sentences that carry readers from section to section, pointing the way. Among novices, transitions are probably the writing tool most often overlooked. They themselves understand where their narrative is heading, but do not realize that they need to mark the way for readers. Writers need to signal to readers how the new thought connects with what has gone before, what the new section will cover, or how it all ties in to the main theme. Inexperienced writers should go over any piece of their work one extra time just to inspect transitions — to consider where linking ideas need to be added. If the theme of the story is thought of as its backbone, transitions are the sinews that tie new ideas to it.

LEARNING TO PROJECT

If story structure demands creativity, so, too, does the crucial act of projection — of getting into the reader's mind, to divine what level of explanation the reader needs, or what questions the reader may ask. Projection thus means *locating* readers, making assumptions about their level of knowledge, their expectations, their attitudes. As Barbara Tuchman says, the reader is the essential other half of the writer: "if it takes two to make love or war or tennis, it likewise takes two to complete the function of the written word" (1982, 81). That means the writer must constantly sense the reader's presence at the other end of the communication line. One journalist of our acquaintance writes with her mother in mind. If there's a tough concept to be explained, she considers whether her mother will have any trouble with the wording she's using, whether she'll need any more detail, whether particular terms will have to be explained. Another writer speaks to an imaginary reader on a bus, a tired and hot commuter — a reader who has some built-in interest in the topic but little patience for ambiguities. In both cases, the crucial point is that the writer is not trying to pass material on to a mass audience but to *one* other reader.

Traditionally, persuasive writers and speakers have well understood the importance of locating the audience, of finding out their concerns, and of making contact with them on that territory before trying to bring them to change their attitudes. Politicians speaking on the Prairies during a severe drought, for instance, would probably begin by commiserating with farmers about the lack of rain before bridging to their own concerns. The same principle applies strongly to persuasive writers: they, too, must be sensitive to what the audience is thinking, even though it's more difficult to do so when the audience isn't even in sight. The principle applies as well to writers who simply want to report, not persuade. They must have some working idea of what is going on in the reader's mind, of how the new information will fit with what's already there.

PICKING UP THE RHYTHM

Appreciation for the rhythms of language is a talent of infinite subtlety, developed only with time and intense interest. Journalists are often drawn to their craft because they have grown up with an attraction to writing, perhaps because they developed a passion for reading as teenagers. Robert MacNeil is only one of many writers who say that a feel for the weight and rhythm of words comes out of the childhood experience of reading and being read to. Writers, MacNeil says, read more than most people and listen more than most people: "they listen to language the way artists look at paintings" (1989, 225).

Those who have not developed this language sense in childhood find it difficult or impossible to develop artificially the necessary feel for diction or rhythm. It may help, though, before you sit down at the keyboard, to tune in even briefly to writers you admire. A few pages of Orwell, or of Churchill, or of Hemingway may help you orient the complex mental tools by which your mind controls language. Reading poetry may also help. Writing coach Kate Long of the *Charleston (W.Va.) Gazette* says reporters can improve the rhythm of their writing by reading poetry aloud for even 10 minutes a day. Reporters who write and read poetry, she says, "seem to be especially conscious of unnecessary words and the rhythm of their words" (quoted from Coaches' Corner in *Washington Journalism Review*, September 1990, 52).

TOUCHING MYTHIC CHORDS

All writers, in fiction or non-fiction, write with some appreciation of the mythic fabric of their societies. That is, they are attuned to the basic stories that help people make sense of the world. On a simple level, one can quickly identify a number of the popular myths of western society: the Robin Hood myth (a rebel against the establishment); the Cinderella myth (an overlooked and ill-treated person who soars to fame and success); the King Lear myth (an arrogant person destroyed by blind pride). These, and many others of the kind, combine to create a cultural understanding of the world. That understanding is shared by writers and readers — as in Spears's linking of Canadian painters and the Canadian wilderness. Like any aspect of writing, the invoking of classic myths can be overdone, producing clichés and stereotypes. But all writers know that their work will be richer as they develop familiarity with the mythic fabric. To cite just one narrow instance: it is hard to imagine anyone working effectively as a Canadian journalist who lacks appreciation for Canada's myths of travel and of distance — of the Atlantic schooners, the *coureurs de bois*, the transcontinental railway, the cattle drive. In subtle ways such mythic material permeates good journalism. For that reason journalists must steep themselves in their country's history and culture.

USING MODELS

These are only a few of the many dimensions of writing technique, which can cover everything from the brilliantly creative connections that sometimes leave us in awe, down to the tiny elements of craft (like treatment of commas) that are normally ignored unless they're handled badly. The complexity and richness of these techniques emphasize again the basic paradox: when writing is done well, it looks simple. It's easy to make the mistake of thinking, as you read a Rosie DiManno or Joey Slinger column, that this kind of thing must be easy. It isn't.

It takes time and a good deal of practice even to learn to evaluate writing. It takes time to learn to break down the work of able writers in order to see how they craft anecdotes or establish suspense, or rhythm, or contrast, or presence. It takes time to develop a measure of self-criticism, an ability to look at your own work as though you had never seen it before. (Gay Talese is said to pin stories on the wall and look at them through binoculars, so he can see them with fresh eyes; many writers read their material aloud, to listen for rough spots.)

Some people may think that this kind of study of craft is unnecessary, that they can somehow make an intuitive leap to the highest levels of writing skill. If that were true, it would be unique: in every other craft or art, beginners begin by *modelling* — by studying and imitating the styles and forms of the best practitioners, and gradually developing their own approaches. So all beginning writers ought to save and analyse pieces of writing they admire, in the process of developing the difficult skill of looking critically at their own work.

MODELLING

In the early stages of learning any craft, students use models, identifying techniques and analysing why one works and another doesn't. In the following lead, for instance, these are some of the noticeable techniques:

Gerald McKendry is sitting in the television room of his big lakefront house collecting unemployment benefits and explaining what happened to his dream of building plastic engines in Kingston, Ont. In chinos and a new-grown beard he looks at the age of 65 like a well-heeled beachcomber. In fact, he is a failed entrepreneur, fired public servant and pardoned ex-convict,	Present tense for immediacy Setting Irony Specific-to-general Main theme hint Symbolic detail for "presence" Creative connection Contrast/irony Suspense — we expect to find out more later

(continued)

items that came as a surprise to believers who lost millions betting he would revolutionize the small-engine business.

Dramatic irony
Main theme
Rounding off anecdote — from hope to despair

In his latest career, he was the father of Plastic Engine Technology Corp., also known as Petco, a company that entered the world in 1985 and died in 1989 without selling a single plastic engine. As a manufacturing venture it was a flop — the little engine that couldn't. But as a stock promotion it was just wonderful.

Bridge/summary sentence
Metaphor

Irony

Allusion — creative connection
Sarcasm signals writer's stance will be critical
Bridge/transition

This is not to say that McKendry, a man of great persuasive power, did not believe in it. His intentions may be forever a mystery, like the practical value of the engine and whether he made money on the deal. It is a measure of his salesmanship that investors and creditors bought the concept, and paid such a heavy price. He maintains that they were not deluded. Whatever the skeptics may think, he says, "Petco was very real. Its products were very real; its employees — no complaint, excellent people all the way through. We faltered for lack of money."

Main sub-themes: writer indicates the article will cover (a) McKendry's motivation, (b) the practical value of the engine and (c) whether he made money on the project

Symbolic quote — shows subject's style

Yes, Petco did run out of money, but not before going through a good deal of it. In round numbers, it raised $10 million by selling shares, borrowed $6 million, found a landlord willing to erect a made-to-order factory at a cost of $7 million and left behind another $3 million in unpaid bills. ...

Topic or summary sentence, indicating what paragraph will cover

Rhythm

Every stock promotion needs a story and Petco's was ideal. It was about a little one-cylinder engine,

Topic sentence

(continued)

the kind you find in chain saws and weed trimmers, something the average stock-market investor figures he more or less understands. According to the story, Petco had a way to make these engines out of plastic, or at least a way to use more plastic than other manufacturers. Thanks to an ingenious fuel-control system, the engine would run cooler than most — cool enough not to melt the latest heat-resistant plastics ...

Source: John Saunders, "The Little Engine That Couldn't," *Report on Business Magazine*, November 1989, 85–91.

Concrete example

Simple explanation of complex technical matter

WRITING TECHNIQUE

A checklist of reminders on writing technique:

✔ Show, don't tell. Illustrate your stories with anecdotes, examples, cases, analogies, parables.

✔ Study writing technique constantly. When you read news stories or articles, analyse what kind of material the writers gathered and how they shaped it.

✔ Project. Write always with audience members in mind, considering what they already know and what will make them react.

✔ Use the full range of writing experience. Study classic literary tools like suspense, irony, surprise, rhythm, creative connections and so forth, and note how they can be used in journalistic work.

✔ Develop an eye for theme — the reason a story deserves to be written and read. Learn to identify thematic structure in your own work and in others'.

RECOMMENDED READING

Barzun, Jacques. (1971). *On Writing, Editing, and Publishing*. Chicago: University of Chicago Press.

Blundell, William E. (1988). *The Art and Craft of Feature Writing*. New York: Plume/Penguin.

Franklin, Jon. (1986). *Writing for Story*. New York: Plume/Penguin.

Koestler, Arthur. (1964). *The Act of Creation*. New York: Macmillan.

Strunk, William, Jr., and E. B. White. (1979). *The Elements of Style*. 3rd edition. New York: Macmillan.

Zinsser, William. (1994). *On Writing Well*. 5th edition. New York: Harper & Row.

CHAPTER 6

Story
Structure

WHEN REPORTER JOHN IBBITSON OF THE Ottawa *Citizen* covered a council meeting in rustic West Lanark Township, he could have started his story with this conventional lead, summarizing the "who, what, where" of the affair:

MACDONALD'S CORNERS — West Lanark Township Council last night approved in principle the opening of a controversial gravel pit between Elphin and Snow Road Station.

Instead, he wrote:

MACDONALD'S CORNERS — The seven councillors who filed into the township hall looked distinctly unhappy.

The place was packed. People in bulky sweaters and jeans, beards and braided hair, leaned against the plywood-panelled walls, perched on the upright piano, sat cross-legged on the floor. They were anti-pit.

They were outnumbered by the ones in chairs — mostly big men in jackets with crests on them that spoke of fire departments and hockey teams. They sat silently, impassively, staring at the councillors. They were pro-pit.

That it should come to this. ...

— JOHN IBBITSON, "THE PIT: ZONING SETS NEIGHBOR AGAINST NEIGHBOR," OTTAWA CITIZEN, APR. 21, 1992

Ibbitson's decision reflects a change and enrichment in journalistic forms. Traditionally, the most common structure of a news report was the inverted pyramid, which summed up the essence of the story in the first paragraph and then added supporting facts in descending order of importance. The rationale was that readers could stay with the story or not: they could read only the lead and move on to something else, or hang in if they wanted detail. Editors could do the same, cutting the story off at the end of almost any paragraph.

That form was, and still is, a newsroom staple. It is a distinct aid in the organization of news pages and news broadcasts, allowing editors to trim a number of stories to fit the space available. It is also an aid to readers, allowing them to cast a quick eye over a page and sample many stories. And for writers, especially newcomers to journalism, the inverted pyramid is a good way of putting news judgment into practice. More than any other form, it requires reporters to make a quick and certain judgment about the most significant aspect of a story, to analyse and set priorities on what they've collected. More than any other form, it requires the writer to cut to the essence of the matter, which helps explain why it is a basic element in news-writing classes. In a sense it is the most natural news-telling form, because it most closely resembles the way people *tell* news face to face.

But as a story-telling method, the inverted pyramid has problems. For one, it gets in the way of narration, making it almost impossible for the writer to unfold a sequence of events, to exploit suspense and surprise. Typically, it deals with effects before causes, which makes for a disjointed feel. It often puts an unnatural stress on one element of a story, throwing other important elements into obscurity. And because each successive paragraph deals with information that is less and less important, it offers readers less and less incentive to stick with a story to the end.

Partly because of these flaws, the trend in recent years has been toward more variety in form. This trend has been encouraged by the flexibility of computer editing, and also by the increased competitiveness that encourages each medium to emphasize its strengths. For newspapers, that means depth, explanation and story values — a consistent effort to offer dimensions a brief TV or radio summary can't match.

The expanded choice of forms includes some that were once more typical of magazine articles and essays. Even on more routine news, it has led to stories constructed not in inverted pyramids but in topic segments, in chronological order or in the suspense-based "once upon a time" story-telling form. Broadly speaking, these forms lend themselves to pattern stories, to reports that get at underlying meanings, rather than simply the superficial facts.

These new forms also work well for reporting that tries to go beyond the rather bloodless, detached tone of most hard news writing. Consider the merits and defects of this "hard" or summary lead, typical of the kind developed in wire service writing, for the top of an inverted pyramid story.

> NEW DELHI — At least 58 Hindu pilgrims were crushed to death or drowned and more than 50 were injured, many seriously, in stampedes in two holy cities in central and northern India on Monday.
>
> — RAHUL BEDI, *DAILY TELEGRAPH*; REPRINTED IN THE OTTAWA *CITIZEN*, JULY 16, 1996

The lead efficiently summarizes the situation. As you read it over a second time, it is hard to imagine taking out a single word. It is easy to imagine a radio or television report based on that one paragraph, without any further detail. It is also neutral in tone, without emotion or involvement — without any effort to transmit the full horror of the scene. Some would call it sterile, a mechanism designed to inform without upsetting readers. The writer of the following story, confronted with the same facts, was impelled to try to transmit the horror:

> The first crush comes from the heat, then from the push of a dozen hands on the back and shoulders and arms, and finally from the realization that there is no thought in a crowd: there is only movement.
>
> As the temperament swirls insanely into a mad, desperate current of chaos, there is terror, fright, fleeting hope, hysteria and above all, the mighty animal instinct for survival.
>
> It can engulf rich U.S. kids at a Who concert in Cincinnati or hungry refugees in a tented camp in Somalia. But almost nowhere is the titanic weight of crowd greater than in India, where the terror of a stampede struck again yesterday in two places, killing 60 people.
>
> All the dead were Hindus on pilgrimages to celebrate an auspicious new moon. ...
>
> — JOHN STACKHOUSE, *GLOBE AND MAIL*, JULY 16, 1996

The question of which lead is better is moot. The first clearly serves a function, advising readers quickly of the essence of the disaster. The second comes nearer to *showing* something of the true quality of the event. Indeed, it could be argued that the hard, summary lead disguises the reality. John Carey is one of many writers who have observed that one function of language is to neutralize or conceal experience. When a report says "more than 50 were injured, many seriously," the phrase does nothing to convey the screams of injured, the smell or feel of mingled blood and dirt. In Carey's terms, this kind of language is used to "keep reality at bay" (Carey 1987, xxxii).

Of course, it is hard to imagine a newspaper covering all the news of the day with heightened language and emotional description. At the least, it would take too much space and become impossibly wearing for readers. Dramatic writing too easily slides over the line to melodrama. Emotion also leads to controversy: the reporter's personal emotional reactions may clash with those of the readers. Traditionally, editors (and readers) have expected reporters to concentrate on the news "out there" rather than on the way they feel about it.

Journalism classes, like reporters and editors in the news business, may debate which version of the New Delhi story is better. But it is clear that more and more newspaper writers are trying to go beyond a flat, just-the-facts style of reporting. For newcomers to journalism, these changes offer increasing scope and challenge.

To deal with this increased complexity, it is useful to start this study of journalistic forms with a closer look at the distinction between hard and soft leads. The hard (or direct) lead sums up instantly the main point or points of the story. The soft (or indirect) lead uses some device to draw readers down to the main themes, after two, three or 10 paragraphs. In each case, the form is signalled in the lead — the first paragraph or the first block of paragraphs — and this lead both reflects and governs the shape of the story. The hard lead is often used on "spot" news: on the sharp, easy-to-summarize development that must be told today, as opposed to the "feature" that can be used any time. But, as Ibbitson's or Stackhouse's stories show, this division is no longer as clear as it once was. The soft, indirect or "featurish" approach shows up often on major news stories. It is an easy exercise to go through a newspaper and identify which leads are hard and which are soft. (The term "soft" lead should not be confused with the idea of soft or frivolous news; it simply designates an indirect approach of some kind to the main news.)

EXAMPLES OF SOFT AND HARD LEADS

Typical Soft Leads

It was going to be a weird day in courtroom number 11.

You could tell that from the beginning.

First there was the toilet. Then there was the snake.

The gleaming white American Standard was brought into the courtroom by defence lawyer John Hale, placed on a table at the front, and filled with lukewarm water. Hale's client, Dave Rodgers, is charged with flushing his pet python down a similar toilet …
— ELIZABETH PAYNE, OTTAWA CITIZEN, JAN. 30, 1992

Bryan Adams spoke and the fans listened.

"Be good to Osoyoos," Adams told the crowd of 30,000 who gathered in the Okanagan town Sunday for the only B.C. stop in his Waking Up the Nation tour.

"Osoyoos has been good to you tonight. So have a good time and don't wreck the place."

Then the clean cut kid from North Vancouver gave the fans what they had come for. He stomped, kicked, strummed and screamed his way through almost two hours of high-powered rock tunes.

And in return the fans kept their end of the deal — they didn't trash the town.
— STEWART BELL, VANCOUVER SUN, SEPT. 8, 1992

(continued)

Typical Hard Leads

Vancouver has at least five crack houses where drug users can buy and smoke cocaine derivative, city police say. And they claim the number is growing.
— MARY LYNN YOUNG, VANCOUVER SUN, SEPT. 4, 1992

If Canada and France don't reach an agreement on fish quotas by Sept. 30 Ottawa will unilaterally impose one, Fisheries Minister John Crosbie says.
— RYAN CLEARLY, ST. JOHN'S EVENING TELEGRAM, SEPT. 16, 1992

A single pack of matches saved a Winnipeg psychiatrist and his young family from death on a small Lake Winnipeg island where they were stranded for nearly two days, police said yesterday.
— LINDA QUATTRIN, WINNIPEG FREE PRESS, SEPT. 17, 1992

Surrey council members are voting themselves another raise — just eight months after the last one.
— HAROLD MUNRO, VANCOUVER SUN, SEPT. 8, 1992

Fuelled by the aging population and carcinogens such as smoking, cancer rates in Manitoba are set to soar 30 per cent this decade.
— ALEXANDRA PAUL, WINNIPEG FREE PRESS, SEPT. 20, 1992

CHOOSING THE THEME

The first task in deciding how to write a story, however, is *not* to choose the form, but to define the theme or thrust of the story. The form can then be made to serve the story, rather than obscuring it. This point is underlined by an exercise done in several reporting classes, on the case of a man who was sentenced for drunk driving even though he'd suffered what he called poetic justice — he himself had been run down by a drunk driver. (Names and other details have been changed in this example and in others where repetition of the story might cause hurt or embarrassment.) Natural storytelling would demand that this point, the irony of the man's "justice," should be central in shaping the lead, as it has been in the above summary. Yet a surprising number of students tell the story in a way that would be news only to the man's relatives. For instance:

> A 44-year-old X-ville man pleaded guilty today to two charges of impaired driving, possession of a stolen licence plate and driving without insurance.
>
> Robert Brown, 44, was given six months for impaired driving with a one-month consecutive sentence for having the stolen licence plate. He was also fined $300 for driving without insurance and prohibited from driving for two years. ...

Since anyone telling this story orally would fasten on the ironies of the case, the first task of lead writing is to *impose that same kind of natural selection on your news judgment*. A natural hard lead would read something like this:

> An X-ville man with a long record of drinking and driving was sent to jail today, even though he said he'd given up drinking after he himself was run down by a drinking driver.

This lead contains three separate ideas and is therefore somewhat hard to assimilate. It also fails to exploit fully the dramatic irony. So a soft approach may be better, catching the reader's interest and building up to the point, as did the original CP story on this case:

> Two weeks after his ninth drinking-driving charge, Robert Brown was hit by a car.
> The driver had been drinking.
> This "poetic justice" caused him to stop drinking last May, Brown told a provincial court judge on Wednesday. Brown, 44, had one leg crushed in the accident and has a steel plate holding the bones together.
> Judge Frances Leung praised him for his sobriety, but in dealing with previous charges against him, said a jail term was still necessary, and sentenced the man to six months in jail. ...

The crucial point in comparing these contrasting leads is that both have the same central ideas, the same theme. Those same elements would be emphasized as well in a radio lead, with a more conversational flow and more emphasis on the punch line:

> ... Finally, there's a touch of poetic justice in this story about a drinking driver: An X-ville man with nine drunk-driving convictions got six months in jail today ... even though he said he'd stopped drinking. Robert Brown said the

FEATURE FORM

A stripped-down version of the classic feature form includes these elements:

- a lead device to catch interest (a scene-setter or a bit of description or a story about an individual, usually building to a point that connects with theme)

- a theme paragraph (or "focus" or "nut" paragraph) setting out the main themes and sub-themes

- sections developing each theme in order, often starting with an indication of how the section connects with the last one, and with the main theme

- a return to the main theme and the "kicker" — the windup quotation or point or anecdote

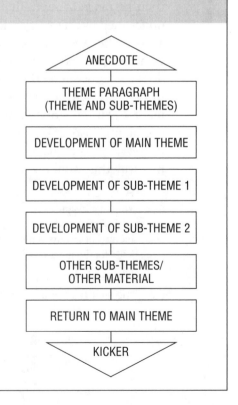

In capturing dramatic moments, a picture sometimes says it best. But often the picture will prompt questions that lead to a background story — in this case the growth of the Special Olympics as both a sporting event and a social phenomenon. (David Bebee/Loyalist College)

reason he stopped was that he himself had been run down by a car last May ...
And, yes — the car that hit him was driven by a drunk driver.

The moral, then, is that when you're confronted by a lead-writing problem, you should ask what you might tell to one other interested person, and then shape the story accordingly. News judgment must be quick and confident, reflecting your best instincts on what deserves to be reported. If it isn't quick and confident — if you agonize about what the textbooks might say or what your editor may want — you're abdicating your basic function as a journalist. If your judgment is challenged and the challenge makes sense, of course you should accept it and adjust your selection process as necessary.

Hard Leads

Of the two main approaches, the hard lead is probably the easiest — though by no means as easy as it looks. The hard lead follows some very clear conventions. These dictate that the first paragraph should be short — not more than 35 words or so, often fewer than 20 — summing up the central idea in simplest possible form. Almost always, the first paragraph has only one sentence. Almost always, it is in simple, declarative form. Sentences opening with dependent clauses are frowned on, as are questions and quotations. (The aim is to let readers grasp the central idea with no difficulty; questions and quotes force them to go farther, to get at context.) Very often, the lead is simply a slight expansion of the headline, stated somewhat differently. (Headline writers try not to take away the punch of a lead by stealing its language.)

Because of the crucial importance of the first dozen words, reporters writing hard leads often go through several versions, mentally or on the screen, stripping out every possible word and testing whether the idea can be stated more crisply. Often writers (and not just those in broadcasting) will read their leads aloud to make sure the idea can be stated in one breath.

Newcomers to journalism who examine a front page will quickly note that the average length of the first paragraph of hard leads is indeed short, and that all sentences and paragraphs are much tighter than they're used to writing. But they're not likely to appreciate at first the discipline that goes into the simple form. Students in first attempts often write something that *looks* like a hard lead, but actually says nothing that is significant, interesting, new. The following lead is typical of the pattern:

> On Thursday the region's social and health policy committee met to discuss a number of issues affecting the area.

This is short enough, but says nothing of what *happened* at the meeting, showing the reporter has made no choice among the significant, interesting, new elements. It is a cop-out of sorts, perhaps reflecting the reporter's own indecision about what to choose for lead attention. From an editor's point of view it's a non-lead. It was rewritten to this form:

> A plan to expand AIDS information clinics was endorsed by a regional committee last night.

The same failure to choose shows up in this lead:

> Taxi zones, the intersection improvement program and the closing of North Street bridge were the main topics of discussion at the transportation and works policy committee meeting.

The lead was rewritten as follows:

> The North Street bridge, described by one official as "totally unsafe," will be closed immediately for repairs that won't be finished until September.
>
> The decision was taken Thursday night by the regional transportation committee after operations director Jacques Bertrand said …
>
> The meeting also …

Cutting to the Essence

Even if a satisfactory lead *idea is* defined, it may still be necessary to hone the wording, to get it down to the tightest possible summary and to use the first words effectively. The following lead chooses a valid theme, but starts with an oppressively heavy name and makes the point in extremely awkward language:

> The city's administration, policy and priorities committee recommended to a meeting last night to approve payment of $34,160 to the government of France for repairing the damage sustained by the French Embassy on Sussex Drive last March from river blasting operations on the Ottawa River.

All of this can and should be stripped down to something like:

> Spring ice-blasting on the Ottawa River that broke windows in the French Embassy is expected to cost the city $34,000.

Any other detail from the original lead that must be used can be subordinated.

The pattern of declining to make a judgment (along with several other problems) shows up in the following court story about the alleged sexual assault of "Christine":

> Testimony continued in District Court this morning in the sexual assault trial of John Robert Smith. The Honorable Judge McWhellan will reach a decision later this week. Smith elected to be tried by judge alone.

Features editor Claire McIlveen of the Halifax *Chronicle-Herald* goes over stories and graphics gleaned from a trip to Somalia by reporter Parker Robinson. At its best, the relationship between reporter and editor can be intensely creative and constructive. Editors can help at every stage, by suggesting (or reacting to) story ideas, research plans and writing approaches. (Len Wagg)

> The complainant testified that the attack happened last Oct. 14. She had been drinking at a party before going to a friend's apartment, described as a hangout where alcohol and drugs were used regularly. ...
>
> Smith's lawyer, Robert Munro, cross-examined the victim, focusing on her heavy alcohol consumption and uncertainty about several events of the night.

This story shows several patterns that would give an editor difficulty. For one thing, it violates evidential rules. (Who *says* her alcohol consumption was heavy? Who *says* the apartment was a hangout where drugs were used regularly?) Phrasing like "the Honorable Judge McWhellan" suggests the writer doesn't read newspapers analytically, to identify how they *do* things. (Newspapers don't use titles like "honorable" for judges or cabinet ministers, but they do identify people by first name or two initials.)

More important, in this discussion, is the way the reporter did not try to define the most significant, interesting, new things that happened. What actually *should* be in the lead is difficult to say, for anyone who wasn't there. But in view of public controversy about the transfer of guilt to victims in sexual assault cases, it might be valid to focus on a lead like this:

> The defence lawyer in a sex assault case closely questioned a 16-year-old girl today on how much she had drunk before she woke to find a man trying to have intercourse with her.

This lead may or may not be defensible as the most important aspect of the matter being covered. But it offers, quickly, a reason why readers might be interested. It meets the conventions of a natural hard lead.

THINKING EDITORS

BY DON GIBB

Don Gibb, director of the newspaper program at the Ryerson School of Journalism, is a former reporter, editorial writer and city editor at the London Free Press. *He is also a "thinking editor."*

We've all had them or heard of them.

Editors we prayed would end their shifts before we filed our story. Editors who niggled over the misplaced comma or muttered a profanity because we misspelled accomod ... acommod ... accommodation.

They had their place in the newsroom, but they could never explain why the lead should be rewritten or why the story was boring. "Just fix it," they'd snarl ... but never tell you how.

So we would stare at the story

(continued)

for a while — add a word here, delete another there — hoping something would give us a clue on how to "fix it."

Reporters eventually learned from these editors. Lesson 1 was, Never write a story a certain way if those editors were on the desk. And lesson 2? Always make sure their pet routine questions were answered before turning in a story.

Such editors ruled by fear. They were not destined to be writing coaches. They didn't respect writers; they lacked enthusiasm; they were uninspiring; they were more concerned with processing copy than motivating writers.

They're the kind of editors humor columnist Dave Barry had in mind when he reported that work on the copy desk has been shown to kill brain cells at the rate of four million a day.

Fortunately, there's another kind of editor, the "thinking editor." Thinking editors are the kind you'll want to work for — and the kind you should want to be, if you're heading toward desk work. How do you become a "thinking editor"?

Begin by thinking of yourselves as story editors, not copy auditors. Think of yourselves as the content controllers on the paper. The thinking editor asks questions like these:

- Is the lead buried?
- What's the point of the story?
- Is the story interesting and informative?
- Is important information missing?
- How effectively has the reporter used quotes?
- Of what significance is the story to ordinary people?
- Should information be deleted because it's irrelevant, boring or tasteless?
- How can you eliminate dull, routine institutional news?

Thinking editors don't settle for checking grammar, spelling and style book errors — though of course those checks are part of the job. Thinking editors stretch their senses beyond the basics.

Good writers will concede they need a good editor. At times, writers can get too close to the story. They need another set of eyes — not to tamper with their style but to enhance it by asking questions, clarifying content and improving structure.

Telling a writer something "doesn't work" simply doesn't work.

Editors need to read with a critical eye and learn to explain clearly what writers need to do to improve their work. They need to think like writers, too, and understand the pitfalls and frustrations of reporting.

Editors need to get excited about good work and to encourage and challenge writers — not an easy task in such an egocentric and sensitive craft.

In an ideal world, editors and reporters would have plenty of time to discuss stories over coffee.

(continued)

Instead, they often have to do it over the telephone or across the computer screen two minutes before deadline — if they talk at all.

Editors need to work constantly at breaking down the wall between editors and reporters. They can do their part by respecting the piece of work over which the reporter has agonized. It may be tempting to forge the piece in one's own image, but it is the editor who treats the story and the writer with respect who gains trust and respect in turn.

In learning how to become a thinking editor, start by looking for patterns in the copy you read:

The buried lead: It's a word, a sentence or a paragraph that piques your interest. Something you didn't know. It surprises, shocks, excites, informs. It may require the writer to get more information to develop a stronger opening sentence or paragraph.

The point of the story: After reading the story the first time, ask yourself: does the story contain important, new information for our readers? Does it have a clear focus? Too often, writers write stories because they've been assigned, and editors edit them because they've been handed in.

Interesting and informative: Providing information is our raison d'être, but if it's not done in a lively way, it's a wasted effort. Help writers tell their stories through simple but powerful use of words. Help them write in a more relaxed, conversational style.

Missing information: If you have questions, you can safely assume the reader will too. We don't need to bog down stories with needless detail, but we need to ensure the reader isn't miffed by a lack of detail. Ask: how important is the information to the reader's understanding of the story?

Effective quotes: They liven up a story. Dull ones kill it. Writers who use tape recorders extensively fall into the trap of running paragraph after paragraph of tedious quotes containing factual detail that can easily be paraphrased. Quotes should be earned. A good editor often can salvage long-winded quotes, but the job must be handled with care.

Significance to readers: Encourage reporters to write with the reader in mind. Their job is not to impress colleagues or satisfy contacts. What impact does the story have on real people?

Irrelevant information: Paragraphs of needless information are the weeds that suffocate the grass in the writer's garden. Nothing hurts a story more. Tell readers only as much as they need to know to understand the story.

The boring and the institutional: Start by dropping the procedural wrangling, the bureaucratic bafflegab and the political posturing that often dominate school board and municipal meetings. Remember, the job is to tell readers what it means to them.

Hard Lead Hazards

No less than a limerick, an ad slogan or a song lyric, the hard lead looks like an easy bit of writing. Almost always, it is not. Nor is it free of hazards: some people argue, for instance, that the systemic pressure to select *just one* aspect of the story for lead attention automatically means downplaying a number of other developments. What right, they ask, does the journalist have to decide who or what will get attention? Part of the answer is that this is what journalists *do*. Journalists decide what will be on the front page or in the TV headlines. The decisions may have to be defended, inside or outside the trade, but they must be made.

In many ways, though, the hard lead is indeed a hazard. Critics suggest that anything that can be reduced to a 30-word nugget of information must have been over-simplified, losing necessary qualifications or cause-and-effect context. They also say that the form puts pressure on reporters to come up with something that looks like a hard development, even if the material doesn't justify it. One former Toronto reporter recalled being flown at considerable cost to a small northern town that was supposed to be threatened by forest fire. When he arrived, all was calm and there was no immediate threat. He quickly filed a story starting out something like this:

> A pall of fear hung over this little northern town tonight. ...

The demands of hard lead writing, then, can encourage gross distortion. Even in the best circumstances the selection can never be defended as a perfect distillation of the significance of the issue or event. However, the process also reflects a basic function of the journalist: to absorb complex matters and define their essence, to sort out and assign priorities to some of the patterns and happenings drawn from the world's "buzzing confusion." That means defining not just the essence of the story, but also the most relevant *context*. Whatever the form used, this defining task will remain, demanding all the intelligence and intensity reporters can bring to it. Furthermore, the demand to choose and to condense applies not just to hard leads but, perhaps less acutely, to all journalism.

Lead Blocks

At times hard lead writing is not just a matter of selecting the best, but the more difficult task of *synthesizing* the best — bringing together a number of elements in a pattern that makes sense. The following story, for instance, makes very hard reading, because the writer hasn't condensed it into a pattern of meaning:

Last evening the department of planning and development held an open house at St. Mark's Church Hall to present the proposed Henderson Street West Planning Study. The plan calls for the creation of a "multicultural village," which would require the demolition of at least two houses.

Joan Koutsaris of the planning department was present to explain the plan to local residents like Joe Martin. Martin walked through the display area shouting to anyone who would listen, "If I sell my house, I want it on my terms. I want to protect my property." Other residents were worried about "subtleties" that were not immediately apparent in the colored maps and schematic sketches tacked around the room.

Richard Burak, who is running for alderman in East Ward, stated his objection succinctly. "It stinks! Business people want more parking, but don't want to pay for it."

If parking was the issue, it was not evident from the discussion among agitated residents. Housing was their concern. ...

The most serious criticism that can be made of this lead is that readers who stopped at the fourth paragraph would simply not know what the story was about. And that writing pattern is not as uncommon as might be expected. The problem is that the reporter *did know* how all the information connected, and erred in thinking readers would also understand. That is why reporters must try to pull back, to see the story not as writer but as reader, to consider what readers will take from it. In this case, a reading of the whole story suggests that the synthesis should have been something like this:

A city plan to relieve parking pressure by building small, underground car-parks camouflaged by groups of townhouses got a cool reaction in the Henderson West area last night.

Plans for the project, described as a multicultural village, were unveiled at a meeting in St. Mark's Church Hall, and drew objections of several kinds.

Some residents feared the development might squeeze them out of their homes in the area, while others objected to the cost of the car-parks. ...

The essence of the story is thus spread out over a lead block of three paragraphs and combined with a good deal of context. The same pattern shows in the following *Globe and Mail* lead (which, incidentally, also offers an indirect comment on the dangers of both the hard lead and pack journalism):

STUDY DIDN'T TELL WOMEN TO GO HOME AND HAVE BABIES

The author of a report on women in the work force that has attracted media attention across the continent says the instant fame is being bestowed for the wrong reason.

When the report by University of Montreal psychologist Ethel Roskies was released Saturday in Washington, journalists focused on its discovery that unmarried, childless professional women are less happy with their lives than married career women with children.

But a more significant finding, Prof. Roskies said yesterday in an interview from Montreal, is that even if women forgo marriages and children, they still will not necessarily get to the top. …

— ALANNA MITCHELL, *GLOBE AND MAIL*, NOV. 24, 1992

The Body of the Story

As already noted, the hard lead may be followed by a variety of overall story forms apart from the traditional descending order of importance. One variant is the so-called hourglass form, which tries to retain some of the flavor of sequential, suspenseful storytelling, while still giving readers the essence of the story quickly. Consider the following soft lead, illustrating a weakness that can be fixed with the hourglass form:

For Smith Township firefighters, one of the toughest nights of the summer began with a minor mishap, when a camper's kerosene lamp was knocked over on a windy night.

This lead suggests a strong plot line, a clear element of suspense — but it does not tell readers quickly *what happened*. Editors may therefore prefer the lead to present a tight summary, before tapping into the plot line. For instance:

A brushfire driven by high winds destroyed the Loon Lake Boat Club and five nearby cottages last night.

One volunteer firefighter suffered minor injuries when part of the boat club roof collapsed.

For Smith Township firefighters, one of the toughest nights of the summer arose from a minor mishap, when a camper's kerosene lantern was knocked over in high winds. Fire chief Dennis Lang reported this sequence:

At about 8 p.m. …

From there, the story can unfold in a natural, chronological order, building from the casual beginning to the climax. A variation on this approach is simply to run two stories side by side, one of them a tight summary of the news and the other a "featurish" version that catches the buildup of drama.

More usual, perhaps, is a pattern of organizing the body of story in "theme blocks." The writer of the fire story, for instance, might look at the lead and define natural segments: how was the fire brought under control? Whose cottages were destroyed? What group of campers set off the blaze, and how did they respond? Each of those segments can then be written, under a theme or summary or topic sentence that introduces the segment and relates it to the theme:

The five cottages destroyed, all vacant at the time, were located …
Fire Chief Lang said the fire apparently got out of control because …
Firefighters took more than five hours to check the blaze. …

These sentences serve as transitions or guideposts, orienting the reader by signalling what material is coming up and how it relates to what has gone before, and to the main theme. The "theme blocks" that flow from them can often be moved around (especially in the era of word processors) if the writer or editor decides a different element should be stressed.

ORGANIZING THE LONGER STORY

One of the most overlooked — and perhaps most difficult — stages in doing any major story lies between the research and the writing: organizing and synthesizing the material you've gathered.

Different writers tackle this stage in different ways, from shuffling file cards to cutting and pasting notes. Some writers organize by instinct — or perhaps by a good deal of mental work before they go near their computer. Others outline meticulously. Whatever system you use, you will probably find that these four basic steps make sense:

1. Define your main theme or focus.

2. Get rid of superfluous material quickly.

3. Sort out your main sections or sub-themes.

4. Consider whether your material is all in place, or whether you have to move back a step to plug research holes.

Some of these steps can be illustrated by a long *Maclean's* cover story on the "fearful nineties," written by Mary Janigan and quoted here in part ("Mad as Heck," *Maclean's*, June 8, 1992). The structure of the story shows, to anyone who reads it analytically, at least some of those organizing stages. Certainly the theme is clear. It's hinted at in the first sentence and then spelled out explicitly in the second paragraph: that Canadians share an erosion of faith in their economic future.

In her cozy split-level home, amid her plants books and cats, Iris Kreiger can testify to the uncertainties — and insecurities — of the 1990s. The former office manager lives with her two children, John, 26, and Lisa, 23, in Kitsilano, a sprawling Vancouver neighborhood that embraces the tavernas of the Greek community and the vegetarian restaurants of aging hippies. Last year, after her employer died, Kreiger, 52, lost her job. She now lives on income from her savings and her children's lodging payments: John is an unemployed cabinetmaker; Lisa is an assistant supermarket manager. The three family members insist that they live contentedly with little money and few expectations. "I do not need a lot of things," says Iris. But she wistfully recalls past decades of prosperity — and her simple belief that those times would never end. "We had a nice rosy life," she says. "People had lifetime jobs. Everything was possible. Unfortunately, we screwed it up. The young people of today have it very differently."

Across the nation, Canadians share that troubling erosion of faith in their economic future. There are few lifetime jobs in the Canada of the 1990s. Familiar manufacturer's such as auto parts firms are scaling down or moving south. ...

(continued)

The structure so far is a familiar one: the lead anecdote (which in a newspaper story might take six or eight short paragraphs) builds to the theme statement.

Also clear is the organizing of sub-themes. This shows up in the topic sentences that introduce each section, as the story continues:

> The immediate targets of that despair are politicians. …
>
> The national anxiety appears startling when Canada is compared with other countries. …
>
> The tax burden has become unmanageable for many taxpayers. …
>
> Finally, there is the new generation that is under 30: pessimistic Canadians who already accept that their future is dim. …
>
> For many, the social safety net has become the focus of those fears. …

At the end, the writer returns to the main theme of the bleak view ahead, winding up with the kicker — a sociologist's comment on the new selfishness.

In the end, the 1990s may become known as the decade of transition. Unfortunately, few Canadians believe that their political leaders have the will or the skill to lead them into the future — and to make that future less uncertain. They want a more responsive government with a more efficient safety net. Instead, they fear that they will simply emerge with higher taxes, fewer benefits, reduced prospects, meaner governments and a growing underclass. As University of Toronto sociologist Raymond Breton says, "In the postwar era, there was money all around. You could give money to the poor and still have money for yourself. We have realized that this is not possible anymore. I see a period of transition, of trying to accommodate our values of sharing while maintaining our individual security and standard of living as much as possible." This is the lament — and the challenge — of the fearful 1990s.

After finishing the story, the analytical reader can tell that Janigan has either organized it instinctively in her mind or outlined it according to a plan like this:

Anecdote: Kreiger family …
Theme: Canadians share erosion of faith in economic future.
Sub-theme 1: Immediate targets of despair are the politicians.
Sub-theme 2: Despair exists even though we compare well with other countries.
Sub-theme 3: Tax burden is becoming unmanageable.
Sub-theme 4: Generation under 30 is especially hard hit.
Sub-theme 5: Social security nets are under attack.
Conclusion: Canadians look ahead to higher taxes, fewer benefits, reduced prospects, etc.
Kicker: Breton quote.

In fact, when she was asked to recall how she actually organized this story, Janigan confirmed that it had indeed fallen out on those lines. Her chief problem, she recalls, was that the sub-theme on the under-30 generation emerged late. When she'd gone through her material to flag topics, she had not defined the under-30 material as a sub-theme, but she found as the writing progressed that it demanded more attention. During one of five rewrites she added it as a sub-theme, at the same time going back to recast the lead block (which she calls the "billboard").

(continued)

In stories like these, of course, the original mass of material is always much larger and more diffuse than the neatly organized final result would indicate. It is in cases like these that you need a systematic approach. Here you may find it useful to turn to the four points summarized above.

1. Jot down a quick sentence — the "theme" or the "nut" or the "focus statement" — to help you clarify in your own mind the thrust of the story. Don Fry of the Poynter Institute for Media Studies suggests you ask yourself two key questions: what is the story about? What's my point? (Clark and Fry 1992, 60–76). The first question addresses *content* and helps ensure that the nuts and bolts of the story don't get lost. The second defines *why* the story is being done.

2. Do an initial sorting job. Before you sit down at the terminal, run through your material and ruthlessly strike out anything you're not going to use — probably a good part of your material.

3. Define your material according to sub-themes. This can be done by color coding, by scissors and paste, or by a code word in the margin. (In the Janigan story, for instance, anything related to sub-themes 4 and 5 might have been flagged "under-30" or "SocSec.") Order your sorting in a brief outline, perhaps like the one given for Janigan's story, but expanded to note in point form under each sub-theme the best material you have.

4. Consider whether there are holes in the structure that show your research is incomplete.

A key benefit of this kind of outline is that it reorders your material in a way that fits with the *story*, rather than with your research pattern. If you've spoken to five people, for instance, it may be tempting to write the material from one interview and then another. But each source may have commented on a variety of *themes*. The organizing stage should make the necessary connections and show the new order that the story demands.

Once the story is organized, a substantial part of the writing work is done. From here on it's a matter of implementing your plan. (Janigan says she makes point-form outlines, but spends half her writing time on the first three paragraphs, feeling that if she gets that part right, the organizing task is virtually complete.)

You may feel that spending time on organizing takes away from writing time. But consider: if you know what you want to say, and how you want to say it, you'll be able to say it quickly. If you're still having difficulty, it may be that you have not completed the job of reporting. You may discover a point you need to clarify or an interview you need to do. With the new material in hand, you may find that the organizing and writing stages fall into place.

Soft Leads

While the conventions of the hard lead are fairly rigid, more latitude is possible with the soft lead, which uses some device to build up the main point or points. Typically, writers use the soft lead when they have a broad, multifaceted story rather than a short, sharp development whose implications are immediately clear. In general, soft leads are associated with a more detailed or spacious approach to a topic than is possible in hard news writing. They may be said to differ from hard leads not only in tone but in intent. Soft leads signal to readers that the story is a complex one, deserving of their undivided attention. They are an invitation to readers to put aside the kind of hasty scanning they bring to hard leads, and absorb the story thoughtfully. They are considered a good form for *pattern* as opposed to *event* stories. As John Ibbitson's soft lead at the start of this chapter shows, they may work well when the reporter decides that an event such as a meeting or court case shows a pattern more significant than any decisions taken.

Typically, the soft lead fastens on one small piece of action that symbolizes the larger theme. It might be called a "specific-to-general" or "problem-to-solution" or "cause-to-effect" approach. Student reporters wrestling with a broad, complex story are sometimes reluctant to use this approach. Because of their experience with essay writing (or perhaps with hard news writing) they want to sum up the significance of the story immediately. The following lead, for instance, is much closer to essay style than to journalistic style:

> In a move consistent with the federal government's endorsement of native desire for self-government, April I is the projected date for dramatic change in child welfare in Canada, with the kickoff of a series of child welfare agencies run by native communities. Four Ontario agencies and one in Alberta are in the development stage now, and by April will either have signed agreements with federal or provincial governments giving them power to provide child and family services, or will get an extension of the powers they already have.

This lead shows sound theme selection, but is complex and hard to assimilate. Asked to do a rewrite, the reporter came up with this optional lead, falling into the soft, specific-to-general type:

> Native leaders call it "scooping."
>
> Over a 25-year period, one band in British Columbia lost 150 of its children to outside adoption — almost an entire generation.
>
> In Manitoba, 54 native children were adopted into the United States in 1980 alone.
>
> That pattern of "scooping" children from the reservations lies behind major changes in the child welfare structures that will come into effect April 1.
>
> They're part of a trend toward greater self-government. ...

The form of the rewritten lead isn't necessarily *better*, but it does more closely reflect the usual tone of "featurish" leads. The first might be preferable on an essay or government report, while most newspaper or magazine editors will prefer the specific-to-general (or problem-to-solution) approach.

The typical soft lead, with one anecdote (or three short anecdotes) followed by the theme, or a "then-and-now" suspense pattern, is in its way just as stylized as the hard lead. Originally considered a magazine form, it moved first to newspaper features and then to news. It was perhaps brought to its clearest definition by the *Wall Street Journal*, a newspaper whose qualities of writing are as outstanding as its makeup is bland. Student journalists can usefully spend a few hours studying the *Journal*, simply to analyse the crafting of *its* lead anecdotes, and especially the way those leads build to a clearly defined *theme* or *summary* or *"nut"* paragraph — the paragraph that sums up what the story is all about — followed by segments that develop each sub-theme. The following *Wall Street Journal* intro builds quickly to theme statements covering the main theme and clear sub-themes:

> Joseph Mercurio has two children in Boston University, which now charges $21,970 a year for tuition. But he doesn't worry about the cost, because his employer picks up the tab.
>
> That perquisite is even better than it first appears, because it is tax-free. He estimates he would have to earn $80,000 in pretax income to cover his kids' tuition. "It's a benefit of enormous value to me," he says.
>
> Mr. Mercurio earns a healthy salary — $325,000 in 1995, according to the most recent records available from the state of Massachusetts. So how does he get such an unusual perk? He is executive vice-president at Boston University, one of hundreds of colleges and universities that subsidize the cost of education for employees' children, and sometimes spouses. It is a benefit that pervades the world of academia, and it enjoys a special exemption in the tax code. ...
>
> — STEVE STECKLOW, WALL STREET JOURNAL, APRIL 15, 1997

Most readers will not consciously identify these last points as sub-themes, but subconsciously they will expect development of each, probably in the order indicated. Again, these sub-theme blocks likely will start with a subtle indication of what the section will cover, and how it ties back to the main theme. At the end, too, there's likely to be a reprise of the main theme.

The following point-of-view article on the Gulf War from Britain's the *Independent* uses exactly the same model, with sub-themes defined even more clearly:

COMMENT: UNCRITICAL PRESS FAILS PUBLIC BY COSYING
UP TO MILITARY

A colonel commanding an American air base in the gulf last week decided to honor the "pool" reporters who had been attached to his fighter-bomber squadrons since the day the war broke out.

He produced for each of them a small American flag which, he said, had been carried in the cockpits of the very first U.S. jets to bomb Baghdad.

"You are warriors, too," he told the journalists as he handed them their flags.

The incident said a lot about the new, cosy relationship between reporters and the military in the gulf war. So thorough has been the preparation for this war, so dependent have journalists become upon information dispensed by the western military authorities in Saudi Arabia, so enamored of their technology, that press and television reporters have found themselves trapped. ...

— ROBERT FISK, THE *INDEPENDENT*; REPRINTED IN THE *OTTAWA CITIZEN*, FEB. 6, 1991

The best writers, of course, vary the form and end up with a seamless story, although close analysis may reveal the underlying design. The following lead, for instance, reverses the usual soft pattern, signalling the theme before turning to an extended anecdote:

JURY SELECTION CAN BE MOSTLY A CASE OF ... TRIAL & ERROR

Is it a crap shoot, with people instead of dice?

Or is the picking of juries in Canada a sophisticated science of sexual politics, ethnic loyalty and demographics?

The subject is something lawyers casually discuss over coffee, but brood over with increasing anxiety as the minutes limp by while they wait for juries to come back with verdicts.

Take the recent case of the female skating coach on trial for sexually assaulting her pubescent boy student by touching him through the clothes and sticking her tongue in his ear.

The first day the jury was out, defence lawyer Jim Brimacombe sat calmly, his lanky frame bending around the back couch outside the courtroom.

By the second day that the eight-woman, four-man jury was out, Brimacombe was starting to get antsy. He was musing aloud, his legal mind becoming seduced by what-ifs. What if that woman I picked hates me, and she wants to send my client down? What if I'd had more men, more rig-working Real Men on my jury? They wouldn't convict.

But whether a sexual assault victim will get a more favorable response from a certain sex is a matter of debate. ...

— KATHLEEN ENGMAN, *EDMONTON JOURNAL*; REPRINTED IN THE *OTTAWA CITIZEN*, AUG. 8, 1992

The same pattern of theme followed by anecdote shows in this feature — a story more relaxed in tone, but with an intro so tautly written no word is superfluous:

GENTLE ELMORE LEONARD WRITES HARD-BOILED BOOKS

Elmore Leonard's books are hard-boiled. Elmore Leonard is not.

During an interview, he fusses like the grandfather he is. He worries that the tape recorder isn't close enough to pick up his soft voice, asks the photographer what he should wear, jumps up to pull a book from his backpack. The book is by a younger writer and bears a fond inscription to Leonard, who "taught us all." Leonard shows it off proudly.

Frankly, Leonard, 65, is the sort of gentle man his characters would beat up. ...

— STEPHEN WHITTY (KNIGHT-RIDDER) IN THE OTTAWA CITIZEN, AUG. 16, 1992

More commonly, soft leads hint at the theme off the top rather than stating it baldly. Occasionally, writers for magazines like *The New Yorker* seem to resist using any definable form, as they start nowhere ("On a recent rainy Friday, a friend suggested lunch in a new German restaurant off Washington Square ...") and gradually ramble toward the most interesting material. This "non-form" is, however, treacherously difficult: amateur writers trying to use it may end up in the quicksand.

REVITALIZING ROUTINE FORMS

While the straight anecdotal lead or the classic variant of three tight anecdotes followed by the theme is sometimes satirized, it can also be effective, depending on how well the anecdotes are crafted and how well they set up the theme. The point may be illustrated by the "Christine" court case cited earlier. The student who failed to find a hard lead in the case used it later as a starting point for a pattern story on changes in sexual assault law. Her first attempt stated the theme off the top:

Not many people are convicted of sexual assault. It's one of the hardest to prove, least understood of crimes.

In the past few decades feminists and victims' rights advocates have worked to reform the Criminal Code sections dealing with sexual assault. They have had some success, notably with protecting a victim's sexual past from cross' examination.

Still, the experience of the average sexual assault victim is traumatic. The justice system doesn't help much.

Take for example "Christine."...

While this is a clear and logical introduction, it is somewhat bland and offers little that is not already known to readers most interested in the topic. A second attempt focused on Christine's case and used suspense to build to the point:

"Christine" is 16 now, but was only 15 when she reported her attack. It's been almost a full year.

Christine is a fairly typical high school student. She likes to shop and party, and has a part-time job. She quarrelled with her family last November and went to live at a friend's house.

That weekend (as she told her story in court) she got drunk at a party, and passed out in a bedroom.

She awoke to find herself partly naked, with an acquaintance attempting to have sex with her.

LEAD-WRITING

A checklist of key points on leads:

Hard Leads

✔ Make sure your lead selection reflects a deliberate judgment about what's significant, interesting, new.

✔ Strip the lead down to essentials. Everything that can be subordinated should be.

✔ Use the first words of the story carefully, signalling the point as quickly as possible.

✔ If necessary, take two or three paragraphs to sum up the essence of the story before you begin the body of the piece.

✔ Once the lead summary is done, organize the rest of the story according to the following:

  • decreasing order of importance

  • segments relating to themes and sub-themes in your lead summary

  • chronological order (The riot began about 7:30 p.m., at the start of the night shift …)

✔ Test your hard or summary lead by asking

  • whether it would stand alone as a front-page item or a radio news item, or

  • whether it summarizes the matter that should be in the headline.

Soft Leads

✔ Remember that soft leads provide an effective way of luring readers into complex, difficult — and significant — stories. In effect you catch interest by focusing in on one aspect of the larger problem.

✔ Start by defining the *theme* — the reason the story deserves to be written and read — and then consider what lead device will set it up well.

✔ Choose for the lead device an anecdote or set of anecdotes, a problem that makes the later "solution" comprehensible, or a tiny element of description that can be used to symbolize something broader.

✔ Don't get carried away in embellishing the lead device. Remember, its function is to catch readers' interest and show them the significance of the point, when that point arrives.

✔ If you find late in your story that you're opening up important material not signalled in the theme statement, go back and amend the theme.

Christine immediately screamed, pushed him off, ran away, and called a rape crisis centre. She went to City Hospital and was examined by a doctor, after a three-hour wait.

She pressed charges and gave evidence as the trial opened Monday. The next day, after testimony from the man's friends about Christine's drinking, the accused was acquitted. The Crown attorney who dealt with the case, Victoria Y.F. Wong, says that despite reforms in the ways courts handle sexual assault victims, the system is still a brutal one. ...

This final story, expanding on the theme struck in the last line of this excerpt, was a good example of *active* reporting — an attempt to go beyond the simple facts of the case to get at a complex issue. As well, it reported the case in a detailed, dispassionate way that forced readers to see it not as a remote abstraction but as something inescapably real. In dealing with stories of that complexity, the soft lead is often more serviceable than the hard lead.

Like the hard lead, though, it contains built-in hazards. The most serious is probably the temptation to embellish aspects that support some of the classic elements of "story": conflict and resolution, obstacles to be overcome or tension rising to climax. The challenge for a journalist, of course, is to make the reality shape the story, rather than the reverse.

Strong elements of "story" are certainly present in the "Christine" report. But they conform rigorously to the account that unfolded in court, and if anything are understated. The important qualities in this kind of writing, then, are precise detail offered in a restrained, understated way. If the case is genuinely dramatic, that drama will come through in a simple telling.

STORY ENDINGS

In most forms, endings are difficult — often as difficult as the lead. In the inverted pyramid form they are usually not a problem, since the writer simply stops when there is nothing more to say. In any more complicated form there is usually an urge to bring the story back to the main theme, to choose a punchy "kicker" (often a quote) that leaves the reader reflecting on the essence of the story.

Most hazardous, perhaps, is the strong urge to preach at the end, to belabor and moralize and lecture. That sometimes happens because writers themselves develop a certain anger — when they're writing, for instance, of carelessness that has led to a child's death, or a bureaucratic bungle that has damaged a community. The urge to preach must be resisted. Readers find it unsettling to encounter a sudden change as the writer drops the reporting stance and suddenly becomes commentator. If the story is well told, the point will have been made. If a point-of-view column is justified, the view should be signalled off the top.

It should be emphasized, finally, that while both the hard and the soft lead forms are stylized, the same can be said of most writing forms, from the sonnet to the novel. The craft lies in using the form effectively.

RECOMMENDED READING

Weekend editions of major dailies; the front page of the *Wall Street Journal*.

Clark, Roy Peter, and Don Fry. (1992). *Coaching Writers: Editors and Reporters Working Together*. New York: St. Martin's Press.

Fensch, Thomas. (1989). *Writing Solutions: Beginnings, Middles, & Endings*. Hillsdale, NJ: Lawrence Erlbaum Associates.

Stephens, Mitchell. (1997). A *History of News*. Fort Worth: Harcourt Brace.

P A R T
four

How Journalists Work

The previous parts introduced you to the key tools of the craft of journalism. In Part Four you look at how reporters use these tools in their daily work.

Part Four begins with a description of a day in the life of a newsroom — the *Edmonton Journal's* — that seeks to capture some of the rhythm, pace and feel of news work.

It then looks at a number of common newsroom "beats" or specialties: general assignment reporting, the police beat, court reporting (including inquests), local government reporting (including education), political reporting of the senior governments, sports writing, the arts and entertainment beat and covering business and the economy (including labor).

Part Four concludes with a look at freelance writing, offering advice on how to break into the business.

CHAPTER 7

A Day in the
Life of a
Newspaper

THE *EDMONTON JOURNAL* BUILDING ON 101ST Street is a rarity in the Canadian newspaper business — a modern, downtown office. Many newspapers took to the cheaper, roomier suburbs when they outgrew their downtown plants in the 1970s and 1980s. Those that stayed found themselves retrofitting old plants with new equipment. The *Journal* tried something different. It moved its presses and production facilities to a plant three miles away, then put up a new five-storey building on the old site, within walking distance of city hall, the provincial legislature and the courthouse.

The newsroom, on the top floor, is both cavernous and brightly lit. At 8 a.m. this chilly Thursday in late May, the handful of people here for work are almost lost among the computer terminals. It's a quiet time of the day, after the end of one news cycle and at the beginning of the next. The stories in today's paper speak of events that occupy the city's mind this morning: a federal election less than two weeks away, a murder linked to gang activity, a dispute with the province over funding for local hospitals, and a late-spring snowstorm that caused — as the headline writers in both the *Journal* and the *Edmonton Sun* put it — "May-hem."

Pictures editor Greg Owens has been in for half an hour and is just about finished typing the day's photo assignments into his computer's Skedmaster tracking program. A couple of freelance photographers are here to pick up their assignments. Shaughn Butts is due to go to Slave

Lake, almost three hours away, with reporter Flo Loyie, for a story on young people campaigning against drunk driving. The kids have produced bags with personal messages on them for local liquor stores. Loyie set up the story two days ago and has come in early to pick up the photographer and hit the road.

But there's a hitch. The front of this morning's city section has a photo of a similar paper bag campaign by Students Against Drunk Driving in Edmonton. Owens figures that as a result, Butts's pictures probably won't make it onto a section front. "Eight hours is a long way to go for an inside, black and white print," he says.

Assignment editor Chris Zdeb arrives a few minutes after 8 a.m. As she hangs up her coat, Owens asks her about the Slave Lake shoot, pointing to the picture on the city section and saying he is reluctant to send the photographer with Loyie. Zdeb shakes her head and says the picture ended up on the city front almost by chance. Yesterday morning, local residents woke up to a snowstorm that devastated trees and gardens, and knocked down power lines all over the city. The *Journal* added two extra pages of storm coverage to this morning's paper. But when the editors went looking for a picture of something other than the storm to put on the city page, the best one was of the liquor bag art.

"This picture played bigger than I expected, but Slave Lake is *the* story," Zdeb tells Owens. "I think they should go."

Owens is still reluctant. Zdeb tells him to take it up with city editor Kathy Kerr, who is due any minute.

As soon as Kerr walks in, Zdeb buttonholes her for a quick conference at the city desk. The two women agree that Owens has a point. But they feel the Slave Lake trip is worth doing — pictures and all. "Flo, you're going," Zdeb calls across to Loyie. Kerr walks over to Loyie's desk for a final briefing. She tells the reporter to concentrate on the kids in the community, not on the program.

Butts collects his gear. Owens tells him to take a digital camera. The paper owns two of these cameras, which capture images on a computer disk rather than film. Owens says they're especially useful for out-of-town or rushed assignments because the photographer can send the images directly from the disk by telephone. "We've even had one photographer send us pictures by cellular phone from a helicopter in mid-air," he says.

The discussion over Loyie's assignment seems, on the surface, to be trivial, but it deals with issues at the heart of newsroom decision making: how to make the best use of limited staff and equipment while staying on top of the unpredictable flow of news.

Butts and Loyie hit the road shortly after 8:30 a.m.

———————

Police reporter James Stevenson slips into the newsroom while the editors are sorting out Loyie's assignment. He's an editorial assistant, but is trying his hand at reporting. He heads to a back office known as the cop room, where reporters produce one slice of the bread and butter of local news — police and fire reports. A sign on the door to the cop room says, "Republic of Crimea — where murder is a way of life."

This office-within-an-office is packed with the tools of the police reporter's trade: a fax machine, a special telephone reserved for news conferences with police, a sheet listing police radio codes, a map that lists the names of property owners in the city, and a bulletin board that keeps a running tally of the city's homicides, and fire, traffic and pedestrian deaths.

Stevenson turns on the two-way radios used to communicate with photographers, and unlocks the drawer where he keeps the radio scanners that monitor police calls. "Without these, we'd be dead in the water," he says. He checks the fax machine to see what's come in overnight — three incident reports, all minor. He sits down to make his first round of calls to area police and fire departments, RCMP detachments and the search and rescue squad — 11 in all. He will make dozens more calls as the day goes on.

Stevenson also checks in with his friend and fellow police reporter, Charlie Gillis. While they're talking on the phone, he hears a call on the scanner reporting, "10-13, 10-13" — police code for an officer down. It may turn out to be nothing, but he and Gillis will keep an eye on it. He then returns to his calls.

These calls have always been an essential part of the police beat, but now they're more important than ever. Two years ago, the emergency response system began using a new radio system, which means fire and ambulance calls don't come in over the scanners any more. The scanners can't pick up calls by the police tactical squad either. A little after 9 a.m., Stevenson finishes his first round of calls. Not much is happening so far. Nothing on the 10-13.

———————

Back in the main newsroom, reporters and senior editors start to trickle in for work.

The room is a broad, open expanse filled with desks and computer terminals. There are few partitions, all of them low, and even fewer walls, most of them glass. A row of glass-walled offices along one side of the room houses the senior editors. (The reporters call it "the management boutique.") Reporters and editors are arranged into configurations or pods that roughly reflect the work they do: business at one end, general news and city in the middle, entertainment at the other end. Southam, the *Journal*'s parent company, houses its new media centre next to the entertainment section. The centre runs the Southam Web site and a scrolling news wire for 150,000 cable television subscribers.

A stairwell atrium through the centre of the building acts as a newsroom divider. On the other side of the glass-walled stairwell lie the sports department, the design department and the editors of the weekend Insight section.

If there's one thing that characterizes desks in this newsroom, it's clutter: reporters work amid piles of notebooks, stacks of clippings and tottering piles of news releases, phone books, reports and yellowing newspapers. So much for the idea that computers would create the paperless office.

Snaking through the piles are wires — phone wires, wires connecting telephones to tape recorders so the reporters may record interviews, wires connecting to small headsets so reporters can listen to what they collect or filter out noise.

Many desks carry pictures of babies and families, and souvenirs of reporting assignments. (The tackier, it seems, the better.) A desk near the cluster of copy editors' work stations is covered with ceramic pigs, stuffed pigs, pictures of pigs and food pigs might eat. The editors call it the shrine of the "rim pig," newsroom slang for the copy editors who get little of the glory but do much of the hard work of putting out the paper.

Reporters whose desks are next to a wall can decorate that too. The fashion reporter has taken full advantage of her wall: it's covered with photos and magazine clips of slender models in trendy clothes. In a corner of the main newsroom, someone with a sense of the ridiculous has hung up a collection of clocks, a parody of the newsroom cliché of clocks set to the time in the capitals of the world. These clocks have labels like Vegreville and Detroit. One, marked Beijing, is a clockwork Elvis, whose hips swing as its pendulum.

City columnist David Staples works near the clocks, but seems oblivious to them as he starts work on his column for Friday's paper. He has decided to do a weather piece of sorts — appropriate in light of this week's snowstorm. Staples has just come back from an eight-month Southam fellowship at the University of Toronto and says that since his return, he has been struck by the Alberta sky — it's so much bigger, wider and higher than the sky over Toronto. "I'm going to talk to a physicist and a couple of poets about why that's so, and what it means," he says.

Reporter Allyson Jeffs comes in at 9:15, a few minutes late because she missed her bus. Jeffs is a senior reporter, but new to the *Journal*. She moved here from Southam's *Calgary Herald* earlier this spring. She checks her voice mail and finds a message from a spokeswoman for the Safeway supermarket chain saying that she can have an interview with the company president who is in town today. Jeffs has spent many shifts covering the bitter, protracted strike at Safeway that began eight weeks ago. She has been pursuing this interview for some time and is happy to get the spokeswoman's message. She decides to set something up for the afternoon.

Over at the city desk, assignment editor Zdeb and city editor Kerr are working their way through the day's coverage plans. Zdeb has called up yesterday's reporting schedule on her computer terminal to remind her of who covered what and which stories weren't finished by day's end. She reads the *Edmonton Sun* to see if it has any stories, or angles on stories, that the *Journal* missed. She finds a short item in the gossip column saying *Journal* publisher Linda Hughes will leave the paper for the *Calgary Herald*. "That's a month-old rumor," Kerr says with a snort of contempt. "It's rubbish." Zdeb listens to the radio news as she combs through a stack of faxed press releases. She fishes through a fat, one-month accordion file for notes on events happening today. She flips through another file folder filled with story ideas she collects in case she has a spare reporter or two.

As they sort out the assignments and start talking to the reporters, Zdeb and Kerr work as a team. Sometimes one of them briefs a reporter, sometimes the other. Sometimes they both do, and follow up with further instructions on the paper's internal e-mail system. Zdeb hands Kerr a pile of story possibilities for the newspaper's crew of eight summer students who started work this week. Most are small events that are worth covering but not likely to hit the front page. Kerr flips through them and says, "These are fine." Senior reporter Marta Gold, who has been assigned as mentor for the students, helps the two editors get the students organized.

––––––––––––––

At 9:20 a.m., assistant managing editor Allan Mayer drops by the city desk for a quick meeting. Greg Owens pitches a couple of picture possibilities, including more storm cleanup shots. Mayer suggests sending a student out with the photographer to talk to people who are clearing downed branches. Kerr says another reporter will look into how power outages caused by the storm affected home security systems, and will find out whether people will have to pay for false alarms triggered by power failures. Marta Gold has her own story: a piece on a plebiscite to be held next week in a nearby community on video lottery terminals. Reporter Dave Howell will try for another followup on a weekend stabbing that involved a gang known as the North Side Boys. Jac MacDonald will have to replace the city hall reporter, who is sick today. He's going to do a piece on a report that criticizes a proposed city reorganization plan for focusing too much on cutting costs and too little on finding other sources of revenue.

But what grabs the editors' attention most is a full-page Safeway ad in today's paper. It says it's time for people to start shopping at the supermarket chain again. "It sounds like they're trying to make the strike appear settled," says Kerr. Mayer nods and asks, "Does this mean they're freezing out the union?" Mayer suggests they assign a reporter to talk to replacement workers about whether they've heard anything new. Photo editor Owens says he can get fresh pictures of the picket line. Zdeb learns from Allyson Jeffs that she hopes to interview the company president this afternoon. The editors decide to put Jeffs on the main story. They ask legislature bureau chief Larry Johnsrude to get a comment from Premier Ralph Klein after question period this afternoon on whether the province will step in to settle the dispute.

"This could be a good A1 piece," says Mayer.

Kerr and Zdeb's task of organizing reporters is complicated by a visit from Don Fry of the Poynter Institute for Media Studies in St. Petersburg, Fla. Fry is in Edmonton to do sessions at the Canadian Association of Journalists convention, which starts tomorrow. The *Journal* has hired him to do a set of in-house sessions too and many reporters and editors have signed up for them. Throughout the day, they will disappear from the newsroom to hear Fry speak. (Jeffs is down for the morning workshop.) Thursday is also early deadline day. The production plant needs extra time to insert the weekly *TV Times* in Friday's newspapers, so the last page has to be closed by 11:20 p.m., not 11:50 p.m. as on other nights. The editors know now, long before noon, that everyone will be pressed for time.

Nonetheless, many reporters are working today on longer-term projects. Newspapers come out every day, but they are not made from scratch each and every time. News has a short shelf life, and tends to be produced — and consumed — in a few hours. But many stories take days or even weeks to complete. In addition, section editors work to a

Editors decide not only what to put in the paper, but where to put it. City editor Kathy Kerr, right, confers with Cheryl Purdey, who runs the night city desk, about the layout of the local news pages. (Brian Gavriloff, *Edmonton Journal*)

range of deadlines, to spread the work out over the week. Mayer says the planning for the weekend papers is done on Tuesdays, which allows the writers and editors time to organize their work and meet their deadlines.

Today, Marilyn Moysa is putting together a piece on corporate head-hunters for the Sunday careers page. Health reporter Rick Pedersen is rewriting a story for Saturday about the mysteries that continue to surround the death of a baby girl a year ago. The *Journal* plans to run a piece of the story on the front page, and a full report in the Insight section. Trish Worron is working on a piece for Sunday or Monday marking the anniversary of Edmonton's airport consolidation and exploring whether the promised benefits materialized. Andy Ogle is finishing up a piece for Saturday that looks at how other grocery stores are faring during the Safeway strike. These reporters, and others facing deadlines for longer-term stories, will work largely on their own today, in quiet eddies on the edges of the torrent of news.

Back in the cop room, reporter Charlie Gillis has joined Stevenson. The radio call reporting an officer down turns out to be a false alarm. Because it now looks like a slow news day, both reporters decide to work on some longer-term stories. Stevenson heads to the courthouse to check out the details of a lawsuit filed this week against the Red Cross by a woman who contracted Hepatitis C from a blood donation. Gillis is working on a piece about provincial policy on homosexual foster parents. He heads over to one of the newsroom *Infomart* terminals to look up past stories on the issue.

A little after 10 a.m., a report on the scanner says an object possibly containing picric acid, a chemical used in explosives, has been found at the Bonnie Doon shopping mall. Edmonton has had a rash of pipe bomb discoveries in the last few months. Gillis arranges for a photographer to head to the mall to check it out.

Managing editor Sheila Pratt arrives around 10 a.m. Her job is to keep an eye on all parts of the paper, except the ads and editorial pages. This means meetings — lots of meetings.

With the June 2 federal election rapidly approaching, Pratt's first meeting is an election-night planning session with assistant managing editor Mayer and city editor Kerr. They make no firm decisions, but come away with a general sense of how they will handle the local and national results.

Mayer and Pratt then have a short meeting about Peter Pocklington, a man who seems to have a finger in nearly every sport and business story in Edmonton. Pocklington is expected to release a prospectus soon for selling shares in the Edmonton Oilers on the stock market. This could be a city story, a sports piece or a business piece — or perhaps all three. Starting the planning now means the editors can develop a clear idea of how to handle the story when it breaks in a week or two.

In the editorial suite beyond the newsroom, another meeting is about to start. Editorial page staffers Susan Ruttan, Satya Das and John Geiger head into a small conference room to talk with editor-in-chief Murdoch Davis. But Davis is late, so the others start in on the planning for election editorials. The editorial board has already decided to do editorials on the local races, as well as the national one. Das suggests three editorials on the nine Edmonton area ridings, to run on three consecutive days the week before the election. These will include the paper's picks for who should go to Ottawa. On the weekend before the election, the editorials should assess the opposition parties and the government's record. Das says the election day editorial should urge people to vote, and remind readers that Natural Resources Minister Anne McLellan won her Edmonton West riding by less than a dozen votes in 1993.

Davis arrives and listens to the plan. He has a different idea: doing all nine ridings in a single day. He also thinks the ridings piece should run on Sunday, with the opposition and government assessments on Friday and Saturday. Geiger worries that the riding editorial will be too long. Davis says that's OK, and he reminds the writers that they shouldn't feel locked into giving all ridings equal treatment. Some can be covered in a single paragraph. The three writers agree that each of them will draft part of this editorial, and then all of them will go over it.

At about 10:40 a.m., city editor Kathy Kerr gets a call from a man who used his credit card to make a donation to the victims of this spring's Manitoba floods and is now angry because the bank seems to be charging him interest on it. "It's such a good tip," she says to Chris Zdeb. "Now who's going to do it? Not a lot of bodies on hand." She spots reporter Bob Gilmour and asks him to look into it.

Meanwhile, Charlie Gillis gets a radio message from photographer Ian Jackson at the Bonnie Doon mall, saying that the police tactical unit has arrived and has just brought in the bomb squad robot. Gillis decides to join Jackson at the mall.

As Gillis heads out, the section editors gather their thoughts — and their notes — and head into Sheila Pratt's office for a meeting known as the 11 a.m. "goat show." Retired editor Joe Cunningham came up with the "goat show" moniker years ago — so long ago, in fact, that some of the editors have forgotten what it means. But Kathy Kerr remembers. She says it's a chance for the section editors to perform for the managing editor. The one who displeases the boss the most is the goat.

The real goal of this session, however, is to shape up Friday's paper. The section editors take turns outlining what stories they see developing. The other editors add suggestions and ideas for how to handle the stories and which angles to cover.

Business editor Peter Collum is first up. He has a list of local, national and international stories. The one that attracts the most attention — and prompts some good-natured ribbing about each other's coiffures — concerns a new hair salon chain that is selling a six-month "pass" for haircuts for $29.95. "Can we do a nibbly on how much it costs to get a hair-cut?" Pratt asks. A "nibbly" is *Edmonton Journal* slang for a short sidebar. It, too, is a holdover from an earlier era, when Michael Cooke, now editor-in-chief of the Vancouver *Province*, was managing editor here. "Let's do the costs for women *and* men," Pratt adds.

Sports editor Wayne Moriarty says there's only one hockey game tonight, Colorado at Detroit. Because it's in the Eastern time zone, the copy should be in hand in plenty of time to make the deadline. For Friday, he plans to feature a locally written boxing package called "generational warfare." Four boxing fans from two generations compare the strengths of boxers past and present, and talk about what might have happened in a series of dream fights. It will run on an inside page with a large photo illustration of one of these dream fights: Muhammad Ali vs. Mike Tyson.

Barb Wilkinson of the features department previews tomorrow's "10 best things to do this weekend" page and the Wheels section, which features the civilian version of the military vehicle known as the Hummer. Entertainment editor Bob Remington says he has a bunch of movie reviews, chief among them the Jurassic Park sequel Lost World, and a news story on plans for a festival to mark the official opening of the Winspear Concert Hall in the city.

Kathy Kerr says her staff is thin because of the Fry seminars, but she passes around a three-page memo outlining who is assigned to what. The Safeway piece seems to be the strongest local story. Kerr says reporter Jeffs will focus on whether the strike will *ever* be settled, and will interview the visiting company president. Greg Owens of the photography department tells the group that he got a call this morning from a replacement worker asking whether it's legal for strikers to take snap-shots of replacement workers as they go into work. He thinks that's a good angle. Kerr agrees and asks him to send an e-mail to Jeffs.

Owens runs down his list of picture assignments. It now includes a shot of the police bomb squad's robot, sent in to retrieve the suspicious device at the mall.

Network editor Silvio Dobri, who files copy to the Southam network and keeps an eye on what the other papers in the chain are working on, points out that former federal health minister Monique Begin is speaking in Calgary. Since Premier Ralph Klein is embroiled in a dispute with the federal government over plans for a private hospital, the *Calgary Herald*'s story will be worth a look. He also asks whether the *Journal* will cover the Canadian Association of Journalists conference. Kerr rolls her eyes at Pratt. A large number of *Journal* staff will be at the conference, but, until now, they have not given much thought to how to cover it.

Allan Mayer, who is co-ordinating election coverage, says elections reporter Mike Sadava is expected to complete a piece today on voting at military bases. It looks at whether the soldiers and their families will vote in their local ridings or by absentee ballot in their home ridings. Mayer also has a riding profile, the second of nine the paper will run. He adds that the first of a series of "local issues" stories, this one by reporter Ashley Geddes, will be in for the weekend.

Pratt asks whether the Safeway story could be turned into an A1 package. Kerr says she thinks so. As the other editors leave, Kerr, Pratt and Owens begin to discuss picture possibilities for the front page story.

More than many other newspapers, the *Journal* stresses page design and tries to package stories in ways that are visually interesting as well as informative. The theory is that newspapers must be able to meet the competition head-on — and the competition isn't television, but other types of printed material, like magazines. If magazines employ artists and page designers, and pay attention to the visual aspects of reading, newspapers should too.

At 11:40 a.m., Kerr and Owens head out of Pratt's office for a hurried conference with Jeffs, who is back from her Don Fry workshop. They learn that, so far, she has been unable to get the Safeway people to deliver the promised interview, but she will keep working on it. Kerr and Owens run down a list of other angles: the sudden sprouting of lawn signs in support of the strikers; the anecdote about strikers taking pictures of replacement workers; the possibility of talking to some of the replacement workers; the main theme about whether this is a turning point in the strike. Jeffs realizes that this story is flagged for the front page, and digs in.

By noon, most of the senior editors are out of the newsroom at a Don Fry session. The copy editors who work the day shift are in, working on pages for tomorrow's paper. The reporters are out for lunch, or eating at their desks while working on their stories.

Columnist Staples has found the poets he wants to quote for his piece on the Alberta sky, but has so far struck out on the scientist. Asked if he has another scientist in mind, he says, "I've already moved to the backup." He has set himself a 3 p.m. deadline for finishing his research.

As Staples picks up his phone to make another call, about 16 people wander into the newsroom in a tight group and start looking around. "Oh, it's the movie guys," says Gay Carruthers, Sheila Pratt's secretary. The group is with Illusions Entertainment, a Calgary production company that wants to use the newsroom as a location set for a film called *Silent Cradle*. The picture will star Margot Kidder as a reporter investigating her daughter's kidnapping. ("Just another routine day at the office, eh?" a *Journal* editor says of the plot.) One of the group spends his entire time on a cellular phone ordering lunch, which prompts snickers from the newspaper staff who overhear him. The others look around the room and discuss possible shots. After about 15 minutes, they leave.

Charlie Gillis calls the newsroom to report that the device at the mall was indeed a small pipe bomb. The robot has blasted it to pieces with its water cannon. But the story has a twist. It seems a mall security guard found the device near a door late yesterday afternoon and thought it was a firecracker. He casually picked it up, carried it to his office, and left it there overnight. Had it exploded while he was carrying it, it might have killed him. Gillis is on his way back to the office to try to track down the security guard. He's a bit disappointed that the *Edmonton Sun*'s crime reporter was with him all morning. Sharing a story like this with the competition just makes his life harder. He hopes the *Sun* reporter won't beat him to the security guard.

By 1:30 p.m., it's clear that Jeffs's Safeway story isn't developing as hoped. The company president won't be available for an interview until next week. He spoke to a couple of local groups this morning, but the *Journal* didn't try to cover them because Jeffs seemed assured of an interview this afternoon. Now Jeffs will have to call the seniors and church groups to find out what the president told them. She also has calls in to the union and to other Safeway executives. She has checked *Infomart* for names of people interviewed in earlier stories. And she is trying to find replacement workers or union members who have gone back to work.

Kerr is disappointed — and a bit snappish — about the company president. "He's going to stiff us," she says. The followup stories on the storm are a bit disappointing too. The student and photographer duo sent out to find people chain-sawing branches tell Kerr on their return that everything had been cleaned up before they got there. They have an interview with one man whose tree collapsed on his lawn, but he didn't want his picture taken.

Over in the business department, Peter Collum sits down with assistant editor Bruce White to organize the pages. Because the paper's presses can handle only 48 pages at a time, the newspaper is printed in two press runs. Pages in the first run, at 8:30 p.m., have to be out of the newsroom by 7:30. The eight-page business section is in the early run.

Collum and White hope to have some pages ready for the copy editors by 2:30 p.m., and the rest prepared over the remainder of the shift.

The haircut story, which intrigued editors at the 11 a.m. meeting, is ready, complete with its "nibbly" on what haircuts cost elsewhere. It will go on the section's back page. The front will have Bill Sass's "business people" column, which today profiles the chairman of a specialty printing form. The latest development in the Bre-X gold-mining scandal, the issuing of cease-trading orders in Alberta and Ontario, will go across the bottom.

The spectacular rise of Bre-X and its even more spectacular collapse amid reports of tampering with samples has prompted a lot of self-examination by business writers. One of the more troubling aspects of the story is that many reporters covering Bre-X owned shares in the company. Collum says an editor can't tell reporters how to invest their own money, but can try to be aware of potential conflicts. The *Journal's* policy is that reporters who own shares in a company can't write about it, and columnists who own shares in a company must disclose that fact if they write about it.

The staff in the entertainment department are working flat out. Thursdays and Fridays are their busiest days, partly due to the crush of coming weekend events, and partly, as editor Bob Remington explains, because the section has no weekend editors. "This means we have to cram seven days worth of coverage into a five-day week." In the ideal week, he likes to have the Saturday and Sunday entertainment fronts and the weekend TV pages done by the time he comes in Friday mornings, and the Monday front out of the way by Friday's end. But ideal weeks are rare.

The sports department, by contrast, is relatively quiet. Like entertainment, sports is an event-driven section of the paper and the staffers know well in advance what needs to be covered and when. But unlike entertainment, the sports department has reporters and editors in seven days a week.

Editor Wayne Moriarty is looking over a proof of his boxing package, which he had squirrelled away in anticipation of a slow day. Today is it. The design department has done a sensational job cooking up the photo illustration. It really looks as though Ali has decked Tyson — though the Ali picture is from his fight with Sonny Liston, and the Tyson shot is from a bout with Buster Douglas.

Digital equipment and software programs have made it easier to manipulate photographs than ever before. Newspapers are very cautious about tinkering with images, but in this case, Moriarty says, the picture is clearly an illustration for a story that is based entirely on fantasy. "My view is that you label it as an illustration. After that, I don't know how you can argue beyond the idea that this is fun, and the readers like it." The boxing story also has an interactive twist: a teaser on the front page of the sports section will invite readers to phone in their opinions on who would win the fights. The results will appear Saturday.

Web editor Bruce MacKenzie is fighting a cold as he works on JournalExtra, the newspaper's Web site, which opened in 1995. It includes a lot of entertainment listings and a daily collection of stories — about 10 each from the local, world, business and lifestyle/entertainment sections, and a half-dozen local sports stories. The site also invites readers' comments, and offers links to other places on the World Wide Web. The advantage of a Web site is that news can be updated as it happens. But the *Journal* doesn't do that. MacKenzie says the Web editors are careful not to scoop their own paper by putting stories on the Web that the paper hasn't published. After all, that would just help the competition. So nothing goes out until after the paper is printed.

At 2:40 p.m., Allyson Jeffs heads for the picket line. She has found out as much as she can about the president's talks and the advertisement in today's paper. Now she has to talk to the workers. She grabs a cellular phone, some taxi chits and an extra notepad. She is feeling the pressure. "It's almost 3 p.m. and I don't have a story yet, and they're looking at it for front," she says.

Over the next two hours, she goes to three Safeway stores, interviewing strikers and replacement workers. The replacement workers are edgy about being quoted, and she isn't able to track down the lead about strikers photographing replacement workers. The strikers are more forthcoming. Among the things she picks up is anger against "phantom shoppers" — people hired by the company to pose as shoppers and check out how the workers are doing their jobs. Jeffs makes lots of notes. During cab rides between stores, she phones the office to check her voice mail. Nothing from the company spokeswoman. "If this story pans out, it's going to be a long night," she says after the second store.

Somewhere along the way, she leaves her cellular phone in a taxi. This means her first call when she gets back to the office will have to be to the taxi company, to track it down.

Back in the newsroom, many of the reporters are writing. The soft, clicking sound of computer keyboards intensifies as they work toward the

6 p.m. deadline. Most try to get things in earlier. Mike Sadava lets Kerr and Mayer know his election story is done. David Staples has given up on getting a physicist for his column on the elements, but has found a meteorologist instead. "He was great — really knowledgeable and interesting," he says. "In fact, he worked out better than the physicist."

At the legislature, Larry Johnsrude has managed to get comments from Klein on the Safeway story, and from Klein and Health Minister Halvar Jonson on Monique Begin's speech. Begin told her Calgary audience that the proposed private hospital in Calgary could undermine Canada's health care system. Johnsrude writes a new top for the *Calgary Herald's* report on the speech, giving the reaction of the Alberta politicians. He sends it to the office by modem.

Reporter Jack Danylchuk is working on a piece about prisoners at the Edmonton maximum security prison voting in the election. He got the idea from a Southam wire report on the federal court battle over prisoners' voting rights. "But they missed an angle," he says. "This will be the first vote ever in a *federal* election by *federal* prisoners." Danylchuk has interviewed a prisoner at the Edmonton maximum security prison by phone and hopes to cover the special poll tomorrow. In some parts of the country, reporters have difficulty making contact with people inside jails and penitentiaries. But here, Danylchuk says, "We have a pretty good relationship with the prison."

Proofreader Carol Pendleton has settled into her desk. Glasses propped low on her nose and red marker in hand, she is starting through the pile of pages put together by editors who work the day shift. Proofreaders disappeared from Canadian newspapers years ago, when the news desk began setting type by computer rather than sending stories to the composing room to be set in type mechanically. But despite their sophisticated tools, editors working on tight deadlines don't catch all the mistakes — and may make new ones. In addition, editors and reporters know that a reader will spot things on paper that they won't spot on a computer screen. Two years ago, editor-in-chief Murdoch Davis decided to bring back proofreaders as an experiment. He liked the results and the paper now has two.

———————

Roy Wood, like Mayer an assistant managing editor, has come in for his shift. If Mayer and Pratt are the big wheels at the start of the news cycle, Wood and news editor Catherine Carson keep things rolling at the end.

On most days, the second "goat show" story meeting begins at 4 p.m., about an hour after Wood begins work. On early deadline days like today, it begins at 3:30 p.m. But because the copy editors are all at a Don Fry session this afternoon, the meeting has been put off to 4:30 p.m. This means Wood, who runs the meeting, will have to keep things moving if the editors are to get the paper out on time.

This is by far the largest meeting of the day. In addition to Pratt, Mayer and the section editors who were at the morning session, the editors who produce page A1 and the Canada, World and Election pages are here. So is Cheryl Purdey, who runs the night city desk. News editor Catherine Carson, night photo editor Neil Smalian and people from the Web page and the design department also sit in. There are too many people to fit into an office, so the meeting is held in a board room known as "the igloo." ("It has no windows," Wood explains. "And it's got lots of Arctic art.") In addition to making sure everyone knows what's going in the paper, the meeting has a second purpose: the editors are to decide which stories are likely candidates for the front page.

City editor Kathy Kerr says the Safeway story has not developed as planned, but she's confident that the experienced reporter Jeffs will pull together a good piece. "The angle is that we've entered a new phase of this strike — the battle for the shoppers," she says.

Kerr also has a bunch of short storm cleanup pieces. Wood asks whether she has a wrap-up story that could go on the front page. "No," she replies, "but we could put together a simple combo."

The pipe bomb story is also interesting, she says. Though no one was injured and Gillis has not been able to talk to the security guard who picked up the bomb and carried it to his office, he has learned that police have found a number of similar devices in recent months. The police are worried that kids are learning to make explosives from the Internet. Finally, she has the Monique Begin piece from the *Calgary Herald*, with Larry Johnsrude's new top.

Entertainment editor Remington also has a new story to bring to the table: an announcement that a promoter will bring three Broadway-style musicals to Edmonton in the next year.

World page editor Don Romaniuk says he has stories on an Iranian election, the transfer of power in the former Zaire, an earthquake in India, Boris Yeltsin's decision to fire his defence minister and a probe into a Palestinian's death in an Israeli prison. The Canada editor tonight, Helen Metella, offers the latest skirmish in the salmon war with the U.S. — a big national story, but of less interest in landlocked Alberta. She also has a story about Tammy Morrisroe, who has been in the witness protection program after she infiltrated an organized crime gang, appearing in a courthouse in Vancouver to plead for clemency for her father.

Election pages editor Karen Sherlock lists the stories already in hand, including Mike Sadava's piece on military voting and Jack Danylchuk's story about prisoners voting. Another election story that will come in this evening: reporter Ashley Geddes is covering a voters' forum in Reform MP Deborah Grey's Edmonton North riding.

Network editor Silvio Dobri describes stories other Southam papers have produced: a piece from Ottawa on a woman who is trying to sell her kidney; a Vancouver item on kids who play a dangerous choking game with cloth towel dispensers; a Hamilton piece on an Internet kiddie porn bust.

Wood, who has been taking notes as the editors talk, plays with his pen and thinks for a moment, then looks at Sherlock. "What's the best election story — Danylchuk on the inmates, or the military one?" She suggests he look at both. "OK," he says. "I'll also look at the Morrisroe in court story. I want to see Safeway and the storm follows. I'll look at the bomb at the mall. And let me see Monique Begin.

"One last thing: the 5:30 meeting will be at 6."

———————

Now that the editors know the likely candidates for A1, they can start producing their own pages. They hunker down in front of their terminals, ignoring a sudden wash of light from a bank of studio lights Allan Mayer has just flipped on. Every afternoon around 5:30 the *Journal* does a live spot on the local ITV news. It fills viewers in on some aspect of city life — and promotes the paper. Today's performer is movie critic Marc Horton, who will do a quick review of the Jurassic Park sequel, Lost World. He sits on a chair in front of a camera that is screwed into the wall, clips on a microphone and puts in his ear piece so he can hear the director. Horton tells the TV audience that the movie offers "no plot, no character development but plenty of special effects and some dandy dinosaurs." His bottom line: "it's worth your bucks."

Mayer turns the lights off as the segment ends.

Over in the cop room, a loud telephone ring signals the start of a police conference call, a mini news conference for reporters here and at other local media. Gillis picks up the receiver and listens as police give further details on the pipe bomb. He plugs them into his story.

In Roy Wood's office, Neil Smalian calls up today's photographs on the computer where he can view wirephoto shots coming in from around the world, as well as pictures taken by local photographers. It's a relatively new system that is much more flexible than the contact sheets and prints still used at some of the smaller papers. Smalian says he has some photographs to go with the Safeway story, but he has also just sent a photographer out to get a picture of a store manager.

Wood and Carson have read most of the stories flagged as front-page possibilities at the 4:30 meeting. (Jeffs is still writing.) At 6 p.m., Carson and the section and copy editors trickle into his office to make a final decision about the front page. Though Wood has the final say, the editors generally make this decision by consensus.

"Anybody happen to come across a line story?" Wood asks, half-jokingly. But after talking over a number of possibilities — the Monique Begin piece, the fish war, the Safeway story — Wood and the others agree that there *is* no story that clearly deserves top play, so the paper will have to take a different approach. They decide to use the Safeway story as the "main hit," packaged over four columns. Wood also likes the military voting story and says he'll take it too. He likes the Monique Begin story, but thinks it needs a rewrite: he'd rather see it lead with Begin, and then quote Klein and Jonson. And he asks Cheryl Purdey to put together a piece for the front page on the storm cleanup.

The editors think about these choices for a moment, then Wood nods.

"That's a good mix," he says.

"All local too," says Purdey.

Jeffs files her story at 7:15 p.m. She has managed to get hold of the union president. The management side has been more elusive: they didn't return her calls. But she has the company ad to work with, and a good idea of what the company president told the seniors and church groups this morning. Her lead strikes the theme — with the talks stalled, both sides have turned their attention to winning the support of shoppers. Jeffs hasn't used the "phantom shopper" angle. She decides to do a separate story tomorrow. "It's nice to have something in your pocket," she says.

She gets one final bit of good news: a taxi driver has dropped off her cellular phone at the front desk.

By 7:30 p.m., the newsroom is a very different place than it was a few hours ago. The crescendo of clicking computer keys at reporters' termi-nals has passed with the deadline. Almost all the reporters on the day shift have gone home, and the smaller night crew is at work on their assignments. Sheila Pratt, Kathy Kerr and Allan Mayer have also left for the day. Activity at this point in the news cycle centres around the copy editors' desks.

Like many newspapers, the *Journal* is fully paginated. This means that the editors do everything by computer — laying out the pages, editing the copy, writing headlines and putting pictures on the page. The paper uses Macintosh computers running Quark Publishing System software. Roy Cook, the assistant news editor who puts out page 1, says the main advantage to this system is that more than one person can work on the same page at the same time.

Purdey gets assistant city editor Cathy Lord to rework the Monique Begin story, and Randy Hardisty to put together the storm package. She lets Cook know when they're done. She and the assistant city editors and layout people now have to figure out which stories will go where. The bomb story that didn't make the front page will be the main piece on the city front, with a photograph of the police robot. Jac MacDonald's city hall piece on spending cuts runs across the top. Staples's column goes at the bottom. A story on funeral plans for the victim of the North Side Boys gang stabbing goes down the side.

Reporter Don Thomas is having a quiet night. His assignment fell through, so he is working on something that may become a story next week. Canadian election law prohibits the publication of polls 72 hours before election day. Thomas is searching the World Wide Web for sites that publish poll results. When he finds one, he uses his Netscape software to "bookmark" it. Once the polling ban takes effect, it will be easy to check his bookmarks to see whether the sites are complying. Thomas often uses the Internet in his reporting. He's particularly happy that he has figured out how to get into *Infomart* through the Internet. This means he can check news clips from his desk, rather than at a shared *Infomart* terminal in the newsroom.

Ashley Geddes's night assignment has turned out to be much more lively than expected. Almost 275 people turned out for the election forum, booing the Liberal and Conservative candidates and forcing Reform's Deborah Grey to defend her party against charges of racism. Geddes comes back to the newsroom at about 10 p.m. He hopes to file before 11. The story will go on the main election page inside the front section.

While Roy Cook edits the front-page copy, designer Gail Echlin is working on the package for the Safeway piece. It takes a couple of hours, and the final product is visually complex. The main headline says "Round 2." Echlin plays with putting shadows behind it, trying to get it to look like it's reverberating on the page, like a bell at a boxing match. Two

The energies and talents of reporters, photographers, editors and designers come together to produce the front page of the May 23, 1997, edition of the *Edmonton Journal*.

photographs — one of a striker, the other of a manager — frame the sub-head. The pictures are cropped to fit the page, but Echlin softens some of the edges so they fade into a pale mauve-grey background that itself fades toward the centre, and down to the story. The copy is set in three wide legs filling a four-column space — a non-standard width known in the newspaper business as a "bastard measure." The story is also set with a ragged right margin — the lines don't all end in the same place. This layout makes the story look more like a feature package than a standard news story. It stands out on the page and is easy to read.

The other editors are quickly putting their pages together too. The *Journal* has recently decided to adopt Canadian spellings rather than the Americanisms of The Canadian Press's *CP Stylebook*. Cathy Lord says that among other things, this requires putting the "u" back in words like labor and favor. A systems specialist has programmed a command that does this automatically.

As each page is completed, a full-sized printout goes to the proof-reader, and then to news editor Catherine Carson. Carson makes sure everything on the page is the way it should be. She sometimes rewrites headlines that don't work. She keeps an eye on the news wires to make sure the editors don't miss a breaking story in their rush to put out the paper. And she rides herd — gently — on the desk to make sure they meet their deadlines.

Once a page is completed, the editors send it electronically to the page assembly department on the third floor. Here, technicians put together the news and the ads, which are also produced electronically. The completed page is then transmitted to the printing plant. The whole process takes just a few minutes.

As the evening wears on, the pile of proofread pages grows and the number of "live" pages shrinks. So does the number of people in the newsroom. By 11:30 p.m., just a handful are left. Despite everything — the disruptions of the Don Fry seminars, the later-than-usual "goat shows," the unfulfilled promises of the Safeway story, the surprises of the pipe bomb, and the thousands of details and loose ends that mark any news cycle — the paper closes on time, and in good shape.

A few editors head over to the "Green Briar," a tradition on early deadline night. The nearby pub was sold some time ago and isn't named the Green Briar any more, but they still call it that anyway. Beer costs $3 a pint. They've earned it. But the satisfaction of making deadline is a passing joy. They know that everybody will have to come back tomorrow and do it all over again.

CHAPTER 8

Covering
General
Assignments

FOR ANY REPORTER, THE TOUGHEST CHALLENGE is likely to come during first weeks on the job — in those painful days when a city editor's scowl can ruin your day, when you're consumed with frustration because sources won't phone back, or when a wrong command has suddenly wiped your story from the computer screen. No advice can cure all those woes, but it is helpful to anticipate them and prepare for them. This chapter looks ahead to some of the problems (and opportunities) of the general assignment work most likely at this stage: the meetings, speeches, press releases, obituaries and the routine "follows."

If a single unifying thought covers all these basic assignments, it is this: each should be treated as *news*. It's never sufficient to treat an obituary (for instance) as simply a summary of the subject's life, with a lead like this one:

> John Halpert Delaporte, for many years a local lawyer, died Sunday of a heart attack at the age of 83.

Rather, you must find what made Delaporte's life distinctive — why the community as a whole might be interested in his life. Was there anything special about his approach to the law? About his hobbies? His community work? His family heritage? If no such dimension exists, then the paper probably won't run an obituary — but reporters should start with the faith that every story has distinctive possibilities.

For reporters, part of the fascination of their trade lies in simply *being there* — in looking on at scenes where conflicts are fought and decisions are made, where problems are highlighted and patterns identified. At this fee-increase protest by Dalhousie University students, reporter Cathy Shaw is the detached observer. (Len Wagg)

This approach can transform basic assignments into opportunities. It can make the work more interesting and also earn points with your editors, who are likely to be impressed if you produce a fresh dimension to what seemed to be a routine task. The legends of journalism are full of reporters who started with a drudge assignment and turned it into a major story — as did Paul McKay of the Kingston *Whig-Standard* when he was asked to handle a call from a local man with a beef about his workers' compensation. McKay used it as the springboard for an eight-part series investigating the Workers' Compensation Board that won him a National Newspaper Award for enterprise reporting. This doesn't mean you can make an investigative extravaganza out of every "obit" or press release, but it does mean approaching the basic tasks with a desire to find something fresh in them.

Novice reporters should see the variety in general assignment work as a virtue, not a curse. Most — not all — reporters prefer to work in a specialty, but for newcomers the breadth of general assignment provides useful experience. More than most reporters, general assignment people need to read all of their own paper carefully (to avoid the embarrassment of spending time on a story done last month) and to focus their interest on the entire community. Sometimes, too, general assignment means helping a more experienced reporter on a major story — a good way to learn.

Ruth Teichroeb, who has worked general assignment at the Vancouver *Province* and the *Winnipeg Free Press*, says junior reporters should also remember that they may find themselves suddenly thrown into a major story, either because it has broken late when everyone else is out on beat assignments, or because, as so often happens, the story turns out to be bigger than expected. The best way to prepare for those challenges, she says, is to study clips (file clippings) to examine the way senior reporters have handled various kinds of assignments in the past. And the best way to deal with problems when they arise is to ask — to turn to other people in the newsroom for help.

Finally, a reporter on general assignment should keep in mind the immense learning benefits of the experience. Whether you see the job as an end in itself or a stage on the way to a specialty, general assignment work is unique in the way it will help you get a feel for *all* of your community — for its problems and tensions, its ethnic communities and class levels, its culture and its factories, its power structures and its forgotten people. The breadth and intensity of insight this can give you is something few people get a chance to experience.

Beyond this broad advice, the following are some of the guidelines to keep in mind on typical general assignment tasks.

COVERING MEETINGS

Carrie Buchanan of the Ottawa *Citizen* recalls an incident early in her career when the night editor handed her a thick agenda for a school board meeting with the comment that the session probably wouldn't amount to much. Before the evening was over she was juggling two front-page stories. One was obviously controversial — a move to require all children to say weekly prayers against abortion. The other was a sleeper. During the meeting, a trustee and the senior administrator had had a cryptic exchange from which Buchanan heard only a vague comment about "water" and "levels." She asked the administrator later whether it meant there was contaminated water in schools. He said yes, and told her the board had a report showing lead levels in the water supply of two schools were higher than acceptable. The administrator was unhappy that the board hadn't made the report public, and was ready to show Buchanan a copy.

The point is that while meetings may sometimes be boring, they also have their surprises and rewards. The art of covering them often lies in what you do before or after, and in the concentration that allows you to spot the surprise, the bit of business that everyone else has missed or failed to follow up.

Before the Meeting

Especially for a meeting of an organization you don't know well, prepare by looking at coverage of previous meetings, at the agenda and at committee reports. Try to talk to someone who knows what is likely to come up. It's also wise to get to the meeting room early, if you can, to find out as much as you can about who will sit where and what petitioners or protesters may be present. For a council or board of education, it's a good idea to sketch a seating plan, to help keep track of speakers. (This is, of course, an ideal approach. The reality is that reporters are often assigned to a meeting at the last moment, or arrive an hour late and must scramble to catch up.)

During the Meeting

Some reporters who have learned shorthand or speed-writing consider it a crucial skill — the only way to keep up on fast-paced meetings or interviews. Tape-recording helps, but taping full meetings is complicated, so the reporter may try to flick the machine on only when the debate gets brisk, or take note of the counter number at the time of an important exchange.

Especially on smaller papers, a reporter may be expected to write two or three stories, plus briefs, before the evening is over, so speed and efficiency become critical. In time, all reporters learn to organize material at slow times during the meeting. That may mean jotting down point-form outlines of your main stories, and evaluating what you have and what you still need to find out. You may do this by visualizing how you'd like to see the coverage come out in the paper: what headline would work best? What lead? Would you prefer to see two or three separate stories on quite distinct issues? Perhaps one wrap-up story would be best, leading with the top development and then turning quickly to some variant of "The commission also decided ..."

Blocking leads out in your mind or in your notebook or laptop computer will get you started on the evaluation process and help you define what questions need to be asked. Story definition is a process that may start in a tentative way even before the meeting; it should be well advanced before the meeting is over. It's not something that starts when you arrive back in the newsroom.

At times, too, it may be necessary to leave the meeting room briefly to talk to participants — the bureaucrat who has just finished speaking or the neighborhood group that presented a petition. That could mean taking just enough time to arrange a later phone call before you return to the meeting.

After the Meeting

Often, the post-meeting interviews are as important as anything said during the session. You may have loose ends to tie off or intriguing hints to develop, as in the case of Buchanan's story on contaminated water in the schools. And post-meeting interviews can serve a number of longer-range aims. Participants are often on a mild high at the end of a meeting, stimulated by the tension of argument. They may be eager to talk, perhaps to restate points they didn't make as well as they'd hoped or to react to decisions made at the meeting. So even if you don't have a specific reason for post-meeting interviews, it's wise (if you're not on deadline) to join post-meeting scrums or take time for post-meeting conversation as a way of developing sources.

In most cases, though, the post-meeting interviews will be designed to get hard information of the kind that rounds out what has happened at the meeting. The following *Edmonton Journal* story is typical: the lead is pegged to the meeting but the next paragraphs go to outside interviews and background material, before the story returns to the meeting itself.

COUNCIL COMMITTEE APPROVES FUNDING FOR TWO AMBULANCES

EDMONTON — A plan to get two more ambulances on the road next month and improve coverage of southwest Edmonton was given the go-ahead Tuesday.

"I think we can relax a bit," said Don Henderson, general manager of the Edmonton Ambulance Authority, after a council committee approved the request for $116,000.

The plan still needs to be approved by council next Tuesday.

The money will add two ambulances during peak hours, bringing to 13 the units available to handle calls between 10 a.m. and 8 p.m.

But the ambulance workers' union wants 15 or 16 ambulances on duty full time, said spokesman Fred Hyland. "This is just one step in a journey of a thousand miles."

Ambulance coverage and response times in Edmonton have come under fire after four red alerts occurred in the past few weeks, in which no ambulances were available to respond to emergency calls.

There was also a red alert for six minutes Tuesday night.

Two children have died this summer after ambulances took more than 10 minutes to reach them.

"If we get two more units on the street immediately, Edmontonians can feel better about the service they receive," Henderson said. ...

— MARTA GOLD, *EDMONTON JOURNAL*, AUG. 19, 1992

Getting all the necessary post-meeting interviews for this kind of story is an art. Sometimes it means checking with two or three people to let them know you want to speak with them before they leave the meeting site, even if neither you nor they are free at the moment. Sometimes it means getting a home phone number so you can check with them later. Gail Robertson of the *Windsor Star* says she makes a practice of listing during a meeting the interviews she'll need. Then she has a quick word with the people she thinks are most likely to wait for her or to agree to a later phone interview, before she tries for the people most critical to her story or more difficult to interview.

Part of the challenge in covering meetings lies in finding out what's happening behind the scenes — the decisions taken informally or at closed sessions. That works best when the reporter has come to know people in the organization, but even a newcomer can be successful at it. Buchanan recalls being surprised during her apprentice days at how much would emerge from closed sessions: "any number of people are willing to tell you things they shouldn't tell you."

Planning the Story

Post-meeting interviews not only generate new information, but also clarify the significance of decisions taken at the meeting. These interviews will help in the crucial pre-writing stage as you sort out and evaluate your material. As part of that process, you should also be thinking of illustrations. Are there tables, graphs or charts available to illustrate your story? Did your photographer get a shot of the angry protesters?

If possible, the evaluation process should also include a quick check with your editor, to report the main developments and illustration possibilities and indicate how you think the coverage should be handled. It may be clear from the post-meeting questions or casual conversations what tack other reporters are planning to take; this information may help your editor decide coverage plans. Again, though, practice varies widely among papers. Reporters at some small papers tell of carrying out the whole process on their own — the evaluation, the writing, even the photos. At some larger, "editor-driven" papers, reporters tell of close and constant consultation, of having to "pitch" stories to editors, of close supervision on length and focus, and of never going too far with any project until they're sure their editor is on-side. Finally, they tell of repeated phone calls to their home from editors checking on minute details.

Storing Ideas

Whether you're working on a small or large paper, it's important not to leave to chance the crucial post-meeting stage of defining followup stories. Take time to list in your story-ideas notebook or computer file anything from the meeting that might justify a digging story. Even an obscure reference in a school board budget to an industry liaison program, for instance, may be worth putting in your list, which should always contain far more stories than you'll ever be able to do.

COVERING SPEECHES

Speeches are generally not as well covered as they used to be, especially in major media, but they're still a staple in small-city journalism. In major papers, a speech won't be printed just for form's sake — because the mayor will be offended if her Rotary address isn't reported. It will be used only if it contains the edge of an intrinsic *story* — a development that would have been a story whether it came from a speech, interview or report. So if the mayor mentions in passing in her luncheon speech that she's determined to get some reforms in the police department, that issue may well become the focus of the story, complete with amplification in a later interview with the mayor and reaction from police authorities or local interest groups critical of the police. Coverage of the speech thus turns into quite a different kind of challenge, with most of the work done after the luncheon is over. This can be called, crassly, "looking for the angle." It can also be called tough news sense, which leads the reporter to keep constant watch for the significant point that could be overlooked in a routine, stenographic account of the speech.

Looking for the angle does not, however, mean casually ignoring the major theme of the speech. At the least, you must identify that theme and give it a fair hearing before you decide to tilt the coverage in another direction. And even if your story builds on that main theme, it is likely to invert the *order* of the speech, since the rhythm of a speech, building to the main argument in the late stages, is opposite to that of the typical news story. Experienced reporters tend to look for their leads toward the end of the speech rather than at the start.

Checking the Library

For most speeches, as for most interviews or meetings, advance work is important. Whether the speaker is an out-of-town athlete, a psychologist or a mountain-climber, it's wise to check the newsroom library, or the computer databases, to get background on past actions, statements or causes. On small papers without their own libraries, reporters may have to rely on their own files or the public library. The organization sponsoring the speaker is another possible source. Wherever it's found, background reading is likely to provide useful context, and perhaps a basis for questions after the speech.

Advance work also means getting a copy of the text, if one is available. If the speaker strays from the text, it's normal to quote what's said rather than what's written, although in rare cases a divergence from the text may be significant enough to note. Even with an advance text, it's important to listen for nuance and for audience reaction.

WRITING "OBITS"

Unlike speeches, obituaries in recent years have made a comeback in newspapers after a period of neglect. The reason for the revived interest level may be that obituaries, at best, have a special capacity to evoke a response in readers by allowing them to identify with a unique life story. It is axiomatic in journalism that people are more interesting than things; the obituary exploits that interest by showing why a particular life had meaning. Consider these two approaches to the same life — the first flat and sterile, the second capturing the subject's significance:

"PÈRE GÉDÉON" DIES OF CANCER AT 75

MONTREAL (CP) — Doris Lussier, well-known Quebec actor and nationalist, died Thursday of cancer at age 75.

— OTTAWA CITIZEN, OCT. 30, 1993

"DAMN, LIFE IS GOOD!"

Quebec has lost one of its cultural icons, a man who helped ease francophone culture away from doctrinaire Catholicism to the freedom of expression of the Quiet Revolution.

Doris Lussier, who came to be identified with his classic character Père Gédéon, died Thursday at age 75 ...

— ANDRÉ PICARD, GLOBE AND MAIL, OCT. 30, 1993

Often, too, obituaries create nostalgic echoes by bringing back forgotten adventures or controversies. The following two obituaries were published side by side in the *Globe and Mail* and show subtly different rationales.

The first is largely a chance to revisit an interesting story, long forgotten by most people. The second creates a word portrait of a unique individual, easily justifying the decision to give his life significant attention.

OBITUARY / PHILIP GUCKER
PURSER SERVED ON LEVIATHAN

Philip Gucker, one of the few remaining crew members of the USS Leviathan, the ship that ruled the Atlantic between the two world wars, has died. He was 89.

He died Thursday in a nursing home in Wolfville, N.S.

Mr. Gucker was purser aboard the ship during its last years, before it was dismantled in Scotland for scrap in 1938. For 20 years it was the largest ship sailing the Atlantic, with capacity for 5,000 passengers and a crew of 1,200. But the New York Times noted in 1938 that "perhaps the most outstanding thing about the Leviathan was her ability to lose money."...

It was launched in 1914 as the German ship Vaterland but had the misfortune of being docked in Hoboken, N.J., after its second voyage when the First World War started. ...

— DONN DOWNEY, GLOBE AND MAIL, SEPT. 22, 1992

OBITUARY / ROBERT GREIG
OFFICER PROBED WHITE-COLLAR CRIME

TORONTO — Canada lost one of its premier white-collar crime investigators last weekend with the sudden death of Robert Greig. He was 48.

Mr. Greig, who died of a heart attack on Saturday, began his police career in his native Glasgow but spent the past 25 years with Metro Toronto Police, mainly as a fraud investigator.

He specialized in apprehending sophisticated criminals in the brokerage and financial communities, and was an expert on so-called boiler-room operations that preyed on inexperienced investors throughout the world. Those investigations took him to the United States, Britain, the Netherlands and many Caribbean countries.

In recent years he and his long-time partner, Robert Barbour, built successful cases against Brian Molony, sentenced to six years in jail in 1986 for stealing more than $10 million from his employer, the Canadian Imperial Bank of Commerce, to finance his gambling habit, and three executives who manipulated the stock of Consumers Distributing.

The gregarious investigator's main weapons were his charm, wit and skill as an interviewer. He also was a prodigious peruser of complex financial documents who was easily excited by the hunt for business crooks. He was renowned among his colleagues for his ability to fit in anywhere and to persuade people to co-operate with him.

"He had a great gift for making people comfortable with him," Mr. Barbour said. "He really understood people ... His only weakness was for French fries."

At heart Mr. Greig was an old-fashioned Scots moralist who was often personally affronted by those who abused their wealth and power. He was driven by a strong sense of social justice, and would often go to unusual lengths to try to help those who had lost their life savings to financial criminals. ...

— JOCK FERGUSON, GLOBE AND MAIL, SEPT. 22, 1992

Clearly, both of these people had elements of drama in their lives. It's easy to imagine them as characters in a documentary or a piece of fiction, and thus the obituary writer need have no doubt about *story* values. The task is simply to convey those values to readers. Sometimes in an obit assignment this special dimension will be obvious, if the person was a war hero or a noted local hockey coach. At other times it may emerge only slowly during patient probing on secondary matters: on where the subjects were born, what they worked at, what hobbies, causes or talents they had. The subjects don't have to be famous and successful, as this obituary shows:

"ONE-MAN RESEARCH CENTRE" BOB JERABEK DIES

Inventor and crusader Bohumil (Bob) Jerabek died a disappointed man, never getting into production the goof-proof chain saw he hoped would save many lives.

"He fought for it so long," his wife, Janet, said Friday. "If there is one thing he would have wanted, (it) was to get his chain saw into production."

The passionate Ottawa engineer, who led a movement to ban aluminum wiring in homes, died earlier this week after a massive heart attack at the age of 67 ...

— SHELLEY PAGE, OTTAWA CITIZEN, Nov. 7, 1992

In part, the challenge of obituaries lies in building a profile without being able to interview the central character. This means interviewing colleagues or family at a time of stress. It is important, of course, to let the survivors know that you understand they're going through a difficult time, but you can signal as well that it's in their interest to see that the person who has died is properly recognized. Some obit writers prefer to start the process with a source not in the immediate family. Often the funeral director may be a good guide in defining a source who is close, but not next-of-kin. This person may also help in advising on other possible sources, or even in making contact with them.

Another constant problem with obituaries is the handling of embarrassing episodes deep in the subject's past: the morgue material that tells how the ex-mayor was once accused of corruption, for instance, or how the local author was arrested in a drunken brawl. For this problem there is no one simple answer. Most newspapers lean toward charity, skipping these less savory details unless they are a central part of the subject's life story.

Similarly, the reporting of suicides presents difficulties. Traditionally, Canadian newspapers did not say a death was a suicide unless the subject was unusually prominent or the circumstances were extraordinary — as when a former premier shot himself in his shower, or when a woman leaped from the Peace Tower. In recent years there appears to be a greater tendency to use the fact of suicide, provided it's so labelled by the police. Nevertheless, it's wise to check your paper's policy before going ahead with a suicide story.

Practice also appears to be changing on reporting some causes of death. Traditionally, syphilis and cirrhosis of the liver were not mentioned, and the same practice was adopted when AIDS first appeared. Later the pattern changed, some editors arguing that suppression might imply wrongly there was something shameful about AIDS, or that it might have the result of obscuring the extent of the problem.

In most cases, the obituary sketch frankly stresses accomplishments, apparently in line with the natural tendency to speak well of the dead. Of all news stories, it may be the kind on which editors most hate to issue later corrections, so careful accuracy checks are crucial. It is not necessary, however, to adopt the mordant language sometimes surrounding death and funerals. As the *CP Stylebook* puts it: "write *die*, *bury*, *coffin* and *undertaker* or *funeral director* rather than *pass away*, *inter*, *casket* and *mortician*" (1995, 70).

BUILDING ON PRESS RELEASES

The prime rule in handling a press release is that it must not emerge in the paper as something that *looks* like a press release. Many press releases generate news, but they should do so only because the reporter sees a legitimate story within them. As with the stylized obit, it's never enough to write a story that simply follows the form and priorities of the press release, ending up as something like this:

> President Frank Campagna of Acme Machine Tools announced today that the company plans to set up a branch in Western Canada.

Again, you must ask yourself why this is a *story*. Is it a surprising success story that Acme is able to expand? Or is Acme getting ready to abandon its Eastern Canada plant for some reason? Will any jobs be cut in the Eastern Canada plant? Are the unions happy or unhappy? These may not be the right questions, but the questioning *process* is crucial.

This *Globe and Mail* story, for instance, started with an announcement but quickly moved beyond it:

CBC, BBC TO SHARE TV NEWS AND BUREAUS

> TORONTO — The CBC has signed an agreement with the BBC's World Service Television to share TV news programming and international news bureaus.
>
> Starting early in November, the two public broadcasting corporations will begin exchanging daily news videos and start working toward operating shared foreign bureaus and possibly opening new ones ...

>   Tim Kotcheff, CBC vice-president of news, was in Ottawa yesterday and
>   unavailable for comment.
>
>   Tom Curzon, senior director of public and media relations at CBC, said the
>   agreement has been in negotiation for a number of weeks but was finalized only
>   this week. Many details remain to be worked out, he said, such as precisely
>   what use the CBC might make of BBC material, and how the shared bureaus
>   would work.
>
>   Asked if the agreement could lead to reductions in staff at some CBC
>   bureaus, Curzon said he could not comment specifically beyond saying it was
>   extremely doubtful.
>
>   "Obviously, having people of our own there puts a Canadian perspective on
>   the reporting of news which is invaluable. So no, that's not in the cards." ...
>
>   — CHRISTOPHER HARRIS, GLOBE AND MAIL, OCT. 1, 1992

Clearly, this reporter was thinking not only of what the announcement
said, but also about what it meant. In evaluating that factor, ask yourself
what the motivation was for issuing the press release. Was it to anticipate a problem? To put a positive spin on something that may turn out
to be negative? You are not required to find something negative about
every story, of course, but neither should you accept the premise of the
press release uncritically. At the least, you need to ask the questions
readers may ask. In the case of the CBC story, the obvious question was
whether the joint bureaus would lead to staff reductions.

Almost any clarifying call to the office that issued the release will
elicit material not in the release, and some queries may disclose important material that is missing from the release, or even errors. The press
release may also provide leverage in getting through to officials higher
than the issuing officer. ("I'd like to get some assessment from your president on what the move to the West may mean for export potential.")
Since the companies or agencies are seeking attention, it's hard for them
to turn down such requests.

COVERING NEWS CONFERENCES

News conferences vary widely in tone and purpose, all the way from routine media events set up by a group seeking publicity for its funding drive
to tense scrums confronting a public figure (an official, an actor or a track
star) who has run into scandal. While the guidelines vary as much as the
events, it's usually wise to keep your questions short and sharp, and to try
to follow up on points raised by other reporters and dodged by the source.

In general, news conferences have all the perils of the interview,
with added intensity. It's even harder to build toward a theme, for
instance, and double-barrelled or complicated questions may be doubly

dangerous. You may get only one question in, so it has to be a good one.

In general, too, news conferences are where pack pressures show up in their most intense form. If you try to ask an open-ended question about topic B when the rest of the reporters want to talk about topic A, you'll feel their disapproval. That may be because the other reporters sense a good theme developing and want to see it fully explored. But individual reporters must guard against accepting uncritically the tone of the pack or the story evaluation of the pack.

Not surprisingly, this problem is probably most acute among novice journalists. Journalism students who have taken part in news conference exercises often deplore afterward the group tone that developed, whether it was hostile or ingratiating. Regularly, too, they will criticize in post mortem analysis the way questions were often calculated to make a point rather than to elicit information. More experienced reporters tend to ask even the toughest questions in a low-key, detached style, and to guard against letting the session become either a love-in or an inquisition.

In some cases news conferences, or scrums, may be useful in allowing a reporter to pose the kind of question that's difficult to ask in a one-to-one interview. In other cases reporters will avoid asking at a news conference the question that reveals the story they're working on. They may instead approach organizers at the end of the news conference to ask for a quick (or extended) interview.

CHASING "FOLLOWS"

For many reporters a routine, less tense, part of the job is the followup story — the phone checks to see if anything new has happened in a labor dispute, for example, or whether the critically injured accident survivor has died. Again, procedure varies from paper to paper. In some cases editors will have set aside clips from earlier stories and will assign a followup check. In others, this may be the responsibility of the beat reporter. For the beginning reporter, the main lesson may be the need to think of news in a continuing way, to take responsibility for preserving clips that need follows and to datebook situations that will need checks at a particular time (when a report is to be presented, for instance, or when a strike vote deadline is to be reached). In effect, this means taking a share of the overall responsibility to see that continuing stories do not slip out of sight.

A variant on this kind of follow is the "localizing" of wire stories. That may mean getting comment from local politicians or business people on a proposal made elsewhere, or inserting local material on a wider story — on anything from dating patterns to an infestation of spruce budworm. Often this is routine, uninspiring work. It becomes more than that when, as sometimes happens, your work uncovers something that clearly supersedes the original story, turning the project from a routine insert or add into a story that stands on its own. That kind of

This *Toronto Sun* photo shows Muslim women preparing a food bank donation to mark Ashura, a day of fasting. It may also represent a trend in Canadian journalism: an attempt to broaden the definition of who and what deserves coverage, and who ought to be doing the covering. For years, critics have argued that the media tended to be run by and for a narrow stratum of society, excluding many significant groups. Those patterns are now starting to change. (*Toronto Sun*)

result is more likely if your knowledge of the situation is broad, so it's best not to rely only on the single clip or wire story provided by your editor. Wherever possible, do a file or computer search to find out more about the situation, to get a better idea of what needs to be asked. The same advice applies if you're asked to "match" a story in an opposition medium: the challenge is to find a fresh dimension rather than simply confirming the competitor's story.

In any case, it is crucial in any followup call not to let the source think the call is routine. In each interview you need specific questions calculated to elicit something new. Reporters who ask in a bored way if there's "anything new on the strike," or if "I can get some kind of comment from you on the Jones report," will get the kind of response they deserve.

WRITING SHORT FEATURES

A part of general assignment work may be short features of various kinds: the news feature linked with a spot story, the news profile or the so-called lifestyle feature. Although these features are defined only loosely, lifestyle features tend to focus on such things as diet, exercise, cooking, home entertainment, back pain, self-esteem, self-improvement and pets — in short, on the things that people talk about.

The lifestyle feature is generally seen as a product of the baby boom era and in the 1990s may be under sharper competition from stories about high taxes, unemployment and deficits, or features on how to get the most for your money. But the light feature is still a major part of most newspapers, and it calls for skills no less distinct than those needed for the more serious civic coverage.

First, it demands good antennae to detect the things people are talking about or want to know about: the new relaxation technique, the new approach to wine-making, the fads in singles ads or the trend to growing your own herbs. Second, it demands a genuine interest in people, a delight in bringing out the detailed personal anecdotes and experiences that allow readers to identify with subjects. Novice reporters may have an advantage in seeking out these stories — in defining genuinely new patterns. They may find that these stories permit (or require) a more imaginative approach than most of their work. They may also be surprised to find that the stories they write about offbeat gardens, music therapy or furniture restoration are the ones that friends are likely to read to the end and to comment on.

As well, lifestyle features often provide advice that is indeed useful — for example, the advice for interviewers contained in this feature:

SPECIALIST TEACHES DOCTORS HOW TO LISTEN TO PEOPLE

When you get home tonight, practice active listening.

That's an assignment given University of Toronto medical students by Dr. Robert Buckman, who teaches them how to communicate effectively with patients.

"The students report back that the results are amazing and have dramatic effects," Buckman said in an interview.

What's the difference between garden variety listening and active listening? Buckman says the technique is simple.

Don't interrupt when another person is speaking. Wait until they finish talking. And repeat one or two words the person said so it is evident you really heard.

Buckman says most of us tend to start talking before the other person has finished but doctors may be especially prone to this. ...

— MARILYN DUNLOP, *TORONTO STAR*, OCT. 6, 1992

News of this kind may not score high on a significance scale, but it does help in the process of disseminating useful advice from specialists to larger audiences. The 1980s slogan of "news you can use" has an old-fashioned ring today, but the underlying principle remains valid.

COVERING DEVELOPING STORIES

At times a news story — a fire, flood, hostage-taking, papal visit — will unfold over a period of days or even weeks. Coverage problems on these "developing" or "running" stories will vary from one news medium to another. Radio or wire service reporters may have to update their material several times a day, while the newspaper reporter writes just before deadline, and the news magazine reporter waits until the whole sequence is over. Because of this variety, no one set of guidelines governs the handling of these stories, but some general points apply to most media most of the time:

1. Don't assume readers know as much as you do about the situation. Keep inserting the necessary background high in the story, wording it so it's there for those who need it while not slowing down readers who already know it.

2. Be careful not to stress the *latest* development at the expense of the *best*. For instance, your first story on a fire may lead with the facts that three people have died in a factory fire burning out of control. When the fire is eventually put out four hours later, it may be tempting to write your new lead on the controlling of the fire. Instead, you should continue to focus on the main news, amending it as necessary. You might end up with a lead like this:

> Three people died early today in a fire at Acme Chemical plant that burned out of control for four hours before firefighters managed to check it.

3. If you expect your story will be outdated by developments, try to group at the top of the story the material most likely to be replaced.

4. Write wherever possible in the simple past tense. For instance, rather than saying

> Fire chief Jan Zareski says two other fire rigs are being called in …

it is preferable to say

> Fire chief Jan Zareski called in two other fire rigs from …

Material in the simple past tense is more likely to stand up.

5. Be extremely cautious about rumors, a special hazard in times of crisis and confusion. At the factory fire, for instance, you may hear people among the watchers insisting that two other people are trapped by the fire, or that there's a danger of chemical storage tanks exploding. Don't report that kind of material until you're certain you have sound reason to do so.

"PICKUPS" — DRAWING THE LINE

For many new reporters, the worst assignment of all is doing "pickups" — that is, being sent out to get pictures and comment from parents whose daughter has been struck by a bus or whose son has been shot in a hostage incident. While some newspapers now de-emphasize that kind of coverage, others, especially tabloids, give it high priority. Their editors put considerable pressure on reporters to get the picture or to get comment from the family. The task is sometimes seen as a test of a rookie's persistence, ingenuity and toughness.

Stephanie Chamberlain recalls that during her work at the *Ottawa Sun*, several assignments of this kind left her with mixed feelings.

On one occasion, she arrived at a home to find other reporters waiting across the street, after they'd been turned away by the parents of the victim. Chamberlain went up to the house anyway, noticing on the way an RCAF sticker on the car parked in front. When a man answered the door she mentioned that she had formerly worked for *Air Force* magazine, then went on to express her sympathy. The man began to talk, and she got the picture. She didn't lie about her purpose, but felt in retrospect she'd used the air force connection in a manipulative way.

Another time, a woman whose child was missing (in the neighborhood of an unsolved child murder) met her at the front door and turned her away abruptly. Chamberlain didn't argue but went around the corner and bought doughnuts and coffee. She came back, handed them to the woman with a sympathetic comment and asked if she'd like to talk. The woman invited her in — and again she got the picture. (The child later turned up.)

On a third occasion, Chamberlain and other reporters were competing in a tense search for pictures of a woman murdered by her husband. After much tracking she located a close friend of the woman working as a store cashier. She made her approach and was turned down, the woman insisting that she couldn't talk to her. Chamberlain responded with a plea on behalf of abused women, arguing that the story needed to be told so that society could do something to stop abuse. The woman eventually tracked down another cashier in the store who had a photo of the slain woman.

In retrospect, Chamberlain ponders her mixed motivation in incidents like these. In each case she feels her response was at least partly genuine: she did in fact feel sympathy and genuine concern about the problem of abuse. But she was also conscious of an element of manipulation that she used to score professional points. She recognized as well a certain triumph in bringing off each coup in a way that would win editors' praise, while at the same time she remained uneasy about the way she went about the task.

This kind of concern is not unusual, and the dilemma it produces has no fully satisfactory answer.

Some reporters argue that shared sorrow is part of what makes a community, so the story and picture of the dead child help in allowing people in a large and impersonal city feel they have something in common. Or they argue that stories like that of the murdered woman must be told so that society can react as it should. Steve Proctor of the Halifax *Chronicle-Herald* says survivor interviews, although he finds them painful and wants to avoid them, give parents a chance to say useful things — to offer a warning on drug use, for instance, or on the stresses of being a teenager. In some cases, too, it gives parents a chance to balance the harsh picture of a teenager who died in troubled circumstances.

While that is no doubt true, it leaves open the question of how far reporters should go in getting the quotes or the pictures. Ruth Teichroeb, who has done many such assignments at the *Province* in Vancouver and at the *Winnipeg Free Press*, says she has occasionally seen other reporters bring flowers to survivors or go to the hospital, pretending to be a relative, but has never felt forced to adopt those tactics or to misrepresent herself.

"I learned what my own limit was and stuck with that," she says. "I would always make the call — the phone call or the stop at the house.

But if the people completely shut me out, said they didn't want to talk to the press, I left it at that. I didn't go on to some of the more aggressive tactics some reporters used."

But she also discovered to her surprise that some parents wanted to talk. "It was important to them. They wanted to have a picture of their child in the paper. They wanted to talk about it. People grieve differently, and this was a different way of reacting to the tragedy. I guess I learned to assume that not everyone was going to slam the door."

For some reporters, doing pickups is simply a professional game, a matter of getting the picture or the quotes before the opposition does, no matter what it takes. Those who don't see it that way often try to move into other areas of reporting. But few reporters escape entirely the problem of balancing their natural sympathies with the desire to get the story.

RECOMMENDED READING

Desbarats, Peter. (1996). *Guide to Canadian News Media.* 2nd edition. Chapter 4, "The Journalists." Toronto: Harcourt Brace Jovanovich.

Fulford, Robert, et al. (1981). *The Journalists.* Vol. 2, Research Publications, Royal Commission on Newspapers. Ottawa: Minister of Supply and Services.

CHAPTER 9

Covering
the
Police Beat

RIME IS, ALMOST BY DEFINITION, "NEWS" — an event that breaks the pattern of ordinary life. When a woman is attacked while taking an after-dinner stroll on a residential street, people in the community want to know about it. Some are simply curious. Others, picturing themselves or their daughters in a similar situation, want to know whether the attacker has been caught and what they should do to ensure their own safety. Should they avoid the area? Is it safe during the day but not after dark? Should the city put in more street lighting?

It is no surprise, therefore, that reporting on crime is a mainstay of journalism. But covering the police beat goes beyond a recitation of criminal acts. More than any other beat, it means coverage of the unexpected: the fire triggered by a dropped cigarette that destroys a downtown business, the highway accident that robs a family of a child, the train derailment that forces people to leave their homes in fear of a toxic spill.

From the writer's point of view, stories from the police beat are distinctive in several ways. For one thing, they have a strong narrative flow, a sequence of events the writer can describe with natural suspense. Unlike stories on social issues such as poverty and housing, most police and fire beat stories have a concrete beginning — an event that triggers a chain reaction leading to a violent or emotional climax. These stories have villains and victims, clues and false leads, and sometimes, heroes and heroines. And finally, many (though by no means all) crime stories have a finite conclusion — an arrest that leads in turn to the drama of the courtroom, which we discuss in the next chapter.

Police coverage often deals with the dark side of the community, with brutality and viciousness and greed and, not uncommonly, with the core evils of society. It is the area where reporters come up hardest and most frequently against what might be called the *dilemma of news drama*: the temptation to exploit misery for dramatic effect.

Reporters often find themselves treading a tenuous line between intense, human reportage on the one hand, and invasion of private grief for exploitation on the other. Any reporter who has ever had to phone the family of an accident victim has felt anxiety over whether the family will tolerate the call or resent it as intrusion — or perhaps worst of all, plead with the reporter to keep news of the accident out of the newspaper or off the 6 o'clock news.

In covering crime and accident stories, reporters justify the intrusion into private grief by arguing that they are providing needed information to members of a community. But every journalist wrestles with the question of exactly what to report and in how much detail. It is important for a community to know, for example, that a murdered child had been sexually assaulted. But does publishing a graphic description of the body serve a purpose? Does it inform, or merely cater to prurient interest? Is it in the public interest or is it an unjustifiable invasion of the private nightmare of the parents?

While wrestling with the journalistic issues of taste and content, the police reporter inevitably runs into one of the central contradictions of the job: the fact that few relationships between reporters and sources are as difficult as those on the police beat. Both groups believe they serve a public need, but they see their roles, and each other's, very differently. Police officers will use the press to get their message out when they feel it will aid an investigation. But, if they feel the investigation will be hindered by it, they will suppress information. Sometimes they'll do both at different times during the same investigation. Reporters, on the other hand, see their job as telling people what is going on in their communities, regardless, sometimes, of whether the police want that information to be public knowledge. In addition, reporters may seek to push an investigation forward, stepping on the investigating officers' toes in the process.

But police reporters don't just cover crime. They also cover the police as an institution. As public witnesses to the business of law enforcement, they point out when things go right, and when things go wrong. When the police make a mistake — an officer fires on a man who turns out to be unarmed; after a night of drinking in a bar, an undercover officer runs down a teenager; a shooting appears to be racially motivated — reporters want to make sure the public will hear about it. And, in the process, they may alienate many of their sources on the force.

Many police officers see reporters as nuisances, and sometimes as enemies. Many reporters see the police as close-mouthed and authoritarian, less willing than politicians or interest groups to deal with the media. Police reporters gradually develop relationships of mutual respect with their police contacts, but they can never escape the tensions those relationships impose.

MAPPING OUT THE BEAT

At first glance, a car engine is a mass of colors and shapes. It is hard to tell which bit makes a particular sound or does a particular job, but with a little effort almost anyone can learn how an engine works. In some

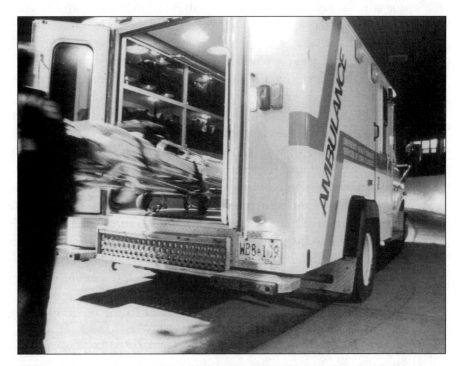

On the night a drunk driver ran down a youth who was crossing the street, photography student David Lucas was shooting pictures at Belleville General Hospital. He recorded the arrival of the ambulance and the ultimately unsuccessful effort to save the young man's life. Many of his pictures could not be published because of privacy considerations. Journalists covering this kind of tragedy face the difficult task of preserving family members' dignity while communicating their despair and sense of loss. (Daivd Lucas/Loyalist College)

ways, working into a beat is much like this: reporters must come to understand the institutions and individual elements of the beat and how they are supposed to fit together before they can report with any confidence on whether the institutions are doing their work well. As veteran crime reporter Bob Johnstone of the CBC puts it, "The first thing you have to do is figure out how things normally go, then look for anomalies."

It is impossible in these few pages to describe in detail how police services are organized in Canada. But some basic concepts serve as a starting point for a reporter new to the beat.

Canada has three main levels of police — local, provincial and federal — plus a number of specialized agencies that deal directly or indirectly with aspects of police work. This last group includes such organizations as the Coast Guard, military police, the Canadian Security Intelligence Service (CSIS), Canada Customs and Ports Canada police.

Each province has some kind of legislation on law enforcement — usually known as a police act — that requires cities and towns to provide police services. Local or municipal police forces have the power to enforce all levels of laws in their areas, including the Criminal Code, many federal and provincial statutes and municipal bylaws.

These forces handle the bulk of urban law enforcement in Canada and are probably the source of information most frequently used by police reporters. Some municipal forces are small, with a chief and a few officers. Others have hundreds of employees. A big-city department may be divided into several branches whose names reflect the complexity of police work — and suggest areas of reportage. Making contacts in all branches can help reporters develop a range of stories, from pieces on hiring women and minorities to articles on budgets and policy changes.

Some areas, including Metropolitan Toronto and the Montreal Urban Community, have regional police forces that handle law enforcement for a number of local municipalities. Other areas may have regional governments but no regional police force. Some municipalities, rather than creating their own forces, contract their policing out to a municipal force from a neighboring city or to the provincial police.

For the most part, provincial police forces operate as full-scale police forces where there is no municipal force. Provincial forces have province-wide jurisdiction in some areas of law, however, such as controlling highway traffic or enforcing liquor laws. Special provincial police branches help their own local detachments and municipal forces with criminal investigations. In Quebec, the provincial police may be given the authority in special circumstances to enforce the law in municipalities that already have municipal forces.

The key federal police force is the Royal Canadian Mounted Police. In Ontario and Quebec, which have their own full-scale provincial police forces, the RCMP mainly enforces federal statutes such as the Narcotics Control Act. Other provinces, rather than setting up their own provincial police, have contracts with the RCMP to provide provincial police service. The RCMP also provides policing in the Yukon and Northwest Territories. In addition, the RCMP says in a fact sheet posted on its Web site, the force provides local police service in about 200 communities, through contracts between the municipalities and the provinces. This means that, in a number of areas, the RCMP is responsible for enforcement of *all* levels of laws, from bylaws to the Criminal Code to federal narcotics laws.

If all this sounds confusing, it is. The odds are that in any urban area, several forces or detachments operate. A reporter tracking police calls on a radio scanner may be baffled at first by the range of calls and bands, and at a loss as to which force to call about a traffic accident on the highway at the edge of town. After a few days on the beat, though, the reporter learns to identify instantly which force to call.

All police forces in Canada are ultimately responsible to a civilian body. This has important implications for reporters. It means you should be able to find sources outside the force who keep an eye on things going on inside the force. In addition, exploring the natural tension between the police and their civilian overseers may lead you to stories.

At the municipal level, most provincial police acts authorize the creation of a local police board or police commission. These have the potential to wield a lot of power over the police, though in practice they seldom do so. (Fights between police chiefs and police commissions are often natural news stories, however.) The commission's biggest job is to set the local police budget, which goes to the municipal council for approval. In Ontario, if the local council and the police commission can't agree on a budget, a higher body, the Ontario Police Commission, is called in to help.

Several provinces have provincial police commissions which, like local commissions, operate independently of government but report to an elected official (usually the attorney general, the solicitor general or the minister of justice), who answers for the commission in the legislature. The functions of these commissions vary from province to province but may include training municipal officers, collecting statistics and serving as an appeal body for members of local forces convicted of disciplinary offences. A number of provinces have police oversight agencies that handle complaints from the public about police actions.

At the federal level, the RCMP is headed by a commissioner who reports to the solicitor general. The solicitor general in turn handles inquiries about the RCMP in the House of Commons. Until the mid-1980s, the RCMP was responsible for most intelligence work. Much of this has been transferred to the Canadian Security Intelligence Service. (*Info Source*, produced by the federal government as a guide to making access-to-information requests, describes the organization of the RCMP and CSIS, the various documents they handle and the laws they may enforce.)

Many police reporters also have to keep an eye on the fire department. This makes good sense: the police reporter has an ear to the scanner and can pick up fire calls. In addition, local police usually play a role when there is a fire — at first, perhaps, only to direct traffic, but also to help in the investigation.

In comparison with the organization of police services, that of fire departments is less complicated and more decentralized. One town may organize its own fire department while another contracts fire service from a neighboring municipality. In some areas, a joint fire department covers two or more communities. Local fire departments may be staffed by professional (i.e., full-time) firefighters, volunteer firefighters or a combination. Volunteer firefighters, who serve on an on-call basis and often receive a stipend for their work, play a major role, particularly in rural or semi-rural areas.

Fire departments are headed by a chief who usually speaks for the department. In larger cities, fire departments may have several branches. The largest branch is the one that actually puts out the fires. Others, dealing with matters like fire investigations, fire prevention and inspection, are important for institutional coverage or pattern stories on everything from arson to smoke detectors to hiring policy.

All provinces have a fire commissioner or fire marshal. In most provinces, investigators from these offices are called in when arson is suspected or in fires involving a death, an explosion or a serious loss of property. These investigators are key sources for reporters covering the aftermath of major fires. Provincial fire marshals also collect statistics on fires and issue an annual report, which can be useful in enterprise stories about the patterns of fires in a particular community or in stories comparing communities. Depending on the province, the fire marshal or fire commissioner may have a part in training local firefighters, in inspections and enforcement of some fire code regulations, and in providing public information on fire prevention and fire safety. At the federal level, the fire commissioner of Canada compiles provincial statistics into an annual national report. It may not be as useful for reporters as the provincial reports, since it is both less detailed and less current by the time it is released.

ON THE JOB

At the Halifax *Chronicle-Herald*, police reporter Eva Hoare begins her workday with a round of phone calls. She checks in with Halifax police, the fire department, the RCMP, the search and rescue squad and Ports Canada. The round of calls, repeated at least twice more during her shift, is aimed at generating two kinds of stories. The first is the quick-hit news item about the latest crime, accident, fire or arrest. These come mainly from a rundown of the police force's daily occurrence sheet, the so-called police blotter. Tracking routine news items takes up 40 to 50 per cent of Hoare's workday. In between the quick hits, she works on the second kind of story — what she calls "the innovative or scoopy end of the beat." Once again, the telephone is her main tool. She has a long list of contacts within the various forces and the police unions whom she calls regularly.

Winnipeg Free Press reporter Paul Wiecek, who spent six years on the police beat, says the police reporter's shift starts with a 10:30 a.m. briefing at city police headquarters, where a police spokesperson goes over the main occurrences the police have been handling in the past 24 hours. These include major fires, robberies, frauds, thefts, traffic accidents and so on, plus any minor incidents the spokesperson thinks may be of interest to the reporters. After the briefing, the reporter phones the RCMP, which polices the rest of province, and gets a similar rundown. By now, he has a half-dozen to a dozen possible stories. Some will be too minor to write. Others will become briefs. Some may develop into the top story of the day or serve as a starting point for an enterprise piece on an aspect of policing or on a public issue relating to law enforcement.

Wiecek, now an investigative reporter, says that once he had an idea of what went on in the past day and what kinds of stories he would write from the briefings, he could turn his attention to tracking other stories. This meant walking around the police headquarters building, dropping in on senior officers to touch base on their current investigations or to find out what's on the officer's mind. "Sometimes we'd just talk about the Blue Bombers," he says. "But sometimes, I'd get a story."

The round of calls and police checks is one of the routine aspects of the job. Another is the use of radio scanners to monitor transmissions from the various police and fire departments in the area. Some police and emergency services departments have begun moving to specially configured digital radio systems whose signals can't be picked up by regular radio scanners. This poses difficulties for reporters trying to stay on top of breaking news. In some areas, however, the police and the local media have made deals: for example, the police may agree to program a select number of scanners for a media outlet to pick up police dispatch channels. In return, the reporters agree to keep these scanners secure, and promise not to tamper with their programming. They may also have to promise to confirm by telephone any information they pick up on the scanners. These deals may seem less than ideal, but reporters feel limited scanners are better than no scanners at all. In addition, reporters can still learn of a breaking story — a fire or a hostage-taking — from the dispatch channel at the same time as the patrol cars. In fact, sometimes reporters get to the scene first.

Rushing to the scene of the crime, however, happens less often than most novices think. The vast bulk of routine police and fire stories come from checking in with the police and fire departments to see what has happened.

Veteran reporters advise those new to the beat to ask specific questions when making police calls, rather than simply asking "Is anything happening?" Harold J. Levy, in *A Reporter's Guide to Canada's Criminal Justice System* (1986, 29), explains that while reporters are supposed to have news judgment, police officers aren't. Their idea of what constitutes a story may be very different from a reporter's.

In addition, Levy says, a police reporter can use these calls to begin developing a reputation as someone who is willing to talk to police officers on the lonely overnight shift and is not out to "'screw' the cops."

ELEMENTS OF COVERAGE

The basic police brief is a quick, simple summary of an event. Many are written almost in a formula style, with a summary news lead and a single source — the police.

The formula looks simple, but even the briefest brief places substantial demands on the police reporter. The reporter must gather the information with care, ensuring that the details are as complete as possible. This usually means putting followup questions to a sometimes brusque and impatient police officer, an experience that can be intimidating to new reporters. Experienced reporters strongly recommend that the novice collect all the information in a single call, since a series of callbacks to check minor details will only annoy an officer who may be swamped with work.

Once a reporter has the basic details, it's a good idea to check for understanding by asking synthesizing questions. ("So what you're telling me is that an unarmed man smashed a display case *outside* the store and made off with a fistful of jewelry. Is that right?") This kind of question is a good way for reporters to ensure that they've written down the sequence of events correctly, and that they haven't missed any key points.

In writing the story, the reporter must draw on news judgment and storytelling skills to craft an item that gives key details simply, clearly and in a way that is easy to follow.

Accuracy is, of course, vital in all journalism, but the demands for accuracy are particularly high in police and court reporting, where an error in spelling a name can have far-reaching consequences. If a reporter identifies the victim of an accident as Thomas Wong rather than Thomas Huang, the reader will be misinformed. Friends of Thomas Wong will begin to grieve his death. Both the Wong and Huang families will be angry at the misinformation going around town. And so will the police officer who gave the reporter the information in the first place.

Experienced reporters make the necessary checks automatically. ("The accused is John Patterson. Is that John with an 'h' — J-o-h-n — or J-o-n? With an 'h'? Uh huh — OK. And does Patterson have one 't' or two? Two? P-a-t-t-e-r-s-o-n? OK. Thanks.") But it is all too easy for new reporters, intimidated by the officer on the other end of the line or perhaps overwhelmed by the task of trying to get the details down, to forget to check whether it's John with an "h," or whether a name is spelled the conventional way (Barry) or has an unusual spelling (Barrie).

Finally, the same kind of careful check must be made when the information goes from notepad to computer screen. Classroom exercises show that a remarkable number of students get the information correctly but make errors as they write the story. Put under stress, perhaps, by the demands of writing to deadline, they forget the basic step of checking for typos.

Police reporters write many different types of stories, ranging from the tiny, one-paragraph brief on up to the major investigative piece. In the sections that follow, we look at some of the basic forms of police reporting, using articles clipped from a number of newspapers. We have changed the names of the people and places in cases where re-publication could cause unnecessary pain or embarrassment.

Accident Stories

The body of a Pennsylvania man was discovered by Ontario Provincial Police Saturday on the rugged shores of Big Rideau Lake.

Police believe Tony Majors, 41, died after his lightweight aluminum boat capsized while he was fishing some time after June 30.

The warden at Murphys Point Provincial Park near Perth reported Majors missing July 5 after he hadn't been seen in five days. He was last seen on June 30, the day he arrived from Philadelphia, Pa.

Majors was vacationing alone and no foul play is suspected, said Sgt. Greg Bulloch of the Perth OPP detachment.

Police conducted a two-day marine search before the body was found Saturday afternoon about 10 kilometres west of Rideau Ferry on the south shore of Big Rideau Lake. Murphys Point is on the north shore of the lake.

The lake is about 85 km southwest of Ottawa.

Bulloch said there have been several thunderstorms in the area in the past week.

Majors's 3 1/2-metre aluminum boat with a 9.9 horsepower Yamaha outboard motor has not been found. Bulloch said it likely sank.

— Ottawa Citizen, July 8, 1991

This story came from a single source, an OPP news release read to a reporter over the telephone. Simple news judgment dictated the lead: the latest development in the story — the discovery of the body — was also the most significant development. With the body found, the mystery of the missing man has been solved.

The story is written in the basic, hard-news inverted pyramid form. It gives the most important information first, in the top four paragraphs. It follows with more details on precisely where and when the body was found, and offers some speculation on how the man died. In this story, the fact that the man was not from the community means people are probably more interested in knowing that he died than in learning about who he was.

Sometimes, however, there is a whole lot more to be said.

Compare the previous account with the following story (again, names have been changed) by Steve Green of the *London Free Press*. Green, who was working the rewrite desk, was given the bare details of a fatal accident and asked to flesh out a story.

Area teen Gordon (Howie) Clark had many friends.

His death in a head-on crash Monday afternoon was all the more tragic because the other driver was one of his closest pals.

Clark, 17, of RR 2, X-ville, died when the car he was driving collided with a pickup truck containing five people on County Road 12, two kilometres south of X-ville.

Clark, who was pronounced dead at the scene, died of massive head injuries, said coroner Jon Greenwood of Y-town, who is also the Clark family's doctor.

"It was a tragic situation," Greenwood said. "They were a close little family. He was very outgoing and had a lot of friends. ... He was a good boy all around."

Clark, a Grade 11 student at Ridgemont District High School, was the oldest of three brothers.

Classmate and close friend Greg Parsons said, "He was very outgoing, the most outgoing guy I've ever met. He was very talkative — he'd talk to all the teachers at school. He had a great sense of humor.

"He and Ron Elgin (the other driver) had formed this crew for the summer that would go around to people's farms and do jobs like picking stones, painting, that sort of thing.

"If you met him once you'd remember him."

Eddie Hill, 18, of Y-town was a year ahead of Clark in school but said he was "the kind of guy you could count on."

Elgin and his four passengers were taken to hospital. Elgin, 17, of RR 4 X-ville, was transferred to University Hospital in London and was discharged on Tuesday. ...

Wingham OPP are still investigating but Constable Rick Schut said there were no signs of alcohol or excessive speed involved.

Clark was driving alone in his Ford Mustang, southbound in the northbound lane at 5:50 p.m., police said. The truck swerved into the southbound lane to avoid Clark but he swerved into the southbound lane at the last moment, colliding with the truck, police said.

— STEVE GREEN, *LONDON FREE PRESS*, JUNE 19, 1991

This story was the first report on the accident the newspaper published. Although the accident occurred on a Monday, the newspaper was unable to get details until well after the deadline for the first edition of Tuesday's paper, the edition that circulates in the rural area where the teenager lived. Green says his editors decided to wait until Wednesday's paper, and go with a fuller story.

As a result, Green had the time to take a far more active approach to reporting. In addition to using information provided by the police, he tracked down people who knew Clark. He decided not to bother the grieving family. Instead, he got the names of the teenager's friends by calling the son of the high school basketball coach, whom Green knew from years of sports reporting. Interviews with the coroner (who by coincidence was the family doctor) and friends of the teen completed the picture of a friendly, outgoing, active young man killed in a senseless accident.

The story of the teen's death is one of those genuinely tragic, genuinely dramatic events that may easily become melodramatic in the telling. The secret in such cases is usually to write in a detailed and low-keyed way. If the event is truly dramatic, the drama will come through in a restrained account.

Green uses "police blotter" material in two places. In the third paragraph, he tells where the collision occurred. The police then disappear from the story until the final two paragraphs, which offer a more detailed description of the accident and answer the question always asked in this kind of accident — whether alcohol was involved.

Green's article combines basic interviewing skills with careful writing to tell a story that has twin aims: informing the community about a death and at the same time trying to capture what that death means for the people who knew the teen. Not all stories lend themselves to this kind of treatment. But done well, these are stories people remember.

Another kind of accident story police reporters always look for is the curiosity, the offbeat incident which, while it may have little broad impact on the community, is so interesting and unusual that people want to know about it. If written well — and indeed, most of these are so interesting that they almost write themselves — this is the kind of story that ends up on page 1. The following, headlined "Dog shoots owner, then saves life," is a classic example of the type of oddball story that can be found on the police beat.

> ST. LAURENT — Despite the bullet hole in his back, Joe Petrowski knows he would never leave Vegas.
>
> Petrowski was shot by his own .22 rifle when his one-year-old German shepherd accidentally caught her fur in the trigger.
>
> But Vegas quickly showed why she's man's best friend, reviving her maimed master by licking his face and tugging at his shirt.
>
> "I made a big mistake putting myself in front of a loaded gun," said Petrowski, who is recovering at home after a stay in hospital. ...
>
> Lundar RCMP Sgt. Lee Wishnowski said Petrowski was knocked unconscious in the accident, but Vegas revived him.
>
> "It's a one-in-a-million accident," said Wishnowski. ...
>
> — KEVIN ROLLASON, *WINNIPEG FREE PRESS*, JUNE 27, 1991

In the course of world events, this "dog shoots man" story deserves barely a mention. But who could resist reading it?

Stories About Crimes

In any given week, police investigate and collect files on a range of crimes, from small break-ins to armed robberies, from bar-room fights to murders. How much of this crime is reported depends on a number of factors, including how much crime there is to report, how much news value the newspaper or broadcaster places on crime, and how accessible the information is to the media. Policies about giving reporters information from the police blotter vary considerably from province to province and from force to force. In Ontario, for example, recent freedom of information and privacy legislation has caused concern among the news media because it allows the police forces to decide whether to withhold information on some crime victims.

Some community newspapers run short items about almost every call to police. In larger communities, reporters tend to limit coverage to major crimes or to oddball stories.

Many crime stories are one-day phenomena. Like reports on an accident, they let the community know what is happening. Some serve as warnings to the public. When a notorious prisoner fails to return from a day pass, for example, or when a fraud artist targets a particular community, news outlets usually carry stories to let the public know a criminal is at large. Other crime stories, such as a report on a racially motivated beating, may serve as the starting point for public debate on broader social issues, and may lead to a number of followup stories.

Since the news value of a crime tends to increase in proportion to its severity, crime stories reported in major cities usually deal with crimes of violence or large property crimes. Some authors suggest that this may lead to public misconceptions about the level of violent crime, creating the impression that society is far more dangerous and violent than it really is (Levy 1986, 12–14).

This sense of fear is exacerbated when editors place a high news value on crime stories. Local TV newscasts in major U.S. cities, for example, are often one long stream of murder, mayhem, violence and death. This is not, of course, for lack of other stories; rather, it's the result of a judgment that crime equals news — that "if it bleeds, it leads." And it's a judgment Canadian news outlets are making more and more often.

Sometimes, a particularly brutal or poignant crime — a serial killing, for instance, or the discovery of the body of a missing child — will seize the attention of the community for days or even weeks. These stories bring into sharp focus the built-in problems of the police beat. It is difficult for any news organ to stay detached from such a story. The temptation to sensationalize, or even to encourage paranoia, is acute.

Typically too, these stories are cases where close rapport between the reporter and the police is vital. Police officers will probably not discuss a case with a reporter they don't know, but they may be willing to talk to a reporter they feel they can trust. And even if they can't discuss a case, they may sometimes direct the reporter they know to someone who can.

Stories on continuing investigations can be of assistance to the police, since the attention can heighten public interest in solving the case. But lawyer Stuart Robertson warns that there are pitfalls in reporting leaks from police about criminal investigations. The information is often unreliable, he writes. "You must always be suspicious when a law enforcement official provides you with information relating to an investigation. If the prosecutor had enough valid information to prove in a court that an offence has been committed, a prosecution could surely take place, and there would be no need to talk to you" (1983, 33).

Reporters writing about criminal investigations need to be aware of several areas of the law that may affect their work (see Bruser and Rogers 1985, 13–18). One is the law covering trespassing on private property. Another is the Criminal Code offence of obstructing justice, or interfering with police investigations. A third is defamation law, which may be of special concern to reporters covering investigations that have not yet led to charges. The *CP Stylebook* points out that the courts consider a false allegation of criminal conduct to be among the worst forms of libel (1995, 98). (For a discussion of libel, see Appendix B.)

Once charges are laid, the area of law that is of most continuing concern is contempt of court — in particular, the prohibition against prejudicing the right to a fair trial. Contempt of court law comes into effect when a case is sub judice, or under the jurisdiction of the courts. In general, this occurs when the charging document, known as the "information," is issued, or when the person suspected of a crime is arrested (Robertson 1983, 52).

Arrest Stories

Writing arrest stories poses a particular set of problems dominated by two social goods that sometimes conflict: the rights of the accused to a fair trial, and the desire to give readers and listeners as full a report as possible about what's going on in their communities. The Canadian news media, working under far more stringent contempt of court and defamation laws than their counterparts in the U.S., have generally erred on the side of the first good: the principle that the right to a fair trial outweighs the desire for a full story on arrest. (Presumably, all the details will come out at the trial.) But that situation is changing. In recent years, Canadian reporters have pushed the limits of the law on contempt in their crime stories — not always, and not in every kind of case, but often enough to concern some people who study media law, and to merit attention even in a basic reporting text.

The base line in crime reporting is easy to draw. In essence reporters should avoid suggesting that the person charged with a crime is guilty of that crime. The job of convicting such people belongs to the courts, not the media. Therefore, reports of an arrest should not include material that might prejudice a jury.

Reporters exercise this caution in a number of ways. First, they avoid linking the individual directly to the crime. The typical arrest story in a Canadian broadcast or newspaper gives the details of the crime and the identity of the person arrested. But a careful reading shows that the report does not say the person accused of the crime actually committed it.

In the following story of a dramatic arrest near a shopping mall, the reporter avoids making a direct link between the man arrested and "the syringe bandit" by putting the name of the accused at the very end of the story.

> A quick-thinking security guard is credited with ending a three-week reign of terror and robberies by an individual Ottawa-Carleton police had dubbed "the syringe bandit."
>
> Bill Cawlishaw, an employee of Burns International Security Service, first noticed a suspicious person lurking around Billings Bridge Plaza about 1 p.m. Thursday.
>
> Cawlishaw then recognized the man from a photo that police had circulated while investigating a theft Sept. 18 in the parking lot at Billings Bridge, when a man carrying a syringe forced a woman from her car and drove off in it.
>
> The suspect is believed to be responsible for at least 15 robberies. In each case, a man, acting alone, pulled out a syringe he claimed was filled with HIV-infected blood and threatened his victims with it.
>
> Police believe he is either a cocaine or heroin addict who committed the robberies to get money to feed his addiction. ...
>
> Once Cawlishaw spotted the suspect, he gave chase while notifying someone else in the plaza to call police. Cawlishaw sprained his ankle during the chase as the suspect bolted out of the plaza and across Bank Street.
>
> But police were able to make an arrest moments later after finding a man hiding inside an apartment building at 1355 Bank Street.
>
> During the arrest, the suspect accidentally stabbed himself in the abdomen with an empty syringe he was attempting to conceal under his belt. His injuries were not serious. ...
>
> Ernest Bryson, 34, of no fixed address, was to appear in court today. He faces 15 counts of robbery and one count of possession of a dangerous weapon.
>
> — DON CAMPBELL, OTTAWA CITIZEN, SEPT. 27, 1996

Though we learn a lot about the bandit — how often he has struck, the suspicion that he's a drug addict, his unusual weapon, the wonderful irony of the injury he sustains on arrest — the reporter does not pin these details on Bryson as an individual, but rather on the bandit. It will be up to the courts to decide whether Bryson and the bandit are one and the same. (We have changed the name of the accused to avoid further embarrassment.)

While putting the identity of the accused at the end works, it is not always the best choice. On a practical level, production editors still sometimes chop stories from the bottom, which means the crucial information about the identity of the suspect and the exact charges against him may be cut. In addition, news judgment may dictate that the identity of the suspect must be higher in the story, especially if the accused is well known in the community. In the following variation on the syringe bandit story, we identify the accused in the second paragraph.

But note that this paragraph does not say that Bryson and the suspicious-looking man are one and the same:

> A quick-thinking security guard is credited with ending a three-week reign of terror and robberies by an individual Ottawa-Carleton police had dubbed "the syringe bandit."
>
> Ernest Bryson, of no fixed address, was arrested and charged with 15 counts of robbery and one count of possession of a dangerous weapon after security guard Bill Cawlishaw spotted a suspicious-looking man lurking around Billings Bridge Plaza about 1 p.m. Thursday.
>
> Cawlishaw recognized the man from a photo that police had circulated while investigating a theft Sept. 18 in the parking lot at Billings Bridge, when a man carrying a syringe forced a woman from her van and drove off with it. ...

Similarly, if a man — let's call him John Doe — is charged with sexually assaulting a woman in a city park, the arrest story may be constructed in one of several ways:

> John Doe, 22, has been charged with sexual assault in connection with an attack on a local woman last night.

> John Doe, 22, was charged with sexual assault after a women was attacked in a city park last night.

> John Doe, 22, has been charged in last night's sexual assault of a local woman.

> A man attacked a woman in a city part last night. John Doe, 22, has been charged with sexual assault.

Many readers — and indeed, many new reporters — might conclude from reading any of these leads that John Doe attacked the woman. But look again. None of them actually says John Doe sexually assaulted the woman. In each construction, there is a small but crucial distinction — a distance between the crime and the identity of the accused.

There are good reasons for this caution. On a professional level, most journalists would agree that their role in reporting arrests is to make information public, not to act as judge and jury. In addition, reporting that "convicts" people of crimes may run afoul of two types of law — defamation (see Appendix B) and contempt of court, especially the category of contempt that deals with prejudicing a person's right to a fair trial.

Determining the risk line in terms of contempt of court is especially difficult because there is no statute spelling out exactly what it is. This means that reporters who wish to understand it must wade through case law. In addition, judges apply contempt law inconsistently, with one judge ignoring material that another judge might find flagrantly prejudicial. But while this ambiguity makes life difficult for reporters, style guides and media law texts, like Michael G. Crawford's A *Journalist's*

Legal Guide (1996), offer useful summaries of the "danger zones" for reporters. These zones include reporting previous criminal records, reporting confessions, publishing photographs of the accused if his identity will be a major issue at trial and interviewing witnesses prior to trial. In general, the closer it is to trial, the higher the danger of being cited for contempt. The question of whether to report that the accused is facing other charges is a grey area. Many media report these charges on the principle that the charges themselves do not imply guilt; but reporting them may suggest that the accused has a bad character, which might influence a jury and be prejudicial to a fair trial.

Increasingly, the Canadian media seems willing to push the limits of contempt law, especially in high-profile cases dealing with attacks on children or sexual assault. For example, some news reports on the arrest of a Vancouver-area man in early 1997 on child-sex charges included his previous convictions on similar charges; the contents of computer disks and videos seized at his home; the fact that he asked people to send him photographs of child pornography over the Internet; and the contents of search warrants. An Ottawa newspaper broke the story of an elderly man charged in 1997 with kidnapping a teenage boy in 1960. The story, which ran the day the man was arraigned, included a long sidebar on his 1951 conviction in a similar case.

A new reporter's problems are further complicated by the growing tendency among Canadian media to pursue aggressive, American-style crime reporting. "It used to be that when there was a murder, we got our information from the police," says Eva Hoare of the Halifax *Chronicle-Herald*. "Now we're out banging on the same doors they are, sometimes at the same time." Hoare attributes much of the change to competitive pressures in the media. Stephen Bindman, legal affairs correspondent for Southam News, sees other factors at work too: changes in the national mood toward supporting a law-and-order agenda, and a sense that individual crimes often have systemic roots that reporters should explore. Bindman notes that news media have become particularly aggressive in reporting criminal records of people accused of crime.

Although standards may be changing, reporters nonetheless need to be aware of law on contempt, even as their editors urge them to push its limits. The best rule for reporters is to be as rigorous as possible in protecting the rights of an accused to a fair trial. This may mean ignoring police statements that the cops finally got their man, that the loot from the robbery was found in the accused's basement and so on. It may also mean ditching good quotes from neighbors and bystanders that impute guilt.

The following story (again, names have been changed) tiptoes through the potential legal minefields of a double killing involving a marriage gone sour.

> X-TOWN — A man and a woman were shot to death early Saturday while five family members slept.
>
> Police have arrested Scott Neill, 25, the estranged husband of the woman killed and a distant relative of the male victim.
>
> Neill is to appear in court Monday on first-degree murder charges, police said.
>
> Dead are Mary-Alice Brown, 19, and Peter Dawson, 27. Each died of a single shot fired from a hunting rifle. They had lived together for only six weeks at Dawson's two-storey home in this farming and logging community northwest of Ottawa.
>
> Relatives said Brown and Neill had been together for about six years. Their children, Sarah, 3 1/2, and Jennifer, 1 1/2, were asleep upstairs when the shooting occurred, as was Dawson's daughter, Caitlin, also 3 1/2. ...
>
> — JOCHEN KESSEL AND ANNE TOLSON, OTTAWA CITIZEN, JULY 7, 1991

These paragraphs tell the reader a lot — that Neill's wife and the man she lived with were both shot and killed, and that Neill has been charged with the crime. The story does not say that Neill did the shooting. That's for the court to decide.

The story then describes the shooting and the arrest:

> Police said the incident began just after 1 a.m. when a man shot at the door of the Dawson residence. Dawson was shot as he came to the door. Brown was shot shortly after.
>
> Neill was arrested at the home of a friend at about 6 a.m. after a phone call to police, said Sgt. Claude Marchand.

Again, the story distances Neill from the shooting. The gunman is described simply as "a man." The fact that a phone call was made to police is published, but there are no details about who made the phone call or what was said. If that information becomes public, it will happen in the courtroom.

But while the story gives the details correctly and carefully, most readers would agree that to this point it has almost a clinical feel to it. Here is a true tragedy; two young parents dead, a father arrested, three children whose lives have been forever changed. The bottom third of the story takes the reader into some of the intensely human details of the case, including an interview with Dawson's estranged and pregnant wife. It concludes with a quotation from a neighbor who describes the relationships in the home as "a tangled web."

Clearly, many readers will infer from this kind of report much more than the reporter says directly. The reporter knows that the readers will

After the heat of a fire has cooled — or in this case, frozen — investigators try to figure out what caused the blaze, and whether anything can be done to prevent similar fires. Journalists are often criticized for being there for the crisis, but ignoring the followup. (Jason Wood/Loyalist College)

make those connections and will conclude that the "Scott Neill" charged in paragraph 2 is "the man" who in paragraph 6 showed up at the door with a rifle. Whether this approach is ethically sound is open to debate, but this style of reporting stays within the strictures of the law. The accused is considered by the law to be innocent until proven guilty, so the statement that he has been charged does not, legally, imply guilt.

Fire Stories

As anyone who lives near a fire station knows, the trucks roll out, sirens blaring and horns honking, with distressing regularity. Odds are, they're not heading to a fire. For example, the Hamilton Fire Department reports that, in 1995, it responded to more than 13,000 calls, or almost 37 a day. Only about 10 per cent of them were fires. Another 10 per cent were accidental calls, including alarms triggered by repair people or broken sprinkler systems. The bulk, almost 60 per cent, were calls for medical assistance.

A reporter monitoring the radio scanner learns very quickly to listen for signs that a fire call is a false alarm or a minor incident. But if the call turns out to be a serious fire, sometimes called a "working fire," the reporter must decide whether to go to see what is happening or to pick up an item by phone later.

It's not always an easy decision to make. A minor fire can quickly get out of hand. In some newsrooms, photographers may be sent to a fire scene first, to take pictures of a rapidly changing situation and keep the news department informed.

A reporter covering a fire does more than watch the building burn. CBC reporter Bob Johnstone says the best fire reporters know something about how firefighters are supposed to do their work. That way, they can figure out quickly whether something unusual is going on. They can also look beyond the smoke and flames for the people involved, for the firefighter who is suiting up to go into a burning apartment, or for the distraught tenant who has had a narrow escape. Better than anything else, the personal stories of these people bring the impersonal event home to the rest of the community.

The Vancouver *Province*'s coverage of an enormous fire on the city's waterfront that took place in 1991 is full of eyewitness accounts and vivid descriptions that make for gripping reading. Interestingly, the main news story begins with a soft lead that describes how a peaceful scene turned into a nightmare:

> Bill Paschal was ready for a quiet sunny day idly cleaning his nine-metre cruiser Blue Water at the Burrard Marina.
>
> But at about 11 a.m. yesterday, a burning boat caught his eye, and he watched in horror as fire destroyed the Canadian Coast Guard's Kitsilano wharf.
>
> "The little boat was on fire and the three people on it just dove into the water," said the 42-year-old Vancouver man.
>
> "The wind caught hold of the boat and it just drifted under the pylons. It went up so fast I couldn't believe it."
>
> Assistant Fire Chief David Cameron said the fire spread quickly because the wharf's pilings were coated with creosote, a wood preservative.
>
> "It's like a tar and once it gets going it gets going pretty good and it's difficult to put out," Cameron said. ...
>
> — MICHAEL KOSLOWSKI, LORA GRINDLAY AND MARC DAVIS, VANCOUVER PROVINCE, JULY 8, 1991

It might seem surprising that the hard news — "fire destroys wharf," — is in the second paragraph of this story rather than the first. There are some good reasons for this, however. By the time the stories appeared, most people in Vancouver had heard about the fire already through television and radio reports or word of mouth. In addition, the tabloid *Province* ran the stories on the inside pages: the front page carried a single, large picture and stacked decks of headlines.

The use of a single eyewitness account as the lead is effective. It's easy for the readers to imagine themselves in Paschal's place. The quotations attributed to him — "the three people on it just dove into the water" or "it went up so fast I couldn't believe it" — have an authentic quality. The quote from the assistant fire chief is also effective, shaky grammar and all. This is just the way a harassed fire official at the scene of a major blaze would be expected to talk.

One of the most chilling stories comes from the man whose boat touched off the fire. The story begins by throwing the reader right into the water with him:

> As How Wong floated beneath the flaming roof of Kitsilano's coast guard station he thought he was going to die.
>
> Minutes earlier, the Vancouver accountant, his wife Cynthia, 50, and his daughter Vicky, 18, had launched their five-metre boat at the ramp adjoining the station.
>
> "I just started the engine to warm up," Wong said from his St. Paul's Hospital bed. "Once I backed the boat up, then I looked at the back and saw the flame of the fire."
>
> He didn't know how the fire started.
>
> Wong, 58, threw overboard a can of spare gasoline before turning back to the blaze.
>
> "I could see with the amount of flame I couldn't extinguish it," he said. "So I told my wife and daughter to jump for it."
>
> Wong swam for the nearby pilings, but was followed by the drifting, burning boat. It lodged in the pilings and within seconds Wong was surrounded by fire.
>
> "There was smoke and fire everywhere. At that moment, I thought I couldn't make it," Wong said. Exhausted, he swam beneath the flames into open water, where another boat spotted him and threw a rope. ...
>
> — CHARLIE ANDERSON, VANCOUVER PROVINCE, JULY 8, 1991

If a reporter covering a fire is unable to find out at the scene the names of the people who own or occupy a building, the information is available at city hall, on the property tax assessment roll. The first estimates of damage caused by a fire usually come from fire investigators at the scene. Initial reports of damage, like initial reports of casualties in a major accident, may be inaccurate, however. Reporters usually err on the side of caution. The reason is simple: if a reporter writes a wildly inflated estimate of damage, the news medium will have to backtrack later. If the initial estimate is low, the release of a higher number is a legitimate news peg for a followup story.

GOING BEYOND THE POLICE BLOTTER

In between writing reports on fires and traffic accidents, police reporters look for stories that, while newsworthy, may have little to do with the crime of the day. At any one time a reporter has a half-dozen stories on the go, plus dozens more leads, story ideas and feature possibilities on the back burner. Some story ideas come as assignments from editors. Many more come from a reporter's own contacts on the force and in the community, and this is where the informal contact with police — like Paul Wiecek's corridor gossip about sports — is important. This end of the beat leads to all kinds of stories, some of them surprisingly at odds with the usual run of crime and fire stories.

Policy changes can lead to interesting stories. In Ottawa, reporters have tracked the development of a new unit that patrols city streets by bicycle and another that uses horses. In British Columbia, reporters have spent months tracking debates over the potential costs and benefits of amalgamating police departments.

Like all beat reporters, Eva Hoare finds there are times when she has to write stories that are critical of her sources on the force. "When there's an incident I have to write about, I tell them I'm going to have to write about it," she says. "If they don't want to talk to me, I tell them there is going to be a story anyway, and this is their chance to tell their side. I'm very forthright. I tell them I'm going to do the fairest story I can."

She recalls a 1989 incident in which Halifax police raided the wrong apartment in a drug bust. For the police officers involved, it was a humiliating experience. For the reporter, it was a story that had to be covered. (We have changed the names in the story to avoid further embarrassment.)

> A Halifax woman and her daughter may take legal action after their north-end residence was raided Thursday by drug officers who later learned they were acting on incorrect information.
>
> Halifax Police Superintendent Arnold Davis said the police department is very sorry the incident occurred, and confirmed Friday narcotics officers "forcibly entered" a residence to conduct a drug search Thursday night …
>
> The apartment was empty at the time, and police discovered that information was incorrect after entering.
>
> Meanwhile, Jane Smith and her daughter are angry about the mistake, saying police "took a sledgehammer" to their apartment door at 9 p.m. Thursday.
>
> "First they tried a separator to widen the door frame. Then they took a sledgehammer to the door. The next thing you know we have two nice holes in the door. My mother heard the bust," said her daughter, who asked not to be identified. …
>
> — EVA HOARE, HALIFAX CHRONICLE-HERALD, NOV. 18, 1989

There can be a cost to the police reporter in writing stories that embarrass individual officers or the force. Hoare recalls using unnamed sources to write a 1994 story reporting that police called off a drug raid because the officers would have had to do it on paid overtime. "That put me in the doghouse," she says. The police restricted her movements in the station, keeping her out of the offices she previously visited unimpeded. Even worse, she learned that many of her sources in the department had been questioned by their superiors about their dealings with her. The clampdown meant "a lean six months, story-wise," she says, but eventually the air cleared and things went back to normal. Though the reaction in this case may appear extreme, all beat reporters know the experience of alienating sources now and then. It's simply part of the job.

Gerry McAuliffe, one of Canada's best-known investigative reporters, says the inevitability of alienating sources means newsrooms should have two reporters on the police beat — one to cover the day-to-day crime, the other to write about the politics of law enforcement. He says reporters need to take a hard look at whether the police system in Canada is capable of dealing with modern society. But this kind of critical reporting naturally angers the people in charge of policing, making it impossible to maintain the personal contacts needed in covering the day-to-day aspects of the beat. McAuliffe thinks the solution might be to set up a separate beat, perhaps attached to city hall, looking at the politics and financing of law enforcement.

He emphasizes, however, that bringing a critical eye to police reporting does not necessarily mean writing negative stories about the police. The key to good reporting is balanced coverage. "You need to report on the successes of police work, not just the problems," he says. "You need to do stories on the really interesting cases the cops break." This is not easy work, McAuliffe adds, since doing a story on how the police broke a case takes as much work as a major investigative piece on something that went wrong.

Paul Wiecek says a successful police reporter has to work long and hard to gain the respect of sources. "Eventually, you get a reputation for being even-handed. I don't think the police expect you to whitewash over things. If they do something wrong and they need a kick in the ass and you give it to them, I think they respect that."

Reporting on the police beat, like any other beat, comes down to reporting about people. All too often, stories about the police read like stories about uniforms rather than the people in the uniforms. All too often, the people whose lives are touched by issues and events on the police beat come across as faceless or as stereotypes. The best reporters look beyond the badge — and beyond labels like "criminal," "victim," and "innocent bystander" — to find the human story.

RECOMMENDED READING

Bruser, Robert S., and Brian MacLeod Rogers. (1985). *Journalists and the Law: How to Get the Story Without Getting Sued or Put in Jail*. Ottawa: The Canadian Bar Foundation.

Crawford, Michael G. (1996). *The Journalist's Legal Guide*. 3rd edition. Toronto: Carswell.

Ericson, Richard V. (1981). *Making Crime: A Study of Detective Work*. Scarborough, ON: Butterworths.

Ericson, Richard V. (1982). *Reproducing Order: A Study of Police Patrol Work*. Toronto: University of Toronto Press.

Levy, Harold J. (1986). *A Reporter's Guide to Canada's Criminal Justice System*. Ottawa: The Canadian Bar Foundation.

Sewell, John. (1985). *Police: Urban Policing in Canada*. Toronto: Lorimer.

Stroud, Carsten. (1985). *The Blue Wall: Street Cops in Canada*. Toronto: McClelland & Stewart.

CHAPTER 10

Covering
Criminal
Courts

EWS MEDIA COVER THE COURTS FOR MANY reasons. Perhaps the most basic is that court stories are interesting — true-to-life accounts of lives gone astray, or miniature morality plays for a modern audience. Like many police stories, court stories have a clear-cut sequence of events, a well-defined cast of characters and a resolution (the verdict). These characteristics all make for easy storytelling. They also help explain why the courtroom is a favorite setting for writers of fiction or drama.

Beyond these simple attractions lies the realization that journalists play an important public role in the courtroom. They are there to see that justice is done openly, before the public eye. Reporting on trials may be seen as a means of social control, a way of telling the community that an individual who breaks the law won't be able to escape justice or keep the crime secret.

Whether this role is beneficial, and how well reporters fulfil it, are still open questions. Some critics argue that the glare of media attention imposes an unfair burden on the individual who is about to pay a debt to society for committing a crime. Others say that publicity surrounding a case can damage people who have done nothing wrong themselves, such as the family or friends of the accused. Still others argue that newspapers or broadcasters focus too much on the small-time criminal and not enough on those guilty of major crimes — the companies that ignore pollution laws and then use a battery of lawyers to fend off charges, for example, or the exporters who sell to people in the Third World products that have been declared unsafe in Canada.

Much court reporting, like police reporting, focuses on stories of brutality, cruelty and pain. Especially troublesome to new reporters is the fact that while decisions made in court are black and white — a defendant is guilty or not guilty — most of the stories that wind up before the judge are made up of shades of grey. Sometimes justice is not done. Even worse, sometimes justice is impossible.

A week spent in the courtroom prompts the thoughtful reporter to reflect on the stark failures of parts of society — on the differences created by wealth, privilege and education, on the effectiveness of social services, on the forces that lead to higher rates of crime (or to higher rates of criminal charges) in some areas and among some groups than others.

This makes the court beat seem grim and forbidding. In some ways it is. In other ways, however, an assignment to the court beat is a tremendous benefit to a reporter. It sharpens a whole range of skills, from observation to organization to storytelling. It opens reporters to a new range of social issues and the people dealing with them — the social workers, legal aid staff and charitable agencies who are trying to make a difference for people in trouble. And perhaps most important of all, it teaches journalists the importance of withholding judgment until all the available evidence is in.

In this chapter we provide a primer-level introduction to the job of covering the criminal courts. Our intention is to give you information that will be of help when you are assigned to cover a court story. Anyone covering the beat full time would be expected to study the legal system in far greater detail — including civil law, which we do not address here. Anyone handling crime news as an editor would also need to undertake further study, possibly beginning with some of the sources listed at the end of the chapter.

MAPPING OUT THE BEAT

Canadian trials work on an adversarial system. They are conducted as confrontations between the state and the individual accused of a crime in which the state seeks to prove that the person accused of the crime actually committed it.

This system can be both a hazard and a benefit for reporters. On the one hand, each side identifies weaknesses in the other's case, helping to broaden understanding. The key points in a case are usually repeated a number of times, in a number of ways. On the other hand, the sequential presentation of evidence and argument by the two sides may tug the reporter to and fro, as it does the jury member. Drawing too much from one side and ignoring the other can create a credible version of events — but an erroneous one. Snap judgments by a reporter are dangerous.

The busiest scene of combat is the provincial court, at the bottom of the court hierarchy in each province.

All criminal cases enter the court system at the provincial court level, and the vast majority of people accused of criminal acts are tried there. Provincial courts are also used for bail hearings and for preliminary hearings on the more serious charges that may be tried in higher courts. (The purpose of a preliminary hearing is to determine whether there is enough evidence to proceed with a trial.) Provincial courts may have a number of divisions, such as criminal court, family or youth court or small claims. (For more on the organization of the court system, see Griffiths and Verdun-Jones 1994.)

Over the last decade or two, almost all provinces have dispensed with their mid-level trial courts, known as county or district courts. The functions of these courts have been absorbed into the superior courts, the highest level of trial court in a province. Depending on the province, superior court may go by a number of names: the Court of Queen's Bench, the Supreme Court or the High Court of Justice. Ontario has reorganized its courts into a two-level Ontario Court of Justice. The provincial division of this court replaces the old provincial court, while the general division combines the trial functions of the former district and superior courts.

Each province has a court of appeal at the top of the judicial hierarchy. The court of last resort for all cases — civil as well as criminal — is the Supreme Court of Canada. There are strict rules governing how cases get to the Supreme Court, however. Very few criminal cases make it that far.

The Criminal Code, the major compendium of criminal law in the country, lists three kinds of offences:

• *Summary conviction offences.* These are fairly minor infractions, tried in provincial court by a judge alone. The maximum penalty for a summary conviction offence is six months in jail or a fine of $2,000.

• *Indictable offences.* These are more serious charges with a wide range of penalties, and they may be tried in a number of ways. Some, such as theft or possession of stolen property, are tried in provincial court by a judge alone. The most serious, such as murder, are usually tried by a superior court judge and jury. The bulk of offences in between —

dangerous driving, sexual assault, attempted murder and so on — are tried by a provincial court judge, a higher-level judge sitting alone, or a higher-level judge and jury. The choice is up to the defendant.

- *Hybrid offences.* As the name suggests, these may be tried by either summary conviction or indictment, at the discretion of the prosecution.

These technical terms are rarely included in news reports on trials. But it's a good idea to be familiar with them, because the nature of the charge helps determine how a case is tried. There are no preliminary hearings, for example, on summary conviction offences or many minor indictable offences. Similarly, people charged with summary conviction offences cannot choose a jury trial.

Most reporters on the court beat cover the trial process at the provincial, county and superior court level, and track appeals to the provincial appeals court. For the most part, newspapers and broadcasters rely on specialized reporters in Ottawa to cover the Supreme Court of Canada.

One other court of note is the Federal Court of Canada, which is not a criminal court but deals with actions brought against the federal government and federal agencies. Appeals of decisions from the trial division go to the Federal Court of Appeal. Again, the court of last resort is the Supreme Court of Canada.

Sorting Out the Players

Between *Law and Order* and *Rumpole of the Bailey,* it's easy to get confused by the titles of the key players in the courtroom.

At the provincial court level, the magistrate in charge may be a judge or a justice of the peace. Judges preside at trials and at preliminary hearings held to determine whether there is enough evidence to proceed to trial on the more serious indictable offences. Justices of the peace have a range of duties, mainly at the pre-trial stage. Criminal charges are laid before justices of the peace through a process known as swearing an information. Justices of the peace also issue search warrants and summonses and preside at many bail hearings.

A provincial court judge is usually referred to on first reference in news copy as Judge So-and-So. A judge from a superior or supreme court is usually called Justice So-and-So. (Some organizations use the more formal Mr. Justice or Madam Justice.)

The lawyer who represents the prosecution is known as the Crown attorney or Crown prosecutor (*never* as the district attorney, which is the title of the equivalent job in the United States). The lawyer who represents the accused is known as the defence counsel or the defence lawyer. Use of the word attorney to describe a defence lawyer is an Americanism.

Reporters whose knowledge of courts is based on watching American TV courtroom dramas will find a number of other differences between the American image and the Canadian reality. For one thing, Canadian lawyers do not berate judges in the manner popular in U.S. fiction. Nor do they "approach the bench" for dramatic consultations. And judges in Canadian courts don't bang gavels.

There are also important differences in what reporters may and may not do in court coverage. Unlike their American counterparts, Canadian reporters do not interview jury members. That's because it's a criminal offence for jury members to discuss the deliberations. Traditionally, Canadian reporters have refrained from giving lawyers a forum for arguing their cases in front of the cameras. This, however, is changing. Some defence lawyers have long been willing to discuss their cases with the media. Increasingly, Crown attorneys are also available for out-of-court interviews. They use these interviews mainly to restate for the cameras and tape recorders what they said in the courtroom, where cameras are barred. (A few jurisdictions are experimenting with cameras in the courtroom, though on a very limited scale.)

At the Courthouse

An urban courthouse is a busy place. On any day, hundreds of people pass through its doors. Some are there for trials, others for preliminary hearings or remands. Some have been called for jury duty. Large contingents of clerks and lawyers work with private law firms. Other groups provide legal aid services, representing people who can't afford to hire a lawyer on their own. Many of the people coming and going are employees of the courthouse, working as clerks, court reporters and so on. Police officers from municipal and provincial forces or the RCMP may be waiting to testify. Finally, there are "court rats," people who just like to hang out at the courthouse.

At any one time during business hours, any number of courtrooms may be in action. The job of the journalist covering the court beat is to be in the right courtroom at the right time.

The way to do this is to keep track of two key documents.

The Information: The public document known as the "information" gives the history of a case in a nutshell. It lists the name, age and address of the accused, the charges the accused faces, the place where the alleged crime took place and the names of any victims. It also includes the names of the investigating officer and the defence lawyer. Finally, it provides a complete record of appearances, including the names of the Crown attorneys and the judges who presided over the various hearings. If the accused is appearing in court that day, the clerk in the courtroom will have the information. Reporters covering the courts check in with the clerk in the courtroom at the end of the day to check spellings and details on the information, and make notes on future appearances. If the accused is not appearing that day, the information will be on file in the central office of the court clerks.

The Court List or Docket: This is a list of all the cases scheduled to be heard that day. A docket is usually posted outside each active courtroom. Its content varies, but it typically lists the name of the accused, the type of appearance (whether it's for trial, for instance, or preliminary hearing), and a reference to the offence for which the accused is on trial. In some places, the docket lists the relevant Criminal Code section; in others, the number of the charging document.

Court reporters often keep in fairly close touch with police reporters. For example, court reporters may begin their day by checking the newest informations, which list the most recent charges laid. They can sometimes pick up good items that the police reporter didn't hear about in the round of police checks. Similarly, if a prominent person is arrested, the police reporter may tip the court reporter to watch for her in court.

Most reporters on the court beat keep detailed lists of cases to follow. It's not unusual for a person accused of a crime to return to the courthouse many times before the actual trial, especially if the person has been denied bail. (This is because an accused may be remanded in custody for no more than eight days at a time.) Depending on the availability of witnesses, preliminary hearings and trials may stretch out over several days, with adjournments in between. And when an individual is found guilty of a crime, the judge often sets a separate date for sentencing. For the beat reporter, this means a lot of paperwork. But it also means that the reporter can cover a case thoroughly, following it from beginning to end.

Beat reporters follow several kinds of cases. Some newspapers in smaller communities have a policy of reporting the outcome of all criminal cases in a weekly list and writing news stories about the most interesting cases. Other news organizations believe that if they run a report on an arrest, they should report on the outcome of the case as well. Court reporters look for stories on major crimes or crimes that have attracted public interest. And they look for the oddball case — the sad, the humorous or the unusual trial that will touch or tickle readers and listeners. They often hear about this kind of case though personal contact — casual conversations with lawyers, clerks, court stenographers, the guards at the door of the courtroom or the "court rats" who love to sniff out unusual cases.

WRITING THE BASIC STORY

The routine court story, like a routine police story, packs a substantial amount of information into a few short paragraphs. The following appeared in the *Kitchener-Waterloo Record*. (Names and locations have been changed to prevent further pain or embarrassment to the families affected.)

> A Y-town man whose driving caused the death of one of his best friends nearly three years ago was sentenced Thursday to two years less a day in jail after pleading guilty to impaired driving causing death.
>
> John Smith, 29, apologized to the family of Tony Morello and told general court Justice Barry Nolan that he "wished it was me who passed away in the accident."
>
> "I feel terrible about it," he said.
>
> Smith and Morello were driving home from a stag in the downtown section of X-town on July 22, 1988, when Smith went too fast into a curve on Ring Road near the airport.
>
> When the car's wheels went onto the gravel shoulder, Smith overcorrected in getting the vehicle back on the road and lost control.
>
> The vehicle went into a ditch and landed in a field, rolling over several times. Both men were thrown from the vehicle.
>
> Investigating regional police Const. Robert Gould told the Record after court Thursday that neither man was wearing a seat belt. He said he had "no doubt" that Morello wouldn't have been killed, or Smith seriously hurt, if they had been strapped in "because the interior of the car was in perfect condition."
>
> A blood sample taken from Smith showed a blood-alcohol concentration of .14. A reading of .08 is considered evidence of impairment.
>
> Defence lawyer John Kelly told Nolan that Smith wasn't a regular or heavy drinker but would only do so at a stag or wedding. He said his client "hasn't had a drink since that night and won't for a long time."
>
> — *KITCHENER-WATERLOO RECORD*, JUNE 28, 1991

The first paragraph includes the major news development — the sentence — and a quick summary of the incident that led to the charges. It also tells the reader that the man pleaded guilty to the charge, rather than being found guilty by the judge. The charge itself is described in ordinary but precise language. In the second paragraph, the reporter identifies the driver, the victim, the court where the case was heard and the judge.

In the original print of this photo, the face of the arrested man was clearly visible. Since publication in that form might prejudice his chances for a fair trial, the picture falls in the grey area between what should and should not be published. In recent years Canadian media have moved closer to the less-stringent U.S. standards on publishing news and pictures that might be incriminating. This makes decision making more difficult as editors balance the rights of the accused against the pressure to be competitive — or against the desire to publish dramatic pictures like this. (Mario Bartel)

The story includes details of the accident, probably from the information, and numbers that indicate the driver's level of impairment. (It might be better to do the arithmetic for the reader, saying that Smith's blood-alcohol reading was almost twice the legal limit.) Quotations from Smith and his lawyer paint a picture of a man who feels deep remorse about what happened.

The paragraph about seat belts is an unusual feature in a sentencing story. It came from an interview with the officer, rather than from testimony in court, and is clearly identified as out-of-court information. Its use is legitimate, although such out-of-court material has to be handled carefully to avoid anything that might prejudice the outcome of another trial or lead to a civil action.

While the writing of the story seems unexceptional, it is clear, concise and coherent — qualities that are harder to achieve than they look, given the legal tangles.

But there are some basic principles to keep in mind when reporting and writing a court story:

- *Don't waffle on the details.* After worrying about how to write police stories without "convicting" the accused or prompting a libel suit, you may feel uncomfortable shifting gears and quoting testimony that is clearly incriminating. But a different set of rules applies in court: roughly, anything said in open court (the term has a precise meaning that will be explained shortly) can be reported.

- *Don't get hung up on the technical terms.* Some reporters, unfamiliar with court terminology, have trouble distinguishing the important points from the minor ones. For example, they may take great pains to track down exact sections and subsections of Criminal Code counts, in the false belief that these numbers have some special meaning to their editor or to the reader. Or they offer elaborate, legalistic explanations of things that should be translated into simple English. This is a mistake. A good test for reporters is this: if you don't understand what all the points mean, your readers (or listeners) won't either.

- *Take careful notes.* During the trial, a number of people — the Crown attorney, witnesses, the defence lawyer and sometimes the accused — speak to the case, all from a different angle. There is a lot of repetition as the parties to the trial work their way through the evidence. In addition, trials feature a lot of back-and-forth exchanges between witnesses and lawyers, posing a special challenge to note-taking. As in meeting coverage, it's crucial that your court notes reflect who made which point. Make sure your notes cover not just what was said, but who made the point and how.

- *Check everything to ensure accuracy — then check again.* As we noted in the previous chapter, accuracy is especially important in crime and legal reporting. The starting point for accurate reporting is to transcribe the details from the information correctly. You need to be aware, though, that the people who type up the information sometimes make mistakes. For example, several students came back from a court-reporting assignment and wrote stories about the trial of a resident of "Arminster" Street in an Ottawa suburb. There *is* no such street — though there is an Axminster Street in the suburb. Interestingly, a handful of students compounded the original error: they identified the street as "Arminister" or "Armister." One even spelled it "Annister." A simple check of the City Directory would have caught both the original error and the variations.

  Check the name of the accused with the defence lawyer, who will know whether the name on the information is correct and also whether the accused goes by his formal name. (Someone named John Bruce Smith may call himself John Smith or Bruce Smith, or perhaps even Jack Smith, J. B. Smith or Buzzy Smith.) The court clerks who compile the official record of each case are good sources for checking names of judges and Crown attorneys. Finally, it's a good idea to double-check all names with guides like the phone book (the Yellow Pages are especially useful for defence lawyers), the City Directory (for addresses), or directories compiled by the law society (for judges and Crown attorneys).

- *Don't bury the story.* It's easy to get so caught up in trying to understand the legal process that you forget to see the court report as a *story.* For example, one student wrote her first court assignment for class this way:

  > After pleading guilty to unlawful possession of a narcotic, John Doe was sentenced to a fine of $100.
  >
  > In provincial court Tuesday, Doe, 26, of Blank Street, admitted that the plant was in his possession but said it did not belong to him. "I found it," he said.
  >
  > Doe was driving in downtown on Sept. 25 when he was stopped by a police officer. He had in his possession a four-foot-high cannabis plant containing 100 grams of marijuana.
  >
  > The maximum sentence for possession of a narcotic is imprisonment for up to seven years.

  The student had the details, but wrote a story no one would want to read. Instead of making a natural judgment about how to tell the story, she got stuck on the *process* — the plea, the sentence, the statute and so on. And that tripped her up.

A more experienced reporter might handle the piece this way:

> A city man who claimed he found a four-foot-tall marijuana plant on the street and loaded it into his car to take home has been fined $100.
>
> John Doe, 26, of Blank Street, admitted in provincial court yesterday that he had the plant on the front seat of his car when he was stopped by police on Sept. 25.
>
> But he said the plant didn't belong to him. "I found it," he said.
>
> Doe pleaded guilty to a charge of possession of a narcotic. The maximum sentence for the offence is seven years in prison.

Or, to emphasize the offbeat quality of the story, a reporter might inject a small element of suspense into the story. For instance:

> A city man pulled over by police with a four-foot marijuana plant on the front seat of his car offered a novel explanation in court yesterday: he said he found it on the street, and decided to take it home.

Court reporter Larry Still of the Vancouver *Sun* is one among many who rebel against the idea that court reporting should follow a formula. He argues that there's room to write stories with a strong narrative line and to break some of the common conventions of reporting. He says, for instance, that question leads are sometimes the best way to tell a court story. For example:

> Did a man accused of the brutal sex-slaying of an elderly Vancouver woman unknowingly drop his bank book at the scene of the crime?
>
> Or did a thief who lifted Richard Paik's wallet as he sat drunk in a bar also steal his bank book and leave it at the murder scene?
>
> The answer to the bank-book question, raised in closing addresses ...

LEGAL RESTRICTIONS ON REPORTING

Courthouses are public places. Reporters, like other members of the public, are free to come and go during most trials and hearings. (One exception is that you may not go in or out while the judge is making the charge to the jury.)

Journalists are free to report on what goes on in open court. The term "open court" generally refers to a court that is in session, and in which there is no order or statutory provision restricting publication of specific evidence. In a jury trial, the phrase usually means the jury is present. Testimony given in open court is exempt from defamation law. In other words, a witness can speak candidly in the courtroom, without fear of a defamation suit. Under both defamation and contempt law, reporters have a privilege to report what happens in court. The privilege has some qualifications: the stories must be fair and accurate reflections of what went on in open court, written without comment and at roughly the same time as the case. (For more on defamation, see Appendix B.)

But free access and privilege should not be interpreted as licence to write about whatever goes on in the courtroom. Indeed, there are a number of restrictions, drawing on contempt of court law and the Criminal Code, on what you may and may not report. A number of the books at the end of this chapter contain detailed discussions about these restrictions. Put two of them on the top of your must-read pile: the latest edition of the *CP Stylebook* and Harold J. Levy's *A Reporter's Guide to Canada's Criminal Justice System* (1986).

Arraignment and Bail Hearing

These are the first steps in the court proceeding. At the arraignment, the accused appears before the judge, the charge is read, and a plea entered. You may report all this. The question of bail may be settled here or at a separate hearing. If the defence requests a ban on publication of evidence at a bail hearing, the judge or justice of the peace must grant it. The ban stays in effect until the case ends.

Even with a ban, however, you may report some things: the name of the accused (as long as the accused is not a young offender), the charge, details of the arrest, names of the lawyers and magistrate, whether the accused got bail and the terms under which the accused was released.

If there is no ban on publication, you should avoid reporting any confessions that may be offered in evidence and any mention of the accused's criminal record.

Preliminary Inquiry

The main function of a preliminary inquiry is to determine whether there is enough evidence to bring the accused to trial. Either the Crown or defence can ask for a ban on publication of evidence presented at a preliminary hearing. Defence requests are automatically granted, and defence lawyers almost always ask for bans. If the charge is dismissed at the end of the preliminary hearing, the ban is lifted and reporters are free to write full accounts.

If the accused is committed to trial, the ban stays in effect until the end of the trial. Even with a ban, though, you may report on the outcome of the hearing: the fact that the accused will go to trial, and the charges.

If no ban has been imposed, you may report on the evidence at the hearing. But you must not report confessions. It's a Criminal Code offence to publish reports of any confessions (including those mentioned by the police or by other witnesses) until they are entered into evidence at trial or until the case ends.

Trial

In an attempt to save victims of sexual abuse from any further embarrassment, the Crown attorney usually asks for a ban on publication of the identity of the victim or any information that could disclose the victim's identity. In many cases, particularly those involving incest, this may mean that the name of the accused cannot be reported either. Many news media don't wait for the Crown to order a ban, refraining, as a matter of policy, from publishing names or other information that would identify the victim of a sexual assault.

The Young Offenders Act imposes strict limits on reporting. The news media may not report the names of children or youths charged with a crime, or any information that might identify them. This almost always means the names of the parents and the address of the family. Sometimes, prohibited information may include the name of the school the child attends, or the grade. The media also may not publish the names of child victims or witnesses, or any information that might identify them.

Finally, reporters at jury trials need to be aware of the perils of reporting what goes on in the courtroom when the jury is not there. Courts sometimes move into voir dire sessions — essentially a trial within a trial — in which the Crown and defence present arguments to the judge on the admissibility of evidence, such as a confession given at the time of arrest. The jury is sent out of the room for the voir dire. If the judge rules that the jury may hear the evidence, you may report the evidence — but only when the jury actually hears it.

"Sometimes the voir dire may be held at the beginning of the trial, or some time from when the jury actually hears the evidence," says Stephen Bindman, legal affairs correspondent for Southam News and a former court beat reporter for the Ottawa *Citizen*. "You shouldn't think that just because it has been ruled admissible it is fair game right away."

If the judge rules that the jury may *not* hear the disputed evidence, reporters must not publish it until after the trial. Reporting such evidence then may raise ethical concerns. Is it fair to the person who has just been acquitted of a charge and to the jury members who acquitted the accused to publish a confession that was ruled inadmissible by the judge? But then if the reason the confession was ruled inadmissible was that the police obtained it improperly, shouldn't the public be told?

Bindman stresses that reporters covering jury trials should remember to limit their reports to only those things the jury sees and hears.

"There is nothing worse than letting something slip into your copy that causes a judge to call a mistrial," he says. "And it's a lot easier than you might think." He tells of a reporter in British Columbia who was severely criticized by a judge for including the maximum penalty for the crime in her story. The jury had not been told this information. In another incident, a judge called a mistrial in a murder case after a newspaper reported that the accused was convicted on the charge in an earlier trial, but the conviction had been overturned on appeal. A third trial had to be set for the man.

Another way for reporters to get into trouble is to describe the security precautions — such as leg shackles — the jury doesn't see. "The accused is always in the box before the jury is brought in so they never see the security," Bindman says. "It is felt they might think he's more dangerous — or more likely to have committed the crime — if they knew he had been brought to the courtroom in chains."

A mistrial is costly to society, damaging to the judicial process and often an embarrassment to the news outlet that is responsible for it.

SCANDALIZING THE COURT

Contempt of court law is designed to protect against interference in the proper course of justice. Most of the time, the key issue for journalists is what you may or may not report about a person accused of a crime.

You should also be aware of another type of contempt offence: scandalizing the court. When applied to journalists, this law deals mainly with commentary or criticism about the administration of justice, rather than with reporting about the accused.

Journalists have been convicted for "scurrilous abuse" of a court, judge or jury — for example, for accusing a court of "iron curtain" tactics, or for describing the judge and jury at a murder trial, at a time when capital punishment was allowed, as being murderers themselves (Martin 1991a, 274). Another way to get into trouble is to impute improper motives to a judge, jury or court — writing, for example, that a judge is biased or on the take (Martin 1991a, 275). This kind of statement is seen as undermining the integrity of the judicial system.

Does this mean you may make *no* comment on court cases? Not at all, says lawyer Stuart Robertson. "A fair and temperate comment on how a judicial proceeding is being, or was, handled is both permissible and an important aspect of freedom of speech. The administration of justice can and must be able to withstand criticism and commentary" (Robertson 1983, 48).

(continued)

During a trial, however, you should avoid comments or criticism that urge a particular result, he writes. You have greater latitude after the trial is over, as long as you stay within the bounds of contempt law. Robertson adds that there are *no* restrictions on commentary and criticism of the laws themselves — only on the people who administer them.

BEYOND THE COURTROOM

As in other beats, reporters assigned to cover courts are expected to cover the institution, not just what it does. This means reporters are constantly on the lookout for feature stories on the court beat, and for stories on the administration — good and bad — of justice.

People who work in or hang out at the courthouse are good sources for story ideas, and a court reporter who works the beat for any length of time eventually gets to know most of the clerks, stenographers, Crown attorneys and judges.

"One thing about anybody in a courthouse — they're all big talkers," Bindman says. "It's a closed little community."

Lawyers are good sources of information, especially about other lawyers' cases, he says. Judges can also be helpful, though it takes time for reporters to build a good relationship with them. Some of the most useful contacts for story ideas, he adds, are the people at the low end of the hierarchy who spend a lot of time in and around the courthouse, or the people who simply like to hang out at the courthouse and see what is going on.

Bob Johnstone of CBC Radio in Toronto agrees. "The lowest-level clerks, or the guys who open and close the door and shout at people — they're the ones you want to get to know," he says.

One way to learn what kinds of stories can be developed is to spend a day at the courthouse looking for story ideas instead of trials to cover. You may run across plans for challenges to the Charter of Rights and Freedoms, discussions of whether court reforms are working, talk of policy changes to speed up the trial process or gossip about how a lawyer's personal problems are affecting her practice. With fresh eyes, you may see things overlooked by regular court reporters — details of architecture that tell a story, or small bits of business in the cafeteria that add a human touch to the proceedings.

The desire to put a human face on criminal justice — to tell readers not just what happened in the courtroom but what it felt like to be there — has contributed to a recent trend in court reporting: the use of columnists as well as reporters. This extra coverage was seen most spectacularly during Paul Bernardo's trial for the torture, sexual assault and murder of two St. Catharines girls. The practice has now become somewhat common in prominent cases. When Calgary socialite Dorothy Joudrie went on trial in 1996 for attempting to murder her husband, the *Calgary Sun* double-teamed the event. Court reporter Kevin Martin wrote daily coverage of the trial itself. Columnist Licia Corbella had a different task — telling readers what it felt like to be in the courthouse, and trying to put the spectacle of the trial in context. On the day the jury was selected, Corbella wrote:

> Exactly 135 potential jurors are packed into the Court of Queen's Bench Room 204 and, despite the proverbial sardine-in-a-can seating arrangement, there is a reverent silence in this room.
>
> No chit-chat here, just the weighty quiet of people who know that what they may be asked to participate in is a civic duty of substantial import.
>
> Justice — indeed, the fate of those they may be called upon to deliberate – could lie with them ...
>
> — LICIA CORBELLA, CALGARY SUN, APRIL 19, 1996

Corbella's columns ranged from how Earl Joudrie felt after testifying, to the effects of the trial on the couple's children, to the emotional costs Dorothy Joudrie paid for a life full of physical comforts. When Joudrie was found not criminally responsible for the shooting, Corbella described in detail both the woman's reaction to the verdict and the effect the case had on her family. Her May 10, 1996, column concluded, "So when you see Dorothy Joudrie smiling, with her face full of promise, it's important to remember that you're looking at a woman who has won a small victory, but lost much of what she holds most dear."

While this kind of material adds a new (and probably popular) dimension to court reporting, it has its risks. Done badly, it over-dramatizes and sensationalizes cases that already have attracted enormous public attention. It may also result in writing that resorts to pop psychology to "explain" crimes. And it may flirt with the boundaries of the law on contempt, especially when columnists question the credibility or character of witnesses. Indeed, Corbella says her columns on Joudrie routinely went to the newspaper's lawyers to ensure they contained nothing that would prompt a citation for contempt.

But done well, the courtroom column pushes reporting beyond the sometimes repetitive and dry drone of testimony and cross-examination, to journalism that takes readers to places they might not otherwise go.

COVERING INQUESTS

The job of covering inquests or *fatalities inquiries* often falls to the court reporter. In many ways this makes sense: an inquest is a formal investigation, usually held at the courthouse in front of a jury, and in some provinces presided over by a judge.

But although on the surface inquests look a lot like trials, these inquiries into violent or unnatural deaths have a unique purpose and their own set of rules that reporters must know and follow.

In essence, inquests examine the cause and circumstances of unnatural deaths and may recommend ways of avoiding similar deaths in future. Inquests are *not* intended to make findings of criminal or civil responsibility in the death, though occasionally criminal charges arise indirectly as a result of an inquest.

For reporters, the recommendations may be the most newsworthy aspect of an inquest. These recommendations often call for concrete, specific changes in the way things are done in a community — how school bus drivers keep track of children getting off the bus, for example, or how police officers keep an eye on newly arrested suspects who are clearly intoxicated by drugs or alcohol.

Inquests come under provincial jurisdiction and therefore vary from province to province. (*CP Stylebook* [1995] summarizes some of the unique features of the Quebec law.) But in general, they are presided over either by a judge or by a *coroner*, also known as a medical examiner. Coroners (usually medical doctors) are appointed by the provincial government and report to the minister in charge of justice, usually the solicitor general or attorney general.

Coroners investigate all unnatural deaths, but hold inquests in only some of them. Some inquests are mandatory — when a person dies in police custody or in jail, for example. In other deaths, the coroner or medical examiner decides whether to hold an inquest. Sometimes, when two or more deaths appear to have a common cause, the inquest will look at all the deaths. Sometimes, too, the provincial solicitor general or the chief coroner will order an inquest. In most provinces, the inquest is conducted with the help of a small jury.

Inquests are open to the public, though they may be ordered closed by the presiding judge or coroner. Reporters covering an inquest should treat it as they would any other public hearing, reporting fairly and accurately on what went on.

The rules and procedures at an inquest are different from those at a trial. For example, an inquest may hear evidence — such as a confession — which would be inadmissible at a criminal trial. Unless directed otherwise by the presiding coroner or judge, the

(continued)

reporter covering the inquest may report it at the time. People who have a direct interest in the death may ask for *standing* at an inquest. This means they (or their lawyers) may call and examine witnesses or present arguments. In addition, jury members may pose questions directly to the witnesses.

These procedures are aimed at helping the jury do its job — to reach agreement on the circumstances of the death and develop a set of recommendations on how to avoid similar deaths. The recommendations are usually made public at the end of the inquest. They also go to the province's chief coroner, who may pass them along to the appropriate agencies or branches of government.

For reporters, inquests have a natural news value. The inquest offers a public inquiry into a tragedy that has affected the lives of many people in the community. The jury's recommendations represent the judgment of a group of citizens about how the people or institutions connected to the death could do their jobs better, and how the community could be spared the pain of such deaths in the future.

Many recommendations, therefore, are pragmatic, action-oriented and concrete. In an attempt to protect other children, a jury investigating a school bus accident might recommend that the local school board buy snub-nosed buses rather than buses that jut

out in front, or that the board install equipment to make sure the driver is able to see the children once they leave the bus. In an inquest into a suicide at a penitentiary, the jury might recommend that guards walk the range of cells at random times rather than on a regular schedule, or that patrols be increased around Christmas, when prisoners are likely to be depressed.

Other recommendations may speak to larger questions of government policy — ideas on licensing or training or safety regulations.

The reporter covering the inquest has the job of conveying to the broader community what happened. In writing inquest stories, as in any other reporting, the challenge is to tell the story as well as possible. Sadly, all too many inquest stories begin with a formulaic lead: "a coroner's jury investigating the death of Indira Knak, 44, of Anytown yesterday recommended X, Y and Z." Don't rely on a formula: make a natural judgment about the news value of the inquest and take it from there.

Coroner's juries are in no position to *order* changes; they may only recommend them. Stories on inquests, therefore, usually lead naturally to reaction pieces — whether school board members think the cost of replacing buses is justified, or whether penitentiary officials see any value in changing guards' schedules. Some recom-
(continued)

mendations are never acted on. Others are adopted, sometimes quickly, by the institutions affected.

Because jury recommendations are collected by the chief coroner, they may also be a source for stories tracing a pattern of deaths. If in- quests in three different parts of a province make similar recommen- dations in similar deaths, the re- porter may be able to see the outlines of a larger problem, one that wasn't necessarily apparent in any one of the deaths.

RECOMMENDED READING

Bruser, Robert S., and Brian MacLeod Rogers. (1985). *Journalists and the Law: How to Get the Story Without Getting Sued or Put in Jail*. Ottawa: The Canadian Bar Foundation.

CP Stylebook: A Guide for Writers and Editors. (1995). Peter Buckley, ed. Revised edition. Toronto: The Canadian Press.

Crawford, Michael G. (1996). *The Journalist's Legal Guide*. 3rd edition. Toronto: Carswell.

Griffiths, Curt T., and Simon N. Verdun-Jones. (1994). *Canadian Criminal Justice*. 2nd edition. Toronto: Harcourt Brace.

Levy, Harold J. (1986). *A Reporter's Guide to Canada's Criminal Justice System*. Ottawa: The Canadian Bar Foundation.

Martin, Robert. (1997). *Media Law*. Toronto: Irwin Law.

Martin, Robert, and G. Stuart Adam. (1991). *A Sourcebook of Canadian Media Law*. Revised edition (new case material). Ottawa: Carleton University Press.

Robertson, Stuart M. (1983). *Media Law Handbook*. Vancouver: International Self-Counsel Press.

Zuber, Thomas G. (1974). *Introduction to Canadian Criminal Law*. Toronto: McGraw-Hill Ryerson.

CHAPTER 11

Covering Local Government

THE LOCAL TOWN HALL IS THE TESTING ground for many new reporters. It's almost a sure bet that reporters on summer internships or in a first job will spend some time sitting in a council chamber somewhere, covering a meeting. If they do it competently, learning how to see a story among the bylaw numbers, agenda items, staff reports and so forth, they may be on track to permanent work. Those who can go further and spot developing issues and then draw out the full details may be making their first moves toward a career in political reporting.

Though covering local government may appear to lack the glamor of covering Parliament or provincial legislatures, it offers many rewards to reporters. Key among them is the chance to cover the level of government that has the most direct impact on the public. From snow removal to trash collection, from sewers to subways, from parks and recreation to property taxes, decisions made by local governments affect the lives of communities day in, day out.

Consider: a proposal to restructure federal departments will draw varying degrees of interest (including some yawns) from people living on any residential street in any city in Canada. A proposal to put a highrise apartment on the vacant lot at the end of that street, on the other hand, is almost guaranteed to grab residents' attention and perhaps spur them to action. People who would never think of demonstrating on a national issue will turn out in force at a council meeting when neighborhood issues are at stake.

Reporter Pam Sword of the *Chronicle-Herald* takes notes at Halifax city council. In circumstances like these it's often difficult for reporters to hear, or to keep track of, who's saying what. Checks after the meeting, to confirm and clarify material, are routine. (Len Wagg)

For reporters, this means that stories on local government issues have an immediacy and an impact on their audiences that are sometimes lacking in national and international stories. While they may have complex dimensions, the issues themselves are usually concrete — things like road widenings, sewer work, police service, public transit and spraying parks with insecticide. People are quick to speak out on these issues. It's easy to get comments from shop owners who think that six months of road construction will drive them out of business, from parents who worry about increased traffic on their street, or from politicians who see a road-widening project as an essential service to commuters.

Decisions made by council can literally change the shape of the community. Covering these decisions is the essence of public service reporting, the kind of journalism that gives people information they need to live their lives better. But a city hall assignment offers reporters something else — the chance to see politics and policy making played out at the most accessible level. Politicians learn by doing. At the local level their education takes place in public, before a reporter's eyes.

The reporter on the local government beat is witness to the beginning of many a political career and the end of countless others. At times, journalists help bring a political career to an end. Stories exposing scandals — violations of conflict of interest laws, for example, or illicit attempts by developers to influence zoning decisions — sometimes trigger resignations and even criminal investigations. Other stories, detailing a councillor's lavish spending habits on trips paid by public funds, or raising questions about whether an absentee councillor is really earning a councillor's salary, can have an impact at the polls.

Many new reporters know very little about local government. They may have vague memories of high school classes on how city council passes a bylaw. They may have taken political science courses, but they probably studied federal politics, not local government. They are probably aware of the latest books by Ottawa insiders on the cabinet and prime minister's office, but would be hard pressed to find a current book on the workings of local government on the shelves of most bookstores.

It is little wonder, then, that a reporter assigned to a first council meeting often finds it a bewildering event. With solid preparation and backgrounding, however, the reporter quickly gets caught up in the issues and in the drama of politics played out at the local level.

MAPPING OUT THE BEAT

A reporter assigned to a new beat needs to spend time "reading in," becoming familiar with the issues and the key players. Each local government has its own history, problems and cast of characters, but we hope this brief discussion will provide some context and point to some general patterns underlying municipal coverage. Four interconnected pieces of the puzzle quickly become evident: the municipal story involves struggles over power, money, land and, increasingly, services.

The Power Clash

Local politicians constantly bump their heads on the limits of their authority. Understanding why this is so demands some knowledge of history. All municipal reporters should know, for example, that independent, democratically elected local governments are a relatively recent development in Canada. Although Quebec City and Montreal are among the oldest European settlements in North America, colonial authorities from France, and later Britain, governed through a centralized and non-democratic administration. A different situation prevailed in the colonies of New York and New England, where the town meeting gave people substantial local autonomy.

After the American Revolution, many Loyalists who came north wanted to continue the town meeting tradition. The British authorities balked, believing that democracy had contributed to the American revolt. The push for local self-government was strongest in Upper Canada, the area that later became Ontario. In 1793, the legislature of Upper Canada agreed to let town meetings proceed, though under strict controls: the only legislative authority the town meeting had was to set the height of fences and control animals running at large (Tindal and Tindal 1990, 18).

The biggest advance toward municipal self-government came when Lord Durham, investigating the Rebellion of 1837, described municipal self-governing institutions as "the foundations of Anglo-Saxon freedom and civilization" and called for their creation in Canada. Over the next few decades, municipal acts were passed in Ontario and Quebec and by the time of Confederation in 1867, the basic structure of local government had been set.

The British North America Act, however, gave no formal status to local governments, saying only that local government is a provincial responsibility. In theory, this means a province can set up any kind of local government structure it chooses, and can change it at will. Municipal structures have their own power bases and are resistant to change, however. When the province steps in, as Ontario did in 1997 by reorganizing the government of Toronto, it often creates a public furore.

In times of change, local government reporters spend a lot of time tracking the tensions between the city and its provincial capital. But like threads on a loom, these tensions pull in many directions. A reporter caught up in an amalgamation battle in Saint John or Hamilton, for example, needs to be aware that similar battles have been fought elsewhere. Some of the best reporting puts the local situation into its larger context, analysing where the conflicts originated and how they might be resolved.

Who Pays for What

Early local governments included urban administrations (towns, villages and cities) and rural governments (townships, municipal districts, rural municipalities and so on) governed by an elected council. In some areas, a second unit of government, the county, was set up to handle issues of shared concern for all townships within the county. Local governments were expected to provide a limited range of services, dealing mainly with property. Property taxes, based on land ownership, paid for those services. Provincial assessment acts set the framework for levying and collecting these taxes.

As cities grew, their governments faced a new and complex set of problems: housing, water pollution, safety, the need for social services, traffic control and so on. Property taxation couldn't pay for it all, and cities began to rely more and more on grants or transfer payments from the provinces. But these payments have been drying up in recent years. As the federal government reins in its deficit and works toward a balanced budget, it has cut transfer payments to the provinces. The provinces, in turn wrestling with their own budget problems, have cut grants to municipalities and tried to get them to take on more responsibilities for services, such as welfare. This shifting of costs down the ladder of government shows up in municipal council chambers, and eventually in resident's property tax bills.

Paying for such services through property taxes is far from easy. For one thing, the cost of services like welfare may vary tremendously depending on the state of the economy — unlike, say, the cost of paving a road. In addition, property taxes are based on what the taxpayers own, not on what they earn. A taxpayer who loses her job will end up paying less income tax for that year, but will still owe the same property tax. As a result, proposals to increase the level of property taxation tend to draw enormous public criticism. The question of how local governments cope with the shifting of costs onto the property tax base has been a recurring story in cities and towns from coast to coast.

The Land Grab

Then, there's the question of land, and it, too, has a good deal of history. During this century, spreading suburbs have blurred the boundaries between what once were separate towns, resulting in wave after wave of annexations and amalgamations. The drive for more land, and the fight over how to get it and how to govern it, constitute another basic theme in local reporting.

Municipalities tend to grow in two ways: by expanding their boundaries or by expanding government structures. The traditional pattern is growth by annexation, in which a city takes over surrounding land. This is still common practice in many areas. In Edmonton alone, there were 19 separate annexations between 1947 and 1980. (See Tindal and Tindal 1990, 119.) Annexation drives are a rich source of story material. These stories may explore the political conflicts between the city that wants the land and the rural areas that don't want to be absorbed, or the impact the annexation will have on tangible items like taxation and services, and on intangibles like the sense of community and the value of neighborhoods.

The second form of expansion — the creation of new governments to cover a larger region — began in the 1950s with the establishment of Metropolitan Toronto. Regional governments, a modern variation on the old county form of government, were set up in the 1960s and 1970s in many parts of Ontario. Under a regional government system, two levels of government operate in the same area. The local municipalities, known as the lower-tier governments, have their own councils and are responsible for local issues such as snow removal and trash collection. The regional or upper-tier government handles issues that concern the broader area.

The drive to create new levels of government stalled in the 1980s, and in the 1990s seems to have switched gears into reverse. The trend now is toward amalgamation of power structures, not simply of land. The new city government in Toronto is the most high-profile example of this trend, but by no means the only one. In recent years, Newfoundland has eliminated 20 municipalities and Prince Edward Island has reduced the number of municipalities around Charlottetown and Summerside. In Alberta, regional planning commissions were eliminated and a number of merged municipalities were created, including Wood Buffalo, which is almost 42,000 square kilometres — twice the size of Belgium. Municipal reporters who cover these mergers look at them from a number of angles: is the merged municipality cheaper? Is it more efficient? Does it preserve the local community, or damage it? Is bigger (geographically) really better, and if so, for whom? Is smaller (governmentally) really better and, again, for whom?

The Service Issue

Finally, there's the question of services. The traditional function of municipal government is to provide hard services for property owners like roads, sewers, snow removal and water. But municipalities have been steadily taking on the administration of an enormous range of services, from welfare to public transit. Now they're being asked to pay for these services too.

Municipal columnist David Lewis Stein of the *Toronto Star* says the cities are arguing that if they're going to have to pay for a larger share of these services, they want more control over them too — "say for pay," as he puts it. As a result, municipal councillors and their constituents are waking up to the enormous role municipal governments play in civil society. "The old idea of the alderman as the good burgher who manages property is changing," says Stein.

A number of cities have experimented with contracting out services in an attempt to keep costs down. This pattern offers a rich array of story ideas, from how the initial decision is made to whether the savings promised from contracting out are delivered now, and whether they will continue to be delivered three or five years down the road.

The fight over services often comes down to an ideological debate between councillors who campaigned on promises of keeping taxes down and those who feel that services must be provided even if taxes go up; between those who believe the role of the municipal government is to take bids and tender contracts and those who support the idea of public service.

"Cities are the last battleground for the social responsibility ideal," says Stein. "We're beginning to get more and more demands made on the cities, then they have to make really tough decisions, which they haven't had to do in the past."

STRUCTURES OF LOCAL GOVERNMENT

Most local governments have a number of features in common.

A Head of Council. The job goes by a number of titles, such as mayor in cities and towns, reeve or overseer in townships or villages. Mayors are chosen in regularly scheduled municipal elections. They chair meetings of council and have the highest profile of any politician in the local structure. This means they are key contacts for reporters on the municipal beat.

A Council of Local Representatives. The composition of councils varies. In some municipalities, one councillor or alderman is elected to represent each district or ward. In others, more than one councillor may be elected per ward. A second form of election is by a vote "at large," with the top vote-getters winning the seats. Some municipal councils combine the two forms and have some councillors representing wards and others elected at large. Depending on the size and organization of a local government, councils may be divided into standing committees, which handle particular policy areas. Some councils have an executive committee, the most powerful form of committee. A council will often divide itself into informal blocs or coalitions, in which groups of like-minded councillors tend to vote the same way. These coalitions can be extremely fragile, however. Good stories may be found in the shifting alliances of council members.

Agencies, Boards and Commissions. These bodies handle specific areas, such as policing, libraries, hospitals and utilities. Some, particularly public utilities commissions, may be filled by election. Others are filled by appointment.

A Civil Service. The council sets policy and passes legislation known as bylaws. The civil service administers the law, collecting taxes, keeping records and so on. Staff also help develop policy for the bylaws passed by council. Some local governments have a chief administrative officer or manager who is the single most powerful figure in the civil service (and may, in fact, wield more actual power than the mayor). In others, individual department heads work with standing committees of council. Reporters newly assigned to the beat should track down an organizational chart to figure out which are the key jobs, then arrange to introduce themselves to the senior officials.

Regional and county governments also have councils. In some, the councils are directly elected; in others, they are composed of elected officials from the local municipalities that make up the county or region. These governments also have their own public service and their own set of agencies, boards and commissions.

Sorting Out the Coverage

For the two full-time city hall reporters at the *Calgary Herald*, the work week starts on Friday morning. That's when they drop by the city clerk's office to pick up the agendas for the next week of meetings. "The agendas can be humongous, sometimes 200 or 300 pages long," says Don Martin, a longtime *Calgary Herald* city hall reporter who now writes a column from the Alberta legislature. Reading them may be "pretty mind-numbing," he adds, but well worth the effort.

The agendas include all the items coming up before council or its committees, including proposed bylaws, land-use changes and so on, plus background reports and recommendations from city staff. They provide story ideas for weekend features and scene-setters that fill readers in on imminent decisions that are likely to affect them.

Monday is meeting day at Calgary's city hall. Reporters spend the morning covering meetings of standing policy committees, which are usually lively and sometimes contentious. They then cover the full council meeting, held later in the day.

"The committees hear the issue out from the administration stand-point and receive public input," Martin explains. "Full council meetings, on the other hand, do not allow public input on most issues. So reporters can often get better stories at the policy committee meetings than at full council meetings because both sides on an issue can present their views."

City hall reporters pick up stories from committee meetings as they surface. They may make followup phone calls to people whose views were not represented at the meetings. "Then they chase political reac-tion, perhaps from the mayor or other aldermen not on the committee, and file accordingly before the full council meeting starts."

This means reporters are often working on five or six stories in a very short period of time.

Reporters need to stay at the council meeting until the end, because some of the best stories come up at the end of the session. Former city hall reporter Bob Bergen writes in a 1987 guidebook for his successors that so-called matters of urgent business are usually the last items on the agenda. "Council's most recent gift to itself, i.e. a pay hike, was introduced as a matter of urgent business," he writes. "Similarly, important matters dealt with by council committees early in the day can be 'blue-sheeted' to council and dealt with on the same day. If that's the case it's usually a good story, but again will be one of the last things council does."

Space and time constraints mean that a lot of council decisions appear in Tuesday's papers as briefs, or what Martin calls "bite-sized pieces of information that give just the essentials."

Tuesday is spent fleshing out some of those briefs for Wednesday's paper, tracking down people who will be affected by a decision or will have something to say about it. The goal is to tell people what a deci-sion means, not simply how it was made. "Wherever possible, you should take an issue and relate it to the average reader, as opposed to writing just what the politicians are saying," Martin says.

On Wednesday and Thursday, Martin says, "you're sort of scram-bling on your own." Sometimes, there are meetings to cover, such as the Calgary planning commission, which handles major development pro-jects, or the development appeal board, which rules on appeals from either the public or a developer on a planning decision.

"I've always encouraged city hall reporters to walk away from city hall on the last two days of the week and find out what issues council may be expected to deal with," Martin says. "For example, we have an extensive bicycle path network. If there's an accident on a bike path, we might do a story that asks questions about the use of these paths and how the city could improve them."

On Fridays, the next set of agendas comes out, and the round of coverage starts again.

This pattern of writing from agendas and meetings, followed by more agendas and meetings, is repeated in newsrooms across the country. Some local government reporters have to cover only one meeting a week. Others have a list of a dozen.

But while many meetings must be covered, reporters don't have to let a meeting schedule drive their news judgment. Through contacts with community groups, bureaucrats or politicians, they know where trouble or controversy is brewing, or where a push for change in land-use laws is likely to be made. They try to catch issues before they get on to the agenda for a particular meeting and write about them in a way that puts the anticipated development in context.

These stories serve an important public purpose: they let the community know in advance that council is about to make a decision on an issue that may be of crucial importance to them. People can then respond — by sending delegations to meetings, lobbying councillors, writing letters to the editor of the local newspaper or holding demonstrations to press for changes. For the reporter, this kind of reporting has an additional bonus: the satisfaction of beating the competition to the story.

Jock Ferguson of the *Globe and Mail* offers another reason for looking beyond the meeting schedule. He points out that meetings are for public show. The hidden side of municipal politics, including decisions made in secret before the meetings, is far more difficult to track. "The secret activity — *in camera* meetings, caucus or lunch meetings of a faction of council, dinners, office meetings — often reveals the real agenda of the politicians and shows in whose interests they are operating," he says.

Contacts and Sources

Of all politicians, local government representatives tend to be the most readily accessible to reporters and the most willing to talk.

In part such accessibility is a byproduct of the structure of city governments. Though there are notable exceptions, party politics plays an unimportant role at the local level. Where parties exist, they tend to be local creations — civic parties, if you will. The relationship between national or provincial parties and local councillors is, on the whole, tenuous: the parties avoid direct involvement, but voters usually know the political leanings of the councillors.

The structure works to the reporter's advantage. "There is no cabinet solidarity or caucus solidarity in a civic government, so leaks can be abundant," Martin says. "It's imperative to understand when you're covering the city council that various forces are at work, with very different agendas."

Local politicians live, eat, work and sleep in the communities they are elected to represent. Unlike MPs, who may disappear in the mists around Parliament Hill, or MPPs, who divide their time between their constituencies and the provincial capital, city councillors are on hand. It is relatively easy, therefore, for reporters to track them down. This means that politics at the local level has an intensely human face, and covering it involves daily contact with the people making the decisions. It also means dealing with their secretaries and aides — valuable contacts in their own right.

Reporters quickly learn the strengths, weaknesses and political orientations of councillors. Some councillors take a strongly pro-business and pro-development stand, while others are more preservation-minded and concerned about social services.

"I find it useful to play these opposing viewpoints off against each other," Martin says. "You know who to go to for one comment. You take that comment to someone else who says, 'Well, my information is different. Here's what I think, and here's why and here's my scenario.' then you have two scenarios from the politicians and you often have the story right there."

Does this approach mean the reporter acts as agent provocateur? Not at all, says David Lewis Stein of the *Toronto Star*. These debates are going to come out anyway, usually at a council meeting. "But you've got the story first, that's all."

Jock Ferguson of the *Globe and Mail* says reporters have to do their homework to avoid what he calls "he said-she said" reporting. "In my experience many municipal reporters are poorly informed about the issues discussed at committee and council meetings and have a hard time asking decent questions, let alone catching untruths." Knowing the documents helps. "Documents are untruthful less often than politicians," he says.

Developing contacts in the civic administration is particularly important. The municipal bureaucracy is powerful, particularly in areas with part-time city councillors. Councils set guidelines for the city, but the senior administrators are the ones who chart the course. And while politicians may come and go, the administrators are in for the long haul. This means they tend to be more knowledgeable than many politicians.

And their work is free of some of the political pressures that influence councillors.

"If you can build any contacts in the administration, it can pay off in spades," Martin says. "Often if I sense council is going against what the administration wants to happen, administration sources can be extremely useful in giving me information to fortify their viewpoint."

Stein says the most useful contacts in the city bureaucracy are the mid-level staffers, who tend to be both ambitious and well educated. The high-profile senior department heads or commissioners, on the other hand, may be more defensive of their own positions. How does a reporter figure out the right people to talk to? Stein answers: "you get to know them because when a commissioner appears at a meeting, they're usually sitting behind him, whispering to him. The guy feeding the commissioner the answers is the guy you want to talk to."

The municipal affairs beat doesn't begin and end at city hall. More than any other area of political reporting, the local beat is about people — those who reap the benefits (or pay the costs) of a vote on zoning or user fees or property tax or dog licences.

Ratepayers groups may be active at budget time and dormant the rest of the year. Other citizens groups organize around a single cause such as water fluoridation or a proposed highway through a residential neighborhood. Still others concentrate on a broader social issue — affordable housing, heritage preservation or public transit. Some groups, such as home builders associations, lobby council on behalf of developers. Others, like chambers of commerce or downtown merchants associations, speak for businesses.

Each group has its own bias, and it can be an easy and cynical game for reporters to pit one against the other. But these groups are also a legitimate part of the municipal process. Fair and balanced reporting will include the views of as many of them as possible.

PATTERNS OF REPORTAGE

Watching the Developers

One of the most intricate and important parts of municipal reporting is keeping watch on land use and development. Provincial planning acts determine what a municipality may do with the land within its boundaries. They require municipalities to draw up a plan — usually known as the Official Plan — setting out what kinds of development may take place, and where. These acts also create the legal tools for carrying out the plan, such as zoning bylaws, building permits and subdivision controls.

The value of land and the profits that can be reaped from it tend to increase according to the level of development allowed. A plot zoned for single-family housing, for example, is usually worth less than a plot zoned for multiple-family highrises or commercial use. As a result, local governments face constant pressure to amend or bend the official plan and local zoning bylaws.

These changes may come about through rezonings, which alter the allowed uses of land in a specific section of the city, or through "variances," which are exceptions to the rules approved by a body known as the committee of adjustment. Committees of adjustment are intended to decide on minor deviations from the zoning. Sometimes, however, developers try to slip major changes through the committee. In places like Toronto, the practice of "bonusing" — allowing developers to build oversized buildings if in return they include some kind of public use such as park space or room for a day-care centre — has been a common way to bend zoning requirements.

Patterns of development vary with the state of the economy and the age of the city. In the so-called edge cities — those at the fringe of a major metropolitan area — the task of tracking the developers may occupy much of the municipal reporter's attention. Inevitably, development creates tension in a community between the long-time residents and the newcomers; between rival development companies; and between councillors who see development as good in and of itself and those who fight for community preservation. Development tends to be cyclical, with most pressure felt during times of economic growth. In the recessions that follow periods of growth, reporters often find themselves writing about the unfulfilled promises of developers.

In the urban core of older cities, Stein says, development activity tends to centre on finding new uses for industrial land, or on the practice known as "infill" or "intensification," whereby buildings go up in the blank spaces between other buildings. "The heroic days when people would buy up whole blocks, raze them and throw up monster apartment towers are gone," he says.

Stein says the edges of a zone are the places to watch. "If the official plan says the downtown stops at A street, for sure some guy has bought property on B street and he wants to get the plan moved over just a little bit to include his corner," he says. The owner's attempt to change the zoning on B street may be a story in itself, or it may be used as part of a larger story tracing patterns of development.

Changes in land use create a paper trail that reporters can follow. Most municipal acts say that materials in the hands of the city clerk are public, although what exactly this means has been open to interpretation. Nevertheless, a reporter can usually count on being able to look at the minutes of council meetings, copies of bylaws, tax assessment rolls that list the name and address of the owners of land, voters' lists, building permit records, committee of adjustment records and so on.

Jock Ferguson has used these records to research stories on local development. A series he wrote in 1987 with Paul Taylor traced some disturbing patterns: the developers of nine major buildings going up on a seven-block stretch of Bay Street in downtown Toronto either had obtained or were seeking rezonings that would substantially enlarge their projects; the rezonings, if successful, would generate a windfall profit of at least $80 million for the developers. In addition, the reporters, using voluntary campaign finance disclosure records, found that the Bay Street developers were part of a larger group that had made substantial campaign contributions to city politicians. (See Ferguson and Taylor 1987. This story was part of a series that won the Centre for Investigative Journalism's best newspaper investigation award for 1987.)

A year later Ferguson, this time working with reporter Dawn King, used land ownership records, corporate records, planning reports, engineering reports and building permits to trace the close relationship between politicians and developers in York region, then Canada's fastest-growing community. The result was an eight-part series that exposed a range of questionable activities and had a major impact at the polls. (See Ferguson and King 1988. The series won the award for best newspaper investigation, 1988.)

These two series were major investigative pieces that took months of research. But the lessons these series offer on the value of tracking the paper trail and watching for patterns in development decisions can lead reporters to stories. For example, a reporter might notice that a construction company is at work down the street, building a new house on land that used to be the back yard of an older house with a large lot. The addition of one "infill" house to the neighborhood is probably not worth a story. But if a check of building permit records reveals that dozens more are being planned, the reporter has uncovered a pattern and found a guideline into a number of stories. (What will massive infilling mean for property values? For the quality of life in the neighborhood? Will it cause overcrowding in schools? What do the neighbors think of the practice?)

Municipal Budgets

Once a year, local governments draw up their budgets, deciding how much money they need to collect in property taxes and how much to spend on local services. Journalists like Don Martin of the *Calgary Herald*, who says he went into journalism "because it didn't require math," find their first glimpse of municipal budget books daunting. But budget books are not hard to follow. And there are a lot of fascinating stories hidden in the numbers.

There are actually two kinds of budgets:

- *The operating budget.* This pays for the day-to-day expenses of running of the city, such as policing, fire prevention, street maintenance, servicing the debt and so on. Most of the money comes from local sources — property taxes, fees and permits, surcharges and so on. Some comes from provincial transfer payments. This is the budget that gets ratepayers upset, since the rate of property taxation is set under the operating budget.

- *The capital budget.* This pays for major projects, such as new municipal buildings and major public transit projects. The money usually comes from borrowing or grants, and spending is projected over several years.

Budgets are put together in many ways. The traditional way starts with last year's spending as a base. The various departments examine what was spent where, and then predict how much money they will need this year. The individual estimates, which may be reviewed by the municipal treasurer and a standing committee, are put together with other spending commitments made by the municipality. Finance officials calculate the revenues expected from non-tax sources such as provincial grants or user fees; then they pull together a draft budget that estimates how much property taxes will rise.

Reporters often have only a few hours to go over a municipal budget before they must write their first stories on it. They usually turn first to the part of the operating budget that outlines how much more in taxes people are going to have to pay. The property tax increase may be expressed in a number of ways: as a percentage increase from the previous year; in dollar figures for the average ratepayer, based on the assessed value of the average house; or as a new mill rate. The mill rate is a technical term used in the calculation of taxes. One mill is 0.1 cent. The amount of property tax comes from multiplying the number of mills in the mill rate by the assessed value of a property, dividing by 1000. Since mill rates are difficult to explain, and difficult to understand, reporters try to put the numbers in terms most people in the community can grasp quickly.

In addition to tax increases, reporters also look for increases in existing fees such as dog licences and the cost of applying for permits, and for the creation of new user fees. Some new user fees (the introduction of fees for using public swimming pools, for example) are probably worth stories on their own.

While trying to figure out what the new budget will cost taxpayers, reporters also look for the reasons for tax increases. Have the debt charges gone up? Have grants from the provinces gone down? Has growth prompted the need for more staff?

"Look for something that doesn't quite fit," Martin says. "If taxes are going up three per cent, you want to find out why spending in a specific area is going up 23 per cent."

Once the rush of filing the initial reports is over, reporters can sit back and go over the budget with a fine-toothed comb. "You may find all kinds of things in there," says Stein. "Training sessions. Trips to Japan to study solid waste. Trips to Tahiti to study wave pools. Then you go to the ratepayers groups and say, 'Do you realize this stuff is in the budget?' They say, 'No, and we don't like it one bit.' And you have a story."

The tax increase finally approved by council is often considerably less than the increase in the draft budget. Some councils impose an across-the-board reduction in the draft budget in an attempt to keep taxes down. Others go through the painful process of making cuts to areas that are considered inessential, such as grants to local arts groups. Budget-cutting hearings can be emotional, confrontational events. News coverage of these meetings tends of necessity to skim the surface. But the hearings are also a tremendous source of ideas for followup stories on the winners and the losers in the battle over the budget.

A final note on municipal budgets: they are not the only cause of property tax increases. Cities and towns act as tax collectors for school boards and regional municipalities. In some areas, taxes set by the boards of education account for half the total property tax bill. In areas with regional governments, the local municipality's share of property taxes may be as low as 25 per cent. This means newspapers and broadcasters carry budget stories on any number of governments and school boards — a situation that is bound to cause some confusion for the audience. Sorting out that confusion is a major job for reporters.

BOARDS OF EDUCATION

The municipal council is the most high-profile local government organization in any city or town. But boards of education wield tremendous power over how the children of a community are taught and at what cost. For this reason, most newsrooms of any size have at least one reporter assigned to the education beat.

Canada has no national system of education. Under the Constitution, education is a provincial responsibility. Each province has its own program of primary and secondary education, with its own education minister and set of rules and regulations. The school systems vary substantially, even in such basics as the age at which formal education begins or the number of years a student spends in high school.

School boards run publicly controlled primary and secondary schools in almost all provinces. (New Brunswick eliminated local boards in 1996.) These boards usually include elected trustees, a professional bureaucracy headed by a superintendent or director of education, and the teachers and administrators at the schools. Nearly 95 per cent of Canadian children attend publicly funded schools.

According to arrangements as old as Confederation, some provinces have dual sets of school boards — one running the so-called public schools and the other running publicly funded religious schools, sometimes known as separate schools. These separate schools were originally intended to protect minority language rights as well as religious freedom. But this meant, for example, that Ontario francophones who wanted French-language education had to send their children to Roman Catholic schools, regardless of whether they were Catholics. In recent years, both Ontario and Quebec have begun moving in recent years toward the creation of boards based on language. In Newfoundland, where public schools have always been denominational, educational reform has been directed at a rationalization plan that will create some single-denomination schools and some inter-denominational schools.

Changes in the provinces are occurring within a national context that favors fewer, but larger school boards. Province after province has forced board amalgamations, apparently in expectation of savings through economies of scale. Between 1992 and 1997, the Canadian School Boards Association estimates, the number of school boards in Canada dropped to about 550 from almost 800. (Andrew Nikiforuk, "Why Bigger Boards Are Never Better," *Globe and Mail*, May 17, 1997)

The provinces also exert a lot of influence over the content and context of local education. In general, the province sets education policy and the local board has to implement it; the province determines a level of funding and the
(continued)

local board has to live with it or supplement it through property taxes. Boards have traditionally had substantial autonomy in areas like textbook selection, curriculum development and the hiring of teachers. Recently, however, some provincial governments (especially in New Brunswick and Ontario) have sharply curtailed local autonomy in these and other areas.

The education reporter, even more than the local government reporter, works in an area that is characterized by strain between the local board and the province. These strains play out not just in the big issues, like funding or standardized testing, but in the smaller issues as well, like classroom size or when to introduce algebra. In addition, education issues genuinely cut across electoral boundaries. For example, groups seeking changes know that they must lobby both the local school board and the provincial education ministry; and parents or ratepayers groups angry with what might appear to be a strictly local problem will bring their campaigns to the provincial capital.

A reporter who spends any time on the education beat quickly discovers the inherent tensions that make education reporting so fascinating. In addition to the strains between the board and the province, these include tensions between trustees who face re-election every couple of years and the board staff who are in for the long haul; among teachers and administrators, parents and officials; and between groups of parents with

different ideas about how the schools should be run. Others in the community also have something to say about education, especially the businesses that employ high school graduates and worry about whether they are educated adequately for the job market.

Like city councils, some boards of education operate on a committee system. Angela Mangiacasale, who has covered education for the Kingston *Whig-Standard* and the Ottawa *Citizen*, says many issues surface first at committee meetings. Even if you don't cover the meetings, she says, it's useful to keep an eye on the committees and to follow the paper trail of reports, preliminary recommendations, notes and comments from staff that accumulates as an issue develops.

The full board holds public meetings on a regular schedule, following an agenda reporters try to receive in advance. Sometimes, especially when controversial issues are on the agenda, board meetings attract large numbers of parents. Emotions may run high at such meetings, with parents arguing passionately against a plan to close a neighborhood school, or in favor of retaining an outdoor education program that is on the budget chopping block.

For the reporter on the education beat, the round of board meetings gives a rhythm to the coverage. You may write advance stories that let people know an issue is coming up at a meeting. You may cover what happens at that meeting. And you may do followup stories on the
(continued)

implications of a decision made by the trustees. Some stories are of interest mainly to parents and children, the key consumers of education. Others, especially those dealing with taxation, have a built-in interest factor for all taxpayers, not just parents.

But education reporting should go far beyond the board meeting room. It requires an ability to spot trends or to see the links between seemingly unconnected events at disparate schools. And because education reporters deal with a broad range of people — politicians, bureaucrats, parents and children — the beat demands stronger people skills than many other reporting specialties.

Education writers deal with a whole range of issues — violence and drug use in schools, AIDS education or breakfast programs for poor children — that are part of the larger mix of local coverage. They also have the opportunity to look in depth at one of the core issues in society: how to raise, educate and train the next generation. This leads to examination of education policy, including what is taught in the classroom, how to reduce Canada's dropout rate and what is being done to keep teens in school or to bring dropouts back in. Schools are places where the children of refugees and immigrants are integrated into Canadian society, where the right education can open the doors out of poverty and where the wrong move can slam those doors shut.

School boards can be difficult institutions for a reporter to crack. Because they deal with children, trustees and employees tend to be protective of their charges and suspicious of outsiders. In addition, they operate within a complex set of provincial and federal laws — privacy laws, the Young Offenders Act or the Charter of Rights and Freedoms, to name a few — that do not address specifically the question of educating children but may come into play in the schools.

It takes time to get to know the institutions, the process and the players. Mangiacasale says principals may be reluctant to let reporters inside a school, and may insist that the reporter go through the board's public relations office. But it's well worth the effort to get into the classroom, Mangiacasale says. "Some of the most enlightening time I've spent is in a school. That's the only way to really see what is going on."

When she interviews children, she often clears their quotations with principals or parents. Contacting the parents is useful, she says, in more ways than one. First, the parents appreciate the call and rarely have any objections to her using the quotation. Second, they may have new information to add to the story or they may want to talk about something else going on in the schools that has been annoying them.

Some reporters find trustees particularly frustrating to deal with. Trustees are elected officials, but tend to have a far lower profile

(continued)

than candidates for city council. Trustee contests attract far less coverage than council races and as a result, voters in a city or large town may know almost nothing about the people they're electing.

In general, trustees tend to be less skilled in the practice of politics than city councillors. As a result, the reporter who covers a school board encounters a level of politics that is at times unsophisticated, and occasionally raw. Many trustees have no ambition to move on to other political jobs: they run for re-election term after term and develop a good deal of expertise. Others see it as a first step toward a political career. And they may make embarrassing mistakes while they learn the ropes.

It also takes time to learn the jargon. School board reports are littered with acronyms and weighed down with tremendously dense language. Many school board officials use similar jargon in interviews. ("We're trying to foster improved interaction between the children and their peers during the noon-hour period.") This means reporters have to be particularly adept at asking synthesizing questions. ("So what you're saying is, you're trying to get the kids to use better table manners at lunch. Is that correct?")

Education reporters have a number of avenues beyond the trustees and the board administrative staff to get at information. A key one is teachers unions, which tend to be strong, well organized and able to provide articulate comment on many issues.

Advisory committees and parents' organizations are also valuable. Both groups tend to be well informed about board business, but have their own ideas of how the board should operate. Principals, librarians and individual teachers are important contacts, as are support staff at the board offices who can fill you in on meeting agendas.

Officials in the provincial education ministry are also good sources of information, as are local members of the provincial legislature. Finally, there's a broad range of people who have a special interest (and expertise) in education issues: business groups, organizations specializing in immigrant services, consultants, university experts and many others.

"Education is like any other reporting," says Mangiacasale. "It means talking to people. Lots of people. And not always the same people."

Municipal Elections

Municipal elections are held on a regular schedule every three years or so, and they offer local reporters a chance to shine. National or provincial elections are fought out in events staged for the TV networks. At the municipal level, on the other hand, local newspapers, radio and TV stations play a vital role. The politicians depend on the local media to get their message across. The voters depend on the local media for information on the candidates and the issues. In addition, reporters covering the elections find that local contests can be tight, intensely competitive and full of odd twists and turns.

Election stories can take many forms. But in general, there are three basic types.

Stories that Focus on the Candidates. These stories may be personal profiles or may examine who the candidates' supporters are (including, perhaps, the party affiliations of their major backers), and what local interests they represent. Stories about incumbents may examine their attendance record at council or the records of their fund-raising for the previous election. Stories may also analyse how effective a councillor has been on council or in dealing with the citizens groups in the wards.

Some newspapers run mini-profiles on all declared candidates in a race. These may appear throughout the weeks preceding the election as each candidate files election papers, or they may be collected into a special pre-election section. If done well, these stories help voters identify the serious but unknown candidate and the occasional candidate from the lunatic fringe. Newspapers that run profiles as the election papers are filed say the practice not only informs the public but builds interest in the election. Special pre-election sections, on the other hand, let a voter do "one-stop shopping," reading up at one time on all the candidates in a race.

Stories That Focus on the Contest. Stories covering contests for city council seats are often presented as ward profiles, describing the particular dynamics of the community and how the incumbent and challengers are faring in their campaigns for votes.

In mayoral contests, the number and intensity of these stories grow in proportion to the excitement generated by the race. If a two-term mayor is seeking a third term with no serious opposition, stories about the "race" are likely to be short and bland — mainly because the race is over long before voting day. If, on the other hand, three ambitious councillors are vying for the chair left vacant by a retiring mayor, the race will generate a range of stories. Some are simple news stories covering all-candidates debates. Some are so-called horse-race reporting, focusing on who is ahead. In contests where the candidates hold markedly different political views, stories on the race may focus on ideology.

Stories That Focus on the Issues. Sometimes a single issue will decide the fate of a candidate. A pro-development candidate running for council in an area known for its love of heritage preservation is not likely to go far. In another community one unpopular vote by council — a tax increase or a spending decision that offends a large segment of the community — may mean defeat for several councillors on the next election day.

More often, though, elections are fought on a range of issues — spending, development, housing and so on. One revealing form of reporting on such issues is the "key-vote" story. Here, a reporter looks back over two or three years' worth of clips to pick out the half-dozen or so major decisions of the previous council. This kind of story serves two main purposes: reminding voters of what happened, and setting out a record that shows how the councillors voted. The possibility of doing a key-vote story is a good argument for keeping track of all votes at council and developing a system for filing these notes in a form you can retrieve easily later.

The major drawback to key-vote stories is that they take into account only the views of people already on the council and ignore the challengers. Some newspapers in smaller communities get around the problem by including all candidates in their key-vote stories, asking challengers how they would have voted had they been on council. Another approach is to survey all candidates on the issues. In 1988, the Kingston *Whig-Standard* printed results of a candidates' survey by a citizens group. It found strong disagreement among candidates over where affordable housing should be built and whether the city's public transit was adequate. These answers gave voters a revealing glimpse of the ideas and attitudes of the people they were going to elect.

All good campaign stories help voters make intelligent decisions. They also can help reporters overcome one of the biggest criticisms of their work — the idea that journalists have no long-term memory. If a candidate wins on a heritage platform but flip-flops on heritage issues as a city councillor, it's a reporter's job to remind voters of the record at the next election. This means reporters have to go the extra mile at election time, going beyond the platitudes of the election pamphlet to analyse what kind of local government the candidate wants to create.

RECOMMENDED READING

Dolan, Rob. (1994). *A Reporter's Guide to Municipal Government.* Toronto: Association of Municipalities of Ontario.

Higgins, Donald J.H. (1986). *Local and Urban Politics in Canada.* Toronto: Gage.

Overbury, Stephen. (1989). *Finding Canadian Facts Fast.* Revised edition. Toronto: McGraw-Hill Ryerson.

Stein, David Lewis. (1972). *Toronto for Sale.* Toronto: New Press.

Stein, David Lewis. (1993). *Going Downtown: Reflections on Urban Progress.* Ottawa: Oberon.

Tindal, C.R., and S. Nobes Tindal. (1990). *Local Government in Canada.* 3rd edition. Toronto: McGraw-Hill Ryerson.

CHAPTER 12

Covering
the
Capitals

N THEORY, THE CAREER PATH FOR POLITICAL reporters is clearly defined. After a brief stint as a general assignment reporter, they transfer to city hall, then to the provincial capital and eventually, after several years of seasoning, to Parliament Hill. This path has a certain logic: at each stage they develop technical knowledge and skills (how to read a budget, how to interpret a government report, how to use access-to-information laws) and a deepening understanding of politics and the process of government.

In view of this pattern, it might seem that a basic reporting text could safely ignore the topic of political reporting at the senior levels. However, the career path is by no means uniform: Canadian journalism is full of examples of reporters who made the leap from city hall to Parliament Hill, or who landed an assignment to the legislature after only a few months on staff. More important, journalists who work far from the capitals need at least a basic knowledge of how political reporting works. They need it if they're handling national news on a radio newsdesk, for instance, or if they're interviewing an MP or a visiting cabinet minister, writing an editorial for a specialized magazine, or exploring a local story that demands added material from higher levels of government.

The previous chapter looked at covering government at the local level. This one introduces some of the basic concepts and components of covering government at the higher levels, without getting into more intricate matters such as analysis of budgets and spending estimates. The recommended readings at the end direct you to sources for more in-depth study.

Any analysis of political reporting must begin with the recognition that government operates on two levels. There is the public show — the daily scrums, question period, news conferences or "photo ops" — and behind it a private world where the real decisions are made. As a rule, the higher the level of government, the more sophisticated and extensive is the public show. Ironically, many of the very politicians who provide the show complain that the media pay too much attention to it. And reporters who complain about being manipulated still find it difficult to avoid the staged events.

The maturity of many reporters is judged by their ability to put the public show in perspective, to get behind it for thorough reporting and explanation of the real decisions. This means staying detached from the

(Ross Allard/Loyalist College)

It's hard for journalists not to choose sides — even in the images they publish. These pictures from the 1995 Quebec referendum tell quite different stories. Each is valid, but neither tells the full story. For the writer, telling the complete story means selecting details that accurately reflect the tone and texture of the event. (Jeremy Ashby/Loyalist College)

manipulation of sources and from the conventional wisdom of colleagues. It is no easy task.

Journalists covering the capitals fill an uneasy but important social role. In part they are simply chroniclers of government decisions. In part they are tools of accountability — acting as outside invigilators, public scolds or watchdogs on government action. They act as a connective among the diverse and often clashing players in and around government. They make important decisions on what to cover and what views of an issue will be considered respectable. Within any press corps, a few journalists emerge as leaders, shaping private opinion among their colleagues who in turn shape public opinion.

Other players in the political world treat journalists with a mixture of benevolence, fear and contempt. Some politicians blatantly court their attention. Others treat reporters with disdain — but nonetheless never make a move without considering what kind of press it will get. Public servants tend to regard journalists as nuisances, always demanding too much, always over-simplifying, always stressing conflict and error. At times, though, some public servants see reporters as useful weapons in fighting their own battles against a wrong-headed policy.

Perhaps more than any other group of journalists, political journalists become masters in the art of leverage. On a basic level, they use the revelations of opposition members to get government people to react. On a more complex level, they use whatever they learn — in specialized journals or committee transcripts, or in cocktail party conversation — as material for a constant, subtle game of information bartering. No manual exists that describes how this process works. But at the top of the list of job requirements are a fascination with the intricate ways in which governments operate and an understanding that the exercise of power brings out both the best and the worst in people. Political reporting deals with genuine efforts to create a better world, and with corruption and greed and waste. The task of reporting on all this is seldom easy, but always engaging.

MAPPING OUT THE BEAT

The legislature-style government in Ottawa and the provincial capitals is markedly different from local governments. Local structures may be changed at the will of the province. By contrast, the provincial and federal governments have constitutional guarantees, defined in the British North America Act of 1867, reinforced in the 1982 Constitution Act and subjected to a steady stream of renegotiation and redefinition in the

1980s and early 1990s. A province is *not* a federation of municipalities; in a very real sense, Canada *is* a federation of provinces, which are also political entities in their own right.

In addition, the party system that permeates the legislatures and Parliament dictates a different way of obtaining and exercising power. In most cities and towns, the mayor is elected as an individual, with no control over the selection of the council. Prime ministers and premiers, on the other hand, govern by choosing a cabinet of party colleagues, and last as leaders as long as they can maintain cabinet solidarity and caucus support. Prime ministers depend on the loyalty of their people — and their people in turn depend on the leader for hope of advancement. That mutual dependence creates a cohesion, a "circling of the wagons" that is difficult for reporters to penetrate. One way to break through is to keep track of two groups: the rising stars (the new MP who is destined for a cabinet spot in the next shuffle) and the potential dissidents (the disaffected cabinet minister who is soon to be an ex-minister, or the backbencher who feels excluded from the centre of power).

Opposition parties follow arrangements similar to those of governing parties. Opposition leaders set up a "shadow cabinet" of caucus members who serve as critics in specialized areas. Opposition parties share with the news media a similar outlook on the government: both see themselves as instruments for ensuring government accountability. Reporters and opposition politicians thus often share a natural but dangerous affinity. Members of an opposition party are key sources of information about government misdeeds. But opposition parties, too, have systems to ensure solidarity and loyalty, and they quickly turn off the flow of information when attention turns to the internal stresses and strains of their own party. The natural affinity between reporter and opposition politician often comes to an abrupt end when the opposition party becomes the government.

In general, the reporter covering a provincial legislature and the reporter covering Parliament do roughly the same kind of work. At the provincial level, the focus of political activity is the legislature, where legislation is proposed, debated, approved in principle, referred to committee, returned to the house with amendments and eventually approved. At the federal level, there are two chambers to track — the House of Commons and the Senate. In many federal states, the upper chamber's role is to represent at a national level the constituent parts of the federation. In its own odd way, the Canadian Senate fulfils this role. It operates on a democratic model of debates and votes, though its members are appointed, not elected. And the appointment system for senators has a regional basis, though provincial governments play no part constitutionally in the selection of senators.

For many years, the Senate was almost a forgotten chamber. Reporters paid little attention to it unless something unusual occurred. In recent years, however, the Senate has taken a more active — and at times fiercely partisan — role. As a result, it is an increasingly important source of stories.

Much of the real work of government is done by members of the professional public service, however. Reporters recognize this by spending a good deal of their time away from the legislatures, reporting on administrative decisions and problems. In this area they deal with several forms of bureaucracies — including government departments, Crown corporations and independent regulatory agencies. Government departments, such as Health Canada or Citizenship and Immigration Canada, are headed by a cabinet minister and are responsible for running programs and providing services to the public. Crown corporations, such as the CBC or Telefilm Canada, are created by government for a special purpose and have far more autonomy than government departments. Regulatory agencies, such as the Canadian Transportation Agency or the Canadian Radio-television and Telecommunications Commission, operate autonomously from the governments that create and fund them. Many of these agencies have quasi-judicial powers.

The structure and operation of the bureaucracy have some important implications for reporters. First, there's a built-in tension between the minister and the department the minister runs. The cause is simple: ministers are transients who may have no specialized knowledge of the department; bureaucrats are experts, people who have built a career in the department. Exploring this tension is a natural point of entry into many stories. In addition, because they do so much of the work of government, the bureaucratic institutions are newsworthy in their own right. Some reporters make careers out of mining one or more departments for, say, developments in agriculture policy or trade policy. They rarely set foot in the legislative chamber.

The reporter preparing to cover the capital can't just walk in cold and expect to start producing stories at top speed or quality. It takes time and energy to figure out how things work and where to find solid information. The *Parliamentary Guide*, government phone directories, guides to programs and services, and materials prepared for use in access-to-information requests are basic reading for the new reporter. For a fuller discussion of obtaining and using government documents, see Chapter 3, "Research Sources."

SORTING OUT THE COVERAGE

The *Toronto Star*'s Ottawa bureau occupies a suite of offices in the National Press Building, across Wellington Street from the Parliament Buildings. With nine staff members, the bureau is one of the larger ones on Parliament Hill, but like all other bureaus seems never to have enough people to cover all the potential stories.

On any day, committees may be meeting, examining legislation or hearing experts or public interest groups. Royal commissions and regulatory agencies may be holding hearings. Lobby groups may be giving press briefings. The Senate may be in one of its periodic revolts, demanding attention. Demonstrators may be parading outside the Peace Tower. In the Conference Centre nearby, federal-provincial negotiations of one kind or another may be under way. Down Wellington Street, the Supreme Court may be handing out a batch of decisions. In the House of Commons itself, the opposition parties prepare for question period, their daily attack on the government. Reporters for The Canadian Press/La Presse Canadienne (CP), the national news agency owned by the newspapers, provide much of the bread and butter coverage of these happenings. But news outlets can't rely on CP the way they once did: in the wake of threats by some newspapers to pull out of the co-operative, CP has made deep cuts in its budget and staffing. The Ottawa bureau has been reduced to fewer than 10 reporters from 35 just five years ago. As a result, CP reporters have had to combine beats and policy specialties, sacrificing depth of coverage.

The *Star*'s Ottawa bureau works on a beat system that encompasses policy areas and politics, says Rosemary Speirs, former Ottawa bureau chief and now Ottawa columnist. For example, one reporter covers external affairs, defence and immigration while another covers economic policy, free trade and taxes. Each reporter also follows a political party. Since there are more reporters than parties, every party gets the attention of more than one reporter.

Speirs says reporters usually have a pretty clear idea of what they plan to cover before they arrive at the office. They know what's coming up on their beats this afternoon, this week and next month. They know committee schedules, and which meetings are likely to produce background or live stories. They know that if a group is testifying before a committee, odds are it will also hold a press conference. They know which issues the opposition parties are eager to bring up in question period. Editors back in Toronto have their own ideas about stories they want chased. And there are often surprises. A daily organizing session, therefore, is essential. At 9 a.m. each workday, the entire bureau gets together to map out the day's coverage plans. The columnist tracks the news too, but is less caught up in the day-to-day flow of events. Carol Goar, now a *Star* editorial writer in Toronto, says that when she was the paper's Ottawa columnist she wrote about things she thought the readers ought to know more about, or that she found interesting. She describes the job as cherry picking — selecting what's most attractive or tasty from among the weekly banquet of news.

When Parliament is in session, the work week for MPs (and reporters) follows the rhythm of the House. The policy and priorities committee, the so-called inner cabinet, meets Tuesdays. All three parties hold caucus meetings on Wednesdays. Cabinet meets on Thursdays and so on. Question period occurs daily at 2 p.m., except on Fridays when it starts at 11 a.m. It is followed by the scrum — the chance to interview ministers or opposition members in the hall outside the chamber. The *Star* always has a reporter in the House for question period. Three or four others go over for the scrums.

Reporters who cover provincial legislators follow similar rhythms on their jobs. Don Campbell, now an assignment editor at the *Calgary Herald*, recalls that when he covered the Manitoba legislature for the *Winnipeg Free Press* his day usually began with a committee hearing. Question period and the inevitable scrums followed. The day ended with an ear tuned to the debates in the legislature.

The tone and pace of a chamber — and therefore of the job of covering it — vary according to a whole range of factors. In the early days of a session, there is little legislation for committees to examine. Near the end, as government presses to get its legislation through, the work intensifies. Other things also exert an influence: the proximity of the next election, plans for a party leadership convention, new polls showing a change in public opinion, a change in the state of the economy, a looming international crisis, a scandal in caucus and so on.

While reporters follow the timing of the people they cover, governments and parties are also keenly aware of the time constraints of the reporters, and so they time things for best coverage. "Good news" announcements, typically, are timed to catch the evening news or the first deadline of the major dailies. "Bad news" is released on Friday at about 6 p.m., perhaps in the hopes that reporters will miss it, news organs will not be able to make a big splash of it, or readers and viewers will be more interested in their weekends than in the news. A cabinet minister may leave the capital to make an announcement, in the hope of getting more coverage or more favorable coverage.

Parliament and the legislatures are in session for only part of the year — roughly six months for the House of Commons and some legislatures, less in other provinces. This doesn't mean, however, that the business of government comes to a stop when the House rises.

"When the House isn't sitting, people have a bit more time to develop their beats independently, rather than being driven by events," says the *Star's* Carol Goar. "But you still get the daily onslaught of press conferences and so on. You almost always find that when Parliament isn't sitting, something moves in to fill the vacuum."

Dale Eisler, who covered the Saskatchewan legislature for the Regina *Leader-Post* and now is a senior writer for *Maclean's* in Calgary, agrees. "Sometimes the government does major initiatives when the legislature is *not* in session, because there's no question period. Essentially, you're covering the government, not the legislature."

When the House is sitting, coverage includes some routine elements, such as those that follow.

Covering Question Period

For a brief period each day, government ministers, including the prime minister or premier, submit to questions on any subject the opposition decides to raise. The questions range from serious challenges on policy issues to thinly veiled partisan attacks; the answers range from revealing to comedic. In the House of Commons especially, it is an event played out for the TV cameras, and politicians and reporters recognize it as such. But the theatricality of the event does not mean it is insignificant.

"The fact that we can look the prime minister in the eyeballs for 45 minutes every day is an important part of the functioning of our parliamentary democracy," Carol Goar says. "Even if it isn't all you'd like it to be in terms of an intelligent debate about issues — which indeed, it isn't — the fact that it exists at all is important. We should do everything in our power to hang on to it."

Nowhere else will a reporter get as clear a picture of what the opposition sees as the issue (or issues) of the day. This is an important factor in a governing system where the deck is stacked so highly in favor of the governing party. Governments have blind spots, places where ideology camouflages reality. Question period serves in some ways as a reality check on government, bringing to the forefront a range of issues that are not on the government agenda.

Rosemary Speirs says question period occasionally turns up something new. "More often, it gives you a part of a story," she says. Reporters who already have stories on the go find that question period produces a comment or two to incorporate in the story, a new and timely element to top the story or an angle to a develop in a continuing story.

The same is true of the scrums that follow question period, when opposition politicians and ministers step outside the chamber for a series of interviews or mini news conferences to elaborate on what was raised at question period. Speirs and some other reporters call this the daily news bazaar, a place to shop for stories or details to add to stories. The scrums are often criticized as shallow exercises in pack journalism. "It's extremely difficult to sidle up to a cabinet minister in the hall for an exchange that might be off the record, or might be on background," says Speirs. "The cameras go on; everyone moves into a circle around the politician to see what's happening. And that just stops any kind of discourse."

Another difficulty with scrums, says former legislature reporter Don Campbell, is that there are so many stories to chase. Most question periods offer reporters dozens of potential stories. It takes maturity, judgment and an ability to focus to decide which one or two to pursue and, equally important, which stories to leave alone. In scrums, inexperienced reporters may find themselves scrambling for so much that they end up with bits and pieces of several stories, rather than enough material for one solid one.

Despite all their problems, scrums offer reporters something their colleagues in other countries rarely get: face-to-face contact with the most senior people in government. Campbell notes that reporters have a hard time getting access to cabinet ministers. The scrum helps.

Covering Committees

While question period is the most high-profile part of the legislative day, committee meetings may have more substance — more solid information on what government is actually doing and what critics would prefer to see done instead. The two key types of committee work are the clause-by-clause study of bills and the more wide-ranging review of the government mandate and operations.

Committees are partisan; their composition reflects that of the legislature. In addition, committees can compel officials to speak before them. Both facts of committee life can work to the advantage of the reporter.

Dale Eisler uses as an example the Saskatchewan committee that reviews the operations of Crown corporations, which are the focal point of ideological debate in the province. The committee includes people who come at the Crown corporation from vastly different points of view and aren't shy about asking tough questions. As a result, he says, the committee meeting may generate serious, substantive discussion about key government policy.

Don Campbell sees committees as time consuming, but essential. Occasionally a committee generates a hot story. More often, though, "their primary value is that you can get schooled in the background on the issues." The reporter who is thoroughly backgrounded in an issue will do a better job of covering breaking stories.

As we mention in Chapter 3, the reports and transcripts that committees publish are full of useful background material. They are also a tremendous source of information about issues and developments that lead naturally to followup stories.

Covering the House

Reporters covering Parliament belong to the Parliamentary Press Gallery, but these days they spend little time in the actual gallery. The business of the Commons still merits attention, however, and most reporters have TV sets in their offices tuned in to the parliamentary channel. Reporters in legislatures that are not televised sometimes keep track of votes or debates by audio speakers in their offices.

Don Campbell says that in Winnipeg, the job of tracking the debates into the evening usually falls to newspaper reporters rather than to broadcasters. The broadcasters have to file early, and tend to clear out soon after question period. Campbell says that while much of the debate is neither interesting nor newsworthy, it must be tracked and can occasionally lead to stories.

Dale Eisler agrees, adding that this is the realm of legislature coverage where news judgment becomes crucial. "Unlike question period, where things are sort of packaged for you and where things unfold in front of you, covering the legislature itself is really the toughest part of the job," he says. "Very often, the debate is dry, back and forth, not much news value, but then, unexpectedly, something might arise — a piece of information that is the germ of a story. That's the less glamorous part of covering the legislature, but it's equally important as question period, or maybe even more important in terms of substance."

Eisler says that instead of simply sitting and listening to dry debates, reporters or columnists can use this time to seek out sources and information. He recalls that he sometimes sent notes into the Saskatchewan legislature asking a backbencher or cabinet minister who was doing "house duty," but not caught up in the debate, to come out into the hall for a talk. "They're usually happy to get out of the legislature, and they'll sit down and discuss all sorts of things." These discussions generate story ideas or new angles on existing stories. Sometimes they have no direct connection to a news story; their value lies in developing a working relationship built on mutual respect between the reporter and the politician.

Eisler says house leaders for the various parties will help reporters keep up with the day's legislative agenda. "And if anything dramatic does happen in the house, you'll hear about it from the government or the opposition, depending on whose ox is gored," he says. Also, if the opposition feels it has uncovered something during the debate — something unusual in the estimates or spending plans of the government, for example — "their press guy will come up to the gallery and draw your attention to it."

Covering Budgets

Federal budgets are much larger and more complex than municipal ones, but at first release they're actually easier to cover. That's because of the system of lockups for releasing major documents. As the name implies, reporters are literally locked into a large room for several hours before the official release of the budget. This gives them time to read the budget document and put together stories. Senior finance department officials also go into the lockup and are on hand to answer background questions. By the time the finance minister starts reading the budget speech in the House of Commons, many news organizations have a package of stories ready to go. Provinces use a similar kind of lockup to release their own budgets.

The lockup is part of the tradition of budget secrecy in Canada, based on the idea that everyone should find out about the budget at the same time. If someone knows what's in the budget in advance, the argument goes, that person may profit unfairly. At one time, secrecy was so extreme that only the finance minister and a few senior officials knew what was in it until just before it was made public. These days, the officials putting together the budget do far more consultation, both inside and outside government. In the fall, the finance minister sets out the broad outlines of where the government is headed and announces new deficit targets. The finance committee then holds hearings, to collect and test spending ideas. In addition to this more open process, government officials are "simply not as paranoid about leaks" as they once were, says Shawn McCarthy, who covers Ottawa for the *Globe and Mail*'s Report on Business. "And there are a lot of strategic leaks," he adds. This means that by budget day, reporters not only have a good idea of the general direction of the budget, but they often know a fair number of the specifics as well.

While the lockup system is no doubt useful for the breaking budget story, it tends to promote conformity. All the reporters, for example, get the same documents and the same "spin" from the finance officials. Some of the best budget stories are those that come out later, written by reporters who decide to look beyond the handouts for fresh or buried information.

Reporters and Sources

In many ways, political reporters are captives of their beat. "We work in a small, closed world, a little bubble in the middle of Ottawa," says Carol Goar of the *Star*. Reporters assigned to cover government look for sources beyond it, but tend to draw most strongly on two key groups: bureaucrats and politicians.

In general, reporters tend to offer political sources far less slack than they offer bureaucrats. Some work on the premise that everything a politician says is on the record unless the politician says specifically, in advance, that it's off the record. Others are less rigid, but are probably far more willing to promise confidentiality to bureaucrats.

Goar says this difference in approach reflects a recognition of the difference in jobs. "Politicians are public people. They stood for office to get these jobs." Bureaucrats are not, and in talking to a reporter they are taking a chance with their careers. "I have no trouble with respecting that," she says.

Politicians have always favored, and will always favor, journalists who are seen as influential, or as relatively sympathetic. These journalists are a prime target for news leaks or invitations to private events. They're the ones whose calls are returned first, or who get through to the minister while another reporter is shunted to an aide. Each press corps has a well-recognized hierarchy, with the national TV people and prominent columnists at the top and the correspondents for the regional newspapers at the bottom. Journalists may resent it when their more high-profile colleagues go to lunch at 24 Sussex, but few would turn down an invitation themselves. To do so would mean missing an opportunity to learn, at first hand, things the reporter has so far picked up only at a distance. It is, however, difficult not to be beguiled by proximity to fame and power. (For a description of the Ottawa press corps see Cameron 1989.)

It is also difficult, at times, to turn down offers of genuine friendship from the people in power. The question of how friendly reporters should be with politicians and their aides is one of the most sensitive in journalism. Some reporters take a purely professional approach, treating politicians as they would sources on any other beat. The problem with this approach, of course, is that a politician may offer far more access to reporters who are seen as friendly — to the individual politician or to the party — than to reporters who are seen as neutral or as enemies. Some journalists feel it's to their advantage to be chummy with politicians and their aides. Others exert power through fear: they get through to sources because people are afraid not to talk to them.

In every press corps, too, are some journalists who dive into partisanship. John Sawatsky's fascinating biography of Brian Mulroney describes one such example — the Breakfast Club of dissident Progressive Conservative MPs who shared Joe Clark jokes over bacon and eggs. A sizable group of journalists often joined the table, not to cover the meetings but as participants. "Within days the same gossip and innuendo began popping up in newspapers — all unattributed, of course, since everything said at the Breakfast Club table was off the record" (Sawatsky 1991, 403–404). The club did tremendous damage to Clark's image and reputation.

Some journalists develop closer, personal ties with politicians, sometimes offering advice or even (though it's very much frowned upon) doing work for them on the side. A few journalists have even taken literally the idea of "getting into bed" with a politician.

Most reporters fall between the extremes, though these days they lean toward keeping their distance. They have strong ideas on what's acceptable, and work to live up to them. "I, personally, would not go out socially with a political aide," says Carol Goar. "I probably would not go to a politician's house. I probably wouldn't divulge details of my personal life to a politician in the expectation that they would do likewise. It's hard to put it in words, but I think I intuitively know the limits. The red lights would go on."

Rosemary Speirs says it's important to set out some ground rules and stick to them. "At the outset of an interview, you decide whether it's on the record, all of it, or on the record but off on some points," she says. She lists other possibilities: "it's off the record but I might ask you later for on-record material on some points; it's off the record but I might write about it without naming you; it's off the record, which means I won't use it at all." Goar adds that if a reporter gets too friendly with a politician, it's easy to forget to set the ground rules. Much of the bad feeling between a reporter and a politician arises when one believes he or she has been "burned" by the other.

Dealing With the Bureaucracy

By tradition and practice, bureaucrats are supposed to be non-partisan. For a bureaucrat to go on record on a political issue is to risk career suicide. But bureaucrats are often the most knowledgeable sources of information about government policy. They may also be the first victims of changes in policy. And like everyone else, they have their own views on how things should be run.

USING GOVERNMENT INFORMATION

BY JIM ROMAHN

Jim Romahn, former agriculture editor of the Kitchener-Waterloo Record, *has built a national reputation for his skill in exploiting government information sources, despite the fact that he doesn't work in a national or provincial capital. His many honors include two Michener Awards for stories based on information obtained via government access systems in both Canada and the United States. In this column he offers basic advice about use of access law.*

The federal government has set up an Access to Information system and most provinces now have Freedom of Information laws that apply to their departments and often extend to municipal governments. But most civil servants remain secretive. That means these systems are bureaucratic and slow.

It also means that reporters should try every easy alternative they can think of before resorting to an application under these systems. Try cajoling civil servants or politicians to get the information quick and free. Consider whether more than one department might have access to the information you seek, and whether it might be easier to wheedle it out of one than the other.

The good news is that bureaucracies can work for you, even though the process is slow. For example, they can work wonders in situations where you have reason to believe civil servants and politicians will be embarrassed about releasing a particular document. But it's also important in those cases to take time to understand the rules, and to follow them to the letter. Any mistake will cost you time and maybe even failure. I have experienced cases where it took five years to get information, but it turned out to be worth the wait, both in terms of the information that was eventually released and in establishing precedents that made it easier for others to get at this type of information.

(continued)

Start the process by finding the person in charge of Access to Information or Freedom of Information requests for the department or agency that has the information you seek. Many of these people are committed to public service, and have an attitude that sets them almost at arm's length from the department or agency that employs them. In other words, they can be recruited to be on your side of any battle to get at information that the law sets out as properly open to the public. Ask them for advice on how to frame your request. Be as specific as possible because if it comes down to a stubborn bureaucracy, they're going to follow the letter of the law. And they're going to take any interpretative escape that the wording of your request allows them.

Many types of documents can cover one thing. For example, meat inspectors working for Agriculture Canada conduct audits at every plant at least once a year and their audit reports detail all the problems. Most reporters have limited their requests to those audit reports, but might have learned more had they also asked for copies of the "plan of action" the company management is required to file in response to every audit report. More can be added by asking for copies of any inspection reports that detailed any fault found with that plant's products arriving at other federally inspected facilities, and for the documentation detailing what happened after those faults were identified. Another set

of documents covers problems with meat that is exported and imported. If the shipments are to and from the U.S., it's going to be faster, cheaper and easier to get the information from the U.S. Department of Agriculture, using the U.S. Freedom of Information Act.

In filing with the federal government, be sure to include a personal cheque for $5, payable to the Receiver General of Canada. And it can speed up the system if you decide, and declare beforehand, whether you have any objections to the disclosure of your identity to any third party involved, such as the owners of the meat-packing plant.

If there is a public interest aspect to your request, specify in your application that you want the department or agency to consider that factor. The courts have been granting rather broad interpretation to this clause in the Access to Information Act, so it might help to pry information out of a secretive civil service.

Consider the reasons why civil servants might be reluctant — or perhaps eager — to release documents under this law. For example, if the information is embarrassing for a politician, some civil servants will be eager to cover their asses, but delighted to see the information become public. By filing a formal request, you give them the perfect excuse to hand over the hot goods. On the other hand, sometimes it's the cabinet minister's office that's eager to fix blame and
(continued)

so seeking the documents from the minister's office, rather than the departmental files, might be the better way to go.

If you're stymied by an unco-operative Access-to-Information officer, try contacting one in another department to get some general guidance and advice. Or contact the office of the Information Commissioner. Provincial departments have similar watchdog and appeal tribunals or commissions. The staff there have experience with a lot of different departments and issues and can provide broader advice. They also work at another arm's length remove from the department or agency that has the information you're after.

Information that's on computer presents a particular challenge. Sometimes departments eager to maintain secrecy will quote ridiculously high fees in an attempt to scare you off. Don't take the first quote as a firm guideline. Negotiate ways you can change the wording of your request to reduce the cost. Or find somebody you can quote as an authority to let them know you have an idea of how searches can be done and what represents a reasonable cost quote.

Obtaining copies is only one way to receive the information. You could also ask to simply view the files or documents, then decide how much you want copied. And you could ask to have the information sent to the department's nearest regional office — for example, from Ottawa to Charlottetown —

to cut down on your expenses.

The federal and provincial systems are designed to let you know about your appeal rights every step of the way, including appeals for time delays, for censorship and for refusal to release entire documents. Take the time and trouble to use them. You will be building not just for yourself, but for everybody coming along after you.

A common reason for using Access to Information is to obtain documentation to back up a story you've already researched. It's not enough to be convinced of the truth; in most cases with any degree of controversy, you need evidence solid enough to stand up in court. Another reason for using the system is to go on fishing expeditions. For example, the minutes of the meeting kept by the Atomic Energy Control Board proved to be a gold mine detailing problems with reactors and radioactive material at everything from big hydro-electric plants to tiny research labs. The *Kitchener-Waterloo Record* used Ontario's Freedom of Information Act to take a random sample peek at health unit inspection reports on local restaurants, cafeterias, supermarkets and farmers' markets. The same could be done for provincial audit reports on local school boards, hospitals, homes for the aged, the condition of highways and bridges, etc. Anything civil servants are supposed to do and regulate will be covered by reports.

Keep in mind, though, that while
(continued)

bureaucratic systems are precise, they are also cumbersome and slow. Often there's a simpler, easier and faster way to get information from government. But if you decide to use these systems, take the time and trouble to learn how to make them work for you. Diplomacy and patience usually work with civil servants, who are often more frustrated than you.

"Bureaucrats have two reasons to contact reporters," says Don Campbell of the *Calgary Herald*. "The first is concern, based on years of experience, about what they see as a boneheaded direction the government is taking. The second is concern about their actual jobs."

Campbell says the key to dealing with public servants is to understand their situation and develop a reputation as a reporter who can be trusted to keep their identities confidential when necessary. Dale Eisler agrees. "As a reporter, you always have to build and develop your credibility. You have to be seen as someone they can trust."

Again, it's important to work out the ground rules. Rosemary Speirs says that in general, the bureaucrat will set the rules. Most of the time, the rule is that the reporter can use the information but not attribute it to the bureaucrat by name.

Even on non-political stories, many bureaucrats are still reluctant to talk to reporters, and may hide behind the complex structures of government. Breaking through to usable information in these structures is mostly a matter of knowledge and persistence, but it helps to remember that some sources are more accessible than others and some are more knowledgeable than others, and that the two are probably not the same.

Most government departments have information offices, but the people who staff them are seldom expert, or privy to the best information. For reporters, the key is to use information officers to best advantage: for information on background reading, access to documents or names of the best-informed experts. By and large, information officers like to deal with reporters without having to pass them on to higher-ups. By and large, reporters who are satisfied with what information officers give them are poorly informed. So the challenge is to pose the questions that will take you past the information office. One former information officer in a sensitive department commented, "I dealt with only two kinds of reporters: those who insisted on getting the information, and those who didn't." Another information officer who, like many of his colleagues, is a former reporter, said, "If I'd known then what I know now, I'd have been a much more demanding reporter."

PUBLIC JOURNALISM

In recent years a popular theme of journalism seminars has been an effort called "public journalism" or "civic journalism," an approach that developed in the United States out of frustration with the democratic process, and more specifically, with the failure of journalism to help people make enlightened decisions.

At the heart of the discussion is a conviction that if people are not taking part effectively in public life, then journalists share the blame. But while many agree on that proposition, fewer agree on what ought to be done about it.

One theme of those who advocate public journalism is that news media should make it easier for people to understand major issues, and then to act to bring about change. As Arthur Charity (1995, 2) puts it, journalists should learn everything they can about "how citizens relate to democracy, how they get drawn into public affairs, what stands in the way of their participation, what information they need that they aren't getting now, what are the root causes of their alienation." Among other things, that would prompt journalists to listen more carefully to the public's concerns and focus news coverage on those concerns, showing clearly what the choices are and how individuals can play a part in addressing them. It would also mean pacing coverage to match public awareness, rather than dropping an issue just at the point when public opinion has come to grips with it. For example, an Ohio paper focused on teen violence for a year or so by taking a number of public steps and doing a number of stories:

- encouraging people to talk informally about the issue;

- helping to organize formal public forums;

- reporting what judgments had been reached in the process;

- taking public soundings again several months later to see how to proceed (Charity 1995, 53).

More controversially, the discussion also includes ways in which journalists can prod the public to act once a consensus has emerged. Debate on that point centres on whether journalists should be pressing for change or simply reporting what is going on. Some critics fear that at a time when reporting staffs are being cut, public journalism may degenerate into publicity stunts in which newspapers pretend to listen to the public and move to fix major problems (such as racism, alienation, delinquency or drugs), but quickly toss the problems back to public servants. Advocates in turn insist that responsible public journalism would stay with the problem until it is resolved, or at least improved.

ON THE CAMPAIGN TRAIL

At election time, some of the worst qualities of both press and politicians emerge. The informal pack — the group of reporters all chasing
the same story — becomes a formal pack, as reporters are jammed
together on a leader's tour. And the tendency of politicians to go for
image and sound bites over policy and substance is accentuated. More
and more, the people managing the tours play for the national cameras.
From the politician's point of view, the ideal campaign day produces
images of the politician meeting workers at the factory gate, a brief bit
of substance on a popular policy and scenes of cheering supporters who
seem to endorse that policy.

Editors and reporters organizing election coverage are of course sensitive to the attempts at manipulation, though that doesn't stop them from
covering the visit to the factory or the rally of cheering supporters. The
leader's tour is still a central element of coverage, though some journalists
try to play down its importance or put it in the context of the campaign.

Political reporters assigned to the leader's tour find themselves in a
small, programmed world, where every basic need is met by political aides
attached to the tour. "They call you in the morning, they make sure your
suitcase gets on the plane," says Carol Goar. "All you have to do is feed
in your stories for deadline." Rosemary Speirs says that although campaign tour organizers take care of a reporter's physical needs very well, life
on the campaign trail is difficult and demanding. "You have to operate
very fast, trying to see the relevance of what the prime minister has just
said compared to what he said on different occasions and what other
party leaders are saying. And then there's that whole question of a reality check — is it true? What does it really mean?"

It's all too easy in a hectic leader's tour for reporters to become part
of the party program. Some media combat this by making sure no
reporter spends too much time on a single tour. Others see advantages
in sticking with a single leader. Don Campbell says the reporter who
stays with a campaign from start to finish has better perspective on the
entire tour. In addition, he says, the reporter can better spot inconsistencies in the politician's campaign.

Carol Goar says the best way to do that is to come prepared. "If
there's any advice I can offer to a reporter covering a leader's tour it's this:
take really good files with you." She carries briefcases full of files and finds
them invaluable in pinning down whether the leader's latest announcement represents a significant change, or even whether a spending promise
is "new" money or a new way of presenting money already budgeted.

THE LIMITS TO CHALLENGE

Journalist and educator Peter Desbarats writes that, while reporters tend to see the struggle with politicians as a built-in part of a free press, a significant school of thought sees these battles as petty skirmishes. This view argues that journalists and politicians share basic assumptions about their societies. And although journalists can be merciless in criticizing politicians, they rarely challenge the fundamental divisions of power in society (Desbarats 1996, 174). An unpublished survey of Canadian newspaper journalists prepared for the University of Calgary by Bob Bergen in 1987 supports this view. It found that more than nine in 10 journalists feel that it is important to investigate government claims and analyse complex problems. A much smaller number — about five in 10 — feel it is important to serve as an adversary of government (128–129).

Rosemary Speirs says her biggest philosophical concern with

THE CANADIAN CONNECTION

Traditionally, Canadians have done well as foreign correspondents. Leading U.S. journalists who trained in Canada include Robert MacNeil, Peter Jennings, Morley Safer, Arthur Kent and many others.

The reasons given are various. The Canadians are said to have fewer axes to grind than British or American journalists. Or they're said to raise less resentment than reporters from some of the more powerful countries. Sometimes, perhaps, they also benefit from the Canadian network.

John Blackstone, veteran of more than a decade with CBS, illustrates the point with an experience from the Ethiopian famine of 1984.

The episode came just after the BBC shocked the western world with the first film on the famine, and other networks were scrambling to catch up. Blackstone, in Paris, was told to get down to Addis Ababa immediately. He recalls:

"CBS had already been scooped on the story since BBC material was available to NBC. It looked like we were about to be beaten again. BBC had returned to the famine areas to get more pictures and ABC had a correspondent in Kenya who beat me into Ethiopia by a full day.

"I arrived in Addis Ababa about midday on Friday, which gave me until Monday to get material for our most important broadcast, the evening news with Dan Rather. I quickly learned from Ethiopian authorities that it took a full three days to arrange press credentials and permission to travel in the famine areas. (There was also a civil war being fought in the famine areas.) If I waited the three days I would have been a clear loser

(continued)

behind other American networks.

"Through Friday and Saturday I put all my efforts into speeding up the Ethiopian bureaucracy. It didn't help much. With my camera crew we explored ways to go without permission to the famine area, but the only means of travel was air and nobody with an airplane was willing to fly without the proper clearance. ..."

By Sunday evening Blackstone was nursing his despair in the lobby of the Red Sea Hotel when a dusty, haggard — and blessedly familiar — figure came through the door: Louis de Guise, a CTV camera shooter based in Beijing. De Guise had his own tale of woe. He'd been covering the funeral of Indira Gandhi in New Delhi and had joined the entourage of Joe Clark, then Canada's external affairs minister, as a way of getting into Ethiopia without much red tape. With the official party, he'd toured the famine area for two days and had great footage.

"'But the terrible part of it is,' Louis said to me, 'CTV doesn't have the money to get the pictures out of here.' To get the videotape out of Ethiopia it was necessary to charter a Learjet from Addis to Nairobi, Kenya, and then buy satellite time and transmit from Nairobi to North America. CBS was already set to do all that, we just didn't have the pictures.

"'Louis,' I said, 'I think this is the beginning of a beautiful friendship' (or something close to that). CTV agreed to share the pictures with us. CBS paid to get them out of Ethiopia. Louis was a hero. And my career was saved ... all because I'm a Canadian reporter."

political reporting is the tendency of the media to fall madly in love with politicians — and then madly out of love a few months later. Reporters often go through a period of admiring a new political leader, offering flattering coverage that ignores or plays down signs of trouble, she says. "Then there's a complete reversal. The feeding frenzy starts, when we're all like sharks after the body." Speirs says both phases are equally intemperate, and unfair to the Canadian voter who has to suffer through the emotional swings.

Speirs says she sees this kind of unchecked pack behavior as a major failing of journalism.

"I think it's really important to have a rule for yourself at the beginning to stay cool. Don't fall for these guys, and don't decide later that they're evil incarnate."

RECOMMENDED READING

Some of the following are basic introductions to the political system. Others look at how reporters work, or the relationship between journalists and politics.

Black, Edwin R. (1982). *Politics and the News*. Toronto: Butterworths.

Cameron, Stevie. (1989). *Ottawa Inside Out*. Toronto: HarperCollins.

Desbarats, Peter. (1996). *Guide to Canadian News Media*. 2nd edition. Toronto: Harcourt Brace

Frizzell, Alan, Jon H. Pammett and Anthony Westell. (1994). *The Canadian General Election of 1993*. Ottawa: Carleton University Press.

Gray, Charlotte. (1990). "Massaging the beast." *Saturday Night*, January–February.

Jackson, Robert J. and Doreen Jackson. (1996). *Canadian Government in Transition: Disruption and Continuity*. Scarborough, ON: Prentice-Hall.

Jackson, Robert J. and Doreen Jackson. (1994). *Politics in Canada: Culture, Institutions, Behaviour and Public Policy*. 3rd edition. Scarborough, ON: Prentice-Hall.

Landes, Ronald G. (1991). *The Canadian Polity: A Comparative Introduction*. 3rd edition. Scarborough, ON: Prentice-Hall.

Taras, David. (1990). *The Newsmakers: The Media's Influence on Canadian Politics*. Scarborough, ON: Nelson Canada.

CHAPTER 13

Covering
the
Sports Beat

SPORTSWRITERS ARE PRAISED AS WORDSMITHS and dismissed as hacks. They are criticized as "homers" when they flatter the home team and attacked as traitors when they don't. The men who write sports — and today, still, most sportswriters are men — are admired by some as the last real men in the news business and derided by others as dinosaurs from a male-dominated past. Some critics like to claim, half-jokingly, that sports journalism is an oxymoron, like military intelligence or jumbo shrimp. In some newsrooms, the "real" reporters — those who specialize in the grimmer worlds of crime, politics or business — look at sportswriters with envy. How nice it would be, they think, to work in "the toy department."

But behind the many myths of sports writing is the reality that sportswriters produce more copy — and more of it on deadline — than many other reporters. They cope with more than their share of the usual reporting pressures: demanding sources, critical readers and second-guessing executives. And they're expected to *write*, not just to set down facts.

In his memoirs of a four-decade-long career as a sportswriter, Trent Frayne writes: "some people with nine-to-five jobs may regard the sportswriter's life as a ride on the gravy train. ... The reality is that working sportswriters actually *work* in a competitive, repetitive field. Most times, meeting tight deadlines, they see about half the events they're attending, often stuffing conditional leads into their computers — if this team wins use this one and if that team wins use that one, occasionally glancing up from the machine to see how the game's progressing" (Frayne 1990, 308).

Adding pressure to the sportswriter's already intense job is the knowledge that the audience is extraordinarily keen. "We have the kind of reader every other part of the newspaper would die to have," says Lynn McAuley, then sports editor of the Ottawa *Citizen* and now

Outsiders see sports writing as the ideal occupation — a chance to get paid for watching your favorite team. The reality is that it is hard work, done under intense pressure. Here, sportswriter Stephen Forest uses a laptop computer to make notes about a hockey game. (Len Wagg)

editor of the paper's weekend magazine. "They are full of passion, they are knowledgeable, they are connected with what you are writing about, they are emotional about what you're writing about. They hunger for analysis and opinion, and they're very vocal. If every part of the paper had that kind of reader, I don't think circulation would be a problem."

The job of covering sports is far more complex and far more difficult than spending Saturday afternoons watching the home team beat the visitors. Game coverage, like council meeting coverage on the municipal beat, is a basic component of the job. But sportswriters are also called on to cover an enormous range of stories — from salary negotiations to land deals, from court proceedings to coaching changes, or from pharmacology to AIDS.

They are also expected to include more opinion and analysis in their copy than are news reporters. For the most part, news reporters are actively discouraged from assessing the performance of the people they cover. Sports reporters, on the other hand, are encouraged — indeed, even required — to analyse what they cover. A court reporter who writes like a sportswriter ("Judge Brown seemed tired and cranky as he took his place on the bench. He rubbed his shoulder, still sore from yesterday's six hours of notetaking …") risks contempt of court. A sports reporter who writes dry and cautious accounts, or who limits the story to exactly what the jury of fans saw, risks contempt of the reader.

Not surprisingly, the best sportswriters tend to be among the best writers in the newsroom — beat reporters who write so vividly the reader can feel the scratch of the artificial turf on bare knuckles, or columnists who can move readers to tears over their bacon and eggs.

For new reporters, the sports department is hard to crack. Reporters on the city side of most newsrooms can often work fairly quickly into a beat such as education or courts and use that as a springboard to other beats. Since beat shuffles are fairly common, news reporters can move in and around the variety of reporting and editing jobs in a fairly short time. Sports departments, on the other hand, tend to be small, stable and tightly knit. A sportswriter may end up covering junior hockey for years, moving up only when the reporter covering the National Hockey League moves on or becomes a full-time columnist. ("Or dies," says McAuley.)

Unlike city reporters who may arrive in the newsroom with little knowledge of who's who at the courthouse or in the city administration, novice sports reporters often know a lot about sports. They may have tried their hand at covering sports for the college press, or perhaps they played sports competitively themselves. In either case, the odds are they are sports fans, people who want to write sports because they love the game.

But being an avid fan is no ticket to a sports writing career. Wayne Parrish, general manager of the *Toronto Sun* and a longtime sportswriter, columnist and sports editor, says good fans make poor reporters. They are so thrilled to be talking to their idols that they have trouble asking the tough questions a reporter needs to ask. They have more trouble than the non-fan in maintaining the perspective and balance that are basic to good reporting.

Parrish says that when he was hiring new writers for the sports department, he looked first and foremost at reporting skills. "I'd prefer to hire a reporter who has an interest in sports and a knowledge of sports but whose primary interest is journalism," he says.

In the past, taking a first job as a sports reporter usually meant following a career as a sports reporter. In recent years, however, cross-overs — news reporters who move to the sports department for a while, or sports reporters who move to news or entertainment — are becoming more common.

In part this reflects growing professionalism in the news business. Most new reporters these days have some journalism training, which helps them move in and out of what were once distinctly specialized areas. Sports departments still prefer to choose their own reporters, though, and may go for people who freelance their way into a full-time job.

Regardless of how they are hired, new sports reporters must be willing to start at the bottom and be prepared to spend a long time there. They pay their dues by covering amateur sports, high school sports, and the occasional tournament, or by working on the desk, putting together the statistics pages. The move up requires skill, talent and luck.

MAPPING OUT THE BEAT

The sports beat of the 1990s crosses local, provincial, national and international boundaries. Depending on the size of the sports department and the season, an individual writer may cover more than a dozen types of sports, and scores of types of stories that touch on sports in some way.

It is impossible to provide any comprehensive map of the sportswriter's terrain, since it varies from writer to writer, from employer to employer and from season to season. What can be said safely, though, is that the job of sports writing is a good deal wider and more complex than most new reporters realize. Newcomers tend to focus on a narrow range of sports — their favorite pro team, perhaps — and on game coverage itself.

But the variety of sporting activity in a community is tremendously broad, and the range of possible stories is equally large. Think, for example, of running. Some people run for fitness and recreation: for them it is a solitary activity. Others are in training for competitions, from local track meets to provincial or national contests, or eventually for international events like the Olympic Games. Both types may come together for mass events like marathons, which are part competition and part recreation. Each type of running may be the source of dozens of story ideas, from equipment to conditioning, from coaching to record keeping, from safety concerns to the maintenance of tracks and running paths.

Most sports departments start with a list of events to cover — tournaments, league games, playoffs — and draw up their staffing rosters accordingly. But the job of the sportswriter is not limited to covering games. Nor is it true that the only sources to talk to are the players and coaches — the people who show up most often on TV.

Around each sport is a constellation of individuals and groups who influence the sporting events directly or indirectly, and may be good sources of information or subjects for coverage in themselves. In the big-time professional sports, like the CFL and the NHL, this includes the hierarchy of coaches, managers and owners of individual teams, topped by a league structure that in essence gives owners a legal monopoly on the sport in their area.

At the amateur level, there are national sport governing bodies, dozens of which are headquartered in Ottawa. These bodies govern the way competitions are held, appointing judges and setting standards and rules. They can provide reporters with a wealth of information about their sport. For example, the Canadian Figure Skating Association produces handbooks with pictures, biographies and performance records of the national and junior national figure skating teams. It also publishes results of all national and international competitions. The national organizations deal with a surprising range of problems — such as training techniques, testing of protective gear, statistical patterns or disciplinary problems — and can provide valuable information for stories tracing patterns.

Governments at all levels play a role in the organization, operation and funding of sports. Municipalities may run substantial recreational sports programs, and their zoning bylaws govern the construction of arenas. Provincial governments may provide grants to amateur sports through lottery funds, or may license sports such as boxing. At the federal level, a massive sport bureaucracy has been created in the years since the adoption in 1961 of a fitness and amateur sport act. Federal money funds the national sports associations and the Canada Games, which were first played in 1967. It is also used to train coaches and fund top athletes, and in the wake of the Ben Johnson steroid scandal, to polish Canada's tarnished image as a "clean" country.

Finally, there is a broad group of agents, marketing specialists, lawyers, accountants, and above all, sponsors and broadcasters for whom sport is not an athletic contest, but a competition for dollars. It is a cliché to say that sport has become big business in Canada, but the reality behind it is an important one for reporters. The business end of the game is an endless source of story ideas.

SORTING OUT THE COVERAGE

The way sportswriters are assigned depends mainly on the size of the sports department. The Ottawa *Citizen*, for example, has three reporters and a columnist on the hockey beat. At the bottom of the hierarchy in prestige and (usually) experience is Tier 2 junior hockey. Junior A hockey comes next and the assignment to cover the National Hockey League is at the top of the line for reporters. The plum job is hockey columnist, a position that offers almost unlimited scope to the writer.

Although there are variations, a reporter assigned to a team generally covers games at home and away, travelling with the players. On days the team doesn't play, the reporter files news and feature stories about the team — personality profiles, items on injuries to players, trades and so on — and may write "advances," or stories that preview the next game.

Alison Gordon, former baseball writer for the *Toronto Star*, says this means the reporters tend to follow the same work schedule as the athletes. They put in extremely long hours during the season, sometimes going for weeks with no time off. They usually take this as time owing for overtime after the season ends, but must be ready to go again in time for league meetings or the start of training. "There's really not much of an off season," she says.

But for every reporter who writes exclusively about major league baseball, there are dozens who cover a broader range of sports. Reporters may be assigned to follow a couple of professional sports — golf and boxing, for example — which do not merit a full-time writer on their own, or to cover a series of popular high school and college sports. Some sports departments assign reporters to an amateur sports beat or to a recreational beat. Others have full-time Olympic reporters. Some reporters are the ultimate generalists, covering whatever needs to be covered; others are full-time feature writers, who never actually cover a game.

Columnists are just as varied as reporters. Some specialize in one sport such as baseball, others in one level of competition, perhaps pro sports or amateur sports. Some write about whatever strikes their fancy — basketball in one column, speed skating in the next, the politics of sport in South Africa in the third. Sometimes, too, sports reporters also write columns, and columnists may act as reporters.

Columnists, of course, have far more freedom than reporters. They confront only a few stern requirements: the column must be credible, it must not bore the reader, and it should not offer grounds for a successful libel suit.

Both reporters and columnists are expected to command (or at least *appear* to command) an encyclopedic knowledge of sport. Some seem to have the rules of any number of games etched into their brains. They are able to switch almost instantly from the rudiments of rugby to the baroque rules for judging gymnastics. Many others, particularly new writers but even old pros covering a new sport, need a bit of help. It is available from a number of sources. Leagues and sport associations put out their own rule books. In addition, big-league teams may produce their own handbooks listing players, rules and records.

Federal fitness and amateur sport information officers put out a looseleaf binder with the rules, contacts and leading participants in a huge range of sports. Individual sport governing bodies — again, let's look at the Canadian Figure Skating Association (1990, 24–25) as an example — produce information on the finer points, such as the difference between a flip jump and a loop jump, or the origin of different jumps. (A glossary of skating terms published by the association will tell you that an axel jump is named after its originator, Axel Paulsen, or that a loop jump means a skater takes off and lands on the back outside edge of the same foot, turning around in the air.)

Popular bookstores sell a range of books outlining the rules and plays of a number of sports, some of them fairly obscure. Lynn McAuley, who more or less fell into sports writing by accepting the only job that was available at the Ottawa *Citizen* at the time she came to Ottawa, says she spent a lot of time studying rule books when she first moved into the sports department.

Finally, university libraries offer a range of academic literature on sport and politics, the sociology of sport and sport history. These can provide good background for new writers and may also be a source of story ideas.

COVERING THE GAME

Television has transformed sports coverage more than any other form of reporting. Television can broadcast complete games, live, with commentary, opinion, analysis, humor and a seemingly endless stream of statistics to enliven the slow spots in the game. TV sportscasts, including the half-hour highlights shows that regular and specialty channels broadcast, show sports fans all the top goals, hits, baskets or touchdowns from the day's big-league games, plus scores from all the major leagues and some of the minor ones as well. More than any other medium, TV transforms athletes into stars. Star athletes then turn their celebrity status into profits by making TV commercials for sneakers or breakfast cereal.

In the days before television, most fans had to read the next day's newspapers to find out the score and to learn how the game was played. Now, says sports columnist Stephen Brunt of the Toronto *Globe and Mail*, "very few people who care to know about a game go to bed at night without knowing who won and how they won."

As a result, print sports reporters (and to a lesser extent radio sports specialists) are under increasing pressure to find the background patterns, the reasons a game or an off-the-field controversy developed as it did. It's not good enough any more simply to report which team won. The reporter faces pressure to explain the hows and whys.

The changes in the way the sports beat is covered, however, should not obscure the continuing basic challenge of *all* sports reporting, which demands a high level of understanding of the subtleties of the game and a high level of concentration. Sports fans transforming themselves into sports reporters may be chagrined to discover just how difficult it is to keep track of the scoring plays, the names, faces and numbers, the substitutions, line changes and shifts in strategy. Only a fraction of this material will be used in the final report, but it is the structure through which the overall meaning of the event is discerned.

Brunt says there are several steps in putting together a game story. The first is to take notes on what happens during the play. The second step — and the most important — is an exercise in judgment. Was one team clearly in control from the outset? Did the leaders run out of steam in the second? Did a nagging injury catch up on a star player? Did a lucky break late in the game rattle the opposition? Did an error by a single player make the difference? Was the opposition able to capitalize on two minutes of confusion on the other side? Did one team play terribly but win anyway because the other team played worse?

"You have to figure out the key moment, or the turning point or the story within the game," Brunt says. "Then you go and talk to the people involved, and write it from that perspective." Often, the critical judgment about the key moment of the game has to be made in a matter of seconds, sometimes as the reporter is heading to the post-game interviews.

For newspaper reporters, the amount of scoring-play material that goes into the story depends on a number of factors, including how close the reporter is to deadline.

Alison Gordon says Blue Jays games usually ended at the same time as her first deadline at the *Star, so* she wrote while watching the game. "Game stories are very difficult in professional sports, and particularly in baseball," she says. "You can be cheerfully writing a game story about how team A is trouncing team B and had it all over them, then you look up from the keyboard a minute and suddenly Team B scores 11 runs in two innings and all you've written is irrelevant."

Gordon says she routinely wrote game stories twice. "You write down the scoring — 'White singled, stole second, went to third on so-and-so's infield hit and scored on Carter's double' — that kind of boring stuff," she explains. "But you do that to fill space. Then, when you find your angle, your lead, you write very fast and file for the early edition.

"Then you race down to the clubhouse, get your quotes, race back up and rewrite the story for the later edition. At that point, you're dumping a lot of that scoring-play stuff."

The game story is a mix of description, quotation and analysis. Here's a fairly typical example.

> KITCHENER, Ont. — The Vancouver 86ers keep on winning — even when they're not at the top of their game.
>
> Looking as though they were headed for a 1–1 tie with the Kitchener Kickers Friday, the 86ers erupted for three goals in the last four minutes for a 4–1 Canadian Soccer League victory before a sparse crowd of 987.
>
> "The scoreline flattered us. We didn't play anywhere near as well as we did against Hamilton," said 86ers head coach Bob Lenarduzzi, alluding to a 5–1 victory over the Steelers on Wednesday.
>
> Forward Mark Karpun, playing in place of the injured John Catliff, opening scoring in the eighth minute and Roderick Scott equalized for the Kickers in the 22nd.
>
> The stalemate held until the 86th minute when Domenic Mobilio scored the first of his two goals on a penalty kick. CSL player-of-the-week Doug Muirhead tallied in the 89th minute to run his league-leading goals title to five, and Mobilio scored his fourth goal of the season in the 90th minute.
>
> The win improved the 86ers' league-leading record to 6–0–2.
>
> — VANCOUVER SUN, JUNE 22, 1991

Even for people who don't follow soccer, this story is readable (though perhaps not gripping). The writer has come up with a theme in the lead and developed it with a quote from the coach and a comparison with the previous game. In a few short paragraphs, the story shows how the final score was a matter of luck as much as skill. It presents the scoring summary in chronological order — the easiest order for the reader to follow — and adds such basics as the winning team's record and the attendance at the game.

The story suffers a bit from the overuse of jargon ("erupted for three goals" … "equalized" … "stalemate held" … "tallied"), though there is less in this story than in many local sports reports. Since game coverage is repetitive and often written to a very tight deadline, it is all too easy to slip into clichés and sports jargon — into using the stylized "tallied" rather than the straightforward "scored," or "equalized" rather than "tied."

The challenge in writing game stories is to avoid this "bop-the-biscuit-in-the-basket writing," as Lynn McAuley calls it. Those who rise above the rest manage to avoid thinking in clichés, not just above writing them. Alison Gordon says she always tried in post-game interviews with players to come up with questions that were a little bit out of the ordinary. "You risk getting the brush-off. But if you're brave enough to ask a question a little bit differently, you can make them think."

Sports reporters have a lot of latitude in deciding how to write the game story. Sometimes, this means going with an angle that defies the conventions of journalism. Here, for example, is a wire service lead from a 1991 NHL game between St. Louis and Toronto:

> The St. Louis Blues aren't just Brett Hull and his entourage any more.
>
> The Blues romped to a 5–1 victory over the Toronto Maple Leafs last night, and they did it without any scoring from Hull. St. Louis is hoping newcomers Brendan Shanahan, Dave Christian and Ron Sutter take the heat off the league's goal-scoring champion. That was the case last night as all three supplied goals.
>
> "Brett's going to score, and we realize he's our top gunner," Shanahan said. "But maybe he's going to get a bit more room now."
>
> Hull had two goals in the Blues' first five games after scoring 86 — second-highest in NHL history — last season. Against the Maple Leafs, his two assists and five shots on goal were plenty.
>
> "I'm just part of the team," Hull said. "I'm just an individual."

The journalistic convention in writing a lead is to tell readers what happened. This lead does just the opposite: it tells the reader what *didn't* happen. (Brett Hull *didn't* score a goal.) But to the sportswriter or the hockey fan, this approach makes perfect sense. The writer could argue that Brett Hull *is* the Blues — or at least, that he has been until now. Therefore, the fact Hull didn't score and that five of his teammates did is worth putting in the lead.

BEYOND PLAY-BY-PLAY COVERAGE

While the game story remains a basic feature of the sports pages, its importance relative to other sports stories is on the decline. Former Montreal sportswriter Alan Richman writes that the game story is the victim of onerous deadlines and the demise of the afternoon paper, "which always had the best stories because its writers had hours to contemplate and compose." Afternoon papers, he adds, are "a direct victim of television" (1991, 261).

With television taking over as the key source for game scores, newspaper reporters must think of new approaches. "The challenge becomes finding a way to deliver that information in a way that is novel — more writerly, perhaps, or more interpretative," says Stephen Brunt of the *Globe and Mail*.

Lynn McAuley of the *Citizen* and Wayne Parrish of the *Toronto Sun* say one of the most promising techniques for sportswriters is to approach a game the same way a reviewer approaches a play or a movie. This encourages the writer to examine the game as a whole — to concentrate on the outstanding performances, for example, or to contrast a player's performance in this game with a previous outing or with earlier credits — rather than simply giving an account of the plot.

The added twist is that the sportswriter, unlike the reviewer, talks to the players afterward. "If a guy flubs a line in an opera you don't go back and ask him what happened," Parrish says. "You do in a sports story."

Brunt sees merit in this approach, as long as the writers keep in mind that a game is an unscripted event, with real players rather than people playing a role. "You can write something stronger than whether it's an artistic success or failure — you can deal with the human beings involved," he says. "When someone hits a home run in a baseball game, you want to know it's a real guy, with real feelings, not someone *playing* a baseball player."

Some newspapers have begun running shorter game stories and longer analysis pieces, or increasing the amount and type of material in the "agate" pages — the page or pages of stats and standings. The demand for statistical material, several sportswriters say, has grown at a tremendous pace in recent years. This is driven in part by the popularity of so-called rotisserie leagues, which feature hypothetical games between teams "drafted" from current players, and of sports betting pools and other forms of gambling.

But while game stories and statistics are basic to most sports reports, a glance through the sports pages of a large daily (in this case, the June

24, 1997, edition of the Ottawa *Citizen*) reveals a broad spectrum of stories. Some look like business stories: Wayne Scanlan's column reviews attempts by Ottawa Senators executives to woo corporate Ottawa; another story deals with ticket discount programs for the NHL team in the coming season; a third piece looks at the challenge to the American all-sports network ESPN posed by Rupert Murdoch's plans for a second network. A story about the opening of the Canadian Football League season the next day leads with the latest departures from the league's head office. There's a good selection of game coverage from major-league baseball and the home-town Triple A team. Other baseball stories look at the latest threat to Roger Maris's home-run record, and the fate of a failing designated hitter. Stories touch on a range of sports: rowing, tennis, golf, boxing, horse racing. One story updates the medical condition of the Red Wings defenceman injured in a limousine crash 11 days ago. There's even a social note of sorts: the announcement that Olympic rowers Silken Laumann and John Wallace are the parents of a baby boy.

Some weeks, says Lynn McAuley, sports reporters spend more time covering lawsuits, business meetings or zoning hearings than they do in the hockey arena. "Some of them tell me they'd kill to cover a game," she says with a laugh.

McAuley sees a need for reporters who are specialists in the business of sports, or in sports and legal affairs. Parrish, by contrast, sees no need for business specialists in a sports department. He says a good reporter is a good reporter, and a good reporter should be able to cover *any* story. "I think your senior beat person in baseball has to have the ability to cover a business story, and to cover it damn well," he says. "He has to understand the collective bargaining process; he has to understand what 'collusion' means; he has to understand what deferred payments mean — just as he has to understand what a hit and run is, or how a second baseman can steal a catcher's signs. If you're good enough to be a full-time journalist earning $55,000 a year at a major Canadian daily, you damn well better be able to understand how annuities work."

REPORTERS, ATHLETES, ETHICS

All beat reporters tend to identify to a certain extent with their sources, but the tendency is perhaps stronger for sports reporters. In part this is due to the amount of time they spend with their sources. A police reporter is likely to check in with key police sources almost every day, often by phone. But when the shift is over, the reporter and the officer go their separate ways. A sportswriter covering a team, on the other hand, may spend weeks on the road with the coaches and athletes, seeing them at all hours and in all circumstances, from the first practice of the morning to the closing of the last bar at night.

Over time, the writer is likely to develop an affection for the players as individuals and the team as a whole, and perhaps even to identify with them. "When a baseball writer starts chewing tobacco," Brunt says, "it's time to get worried."

In addition, a sports reporter's professional success may be tied very closely to the team's success. Reporters covering a team in contention for the playoffs get more room — and better play — for their stories than reporters covering a team near the bottom of the league.

GUN FIRES, RACE OVER

It takes less time for Donovan Bailey to run 100 metres than it took to type this sentence. Unlike a basketball game, a hockey game or even a horse race, the 100-metre dash is over almost before it begins. So how much can a sports writer find to say about it?

Plenty, as it turns out.

The following leads come from two races dominated by Canada's Donovan Bailey: the 100-metre race at the 1996 Olympic Games in Atlanta and the 150-metre "match race" between Bailey and American sprinter Michael Johnson in Toronto, almost a year later.

All these leads show flair and imagination. Several of them also reflect efforts at putting the single, short race in some sort of context. But as you read them, consider these points:

- Which leads are the most imaginative? Which are the most readable?

- Is the tone of the leads justified?

- What does the tone say about the writer's relationships to the athlete and the audience?

- Do any of these writers step over the line from reportage to promotion, or to self-indulgence?

- What techniques do the sportswriters use to grab and maintain the interest of readers who have probably already seen the race on television?

Atlanta, Ga., July 1996

The 100-metre race was held on a Saturday, in the midst of a frantically busy weekend for athletes and reporters, and less than a day after a bomb went off in a park next to the Olympic site. As the sprinters lined up at the starting line, the print reporters knew their readers would be watching the race on television. But they hoped to produce accounts that would feel fresh to readers who already knew the results.

World's Fastest Human. Donovan Bailey wore that title for a year after winning his

(continued)

1995 world championship, but only the few faithful really could say it with a straight face. He was the one-shot wonder who never took training seriously, who had come out of nowhere and — so the experts believed — was destined to return there at these Olympic Games.

But when the 100-metre final threatened to come apart at the seams Saturday night, guess who didn't flinch? When the field had to start over three times, which seemed certain to cost the runners, guess who still had gas in the tank?

When the defending Olympic champ, England's Linford Christie, was disqualified after his second false start, guess who wasn't fazed? And when Christie and Trinidad's Ato Boldon nearly came to blows after the race, while American Dennis Mitchell was decrying it as "the most unprofessional race I've ever seen in my life," guess who was out on the track, doing a victory lap with the Canadian flag held aloft?

The World's Fastest Human, that's who. Now official.
— Cam Cole, Edmonton Journal

Canada Rules.

Best on the water, best on the land. Bring on the air.
— Steve Milton, Hamilton Spectator

It's a hot, wet day in Georgia. The sky hangs low and weepy over bomb-riddled Olympic Park. Soggy tourists wearing T-shirts festooned with Olympic pins like battle decorations slog through the humid air, stunned and sweating.

In the cafeteria at the main press centre — this would be the cafeteria overlooking the stage where the bomb went off at Olympic Park early Sunday morning — someone drops a tray with a bang. Two hundred journalists leap to their feet, ready to run, dive for cover or take notes.

In this atmosphere, bomb scares multiply like fungus. A midtown shop-and-party mall called the Underground is evacuated so the bomb squad can blow up an iron someone left lying around in a duffel bag. (We have questions about this: how did

they know it was an iron after they blew it to smithereens? And who walks around with an iron in a duffel bag, anyway?)

No matter. We will forget the bad parts. Think back on this humid, terror-stricken Olympics two years or 20 years from now and you'll remember one thing: Donovan Bailey's long-legged strides eating track, Donovan Bailey blowing the doors off strong and famous men in a race where even the losers are quicker than a rumor. Donovan Bailey going gold.

What Bailey did Saturday night, a gold medal and a world record, was worth a dozen medals in ping-pong, fencing, mountain biking or beach volleyball put together. Win the men's 100 metres on the track and you're the man. There is no other. Donovan Bailey is king of the hill.
— Jack Todd, Montreal Gazette

Nothing was going to throw Donovan Bailey off stride Saturday night. Not three false starts. Not a temper tantrum by Linford Christie. This was going to be Bailey's moment of glory, his gold medal to lose.

And in one of sport's greatest, most electrifying events, the men's 100-metre sprint, Bailey came through for himself and two nations, winning Olympic gold with a world-record time of 9.84 seconds.
— Allan Maki, Calgary Herald

As he circled the Olympic Stadium track draped in the Canadian flag, Donovan Bailey sent one poignant message.

The legacy of Ben Johnson is dead. The past is buried. All the disgrace, heartache and national embarrassment are gone.

Long live Donovan Bailey. The World's Fastest Human — ever.
— Scott Taylor, Winnipeg Free Press

An Olympic gold medal and a world record.

Give Donovan Bailey credit. It doesn't get any better than that.

The fastest man in the world is a Canadian again. A Jamaican-born Canadian, he insisted. A Jamaican first, he made sure

(continued)

everyone at the post-race press conference understood.

Okay, he can have it his way. Part of the country might have begun throwing things when he said that, but in Canada, he is entitled.
— DAVE PERKINS, TORONTO STAR

One night, Donovan Bailey ran like the blazes and returned the title of World's Fastest Man to Canada.

The next day he spent diplomatically putting out fires after proclaiming himself "Jamaican first."

Bailey gave Canada a thrill on Saturday night that it probably hadn't felt since watching the 1988 Seoul Olympics with his world record of 9.84 seconds in the Olympic 100 metres.

As he crossed the finish line, and he saw his record-breaking time, Bailey's jaw dropped to his chest revealing a mouth the size of a bucket and he screamed with joy. Then he ran to the packed stands where he was handed a Canadian maple-leaf flag.
— JAMES CHRISTIE, GLOBE AND MAIL

Toronto's SkyDome, June 1997

It seemed like a good idea: a race between the world-record holders in the 100 and 200 metres, run at a distance that split the difference. But like many good ideas, it suffered in the execution.

Much of the story before this race had to do with problems of the event's organization. The race itself was equally jinxed. Johnson pulled up lame halfway down the course. This time, the sports writers had a different — and in many ways, more complex — story to tell.

The fastest man in the world is still a Canadian.

"Still," say those who believed what they saw in the Olympic 100-metre final last summer, and had their belief confirmed when Donovan Bailey beat Michael Johnson in their much-hyped match race at the SkyDome yesterday.

"With an asterisk," say those who number themselves among Johnson's supporters, and will maintain that when he pulled up short with an apparent injury there was no more possibility of settling matters on the track.

Afterward, aglow and cocky, he was in no mood to make peace. He maintained he always had said that the race wasn't going to prove he was "the fastest man in the world." It would merely "shut Michael Johnson up."
— STEPHEN BRUNT, GLOBE AND MAIL

The winner and still the world's fastest human: Donovan Bailey.

In front of a delirious, Maple Leaf-waving crowd at the SkyDome that endured three hours of boredom, broken by sporadic bursts of excitement, Bailey capped a week of harangue and hype with an almost effortless 150-metre victory over American Michael Johnson, world-record holder in the 200 and 400 metres.

Bailey — who holds the world record in the 100, the traditional distance by which the world's fastest human is determined — surged to the front out of the blocks and had at least a one-metre lead by the time the two runners came out of the curve at about the 75-metre mark.

Johnson was expected to make his move through the last 50 metres, but with Bailey pouring it on, he pulled up, clutching his leg, at about the 100-metre mark.
— JACK TODD, MONTREAL GAZETTE

Canada's Donovan Bailey gave American rival Michael Johnson a beating yesterday — on and off the track.

First, he beat Johnson in the much-hyped 150-metre race to determine the world's fastest man when the American pulled up lame with a leg injury.

As the SkyDome crowd of 25,000 rabidly pro-Bailey fans roared its approval, the Oakville sprinter draped himself in a Canadian flag, hugged his family and waved madly at his supporters.

(continued)

Then Bailey bashed Johnson again, saying in post-race interviews he didn't believe his longtime nemesis was injured at all.

"He didn't pull up," Bailey told CBC-TV. "He's a chicken. He's just a chicken who's afraid to lose."
— RANDY STARKMAN, TORONTO STAR

Canada zippered the mouth shut of arrogant, loud-mouthed America yesterday when Donovan Bailey whipped Michael Johnson in the match race to prove The World's Fastest Man.

The Yank pulled up lame with an injury that Bailey said he faked to spare himself humiliation from the certain beating he knew was about to be laid on him.

Any notion that pre-match animosity between the two runners was also fake was quickly blown away by Bailey after the race: he spoke with a smile, but the words slapped around Johnson, who was in another room having an ice pack strapped to the thigh muscle that supposedly gave out with Johnson trailing and, in the opinion of Bailey, with the stench of defeat in his nostrils.
— EARL MCRAE, OTTAWA SUN

It was, all in all, not our nation's finest hour.

Donovan Bailey didn't get the chance to beat Michael Johnson all the way to the finish line in the (ahem) race of the century — he only beat him to the halfway mark, and jogged in for a million-and-a-half dollars while an injured Johnson limped off the track behind him.

The Olympic 100-metres champion from Oakville then made it quite clear he'd never heard of the expression, "When you lose say little, when you win, say less," by accusing his opponent of being a choking dog and a quitter.

But the topper was a handful of colleagues I am embarrassed to say are Canadian journalists, who had to prove how manly they were at the post-race news conference by publicly rubbing the American Olympic hero's nose in his ignominious defeat.

"Did you fake your injury?" one asked.

"Next question," Johnson said.
— CAM COLE, EDMONTON JOURNAL

Bawk! Bawk! Bawk!

Chicken! Chicken! Chicken!

Why did he have to go and do that?

Why couldn't Donovan Bailey have taken the high road instead of the low-blow road?

"He didn't pull up. He's a chicken. He's afraid to lose."

That's quote-unquote after Bailey was the only one to finish the One To One Challenge Of Champions at SkyDome yesterday.

Sorry. I know you want this to be a great moment in Canadian sport. And for a moment there — 14.99 seconds on the clock — it was.

I'm sure you at home watching on TV thought this was wonderful, Bailey beating American Michael Johnson to win World's Fastest Man bragging rights and $1 million U.S. in addition to a $500,000 appearance fee.

And it was wonderful. It really was. Don't get me wrong. The lasting image of Donovan Bailey ahead of Johnson at the turn and alone at the finish line, looking back over his shoulder will probably endure after everything else is forgotten.

But what was never better than a sleazy heavyweight championship fight in its build-up, ended up strictly World Wrestling Association stuff.
— TERRY JONES, EDMONTON SUN

Fast. And furious.

But maybe a million dollars richer — if the cheque clears.

Donovan Bailey, the fastest man on Earth — or at least so-considered by track fans outside of the United States — proved yesterday that he is as quick off the mark with his mouth as he is with his feet.
— ROSIE DIMANNO, TORONTO STAR

Sports writers and columnists may get as excited as their readers over the accomplishments of athletes like Donovan Bailey, shown here celebrating after his 1997 match race against Michael Johnson. The more thoughtful among them realize that the tendency to identify with local heroes is an occupational hazard, and should be resisted. (Paul Chiasson)

"Sportswriters say, 'I'm always rooting for a good story, not for a team,'" says Alison Gordon. "But let's face it — your life is a lot easier if the team wins, and a lot more difficult if the team loses." A team with a shot at the championship is innately more interesting for fans and reporters than a team with a middling record. In addition, players who have just won a game are happier to talk about it to reporters than those who have just lost. Sometimes, players may even take out their frustrations on the reporters, a modern twist on the classic idea of killing the messenger who bears bad news.

Sportswriters write for an audience largely composed of fans who identify personally and closely with the team. While some media maintain a professional distance with the home teams, others gladly identify with them. (For example, one newspaper may top a home-team victory with "Sox win" while another may go for the more flamboyant headline "We won!")

All these factors pressure reporters to become "homers" — writers whose preferences (in some cases, biases) toward the home team come through loud and clear in the copy. But many sportswriters see the term "homer" as an insult. They may compensate for the natural tendency to root for the home team by being overly critical.

There is no clear definition, however, of what "overly critical" means. For some fans, the mildest whisper of complaint about a team is unacceptable. Others love to have a columnist they can hate — to a point. (Venom simply for the sake of venom quickly becomes tiresome.) Owners and managers often claim the local media are against them. Occasionally, team management will become so enraged by a sportswriter's darts that it will throw the reporter off the team bus.

Given the conflicting interests of writers and athletes, it should be no surprise that relations between athletes and media can at times be strained. Alan Richman writes of an incident where the response to a sportswriter's innocent question — "Kirk, can I talk to you for a minute?" — was a flood of verbal abuse from the athlete and the threat of physical harm (Richman 1991, 255–256). Alison Gordon says athletes think of reporters as "subhuman invaders of their turf."

Stephen Brunt says the sports world tends to be conservative rather than progressive, and reacts to social change rather than leading it. Similarly, the professional standards in sports journalism, he says, tend to lag behind the news business.

A news reporter covering a labor negotiation, Brunt says, would hesitate to file a story that quotes just one side. A court reporter would never file a story that quotes just the defence lawyer. But some sportswriters have no hesitation in writing a single-source story on a salary dispute, quoting just the owner, for example, or the player's agent.

Similarly, no news editor would stand for a column put together by an Ottawa correspondent who takes part in a regular conference call with other Parliament Hill reporters, then writes up the gossip and rumors into a "notebook" column. This kind of column has been a fairly common staple in sports departments since the early 1980s, though it appears to have lost popularity in the last few years. Indeed, a set of ethics guidelines adopted in 1991 by the Associated Press Sports Editors (APSE) organization says, "Sharing and pooling of notes and quotes should be discouraged. If a reporter uses quotes gained second-hand, that should be made known to the readers." The guidelines also refer reporters to the standards of their individual employers on the use of unnamed sources and verification of second-hand information.

Two areas of ethical behavior are particularly troublesome for sportswriters. One is the question of athletes' privacy. A reporter travelling with a team sees the players night and day, in all kinds of circumstances, Gordon says, and has to put limits on when the workday begins and ends. "I often got good stuff at bars, but it was understood that bars were off the record. I could build on that stuff, but not quote it directly. I think you have to say that what goes on in 'business hours,' as it were, is what you cover." This approach can run into problems, however, if a reporter finds an athlete is spending his off-hours in such illicit activities as gambling or steroid use.

A second troublesome area is the broad realm of freebies and conflicts of interest. "Sports journalists have been inundated with gifts on a much broader scale and into a much later time frame than news journalists," says Wayne Parrish. A single trip to the Super Bowl will net a reporter a full wardrobe of athletic gear, from sneakers to sweatshirts to jackets, all emblazoned with company logos.

The ethics guidelines adopted by the Associated Press Sports Editors say sportswriters should not receive any gifts, deals or discounts that are not available to the general public. They say publishers should pay the costs of tickets and the expenses of sending reporters on the road with a team. Writers should not take part in any outside activities — such as writing program pieces or serving as official scorers — that might present a conflict of interest with their employer, or the appearance of a conflict.

The guidelines, which update and replace guidelines adopted in 1975, seem uncontroversial — even basic common sense. Interestingly, though, they generated substantial debate at several APSE meetings. And some of the strongest prohibitions proposed by the ethics committee, such as a statement that staff members should not gamble on any athletic event, were deleted from the final version.

Brunt says sports writing still lags behind the standards in other areas of journalism. "Sportswriters should be grounded in the real world. The sports world is a subset of the bigger world. You can't deal with it like it's fantasy, or another planet. We write about a lot of things in isolation in sport that are not isolated. Racism in baseball is no different than racism at IBM, but we write about it as though it is."

Alison Gordon says sportswriters have to keep their work in perspective and remember that the games they cover are only games, after all.

"I think we tend to take it all too seriously," she says. "I've written columns that would make grown men weep over someone being sent back to the minors. But tragedy in life and tragedy in sport are something different.

"My best advice to new reporters is this," she says. "Don't take it too seriously. And don't get too comfortable."

RECOMMENDED READING

Frayne, Trent, ed. (1996). *Trent Frayne's Allstars: An Anthology of Canada's Best Sportswriting.* Toronto: Doubleday.

Frayne, Trent. (1990). *The Tales of an Athletic Supporter.* Toronto: McClelland & Stewart.

Richman, Alan. (1991). "The death of sports writing." GQ, September: 254–261, 334–337.

CHAPTER 14

Covering Arts
and
Entertainment

A T FIRST GLANCE ENTERTAINMENT WRITERS
and sports reporters seem to have little in
common. Their popular images are polar
opposites: the tough-talking, rumpled sportswriter who glories in booze,
baseball and bad language; the supercilious, black-clad esthete who
writes witty bits about "Art" (with a capital A) or "the theatuh."

Both images are fanciful exaggerations and, like all stereotypes, grossly
unfair. Indeed, sports and entertainment writers probably have more in
common with each other than with the news junkies of the city section.

For one thing, both must have substantial analytical skills, a fair
amount of specialized knowledge and a distinct flair for writing in addition
to fundamental news-gathering skills. The best entertainment writing, like
the best sports writing, mixes basic reporting and analysis into a rich con-
coction that goes down smoothly, with no gritty aftertaste.

The popular music writer must be able to cover a U2 concert, for
example, as an event. He must also know enough about U2 to be able
to analyse whether Saturday night's performance lived up to past performances, or whether the band was off its stride. He must also keep an
eye on the audience — whether the crowd was wildly enthusiastic or
tepidly polite, or whether the audience noticed that the performance
was flat-out brilliant or unusually bland. And he must put all this material together into a review that can be read, with equal interest, by those
who saw the concert and those who didn't.

Similarly, the theatre writer covering the local Little Theatre production of Agatha Christie's *The Mousetrap* should know the play well and should have a good idea of the abilities of the players. She must be able to explain convincingly why the first act of the production worked but the second act didn't, or why the leading man's performance would have delighted Agatha Christie while the supporting cast would have made her squirm. And if she is really good, she'll be able to write in a way that will inform and interest those who would never think about going to see the performance.

To the novice writer, the job of the reviewer seems temptingly easy — all you have to do, the new writer thinks, is have an opinion. But this kind of writing demands much more. It requires an ever-expanding knowledge of the area, the judgment to examine the film, movie or concert in context, the ability to make and sustain an argument that backs up the writer's judgment, and the ability to write so that even people who *hate* U2 or Agatha Christie will read and enjoy the stories. At its most demanding, it calls for the intellectual breadth to relate the specifics of the work being examined to things that are happening in the world at large.

The people writing for any large entertainment department have an enormous variety of skills and backgrounds. Some are populists at heart, able to bring the common touch to subjects as varied as art exhibitions and rock concerts. Others spend much of their time as consumer reporters, offering advice on the best value for the entertainment dollar. Still others write, often as part-timers, in highly specialized areas like classical music, ballet, modern art and architecture. Many work in what might be called the literary realm, as book reviewers or the authors of critical essays on trends in literature.

Some are first and foremost reviewers; others are critics (or aspire to be critics). David Prosser, who won multiple awards for drama criticism when he worked at the Kingston *Whig-Standard*, explains the difference this way: "the reviewer delivers an instant, off-the-cuff assessment of a work of art almost immediately after he has seen it; he writes with its impact still fresh in his mind. The critic, on the other hand, writes at a distance, beyond the immediate impact of the work of art, taking time to examine it in its cultural context from many angles and perspectives, and taking account of what others have said before him" (Prosser 1989, 234). Reviewing, he says, is akin to "the art of surveying," while criticism is "the art of cartography."

At all levels, though, a review *must* go beyond the simple "I liked it" or "I hated it." It must combine analysis of the work with some other dimension of knowledge, insight or experience. That creative combination in effect produces a new piece of art, perhaps more modest than the work of art under review but still something that stands on its own merits.

Elissa Barnard of the Halifax *Chronicle-Herald* interviews an actor at the Neptune Theatre. For journalists, covering arts and entertainment means far more than just going to the show and telling readers whether or not they liked it. They must be reporters first, adding expert commentary as a second level of skill. (Len Wagg)

Few new reporters can expect to walk into a first job as a full-time entertainment writer. Many, however, work their way in from the edges, doing reviews or features on a freelance basis. Others get in by taking a desk job and writing on the side. Like would-be sportswriters, most bring to the job an area of specialized knowledge or interest, gained off the job, and basic critical or analytical skills, which can be honed on the job.

There are few opportunities in Canada for formal education in criticism in the popular arts. Some universities offer courses or degree programs in film studies or fine arts, and McMaster University in Hamilton offers a master's degree in music criticism. But most writers in arts and entertainment learn the craft by practising it. It is no surprise, therefore, that it takes many years to develop a reputation as a writer of substance. And while entertainment writers place a higher value on clever or witty writing than, say, police reporters, over the long haul it takes substance, not just wit, to succeed.

MAPPING OUT THE BEAT

Entertainment departments at large newspapers include an eclectic mix of writers and beats. The *Edmonton Journal*, for example, has specialists in theatre, classical music, films, popular music, television, dance, visual arts, country music, jazz and world beat music. It also has an entertainment columnist and a books editor who commissions and edits book reviews. Entertainment editor Bob Remington says the qualifications of the writers range all over the map: some are professional musicians, others have graduate degrees, while others have no formal background in arts or culture reporting. The movie reviewer is a former sports columnist. The TV writer used to cover the legislature. Remington worked as a city reporter and a TV writer before becoming the entertainment editor.

At smaller newspapers with fewer writers, each writer needs to wear a number of hats. One might cover pop music, TV and popular theatre, for example, while another specializes in classical music, serious theatre and fine arts.

In most entertainment departments, the writers do news, features and reviews in their areas of expertise. If an all-star rap concert is coming to town, the writer whose beat includes pop music will probably do a handful of stories of differing types. These may range from an initial news story announcing the concert date to news and features on ticket sales, special security arrangements for the concert, or debates among parents about the merits and drawbacks of rap music. The writer, working through the concert promoter or agents, may also arrange an interview with the musicians a day or two before the concert, to use in a final "advance" story on the event. On the concert night itself, she will put together a review of the event, and perhaps short profiles of some of the performers, or news stories about last-minute hitches or unexpected developments.

Similarly, the TV writer may spend a few days each week reviewing tapes sent by mail showing programs that will be broadcast this week or next. He may also file news and features on local production companies or celebrities, or changes in the TV news lineup. He may write columns and analysis pieces on television as a medium — assessments of the impact of Newsworld's live coverage of the latest constitutional wrangles, for example, or thoughts on the ethics of a TV network's decision to broadcast scenes of a motorist being attacked by a mob. The TV writer will also keep track of decisions by the federal broadcast regulator, the Canadian Radio-television and Telecommunications Commission, as well as federal or provincial legislation on broadcasting and advertising.

Given the range of stories each writer must do, it's no surprise that editors like Max Wyman, of the Vancouver *Sun*'s Saturday Review section, say the top entertainment writers are top journalists, first and foremost.

"They must possess all the qualities and qualifications for daily journalism," Wyman says. The specialized knowledge of an individual writer, he adds, is a necessary extra.

PATTERNS OF COVERAGE

While reviews sometimes seem to dominate, the entertainment pages also carry a broad range of news. Some of it is local news, stories that simply tell people what is happening in their home town. Some of it is business news — stories about the opening of new clubs or restaurants, the trouble the local orchestra faces in raising money, or businesses sponsoring concerts and plays. Some of it is political news, from city council attempts to charge for parking at the civic arena to changes in federal funding of the book publishing industry. Some of it is cultural news, from columns on architecture to reviews of museum openings in other cities. And some of it is just for fun — celebrity gossip or accounts of trivial incidents from the lives of Hollywood stars.

In general, the entertainment department has a higher proportion of "booked" events than the news side. In other words, entertainment or arts editors usually know well in advance what their writers will be covering. That's because the entertainment business has a strong, well-organized and highly developed public relations wing whose job is to get the names and faces of performers and productions before the public eye. The ultimate goal of the promoters is to create an audience — or a market — for the entertainment commodity they are trying to sell.

Every entertainment editor in the country gets a daily flood of material on the latest in the entertainment business. Some of it is quite complex. A press kit on a new movie, for example, usually contains press releases about the story, the production, the stars and the director, plus still photographs from the production — in other words, a quarter-inch stack of material designed to provide the kinds of pictures and informa-tion the producers of the movie would like to see in print. Most long-time reviewers use these kits only for accuracy checks of names, dates and previous credits. Of more use are the stills: many newspapers use them to illustrate the review.

The daily mailbag also is likely to contain tapes, albums or CDs from record companies for the music reviewer, invitations to film festi-vals and galas, announcements of concerts, schedules of amateur and professional theatre performances, announcements of book authors' tours and so on. As a result, most full-time entertainment writers can plan their work schedule well ahead. But like all reporters, they need to be able to switch gears suddenly in response to news events.

The relationship between entertainment writers and their sources tends to be mercurial. Entertainers and their sponsors, promoters and agents crave publicity and may sometimes demand publicity — until something comes along they don't want reported. The spokesperson for a symphony may be eager to chat with the music writer, any time of the day or night. But if the symphony fumbles on the year's big fund-raiser, or if the board of directors and the conductor have a falling out, the spokesper-son may shut the door on the reporter who asks probing questions.

The fascination the industry holds for media also raises some tricky ethical problems, notably the question of freebies. The trend in recent years has been for news outlets to pay their own way to more and more events, though this practice is by no means universal.

Another issue is the blurring of the lines between the reviewer and the arts community. Some entertainment writers, for example, also work as directors or actors in local theatre companies, or are married to actors and directors. Others may be professional musicians as well as music reviewers. Still others not only review books but also write them. In these situations, arts and entertainment departments do what they can to avoid conflict of interest (or the appearance of conflict). This is particularly difficult in smaller cities, where the local newspaper's entertainment staff is also small, and where the review in the local paper can make or break the season for the local community theatre. Few journalists in other areas make decisions that are so critically important to the people they cover.

WRITING REVIEWS

Most entertainment writing is a variation on basic reporting, drawing on all the skills of research, organization and writing we discuss elsewhere in this work. Reviews, however, are different. In essence, the review is a critical report on a cultural event. The reporting part tells the reader what the event is all about (without, in most cases, giving away the plot twists or the surprise ending). The critical part is the reviewer's informed assessment of the value of the event. While all reviews contain both reporting and analysis, the analytical element is often the most interesting feature, the thing that makes one review (or one reviewer) more engrossing than another.

Jeff Holubitsky, former entertainment editor at the *Edmonton Journal*, says reviewers can't rely simply on their personal taste. "For example, a music reviewer may *hate* Tom Jones, but if Tom Jones gave a good show, the reviewer has to be able to say Tom Jones was a very exciting performer for the fans who were there." Max Wyman of the Vancouver *Sun* agrees. He says reviewers usually carry a lot of personal baggage about the subject they review, but have to learn to leave it at the door. "Once you're inside the theatre, it's your responsibility to try to respond as openly as possible to what's going on," he says.

For promoters, performers and producers, the review means publicity. And publicity is the key to success. A good review can be recycled into good advertising — as shown by the many movie ads carrying the "two thumbs up" phrase used by popular U.S. movie reviewers Siskel and Ebert. Even a bad review has its uses. At a minimum it says this particular event was important enough to attract the reviewer's attention. As David Prosser of the *Whig-Standard* jokes, "only one thing upsets a theatre group more than a bad review, and that is no review at all" (Prosser 1989, 233). Sometimes, of course, the worse the reviews, the better for the producers: a film like *Basic Instinct* was almost universally panned as vicious and unpleasant, but did well at the box office, in part because it got so much publicity.

For the readers, Holubitsky says, reviews serve two functions. The first is consumer service, or advice on how to spend their entertainment dollars. The second is coverage of the community. "Regardless of whether we write about a movie or not, hundreds of thousands of people are going to go and see it. That makes it an event, something that draws people's attention. By any standard, that makes it worth covering."

Prosser says reviewing should serve a broader purpose. "(Newspapers) should review plays for the same reason they should write editorials or features or anything other than plain information of the who-what-when-and-why variety: because they are striving toward the very best, the most profound that can be written about human life and endeavor" (Prosser 1989, 234–235).

While it is always difficult to generalize, it is possible to sort reviews into a number of categories, based mainly on the purpose or intention of the review. These range from prescriptive or consumer reporting to the descriptive review that combines reporting and analysis to the loftier realm of cultural criticism. But the best measure for success of a review is a simple question: would people read it, even if they missed the concert or have no intention of seeing the movie?

If the answer is yes, then the reviewer has managed to speak to the larger audience.

Reviews and Advice to Consumers

Some people read reviews for a simple reason: is this movie, they want to know, worth my attention? In answering the question, the basic review offers a brief summary of the subject matter without revealing the plot, some short comments on the strong and weak points in the project, and a bottom-line evaluation or prescription: "go see it," or "Don't bother." Within that framework, there's room for individual approaches and for offering the consumer advice in context. (The review may compare this particular Woody Allen movie with his previous work, for example, or it may analyse this particular fact-based TV mini-series in relation to the genre of fact-based TV mini-series.)

The writing of a review — particularly a review of an essentially uninteresting play or TV show or movie — requires a special flair. Most reviewers work hard at producing copy that is engaging or entertaining in its own right. Their writing may be playful or poetic, sharp-tongued or saucy, glib or intensely thoughtful. It reads easily — but it was not easy to write.

Some reviews, like this TV column by Claire Bickley of the *Toronto Sun*, offer a straightforward and light-hearted assessment:

> Pay attention, possums: One day, a programming executive came back from lunch feeling a little wacky.
>
> Hey, what's this? the programmer surely asked of the proposal lying in the in-basket.
>
> Goofy wigs, British royals, Hollywood celebrities, cross-dressing, bad taste.
>
> No it wasn't the one-sheet for *The Adventures of Mark and Brian*. That's another — much uglier — story.
>
> It was *Dame Edna's Hollywood*, finally airing tomorrow night at 10 on NBC, and it's the most unique and uproarious comedy special on network television this season.
>
> Behind it all is a 58-year-old Australian comedian named Barry Humphries who likes to don the lavender wig, rhinestone cats-eye glasses and regal persona that transform him into "megastar" Dame Edna Everage.
>
> After years of success on the London stage, Dame Edna has moved to Bel Air, the better so gal-pals Cher and Beatrice Arthur can drop by to dish.

Dame Edna alternately coos over and belittles her other celebrity guests —
Mel Gibson, who can't get past the security gate; Jack Palance, who disappears
with Dame Edna's septuagenarian nymphomaniac longtime companion Madge
Alsop; and Larry Hagman, who's easily confused and prone to wandering.

This summer Humphries/Everage kept 120 TV critics laughing near to tears
for well over an hour — no easy feat.

All in all, something completely different.

— CLAIRE BICKLEY, *TORONTO SUN*, NOV. 29, 1991

In a few short, breezy paragraphs, Bickley covers all the basic points in
reviewing. The reader learns enough about the show to decide whether
it's worth watching, but not enough to spoil any surprises. Bickley briefly
compares the show with another of the same type and finds it vastly
superior. Her bottom-line assessment: "big goofy wigs, British royals,
Hollywood celebrities, cross-dressing, bad taste," but the funniest show
of the season.

Globe and Mail reviewer Rick Groen set himself a far more challenging task in reviewing a 1997 comedy that many critics didn't find
terribly funny:

FATHERS' DAY COULD MAKE YOU SHTICK

Hollywood has a habit of ripping the chrome off charming French comedies
and retooling them into sturdy American vehicles. For instance, *Trois Hommes
et un Couffin* became *Three Men and a Baby*; *Cousin, Cousine* got whittled down
to *Cousins*; and *La Cage Aux Folles* morphed into *The Birdcage*. In virtually
every case, what gets lost in the translation is the original's elevating charm.
Like most predictable happenings, this can be traced to a predictable cause —
that is, to the ocean's worth of difference between a comic film and a comedic
vehicle. The first finds humor in the characters themselves, allowing it to
bubble up from their flawed natures and human foibles. The second is happy to
stick big stars into wacky situations, pretty much ignoring character and striving for a large-screen version of that American staple — the TV sitcom.

With that in mind, welcome to *Fathers' Day*, a flick that continues both the
trend and the result: it's the Hollywood answer to Francis Veber's 1983
charmer, *Les Comperes*, and it ain't charming. This time the vehicle is designed
for two of the bigger stars in the firmament, none other than Billy Crystal and
Robin Williams (who scored a commercial bull's-eye in *The Birdcage*, and thus,
the thinking must have gone, why not fire away again.) Admittedly, these are
a couple of very funny guys, and you can't go too far wrong casting them
together in anything (hey, maybe even *Hamlet*). Yep, Preston Manning could
have directed this baby and generated a few laughs; instead, Ivan Reitman does
the honors and generates a few more — but not nearly enough to ward off our
lingering disappointment. ...

— RICK GROEN, *GLOBE AND MAIL*, MAY 9, 1997

This review operates on many levels. In a relatively short time, Groen
manages to give a history of the Hollywood makeover of a particular

type of French film. He diagnoses the source of the problem — the Hollywood tendency to see such films as comedic vehicles — and makes a link between the big-screen product and its television equivalent, the situation comedy. In the hands of a less talented writer, Groen's approach might sound preachy or like notes for a film studies lecture. But Groen leavens his analysis with humor, including some that will appeal broadly (the reference to Preston Manning) and some that will reward those with inside knowledge (the oblique reference to Crystal's and Williams's bit parts in Kenneth Brannagh's *Hamlet*).

Groen offers a clear and succinct analysis of the film's few strengths and many weaknesses, but avoids taking the easy way out of merely panning the piece. All in all, the review may be more interesting than the movie itself.

Reviews, News and Analysis

A review of a film, a TV show or the opening night of a theatre run can help readers decide whether to see a show. But many performances, particularly popular and classical music concerts, are one-shot deals. Reviews of this type of performance tend to have something in common with game coverage of a sporting event. Lynn McAuley, former sports editor of the Ottawa *Citizen*, says game coverage offers confirmation to people who saw the game, as well as information and analysis for those who didn't. A concert review provides a similar combination. People who attended the show will turn to the review to see whether the reviewer shared their perceptions of the event. Others may read it for news of what happened. Still others may read it for the simple entertainment value of reading the review (a different kind of pleasure from that of actually seeing the concert, but a pleasure nonetheless).

While there are similarities between the seemingly diverse journalistic forms of sports coverage and arts reviews, Bob Remington of the *Edmonton Journal* argues that reviewing is the more difficult of the two. "When you do a review, there is no score," he says. "There is no winner or loser." The sports writer can always fall back on statistics to support his point and round out the story — the reviewer can't. "Reviewing on deadline is therefore one of the most difficult jobs in the newspaper, and those who can do it and do it well are extremely valuable," he says.

Reviews and Criticism

Beyond the news reporting, beyond the speedy analysis, beyond the quick review is the larger realm of the critical essay. This kind of writing is also beyond the reach of most students, even the most brilliant, because it is based on a depth of knowledge and writing ability that take years to develop. The goal is the creation of a piece of critical writing that stands on its own as a work of art.

"The work of such a critic is illuminating, even if the reader has not seen the work of art under discussion or has no intention of seeing it," Prosser writes. "A great essayist may write about mountain climbing. He is not attempting to promote mountain climbing as a sport. He is not attempting to tell people whether mountain climbing is likely to appeal to them or not. He is not attempting to make them better mountain climbers. He is attempting to capture some of the human experience of climbing; of inching from ache toward agony, clinging bitterly to a contemptuously immobile wall of stone above a crunching drop and wishing to God you were anywhere else; of reaching the very limits of power, then attaining a sudden vantage point on the whole world, flinging your arms to the sun and sobbing with the awful ecstasy of the sight" (Prosser 1989, 235).

In this passage, of course, Prosser demonstrates the very phenomenon he describes: his writing has force and meaning even for those not especially interested in either criticism or mountain climbing.

ISSUES FOR NEW REVIEWERS

When an entertainment writer from an area newspaper gave a guest lecture on reviewing to a basic reporting class, he brought along what he thought was a fairly innocuous half-hour CBC TV drama for the students to review. To his astonishment, 28 of the 30 students wrote reviews that trashed the show, in terms much more savage than he would have expected from established reviewers.

Why did that happen? There are several possible answers, and they illustrate some of pitfalls and challenges facing new reviewers.

When told about the classroom incident, Max Wyman of the Vancouver *Sun* concluded that the students had taken the easy approach to reviewing. "It's so easy to do a total pan, and so hard to write something reasoned," he says.

Many new writers confuse critical writing with writing that criticizes. The former is a type of analysis, in which the writer reasons his or her way to an opinion. True critical writing can be quite complex, assessing a number of variables on the way to the "go see it" or "give it a miss" conclusion. The writer praises what needs to be praised, points out the flaws, and analyses the reasons for both. Some critical writing never comes to a prescriptive conclusion at all. For example, the critic might conclude that a play was an artistic failure, but interesting nonetheless.

Writing that sets out simply to criticize, on the other hand, is a form of attack. And it's far less demanding on the writer, since it doesn't require the same kind of reasoned approach as true critical writing. It comes down, perhaps, to the difference between knowing how to grow tomatoes and knowing how to throw them.

A CODE FOR CRITICS

The Canadian Theatre Critics Association, a national organization with about 50 members, has adopted its own code of ethics regarding the task of reviewing. This is what it says:

Critics' ethics are based on consideration for others, just as is any code of civilized behavior. The Canadian Theatre Critics Association accepts the premise that its members are dealing with contributions to the public by artists and technicians who have worked long and hard on their presentation. It is thus agreed that while such consideration must not inhibit the reviewer in any honest estimate, it does presume respect for the contributors' efforts. Membership in the CTCA offers no licence to insult, ridicule or denigrate artists who are serious about their work.

1. It is expected that critics be as objective as possible to achieve a balanced review. Comments on past performances or remarks on physical attributes of performers are justified only when and if the critic can establish a direct relevance to the production under consideration for description, interpretation, analysis and esti-

mate. The production seen should be the production reviewed.

2. The critic should, wherever possible, prepare in advance of a performance. This includes reading all program and advance material provided by the producing group. Reading a new script before attending its performance is optional but advisable.

3. The critic should attend the entire performance reviewed. If a critic must leave a performance early because of a deadline, this should be mentioned in the review.

4. The critic should behave in an unobtrusive manner, causing no distraction to audience members and performers. Arrangements for suitable seating should be made privately and with decorum.

5. The critic should not under any circumstances exploit his or her position.

(continued)

6. The critic should give full consideration and attention to all elements of a production. The work of supporting players, designers, musicians and technicians is important, as well as that of leading players, director and author.

"TV or Not TV"

Another factor that helps explain why new reviewers tend to write over-critical reviews has to do with the distinctly human problem of making judgments.

Picture this: in many households, the television set is on all the time. But most of the time people spend in front of the set is passive viewing. The shows come and go; the viewer doesn't have to think about the merits of each. Watching TV is often a backdrop for other activities, such as eating or talking. And in these days of cable and remote control, lots of people don't watch *programs* at all — they watch *television*, flipping through the 50 or so available channels at the drop of a commercial, sometimes watching two or three shows simultaneously. Now, what happens if you take people who are passive viewers and assign them to watch *one* show and write a critical commentary on it? The odds are that the viewers, who ordinarily wouldn't notice the small cracks and flaws in the shiny surface of the show, will suddenly see deep crevices in the plot and gaping pits in the performances. Some of them, not sure exactly what critical writing means, will simply seize on the weak spots — "Aha! here's something to criticize!" — and use them as the basis for the review. The result, naturally, will be a pan.

Others get stuck on the question of *how* to judge. What standard, these writers think, should we use to judge this TV show? They may be tempted to judge it in relation to the best they have come across in their cultural education — the plays of Shakespeare, perhaps, or the poetry of T. S. Eliot or the films of Bergman. Measured against these standards, the half-hour TV program will no doubt come up short.

The problem, of course, is that this kind of comparison is fundamentally unfair. "The average TV script *can't* be compared to Shakespeare," says Holubitsky of the *Edmonton Journal*. "It's not meant to be Shakespeare!"

A similar problem occurs when new theatre reviewers try to do reviews of amateur productions. If they attempt to judge the local high school production of *Pygmalion* against the Shaw Festival's version, they have chosen the wrong starting point. The end result is predictable: a highly critical review. The reviewer cannot and should not expect professional performances in an amateur production, or anything approaching the gloss of a big-budget show. However, the writer can and should look for zest on the part of the cast or a level of comfort on stage. She should keep an eye out for flashes of potential in young performers. She can also assess whether the performance holds together and accomplishes what it set out to do, noting where it went right and where it went wrong. In other words, she should learn how to judge the context of the performance, which in turn will help shape her review.

The Problem of Personal Taste

Fans of popular music or TV or movies may, like baseball fans, have passionate feelings about their favorite performers. But just as new sportswriters have to learn how to stop being fans and start being writers, entertainment writers have to learn how to review, fairly, the performers and genres they like in the popular culture, as well as those they dislike.

Two things can help here.

The first is to invest time in learning as much as possible about the art form you will cover, regardless of personal taste. You may never, for example, develop a love of 17th century Spanish drama, but with effort and study can at least develop an understanding of it, and as a result, an appreciation of it and the ability to analyse it. As Holubitsky says, "You have to be able to judge a kick-boxing movie on whether it is a good or bad example of the kick-boxing type of movie. Even if you hate kick-boxing movies, you should still be able to review a kick-boxing film."

The second is to develop a realization that each review is the opinion of only one individual. This realization is at the same time liberating and sobering. The sense of liberation comes from the awareness that if a reviewer has made a judgment and argues it well, it doesn't matter what other reviewers or writers think. The sobering part is an awareness that the reviewer is solely responsible for the opinions expressed. The review carries one name on it — the reviewer's. And the reviewer, as an individual, will be praised for his brilliance, or derided as an ignorant lout (or perhaps both).

"I've Always Wanted to Direct"

Some reviewers seem to write more for the performers than for the audience. This problem is particularly relevant for reviewers who have a strong personal background in the area — years of study as a musician, for example — and look at a performance by imagining how they would do it differently.

This approach can, of course, be useful at times, particularly if it helps the reviewer see relative strengths and weaknesses. But occasionally, reviewers forget that the people who will ultimately read the piece may know nothing about Wagnerian leitmotifs, theatrical blocking or hiphop. And a review that is pitched over the heads of the reader is of little use to anyone.

Jeff Holubitsky says the writing "has to be plain and easy to understand, not esoteric and scholarly."

Max Wyman agrees. "You need to be able to use language in an evocative way," he says. "It should not be pretentious or precious. The review should have all the qualities of good writing — clarity, directness, vividness, color. Don't use specialized language." Wyman adds, with a chuckle, that a sure sign of trouble for an editor is a reviewer who fills her reviews with foreign phrases or technical terms.

The Problem of Maintaining Reader Interest

All reviewers hope that their review will entertain and enlighten a broad audience, including those who *didn't* go to the work being reviewed.

The best way to reach those readers is to write a review that speaks to something larger than the individual performance. A review of a Japanese Noh theatre performance, for example, will probably compare this form of theatre with the better-known Kabuki theatre, or with North American theatre. A review of a children's puppet show may touch on the modern history of puppetry and assess the techniques used by this particular puppet group to engage and entertain the young audience. A movie review about a political thriller will probably draw comparisons to real-life political intrigues.

This means reviewers must be aware of the things beyond the doors of the theatre — the issues in the community, the tensions among various parts of society, the political causes that are hot and those that are not — as well as the specialized area of the arts within which they work. "This knowledge comes from being interested in the world around you," Holubitsky says. "It comes from reading, from getting out and talking to people."

Those writers who see the Entertainment section as a chance to escape from the harder realities of writing about politics and business — a chance to trade in their hard hats and battered notepads for a stint in the "song and dance department" — are probably attracted to it for the wrong reason.

As in any other of journalism, work in the Entertainment section requires the ability to research and write quickly, to juggle assignments, to talk with an endless assortment of people and personalities, to read and learn (in breadth and in depth) about the state of the city, the country and the world, and to bring all these things to bear on the production of informative and interesting writing.

RECOMMENDED READING

Berger, John. (1972). *Ways of Seeing*. London: BBC.

Bywater, Tim, and Thomas Sobchack. (1989). *Introduction to Film Criticism: Major Critical Approaches to Narrative Film*. New York: Longman.

Keith, W.J., and Ben-Zion Shek. (1980). *The Arts in Canada: The Last Fifty Years*. Toronto: University of Toronto Press.

CHAPTER 15

Covering
Business
and the Economy

L evi Strauss' investment in multiculturalism and racial harmony in its Barton Street East plant is about to pay off.

The jeans and clothing manufacturer is changing its production from piece work to a more efficient team approach Aug. 11, a move that would be almost impossible if employees could not get along. ...

— JOHN BURMAN, "RACIAL HARMONY PAYS OFF," HAMILTON SPECTATOR, JUNE 30, 1992

Six giants of the U.S. steel industry will launch what they are calling "the most extensive trade cases in history against unfairly traded foreign steel" this afternoon in Washington.

Canada, Japan, the European Community and a dozen Third World countries are expected to be named as violating U.S. trade laws by dumping highly subsidized steel in the U.S. market. ...

— MARION STINSON, "STEEL FIRMS BRACE FOR TRADE ACTION," GLOBE AND MAIL, JUNE 30, 1992

For two years, Alastair Sweeny quietly worked on Canada, a piece here, a piece there, a Laurier here, a Mackenzie there.

From the first cooling of the sea of molten rock that would eventually form North America millions of years ago, to the volcanic contemporary debate over our 125-year-old Constitution, Sweeny collected, catalogued and filed the pieces of our history on his Macintosh computer. ...

The fruit of 44-year-old Sweeny's quiet toil in the nation's archives and his Britannia home is Canadisk, half-a-billion bytes of point-form Canadiana. ...
— Dominique Lacasse, "Historian Puts Sights, Sounds and History on Compact Disk," Ottawa Citizen, June 30, 1992

Three stories, taken from three Canadian daily newspapers. Which ones are business stories? The answer is: all of them. And all are typical of the kinds of stories found on business pages across the country.

Business writing has a reputation for being dry, packed with numbers, hard to understand unless you have an accounting diploma, and less interesting to write than general news or sports. There is some basis for this reputation. Certainly, business pages carry more than their share of specialized language or jargon. Certainly, too, some of the activities covered in the business pages are far removed from the lives of most Canadians. These factors combined make some business stories virtually impenetrable to casual readers, and even to some journalists.

But much of the reputation for dullness is undeserved. Some of the best writing in the newspaper these days is in the business pages. Business and economics writers cover, arguably, some of the most significant news of the day. And in recent years, many news operations have placed increasing emphasis on making business pages interesting to as wide a range of readers as possible. This means, as Kimberley Noble of the *Globe and Mail's* Report on Business puts it, a constant push for "more professional writing, more polished writing and better storytelling."

The business beat is one of the most wide-ranging in journalism. Business stories overlap every other area of news, from the business of running a major sport franchise to the financial worries of arts groups, from the economic development plans of local municipalities to the employment equity laws of provincial governments and the machinations of the federal Finance Department. The "pure" business areas, such as the stock market and the corporate boardroom, are important to people far beyond Bay Street. A factory closing, a new order for Canadian-made telephones, a takeover of a department store chain or a change in mortgage lending policy all affect the way ordinary people live their lives.

The business press itself also operates over a wide range and serves a wide range of readers. Tim Doyle, former business editor at the *Hamilton Spectator* says business stories should interest everyone who buys the newspaper. "We want to inform members of the business community and let them know what is going on, but we also want them to take the paper home with them for their families to read," he says.

At the *Globe and Mail*, Noble says, "My goal is to make sure that anyone who has any interest in the things I write about has to read the

Report on Business — that if they don't read it, they're going to miss something. My audience is not just people in business. It's people in government, people in environmental groups, or people who are the average workers for the companies I write about."

As a specialized section of Canada's elite newspaper, Report on Business attracts both general newspaper readers and those with a particular interest in business and the economy. Some publications — like the *Financial Post* or the New York-based *Wall Street Journal* — aim specifically at the business-minded audience. Beppi Crosariol, who has covered the high-technology beat for the *Boston Globe* and the defunct *Financial Times of Canada*, says the hard-core business audience wants practical information about how to run a business or invest money. As a result, he says, stories tend to be pitched at a different level than they are in the regular news pages.

The reporter who moves into a business or economics beat must acquire a great deal of specialized knowledge, some of it extremely technical. Business writers have to know how the stock market works, or how to interpret Statistics Canada data, or (at least in general terms) how a forestry firm turns trees into fine paper. This knowledge sets business specialists apart from other specialists in the newsroom.

Other aspects of the beat are also distinctive. Compared with sports reporters, for example, business writers tend to spend time in the office rather than on the street. They do more reading and more background interviews than most general assignment reporters. Most business writers would be lost without their telephones and fax machines. And unlike people on the city hall beat, business writers are not driven by a packed meeting schedule. There are, of course, events to cover — speeches, conferences or corporate annual meetings — but Eric Beauchesne, economics writer for Southam News in Ottawa, says the beat has fewer "staged events" than beats like entertainment and political reporting.

As so often happens in journalism, many business writers get into the beat by happenstance rather than careful planning. Noble, who has won two National Newspaper Awards for business writing, did her undergraduate work in fine arts. After journalism school at Ryerson, she landed a job with a U.S.-based business wire, then moved to the *Globe and Mail* when Report on Business offered her a job. Beauchesne was working on the desk at the *Ottawa Journal* when the paper closed. He took a job with the short-lived business wire of United Press Canada and moved from there to a finance beat at The Canadian Press. Crosariol, who has a master's degree in the philosophy of science, started off as a science writer. And Doyle, a sportswriter before he became night metro editor and then business editor, has circled back to the sports department.

Once assigned to the Business section, good reporters quickly become good business reporters. They put in the time they have to in order to learn their beat. They read voraciously, for both style and substance. They find colleagues they can talk to about their work, or co-workers they can use as sounding boards for story ideas. They don't lose their news judgment; they simply learn to apply it to a new area.

Beauchesne says having a background in economics would be an asset to a newcomer to the business beat, making it that much easier to get a grasp on the workings of the beat. But he draws a great deal on his own general news background to get maximum interest value from stories about the economy.

"A lot of people find economics boring, but if you write it well enough it's exciting," he says. "The trick is to get people to explain things to you as they would to the layman. I'm never shy about saying to a source, 'Now, if you had to explain this term to your 12-year-old son, how would you do it?' or 'Wait a minute — can you go over that last part again? I'm not sure I get it.' If you can do that, if you can find ways to relate what you get to the average person, the average person will find it interesting."

MAPPING OUT THE BEAT

Don McGillivray of Southam News uses the analogy of macroeconomics and microeconomics to describe business journalism. For reporters, he says, the "macro" level means coverage of things like taxes, interest rates and unemployment — things that affect the economy as a whole. The "micro" level means stories about individuals or individual companies, or changes that affect a small geographic area. "Of course, it's not as cut and dried as all that," he says. "The macro affects the micro and the micro can be a symbol of the macro. But it's a good way of looking at how business journalism works."

SOME SIMPLE NUMBERS

Dave Wreford, editor of *Country Guide* magazine, says too many Canadian journalists are "innumerate" — the mathematical equivalent to being illiterate.

"In general they are not stupid. And they are literate and articulate," he says. But far too many of them have no feel for numbers. "In fact, they're afraid of numbers."

Wreford says that when he talks with other journalists, or with

(continued)

students considering a career in journalism, he is always struck by their lack of mathematical competence. "Ask what subject they found least interesting and most difficult at school and the almost invariable answer is: 'math. I hated math.'"

Few people go into journalism because they like math. But knowing your numbers is not a matter of choice.

Here are some key areas where journalists often go wrong:

Per Cent Versus Percentage Point

Many economic indicators — the consumer price index, unemployment figures and so on — are expressed in "per cents." This is a simple-to-understand way of expressing a figure in relation to the whole. An unemployment rate of 10 per cent means that 10 of every 100 people in the labor force are out of work. If you are writing a story about an increase in the unemployment rate, there are a couple of ways to express the change:

1. The unemployment rate rose to 11 per cent from nine per cent a year ago.

2. The unemployment rate has risen by two percentage points, from nine per cent a year ago to 11 per cent today.

So far, so easy, right? But one thing you *can't* say is that the unemployment rate "rose two per cent from nine per cent to 11 per cent."

In fact, an increase from nine per cent to 11 per cent is a whop-

ping 22 per cent increase over the previous unemployment rate. (To calculate a percentage increase, you subtract the old figure from the new figure. Then divide the difference by the old figure and multiply by 100. In this case, 11 minus nine leaves two. Two divided by nine is 0.22. Multiply this by 100 and you get 22 per cent.) But calculating x per cent of y per cent is, in most cases, absurd. It's far better to use "percentage point."

Adding Versus Compounding

A new contract signed by the teachers' union includes a wage increase of five per cent a year for two years for a group of teachers whose base salary is $50,000. Does this add up to a raise of 10 per cent? No. Here's why.

In the first year of the new contract, the teachers get an increase of five per cent (5 x $500), or an extra $2,500, raising the base salary to $52,500. In the second year, the five per cent raise is calculated on the *new* base salary (5 x $525) and is worth $2,625. Over the course of the contract, the salary goes from $50,000 to $55,125. The amount of the increase, $5,125, is 10.25 per cent of the original base salary.

The rule when you get information on a contract is simple: always check the math yourself, to make sure it adds up correctly.

Appropriate Comparisons

Most Canadians don't buy houses in the winter. They tend, instead, to buy in the spring, when the

(continued)

weather is warm and it's easier to move. As a result, the number of houses sold in May and June is usually far higher than in December and January. A new reporter, given raw real estate sales figures for a story, might be tempted to write that house sales rose 400 per cent from January to June. This might be accurate mathematically, but would it paint an accurate picture of the housing market? No. June sales are almost *always* higher than January sales, even when the housing market is in a slump. The reporter would get a better picture by comparing June sales this year with June sales *last* year. Alternatively, the reporter might do a three-month comparison, averaging the figures for April, May and June (the busy spring period) from this year and last, and comparing them.

Seasonal Adjustments

Each May the number of people looking for work jumps as high school and university students finish up their studies for the year. Each September the number goes down as the students return to class. Statisticians are aware of these events, and have developed the so-called seasonal adjustment to cope with them. Essentially, regular events that occur in a particular season are averaged out over the year. When comparing figures from the fall quarter with figures from the winter quarter, it's best to use seasonally adjusted numbers. That's because the numbers are calculated to take into account things like pre-Christmas buying binges that might otherwise change the picture the numbers paint.

Seasonal figures are of less use when comparing one fall with the previous fall. If you're comparing the same season, why do you need an adjustment? Comparing seasonally adjusted figures with those that have not been adjusted is, of course, a bad idea — like comparing apples with oranges.

Most newspaper business pages and most broadcast business reports reflect both aspects. They carry national and international stories — the latest Statistics Canada report, government announcement or decision by an international trade agency — as well as stories that are distinctively local.

National economics reporters like Beauchesne provide a lot of that macroeconomic reporting. "I look for the overall economic story of the day," he says. "I try to explain to people what's happening, in a broad sense, to the economy. And because I'm working out of Ottawa, I look especially at what the federal government is doing and its effect on the economy."

Beauchesne starts his day at 6 a.m. by reading the morning papers from Toronto and Montreal. At the office, he's almost always within sight of a TV tuned to Newsworld. He can call up The Canadian Press wire on his computer terminal any time he wants, to check in with the rest of the world. He also uses Netscape to cruise the World Wide Web for ideas, sources and background. Beauchesne says he sometimes looks for company Web sites. He also gets good results from posting requests on ProfNet (a U.S.-based network of university professors) for experts on specific areas. "You can often get same-day turnaround," he says. He frequently checks the Web sites of organizations like Statistics Canada, the Bank of Canada and the Paris-based Organization for Economic Co-operation and Development (OECD). It has always been difficult for reporters in Canada to get timely copies of OECD reports, he says, so the Web site really makes a difference.

Beauchesne tends to use Web sites to collect background information and track trends rather than for breaking news. "I still get the *StatsCan Daily* faxed to me," he says. "I still get most reports in the paper version. If I'm really in a hurry, I'll use the Web and then download a copy." Many government Web sites have archives and their own search engines, and he often looks up things electronically in previously published reports. But he likes to work with reports on paper. "I print it out, then take it away and read it over coffee," he says. His desk, piled with Statistics Canada reports, old press releases and notebooks, looks as though it suffers from information overload. The flood of material serves a purpose, however. "Part of the job is taking all this in and identifying the contradictions, the spots where what you hear coming from one group is different from what you hear from another," he says. "You think, 'Hey, that's interesting. That's worth looking at. That may be a story.'"

Beauchesne also keeps track of what he calls "the broad numbers" on the economy. Statistics Canada's schedule for releasing economic indicators sets a loose framework for his work schedule. These reports offer snapshots of portions of the Canadian economy and indicate whether Canada is sliding into recession or booming back to prosperity. Beauchesne says some reports — such as the quarterly balance of international payments — always merit attention since they serve as a "report card" on the economy. The relative importance of others depends on the state of the economy at the time of release. The monthly consumer price index report is of strong interest when inflation is an issue, of less interest when prices are stable. Similarly, the monthly reports on employment (the labor force survey, the report on employment earnings and hours, and the report on unemployment insurance statistics) are of most interest when they signal a change.

Beauchesne says the Canadian Composite Leading Indicator, released in the first week of each month, deserves careful examination in times of economic uncertainty. The indicator, based on a collection of 10 statistics, may be the place where the first signs of a change in the economy are to be found. It is an imperfect device, however. Beauchesne points out that the statistics used to compile it are themselves dated.

Other reports look at a specific type of economic activity. The report on building permits, for example, is a good guide to what's likely to happen in the construction business. The manufacturing survey, retail trade and motor vehicle reports look at what's going on in the nation's factories and stores.

Tracking the reports is a basic part of Beauchesne's job. But numbers are not necessarily journalism. "It's one thing to spew out the numbers, and another to ask, What does it mean? How do the retailers feel about it? What do consumers say?" This kind of thinking sends him on the hunt for comments from a whole range of people who think about these questions.

In his search for reaction, comment and context for changes in the economy, Beauchesne deals regularly with a range of non-government sources, such as think-tanks, lobby groups, consumer groups and labor federations. Many of these groups produce reports or position papers, which can generate stories on their own. This story on charitable contributions is an example:

> Businesses that Canadians often love to hate — banks, breweries, oil and tobacco companies — are among the most generous when it comes to giving to charity, according to a Conference Board of Canada survey made public yesterday.
>
> But with the recession, businesses generally held the line on cash donations last year and offered more goods, services and time instead ...
>
> Causes getting the lion's share of corporate cash support are education, social services and health, said the survey of who gave what to whom.
>
> "With government tightening their purse-strings in most areas — particularly health and education — corporate community investment is taking on even greater importance," said conference board researcher Janet Rostami. ...
>
> — OTTAWA CITIZEN, JUNE 30, 1992

As an economics reporter stationed in Ottawa, Beauchesne also tracks what and how the federal government spends. This means covering budgets and spending estimates, keeping track of Finance Department activity, and covering the Commons finance committee. He makes a point of watching question period on the Parliamentary TV channel — not to write spot news but because it tells him what the opposition parties see as the top economic questions of the day. And he covers the auditor general's reports on how well the government managed its money.

Reporters working in a specialized area in the capital face the danger of becoming isolated from the lives of their readers. Beauchesne says making a deliberate effort to keep down the level of jargon helps. So does the fact that he knows he is writing for papers big and small, in cities and in towns, with business editors who don't want stories full of economic bafflegab.

An ability to see the humor in what others might consider a dull report can also be an asset. When Statistics Canada released two studies on the costs of owning pets, Beauchesne wrote:

> A dog'll take a bigger bite out of your wallet than a cat. Put another way, it takes less scratch to keep a cat.
>
> That's the tale of two pets, released this week by Statistics Canada — which, despite a decade of having its budget squeezed, found time and money last year to check out the country's dog domiciles and — dare we say it — cat houses.
>
> What it found, among other things, is that the cost of supporting a dog for a year is — brace yourself — $416. That's about 20 per cent of what's spent by a family on child care. In contrast that cute cuddly kitty (this guy's obviously a cat owner) will cost you only $304. ...
>
> — OTTAWA CITIZEN, JULY 2, 1992

THE LOCAL BEAT

Papers like the *Hamilton Spectator* use a lot of the "macro" material transmitted from Ottawa. But the main concern of the local business editor, says Tim Doyle, is assigning and editing stories at the "micro" level. The *Spectator*'s business staff is small: two full-time reporters, a reporter/copy editor and a local business columnist. The newspaper also tries to take advantage of experts in the community, using them as freelancers and guest columnists, Doyle says. With a small staff, it's impossible to have an elaborate beat system. Each of the two full-time reporters has an area of specialization that reflects the changing local economy. One specializes in steel, the backbone of the Hamilton economy for much of this century, and the other specializes in the growing high-technology field. However, they have to be able to cover just about any story that comes up.

Doyle says there's a lot of cross-over between the news and business departments. The business editor often gets stories written by reporters who work out of the general newsroom, and sometimes stories written by business reporters appear in other parts of the paper. "For example, we did a takeout a while ago on the use of private investigators to check up on people who made Workers' Compensation claims. It could have run either in the news or the business section. It ran in business."

It's impossible to catalogue all the types of stories that run on the business pages. But Doyle says some, such as the local business profile, are easily identified as distinctive to the business pages. "We don't do a story on the opening of a routine franchise," he says. "But if a local entrepreneur launches a genuinely new or interesting business, we'll do a story." In its softest form, a business profile can amount to free advertising for the business owner. Doyle says business reporters don't just talk to the entrepreneur: they attempt to assess the prospects for the company, the number of people who may be employed and so on. "The goal is to let the reader know what's going on in the community — not only whether it will provide a product, but whether it will provide jobs."

The *Spectator is* one of a decreasing number of newspapers with a labor beat. The labor reporter works in the general newsroom, but her stories are as likely to appear in the Business section as in the Metro section. Doyle rejects the idea that business reporters talk only to businesses while labor reporters talk only to the unions. "We feel it's important to get the union point of view on many stories," he says. "For example, if we're doing a story on a business going through a restructuring — and we do a lot of them these days — we *have* to look at what it means to the employees there, and the union."

COVERING LABOR

Many new reporters get the worst possible introduction to labor reporting: they're sent to cover a strike. They probably don't know the company well, though they may have a phone number for the public relations department. They probably don't know the union at all, though they hope they'll find someone to talk to on the picket line. They don't know the law regulating collective bargaining, the history of labor relations at the company, or why the union and management are at an impasse. They may not even be sure how the collective bargaining system *should* work (and usually does work) and why it broke down in this case. At most media outlets, they won't have a labor reporter in their newsroom who can help them sort it all out.

As a beat, labor reporting is in transition (some argue, in decline).
(continued)

A 1990 survey by industrial relations professor Anil Verma found only seven full-time labor reporters at Canada's daily newspapers, and another 33 working on mixed beats with a labor concentration (Verma 1990).

"The typical labor reporter is a person on assignment from a generalist pool who is biding his or her time until he or she can be reassigned to something 'more interesting,'" Verma writes. Odds are this reporter has no formal education on labor relations, and will stay on the beat for less than two years.

As a result, Verma says, a lot of labor reporting is simplistic and inadequate. "Many company and union officials complain bitterly that they must continually educate newcomers in such basics as the difference between an illegal and a legal strike" (1990, 10–11).

Complaints about how labor is reported raise some interesting issues for reporters and their employers. What other group or organization, critics ask, represents close to 40 per cent of the work force yet *doesn't* merit a beat? Why is it that a newspaper will have an entire department devoted to covering "business" but not a single reporter specializing in labor? Why is it that so much labor coverage focuses on strikes rather than the other things unions do? How is it that some reports seem to equate "big business" and "big labor," as though the two groups had roughly equal amounts of wealth, power and status?

In recent years, some newspapers have changed the name of the labor beat to the workplace beat. In part this reflects a recognition that most Canadian workers are *not* unionized. In part too, it reflects rapid changes in the workplace — the drive for employment equity, the arrival of job-sharing or new technology — and in the way unions and managers work on issues of joint concern.

Labor or workplace issues arise on *every* beat, however. The city hall reporter, for example, must keep track of negotiations between the city administration and its outside workers. The police reporter needs to follow what's happening in the police union. The entertainment reporter may have to write about a dispute local theatre owners are having with their projectionists or about how a possible strike by technicians might affect a concert scheduled for next weekend. The sports reporter has to understand the complexities of contract negotiations between players and owners, free-agent clauses, strike votes and so on.

This means that when you take on any new area of reportage, you should keep an eye on labor-related issues. Here are two suggestions to consider:

1. Begin to make contacts with the unions and labor federations that have an interest in the area you are covering. Unions can be a good source of

(continued)

story ideas, not just on simmering disputes that are about to boil over, but also on longer-term matters such as health and safety and day care. Some unions also produce first-rate research on things that affect their members directly (new technology, for example) or policy papers on national and international issues, such as free trade, welfare reform and education.

2. Don't wait until you have to cover your first strike to educate yourself about the collective bargaining process. We include some suggested readings at the end of this chapter.

Here are some of the basic concepts in collective bargaining that you will need to know.

Laws and Regulations

Canada has a national labor code, a set of provincial codes and a range of special legislation for federal and provincial employees or other "public employees" like teachers and police officers. Essentially, the national code covers employees in federally chartered companies (banks and Crown corporations, for example) and in businesses that operate along inter-provincial lines, such as transportation and communication. The Canada Labor Relations Board enforces the industrial relations part of the federal code.

The provincial codes cover workers in the individual provinces.

Provinces also have their own labor boards. (Quebec's labor court covers the functions of the labor board in that province.)

Labor laws regulate the collective bargaining process, from ruling on how a union becomes recognized as the bargaining agent to setting out the steps in contract negotiation. Labor laws also set the legal framework for the process of settling complaints against employers accused of unfair practices.

Certification and Negotiation

Unions aren't imposed from outside; the workers in an organization or plant must begin a drive to join a union, and gain the support of a majority of their fellow employees. It can take many months to complete the process of getting the union "certified" as the bargaining agent for the workers. Once that happens, the union generally represents *all* workers in the bargaining unit, excluding those who do specific management functions.

The relationship between the workers and the employer is set out in the contract, a formal and legally binding agreement drawn up by company managers and representatives of the workers, and ratified by the union membership. Contracts last for a limited time — one to three years is common — and then must be renegotiated.

If the union and management are unable to reach an agreement, either side may ask for help from whichever government has

(continued)

jurisdiction in the area. This help varies from province to province, but it usually includes provisions for conciliation, mediation and arbitration. Conciliation is an attempt to get the two sides talking; mediation, usually done only when conciliation fails, is a special attempt by a go-between to reach an agreement; arbitration is the imposition of a settlement by an outside specialist. On rare occasions, governments will pass legislation forcing public-sector strikers (for example, teachers and police) to return to work. In these cases, a third party resolves the issues.

(Don't confuse arbitration of a settlement with what is known as rights arbitration. The latter refers to the resolution of grievances — formal allegations that one party, usually the employer, has violated or improperly interpreted the terms of the contract.)

The vast majority of contracts are settled without any kind of labor disruption. It would be a mistake, however, to conclude that this means they're not sources of good stories. An examination of a range of peaceful settlements can sometimes show patterns emerging in labor relations — changes in the sizes of settlements, for example, or in the trade-offs made between money and job security.

A look at the labor relations history of a single employer or union can also be revealing, particularly if it shows a history of bad-faith bargaining, exceptional militancy or an unusual reliance on outside mediators. A reporter looking for story ideas will probably find plenty in an employer with this kind of history, particularly if it is a school board or some other public-sector organization.

Strikes and Lockouts

Reporters should never confuse a legal strike with an illegal strike, or a strike with a lockout. All three mean a work stoppage, but of widely differing kinds. Unions move into what is called a "legal strike position" at a particular point in the bargaining process (usually one to two weeks after a conciliation report has been written). A strike before that time is called an illegal strike. A wildcat strike is one for which union leaders deny responsibility. Not all wildcat strikes are illegal. A lockout occurs when an employer decides to deny employees access to their workplace. It is usually ordered to get concessions from workers, or in reaction to a slowdown or work-to-rule campaign. Like strikes, lockouts may be legal or illegal. Employers gain the right to lock workers out at the same point in the bargaining process as unions gain the right to strike.

Strikes and lockouts usually result in picket lines, where workers walk back and forth outside the entrance of their place of employment and try to discourage people from going in. Picket lines can be particularly effective if they persuade other unions and customers not to cross the line. In companies

(continued)

that trade in information rather than commodities, however, picket lines are less successful at halting work. Some strikers at companies that rely on the telephone will set up so-called electronic pickets, trying to tie up the company's phone lines.

While money is often a key issue in a strike, it is rarely the *only* issue. Some of the most interesting stories in labor disputes centre on questions of control over work, or on the issue of layoffs, or on conditions of work.

In reporting on a strike — as in any other report you write — you must take steps to ensure you have a good grasp of *all* the issues. This means you must never take one side's version of events as gospel, and you must tread carefully to avoid being taken in by rhetoric.

Does the fact that many reporters are themselves union members complicate coverage? It shouldn't: as in all good reporting, reporters covering strikes must set aside their own personal views. Problems occasionally arise, however. During and after the 1988 federal election, for example, broadcaster Dale Goldhawk came under pressure because of what the CBC saw as a conflict between his on-air job as host of a national radio show and his role as leader of a union that opposed free trade. Eventually, the network told him to give up one post or the other, and he chose to resign the union job. The Canada Labor Relations Board later found the CBC guilty of unfair labor practices — a decision that was itself a good example of the kinds of stories that develop at the edges of the labor beat.

How-to stories — how to buy an RRSP, how to sell your house, how to buy life insurance and so on — are popular fare for the business pages. They are part of a new and growing realm of business reporting known as personal finance, based on advising middle-class people (as opposed to the wealthy or investors) how to get the most out of their money. "There's some crossover here with the Lifestyles section," Doyle says.

Business writers at the *Spectator* have to handle a lot of "numbers" stories — local breakdowns of statistics provided by Statistics Canada, local real estate sales figures or quarterly surveys by the privately owned Manpower Temporary Services of where the jobs are in the local economy. Doyle concedes that it's easy to get bogged down in them, though the use of graphics — made possible by the development of powerful but inexpensive computers — can help. "They not only convey the numbers efficiently, they brighten up the page," he says.

Doyle says the guiding principle in writing business stories is to project into the mind of the readers. "We don't just report that the bank rate went up or down," he says. "We try to tell people what that means here. What does it mean for the mortgage rates? Is it going to make it harder or easier to buy a home? Is it going to mean more jobs for the people who build houses?"

He says lack of specialization can be an advantage in helping a reporter write at the right level of complexity. "If I can make it understandable to me, if I can keep the stories interesting for me, then I figure I can make it interesting and understandable for the readers."

SPECIALISTS AND SPECIALTIES

If newspapers like the *Spectator* look for the common touch, specialized business publications pride themselves on being at the cutting edge, or perhaps even a bit beyond it. And that makes a difference in the way reporters do their job. Beppi Crosariol says that reporters at elite business publications operate on the premise that part of their job is to predict the future. These reporters not only keep ahead of the competition, but at times keep ahead of the businesses they cover and the brokers who advise their readers.

Crosariol, an experienced business writer, now works in the arts section of the *Globe and Mail* and keeps a hand in the business beat through a monthly high-tech column in *Report on Business Magazine*. He says most business beat stories fall into three broad categories — stories about companies, stories about trends, and stories about people.

At the *Financial Times of Canada*, he focused mainly on so-called public companies, those whose shares are traded publicly. Crosariol says business reporters keep track of the companies on their beat by talking to customers and competitors, as well as to market researchers, managers of investment portfolios, analysts at brokerage houses and so on. "A lot of this is off-record material," he says.

Documentary sources are also important. Press releases, securities commission filings and annual reports to shareholders are useful not so much for immediate news value, but for keeping track of companies and their industry. In addition to using these "public" documents, Crosariol says, reporters may ask their contacts at brokerage houses to pass along copies of analysts' reports. These reports, written by what he describes as "well-trained numbers people," are intended to help brokers advise their clients. Crosariol says these documents contain terrific background material.

STOCKS AND MARKETS

The first step toward understanding the stock market is mastering some of its key terms. Here is a brief introduction to some of the phrases you will come across on the business pages.

Public company: This is a company that has decided to offer shares for sale to the public, in an effort to raise money.

Shares: A share, also known as a stock or an equity security, is a tiny piece of the company. The share purchaser ends up as the owner of a fraction of the corporation. Shares of "listed" companies are traded on a recognized stock market, such as the Toronto Stock Exchange or the Vancouver Stock Exchange. "Over the counter" stocks are not listed on the exchange and are usually traded through brokerage firms.

The shareholder earns money in two ways:

1. increases in the value of the stock. If a stock is purchased at $25 a share and the price goes up to $50 two months later, the owner can reap a profit by selling the stock; and

2. dividends paid by the company. This is a portion of the company's profit, paid out to the owners of the stock.

There are two main kinds of stock:

Preferred shares: These come with the guarantee of earning a fixed dividend. They tend to be more stable than common shares.

Common shares: These shares have no guaranteed minimum dividend. The owner is entitled to a share of the profits the company earns, and usually has a vote at stockholder's meetings.

Most of the shares traded on the stock exchange are common shares. The buyers are gambling that the value of the stock will increase and that the company will make a profit and pay dividends. There is no guarantee that either will happen. If the company makes no profit, the stockholder gets no dividend. And if the price of the stock goes down, the stockholder loses money because the value of the investment has declined.

Bonds: Like stocks, bonds are issued by a company (or a government) as a way of raising money. But bond buyers do not end up with a small piece of the company: instead, they are essentially making a loan to the company, in return for a promise that the money will be returned within a specific period of time and at a set rate of interest. Bonds, therefore, are known as "debt securities." Canada Savings Bonds, the best-known bonds, are not traded. Most other bonds are, and the price varies, mainly in reaction to changes in interest rates. Once again, there are two main ways of making money:

1. trading the bonds; and

2. earning the interest payments promised in the bond.

(continued)

Commodities: These are the raw or partly processed materials — minerals, metals, soya beans or wheat — that fuel the nation's industries. There are three main types of commodities trading:

Spot markets: In spot markets, the commodity is exchanged for cash.

Futures markets: In futures markets, the buyer promises to purchase the commodity at a specific point in the future and at a specific price.

Options markets: In these, the buyer obtains the right — but not the obligation — to purchase a commodity or a futures contract at a specific price within a set period of time.

Reading the Stock Tables

Most stockholders follow the ups and downs of their shares by reading the stock tables in the daily newspaper. The format varies from paper to paper, but if you can read one stock table you can probably read them all.

As a general rule, stock prices are traded in eighths of a dollar (12.5 cents). The Canadian Shareowners Association says this habit dates back to the time when the Spanish *real*, the famous piece of eight, was the accepted international monetary unit.

Here are the key terms used in the stock tables:

52 week high/low: These two numbers indicate how the price of the stock has varied over the last year.

Div.: This shows the actual dollar amount of dividends paid annually, in cash. If there is no figure, it means the company paid no dividend in the last 12 months.

High: The top price for a share of the company's stock during the trading day.

Low: The lowest price paid during the day.

Close: The last price of the day.

Vol: This tells you how many shares were traded yesterday. (It's usually expressed in hundreds.)

Most stock tables also include figures based on ways of calculating potential profits. These may be expressed as Yields, Price/Earnings ratios or Earnings Per Share.

From the "B" list

A few other phrases will improve your understanding of the markets.

Bear: Someone who thinks the price of a particular share or the overall market will fall. A "bear market" is one in which prices in general are on the decline.

Bull: Someone who thinks the price of a particular share or the overall market will rise. A "bull market" is one in which prices in general are on the way up.

Blue chip: The stock of a large, well-established company with a good record of dividends and earnings.

Broker: The firm (or an individual employee of it) that actually buys or

(continued)

sells shares on behalf of the investor. Brokers are paid a fee or commission for each transaction. As a result, they are often the only people guaranteed to make money on any deal.

Buying on margin: An investor who does not want to put up the full value of a share purchase can buy "on margin." On a $10,000 purchase, the investor might put up only $5,000 and borrow the rest from the broker. The investor pays the broker an interest charge on the other $5,000, which is essentially a loan from the broker to the investor. If the price of the stock falls, the broker may issue a "margin call." This means that the investor must put up more cash, or the broker will get the right to sell the stock.

Source: Wayne Cheveldayoff (1978), *The Business Page: How to Read It for Profit, Politics and Peace of Mind.* Ottawa: Deneau and Greenberg; John T. Bart, ed. (1987), *Canadian Investors Manual: The Handbook for Learn-by-Doing Investing.* Windsor, ON: Canadian Shareowners Association; Murray Oxby, The Canadian Press (1991), "Navigating the markets." Ottawa *Citizen*, Sept. 16.

Reporters also rely heavily on market research firms, whose main business is to publish sales and growth figures on a particular industry. The chief clients of the market research firms are companies within the industry being studied, who pay substantial sums to buy reports containing information about their competitors. Crosariol says that, on occasion, he got the reports before they were officially released, which kept him ahead of reporters at other business outlets. The market research companies also benefitted, since the stories he wrote helped create a market for the reports.

"In covering corporate performance, I would try to anticipate where things are going," he says. "Are the stocks of X company poised to go up? Are they about to go down?"

Stories about trends in technology offer similar predictions. How will the latest development affect the economic health of a company's rivals or suppliers? "The goal is to unearth developments just before they become well-known in the investment community." Then, the readers know about the developments before the brokers do. "Again, I want to know which companies are poised to benefit, and which are likely to be hurt."

Crosariol says business beat profiles may focus on an individual or a company, or sometimes both. He advises reporters to look for "someone who has done something quirky, something that may be instructive for another business person." And as with other specialized areas of journalism, business profiles demand a high level of writing skill. For example, Crosariol's profile of a Canadian steel-manufacturing pioneer used a couple of gritty metaphors, a twist on a Frank Capra movie title and a number of well-known company names, to introduce the subject of the story:

> Meet Gerald Heffernan, the man who has all but nailed the coffin shut on Big Steel in North America. Dofasco? Stelco? Heffernan's creation, the flexible, high-quality steel mini-mill, is putting them out of business. ...

— BEPPI CROSARIOL, *FINANCIAL TIMES OF CANADA*, MAY 11, 1992

Private companies are more difficult to cover than public ones because they're not required by law to release financial information. "If people from a private company want to talk to you, it's probably because they're doing well," Crosariol explains. "After all, not too many companies will want to tell you they're losing market share, or they've just had a flop." This means the reporter has to work that much harder — talking to customers, competitors, market researchers and so on — to nail down a story. "Market research reports are critical for dealing with private companies," he adds. "They're often the best source for information about things like sales figures."

For people who know little about business, the kinds of activities covered by the specialized business publications and the language business writers use to describe them are sometimes hard to follow. "It's difficult to get around the jargon — in some cases it's almost impossible," Crosariol concedes. "The virtue of jargon is that it's efficient. Look at a term like 'short seller.' Those two words do a lot of work for you, as long as your readers understand it too. If you used it in a story in a regular newspaper you'd have to define it, but you don't need to keep defining it for people in the business because they know what it means. Sometimes you can even abbreviate it more — you can say, 'What are the shorts doing?'"

A reporter who knows the lingo may also have an advantage in the news-gathering process, he adds. "Using the real, in-house jargon makes you seem more authoritative. The financial community is very clubby. They talk that way to each other, and you feel they want to be talked to that way."

READING FINANCIAL DOCUMENTS

One of the first things a new business writer must learn is how to read two key documents that form part of most companies' annual reports to shareowners: the balance sheet and the income statement. The Canadian Shareowners Association, based in Windsor, Ont., offers detailed advice on how to do this in its *Canadian Investors Manual*. Here are some basics.

The Balance Sheet

This is a snapshot of the company's financial position at a particular time — usually the end of a fiscal quarter or year. One side lists the firm's assets and the other lists the firm's liabilities and the shareowners' equity. All numbers are expressed in dollar figures. The totals on the two sides are always equal.

Assets are the left side of the sheet. "Current" assets range from cash on hand to things like securities and accounts that are likely to be turned into cash within a year. "Noncurrent" assets are things like buildings and equipment as well as "intangibles" — patents or the goodwill of customers — that are of value to the company.

Liabilities and shareowners' equity are on the right side of the sheet. "Current" liabilities are debts the firm expects to pay in one year, such as staff salaries, income taxes and so on. "Long-term" liabilities are debts that will fall due later, such as bonds and deferred income taxes. Shareowners' equity is the net worth of the company — the amount left over when you subtract the liabilities from the assets.

"There are some basic questions you should ask while studying the balance sheet," the shareowners association manual says. "Can the company pay its bills? What would the company be worth if it were liquidated, or sold? How much debt is there in proportion to assets? Have there been any large changes in the items listed?" (1987, 7). One way to analyse the company's well-being is to compare the latest balance sheet with previous ones.

The Income Statement

Unlike the balance sheet, which shows the company's financial position at a specific time, the income statement summarizes a company's activities over the last quarter or the last year. Again, it's a good idea to compare the latest income statement with previous statements.

The income statement begins with the amount of money the company took in from selling its goods or services to customers. (This may be listed on the sheet as "sales," "revenues," "gross income," "receipts" or some other term.)

"Net operating income" is calculated by subtracting the costs of manufacturing (labor and materials, administration, rent and so on) from the sales figure. By subtracting the amount the firm paid in financing charges (interest and other borrowing charges) and in taxes, you get the "net income after

(continued)

taxes" — the basic, bottom-line profit of the company, which can be divided among the shareholders.

Dividing the net income by the number of shares or stocks produces the "earnings per share." Normally, the company reinvests a good portion of this amount, and pays out some to individual shareholders as "dividends" or cash earnings. These are also listed on the income statement.

Source: Adapted from John T. Bart, ed. (1987). *Canadian Investors Manual: The Handbook for Learn-by-Doing Investing.* Windsor, ON: Canadian Shareowners Association.

WORKING THE SOURCES

Kimberley Noble has built a reputation for exploiting an impressive range of sources in a beat that extends (remarkably) from very basic manufacturing issues all the way up the arcane reaches of high finance. When she was hired by the Report on Business she was put on the "trees" part — the forestry industry — of a beat that used to be known as "rocks and trees." She describes this as a "true" business beat since it focuses on the manufacturing, management and sale of a product.

The newspaper also has a tradition of assigning coverage of the country's leading financial families to individual reporters, and in 1986 she was given the task of keeping track of the branch of the Bronfman family that ran Edper Enterprises Ltd. (After Peter Bronfman's death in 1996, it became EdperBrascan Corp.) Covering Edper involves a lot of financial reporting — how money is raised, lent or borrowed. "I do a strange mixture of basic business reporting and high Bay Street reporting," she says.

Noble says the starting point for most business stories is a public announcement by a company. Government regulations require that before a company "goes public," or offers shares for sale, it must file a prospectus, in essence a development plan, with the securities commission of the province where the shares will be traded. The company must also file quarterly reports and make public announcements of any so-called material change, such as the sale or the acquisition of a major asset.

Many press releases issued by companies, she says, are really disclosure documents, written to fulfil government or securities commission requirements. "Most of the time companies go to great lengths to disclose the absolute minimum necessary in any transaction," Noble says.

"This means a lot of our time is taken up trying to decipher the announcements they have to make, get more information and put that in context for the readers."

Business reporters rely on a wide range of documents for story ideas and information, and they work in an area where computerization affects what they can get, and how. Noble says an increasing amount of material is available on the Internet. The U.S. Securities and Exchange Commission, for example, runs a Web site where reporters can get documents that companies are required to file with the commission. These documents include information on Canadian companies whose shares trade in the United States.

Other material is available through specialized databases. Canadian securities administrators are launching a domestic database of securities disclosure documents from all the provinces and territories. In the meantime, business writers must search province by province. In Ontario, reporters who want Ontario Securities Commission documents have to order them through Micromedia. Information on federally chartered companies is available through the federal government, but recent changes in the rules mean that companies can file less financial data than they did before.

Business publications tend to subscribe to specialized business services like the Bloomberg financial wire, which has a wealth of data on companies around the world. It also allows reporters to cross-reference material, do customized searches and construct charts and graphs. Reporters also go through annual reports aimed at shareholders, which sum up the year's activity and offer a handy snapshot of the company. Noble says court documents from lawsuits and bankruptcy proceedings are also useful. Databases like the *Canadian Who's Who* can be used to cross-reference things like company directors' memberships in clubs. "And divorce filings are great — sometimes corporate or financial information you can't get anywhere else will come out in a divorce case," she says.

Much business reporting, like any other kind, means simply keeping track of what's going on in the area. Business reporters may attend the annual shareholders' meetings of a corporation — perhaps to cover them as simple news events, or to use them as ways of making contacts or gathering background for other stories. They develop sources to contact for confirmation of a tip, for reaction stories or for news analysis pieces about a decision that affects the business. When the price of pulp products went up in mid-1992, Noble conveyed the news and explained the context behind it.

Canada's eastern wood pulp producers are taking advantage of the strike that has closed down their western brethren by announcing that the price of their suddenly scarce product will go up substantially a week from today.

Just about every market pulp producer east of the Rocky Mountains has called its North American customers in the past few days, informing them that they'll be paying up to $40 (U.S.) or $50 (Canadian) more for each tonne of northern bleached softwood kraft (NBSK) pulp they buy after July 1. ...

The success of this increase is thought to be a foregone conclusion, given that this month's strike by 12,500 B.C. pulp and paper workers has effectively choked off almost half of Canada's production of NBSK pulp at a time when its buyers are just beginning to enjoy slightly better demand for their own products. ...

— *GLOBE AND MAIL*, JUNE 24, 1992

When U.S. trade authorities imposed a tariff on softwood lumber imports, the news story came out of Washington. Noble's job was to try to sort out what that announcement would mean to Canadians.

Every time a U.S. trade tribunal hands down a decision about how its country should view or treat Canadian softwood lumber imports, people inside and outside the wood products trade ask the same two questions.

First they always want to know what impact this whole process, and the individual decisions made along the way, are having, have had and will have on North American lumber markets — particularly on what Canadian exporters can get for their products in the United States, and how much more or less of those products they are going to be able to sell.

Put simply, the answer is: none — or, perhaps more accurately, none that lasts beyond a very short period of time.

Then they want to know what, specifically, is going to happen to the Canadian lumber business, including the mills that make the products and the nation-wide service sector that helps them get their goods to market.

And the answer to the second question is: nobody knows for sure. ...

— *GLOBE AND MAIL*, JUNE 26, 1992

This kind of interpretation is based on the idea that it's not enough simply to tell people *what* happened — you also have to explain *how* and *why* it happened, and you should do it in a way that makes for good reading. There is a danger, however, in putting too much emphasis on storytelling, Noble says. "Sometimes the content loses — you can write a glitzy little story that rolls along well but doesn't really grapple with what's happening. The challenge for me is to try to keep learning, to find better and better ways to get the basic content out there for the readers."

BASICS OF THE CRAFT

Reporter-editor Cathryn Motherwell of the Globe and Mail *offers these hints with business reporting in mind — although all of them are applicable to any kind of reporting.*

- Never assume anything — ever. Several years ago Jan Wong wrote profiles of business newsmakers for the Report on Business. When she was told that a young up-and-comer at the Toronto Stock Exchange had a master's degree, she made a routine call to verify this with the university. He didn't have the degree after all, which transformed Jan's story from just another business profile into a mini-scandal that led to the man's hasty resignation. One call about a seemingly banal fact created a terrific tale.

- Don't be afraid to ask the stupid question. Other reporters may snicker, but that question often can produce the best quote; interview subjects will often go to greater pains to explain a situation to you than they would if you pretend to know more about the topic. And if you still don't understand, ask the question again. We like to think of ourselves as intelligent people and often pretend to understand a complex situation. But you can't write a story if you don't understand it yourself.

- Don't be cowed by numbers. I cannot stress too strongly the importance of being able to read a profit-and-loss statement and to understand the principles of a balance sheet. From national and provincial budgets to the intricate loan manoeuvring of private companies to sports teams ownership, an understanding of the financial basics is essential.

- That said, numbers can be downright boring. That's why it's important to put a human face on a numbers story whenever possible. If farm incomes are down, try to find a farmer who can talk about the situation. If retail sales are up, talk to a local business person about the reasons. The additional insights will help you write a much better story, and possibly lead to further stories.

- Look for colorful anecdotes. It's not always easy to find color, but in the television age it's an essential tool for the print writer. What hobbies do your interviewees have? What is their favorite anecdote about the subject of your story? Where did they go for their last vacation? Are they active in politics? And before leaving,

(continued)

ask if they have any other stories to tell — often that last
thought will be the most interesting.

- Never be content with a one-
source story. Look for opposing
viewpoints, another witness, or
an expert who can cast new
light on a story.

SOURCES AND IDEAS

Columnist Don McGillivray, who recently retired after a long career as
an economics columnist and a teacher at Carleton University, notes
that little business news is "unalloyed good news or unalloyed bad
news." A decision to put a plant in Brampton rather than Beauce is good
for the former, bad for the latter. The rapid refinements in computer
technology are good for those making and selling the latest gadget, bad
for those selling the next-to-latest. A new technique in robotics is good
for the profit margin of the companies that make it and buy it, but bad
for the workers rendered redundant, and bad for their unions and their
communities. "There's a constant struggle for a share of the pie," he says.
"It's a little like covering a war."

He says reporters need to be aware of this fact, conscious of the
stakes involved in the conflicts, and alert to the interests of their sources.
"You need to ask yourself constantly, 'What does this person have to gain
or lose in this issue?'" he says. Reporters who don't ask themselves these
questions all too easily become the tools of their sources.

The strong self-interest of sources is a constant challenge to the
independence of a reporter's news judgment, especially when the most
powerful elements are able to make their case the loudest. This is seen
nowhere more vividly (or continuously) than on the business beat,
where corporations have enormous resources to spend on getting their
messages across.

It's all too easy for business reporters to slip into the conventional
wisdom of the people they cover — into agreeing almost without
thought that competition is always good and that monopolies are bad,
without critically addressing the issue of *good for whom*. It's all too easy
to accept on faith the idea that no regulation is good regulation, without examining who stands to win if an industry is deregulated, and who
stands to lose. And it's all too easy to accept the euphemisms "downsiz-
ing" and "restructuring," instead of examining the human costs.

Doyle's advice to reporters is to keep in touch with how ordinary people are affected by change. "Listen to what people are talking about on the street, whether it's a store opening, or a store closing, or the price of milk or the price of gas. These are all business issues, all things that affect people in the wallet or the pocketbook. Money's important to people. Always was. Always will be."

RECOMMENDED READING

Bart, John T., ed. (1987). *Canadian Investors Manual: The Handbook for Learn-by-Doing Investing.* Windsor, ON: Canadian Shareowners Association.

Canadian Labor Congress. *Notes on Unions.* This series of handouts, produced by the leading labor federation, includes a useful glossary of labor terms.

Cheveldayoff, Wayne. (1978). *The Business Page: How to Read It for Profit, Politics and Peace of Mind.* Ottawa: Deneau and Greenberg.

Crane, David. (1980). *A Dictionary of Canadian Economics.* Edmonton: Hurtig Publishers.

Heron, Craig. (1996). *The Canadian Labour Movement: A Short History.* 2nd edition. Toronto: Lorimer.

Kluge, Pamela Hollie, ed. (1991). *The Columbia Knight-Bagehot Guide to Business and Economics Journalism.* New York: Columbia University Press.

Morton, Desmond. (1990). *Working People: An Illustrated History of the Canadian Labour Movement.* Revised and updated. Toronto: Summerhill Press.

Tasini, Jonathan. (1990). "Lost in the margins: Labour and the media." *Extra!,* Fairness and Accuracy in Reporting newsletter, Vol. 3, No. 7, Summer.

CHAPTER 16

Freelance Writing

THE JOB OF FREELANCE WRITING IS ONE OF THE last great romantic occupations in today's office-bound society. At best, it conjures images of freedom, of lunches with editors followed by long trips to Majorca. At worst, it's portrayed as a world of long hours in a rented room, with no salary, no pension plan — and plenty of rejection slips. Eve Drobot and Hal Tennant were clearly thinking mainly of free-lancers when they wrote, "Journalism, generally speaking, is writing to live, rather than living to write." (1990, 2).

The reality of freelancing covers both these images, and more, embracing a good deal of discipline and hard work as well as an interesting (or potentially interesting) life.

Newcomers to journalism may see the freelance life as a distant goal, something to dream about between calls to unco-operative sources. But the best time to start thinking of freelancing may be in the early stages of your career. For many journalism students, freelancing is the key to landing a full-time job. Others realize they must start small to build a reputation that can sustain full-time freelancing. Both types, though, must remember this key point: in freelancing, persistence is more important than brilliance. Successful writers are likely to be disciplined, organized — and dogged. Much of the best work done in journalism schools is never printed, because the writer for one reason or another doesn't make the effort to push for publication.

Getting Started

Exploring the Markets

Even for those with the necessary drive, some guidelines for the attack are useful. One is that newcomers to freelancing are almost always too narrow in their conception of possible markets. They think of major magazines like *Saturday Night* or *Toronto Life* and fail to think of the hundreds of other small publications like *Canadian Heritage*, or *The United Church Observer* — or their community newspaper. Many of these pay little or nothing, but provide a way to get started and to build a portfolio.

Another basic guideline is to specialize — to find a niche, to establish a link with a small group of publications in one field. Increasingly, editors want assurance that writers have some real expertise (or at least a strong interest) in the topics they're writing about. Newcomers who work outward from an area of knowledge bring a higher level of confidence to story selection, interviewing and writing.

So a vital first step is to study references (all updated periodically) like *The Canadian Writer's Market* (Bates 1996), *The Great Canadian Magazines Catalogue* (Bazan 1988) and the *Publication Profiles* (Canadian Advertising Rates and Data 1992). Also useful is *Who Pays What 1994–95: A Writer's Guide to Canadian Markets* (MacVoy 1994), put out by the Periodical Writers Association of Canada (PWAC). It gives guidance not just on how much each publication pays, but also on whether it wants photos, whether it will accept phone queries and so on. A look at any of these references will give a quick indication of the variety of outlets available.

Selecting with Care

John Eberlee, who started freelancing science and medicine stories in journalism school and afterward turned to a full-time career in Ottawa, says new freelancers should choose their target markets with a number of specific criteria in mind. It makes sense, he says, to pick magazines that publish frequently, that publish a lot of freelance material, and that don't have staff people in your area.

In his own case, for instance, Eberlee checked the CARD *Publication Profiles* and selected *The Medical Post* as one of his targets. "They're fairly big and they publish 44 times a year, which is a pretty good guarantee that they'll need lots of copy. And their staff isn't in Ottawa. There's lot of medicine going on in Ottawa so I'm in a good position to feed them stories uncompetitively."

WORKING THE GRID

Novice freelancers are often told to specialize. Usually it's good advice, but it doesn't mean you can't sell *from* your specialty *to* other areas. Look at the grid that follows and imagine the kinds of articles that could be drawn from each specialty and shaped for a particular market.

For instance, if your specialty is the law, would the *OHA Hockey News* be interested in something on hockey contracts? Would *The Medical Post* be interested in a piece on trends in malpractice insurance? Would *Campus Canada* be interested in something on admissions to law school? Would *Country Guide* be interested in an article on legal clashes between farmers and other country residents over farm smells?

These questions are only starting points — but they're the kinds of questions freelancers ask themselves as they pore through the magazine racks at their local store or library.

Environment	Sport	Health	Law	
				Campus Canada
				Canadian Lawyer Magazine
				Canadian Gardening
				Computing Canada
				Country Guide
				Food in Canada
				Healthwatch Canada
				Canadian Wildlife
				The Medical Post

It's also useful to concentrate on publications that are part of a larger group, Eberlee says, so your name may be passed on from editor to editor. The same word-of-mouth messages can circulate outside the chains, however: all freelancers know that Canadian journalism is made up of a number of fairly small communities. The groups of people who write regularly on agriculture, hockey, forestry, the environment or religion are relatively small. Reputations can be lost and made quickly.

Eberlee notes that in recent years these specialized networks have been nurtured online. He not only freelances but edits an online magazine for the International Development Research Centre, *IDRC Reports Online*, which draws on a group of specialist freelancers.

Charlotte Gray, who worked as a magazine editor for several years before launching her freelance career, warns that a specialty can become a ghetto, but agrees that defining a niche is useful in the early stages. "Once you're established as somebody with particular expertise in a particular area, whether it's business or child-rearing or politics or bran muffins or whatever, it gives you a credibility that a general magazine writer takes a long time to establish."

Most people, of course, do not launch a freelance career from ground zero. They first serve an apprenticeship in full-time journalism, or they devise some way (unless they're independently wealthy) of covering the household bills while they gradually establish themselves. Most freelancers begin selling on the side, while in university or while working on a small regional paper or magazine, until they have enough assurance and reputation to move out on their own. Others start writing from their background in another area — figure skating, farming, woodworking — and broaden out from there as they gain a track record.

Knowing the Market

Even if they are working in areas they know well, beginning freelance writers must also read target magazines carefully to get a feel for individual style and format. Ian Darragh is one of many editors who say this elementary move is often overlooked by new writers. While editing *Canadian Geographic*, his basic advice to freelancers was to analyse back issues of the magazine as though they were studying for an exam. He found that writers often proposed articles that had been the magazine's cover story only a couple of issues back. Or they would want to do a story on leopards in Kenya, even though it was obvious the magazine focused on Canadian topics.

Each publication, too, has its own flavor. Some highly specialized magazines — or certain sections within them — want crisp, fact-filled writing, very like traditional newspaper style. Others favor a more leisurely, personal approach. Some newspapers now run weekend supplements, or op-ed features, with writing very like the traditional magazine style. (While magazine writers have traditionally disdained newspaper work, Ottawa columnist Roy MacGregor suggested in a talk at the school of journalism, Carleton University, that some of the best magazine writing these days is being done in newspapers.)

FINDING IDEAS

Once you've identified an area of interest and a group of target publications, you can begin to collect and evaluate story possibilities and research sources, using some of the techniques outlined in earlier chapters.

In general, magazines give less space than newspapers to public life (city hall, the courts, Parliament) and more to private life — the things that people dream about or worry about as they're dropping off to sleep. While the newspapers may give close attention to changes in divorce law, the magazines are more likely to be interested in how to avoid divorce — or how to survive it, or help children cope with it. (This is true of general interest magazines, at least. The specialist magazines may cover anything from trends in divorce mediation to special problems of divorce in farm families.)

Beyond that, magazine writers get their ideas the same way as any other reporters. John Eberlee says most ideas come from reading voraciously: they come from reading newspapers carefully and considering what story could be given a different twist for a different market; they come from hanging out at the library or the magazine store and reading everything you can find that will help you keep up with trends in your area and allow you to devise ways of localizing issues. They come from getting on the mailing lists of associations in your field, and reading their specialized reports and newsletters. Eberlee says many of his science and medicine topics (in the early days when he had to produce his own ideas, rather than being handed assignments) came from visiting university departments to talk to the people there and to scan bulletin boards. Other writers look for ideas on a different kind of bulletin board — in the proliferating and constantly changing computer networks that now link people with interests ranging from religion to the environment.

Most writers find it useful to open a set of files in which they can collect raw material for articles. Whatever your interests, you can open files on those topics and drop in clippings or other bits of information you encounter. Eventually, you'll find the background has reached critical mass, and that a serious research effort is justified.

The freelancer's way of finding ideas and background is thus very close to the staff writer's. But after this point, the approach of the freelance writer begins to differ sharply, as considerations of marketing come into focus.

FRAMING QUERIES

Most professional freelance writers don't prepare full articles until they're sure of a market. They thus *query* publications, in one way or another, to see if the editors are interested. The most basic level of querying lies in simply phoning the editor to make your pitch. That works best if the magazine is a small one, or if you and your work are known to the editor. More usual is the query letter, sent by fax, e-mail or regular mail, in which you tantalize by offering a lead for your article and a quick sketch of how you propose to research and write the story. The editor can then indicate whether she'd like you to go ahead with it, or whether she'd like a fuller outline. That doesn't mean an assurance to buy, but most editors who've given a go-ahead will pay at least a partial "kill fee" if they decide not to use the story.

In general, the larger publications that pay the most also make the most demands for detailed queries or outlines (and, later, for revisions, or for source lists to be used by their fact-checkers). Newspapers are more casual in dealing with freelancers. It's usually sufficient to call the relevant editors (sports, finance, religion and so forth) to ask whether they'd be interested in seeing your story.

Most magazines publish *freelance guidelines*, which indicate how much they pay and what they expect of a writer. These range from the very elaborate and detailed instructions of *Reader's Digest* (covering everything from the query and revision process to the types of stories the *Digest* prefers) down to one-page summaries that list the magazine's pay scales and special interests.

The guidelines may also tell you (for instance) whether the editors will read full articles or expect queries, whether they accept work from novices or insist on seeing clips of previous work, and whether they require a full list of sources, with addresses and phone numbers. They may specify that they want copy submitted in CP style or in a particular electronic format. They may insist on stamped, self-addressed envelopes (usually a good idea, whether or not they're required). They're likely to specify length limits — which should be rigorously respected — and to say whether illustrations are welcomed.

While it's frustrating to wait for an editor to accept or reject your work, you should not send a full manuscript to more than one publication at a time. Some "how-to" books say it's proper to *query* more than one, but views differ on the point. Toronto freelancer Kim Pittaway, for instance, says she never queries more than one editor at a time, because she doesn't want to be in the position of getting two acceptances and having to disappoint one editor. If there's a pressing time factor, she'll make that point in the query letter, using it as a lever to get a quicker response. Pittaway says she also makes a practice of querying even newspaper editors by letter and followup phone call, rather than just by phone. She says editors seem to appreciate it, and the act of writing the query puts a better focus on her material, allowing her to make a more effective oral pitch.

Other writers say they send simultaneous queries to more than one editor but are careful to note that they've done so. *The Write Way*, a handbook of the Periodical Writers Association of Canada, says cautiously that "some editors" don't object to simultaneous submissions, provided writers ask them first. This handbook also discourages phone queries, saying they may be permissible when a writer has established a relationship with an editor, but should usually be used only when the writer needs a quick decision.

Unlike Pittaway, John Eberlee operates mostly by phone, after the first contact. But he says the initial approach should always be by mail, because editors aren't likely to be responsive on the phone to someone they don't know. The written query also allows writers to spell out their ideas more succinctly, while letting editors think about the idea at their convenience and pass it to others in office.

Catching Attention

The sample query letter shown in this chapter provides only rough guidelines on how the query letter should be framed. In general, there are two tests of a good query:

• Will it persuade the editors there's a story that should interest them?

• Will it show that you are the best person to write it?

In your early dealings with an editor, it may be useful to pitch three or four ideas at once, in hopes that at least one will catch her attention. It also makes sense to signal to the editor that you're a good prospect for future work, even if the particular story you're offering isn't needed.

The least professional approach is to write editors to tell them first about *yourself* ("I am a third-year journalism student at Penokey College ...") rather than showing what you can do for them. You'll avoid that kind of error if you imagine the editor opening your letter on a busy day as she's trying to get through her paperwork. Will the first words of your letter make her pause, thinking that this is indeed an idea that deserves to be followed up?

Kim Pittaway
8 Strathmore Blvd.
Toronto, Ontario
M4J 1P2
fax/phone (416) 465-4472

Cathy Callaghan
Chatelaine
777 Bay Street
Toronto, Ontario
M5W 1A7

Dear Cathy:
My apologies for t
story proposals to
worth the wait. A
Halifax story wou
the way of expens
place to stay in
I would need is

I'm also lookin
wrong" issue, a
together on tha
you soon.

Regards,

Kim Pittaway

PROPOSAL:
SOMETHING IN THE AIR

It's been called the hospital that's sicker than its patients. But some experts say that the only difference between Halifax's Camp Hill Hospital and other afflicted modern buildings throughout North America is that Camp Hill has been open about its "mystery disease." Some call it twentieth century disease, others label it environmental illness, sick building syndrome or multiple chemical sensitivity. Whatever the moniker, it has affected over half of Camp Hill's 1100 employees over the last six years, with 120 workers still on paid leave because they are too sick to return to their jobs.

The problems started when kitchen employees working in the basement complained about headaches, rashes and eye irritations. The culprit was soon tracked down: stale air laden with cleaning chemicals was being blown out of the basement but was then sucked back in by a nearby air intake vent. The problem was solved and so, hoped the hospital, were the health complaints. But before long, kitchen staff were complaining again. This time the culprit was acid fumes carried in through the air intake. Then, workers on the first and second floors started complaining as well — improperly vented formaldehyde and phenol got the blame. But with each solution came new problems, some that defied explanation.

In news reports at the time, Dr. Rosemary Marchant, an air quality expert hired by the hospital, stressed the problem had no single cause. She — along with many other air quality specialists — blamed the symptoms on the fact that the affected buildings were essentially "sealed shut" to prevent them from losing energy. She compared it to asking people to live in a plastic bag: if the stale air can't get out, or fresh isn't coming in, problems are inevitable, she said.

For some employees, what began as rashes and headaches seemed to set off a chain reaction of chemical sensitivities. People who had never had allergies found themselves having severe reactions to perfumes, detergents, processed foods and synthetic fibres. While it was clear to some that something at the hospital was causing the problems, many doctors remained skeptical: some suggested it was stress.

Others felt the problem wasn't in the hospital's air, it was in the patients' heads. Those afflicted by the symptoms rejected the suggestion that their illness was psychosomatic, and set up a support group to help them deal with illness and its impact on their lives. But there are still many in the medical profession who remain unconvinced that "environmental illness" is real.

Now, after six years with no clear answers, the province of Nova Scotia is funding the first clinic in Canada set up to treat and research environmental illness. Set to open this spring, the clinic is headed by Dr. Roy Fox — a physician who had to leave his post as head of geriatric medicine at Camp Hill because he says the building made him too sick to work there.

I'd like to explore what happened at Camp Hill, and the issues around the environmental illness. What I'm particularly interested in are the psychological aspects: what interplay, if any, is there between the physical symptoms and the psychological issues of work in the 90s? Not everyone at Camp Hill got sick — why were some more affected than others? And why were some not affected at all?

Some research into environmental illness suggests that employees with the least amount of workplace control or clout are ones most likely to get sick — is it because they can't control the conditions under which they work, and so are forced to stay on the job even when it's making them sick, or is getting sick a way of exerting control? Also, the symptoms involved are often quite subtle — could the thought that there's a mysterious illness going around prompt workers to pay attention to symptoms they might otherwise have dismissed? (For instance, recent work on hypochondriacs suggests that their aches and pains are real — but while the rest of us shrug them off as 'aches and pains' hypochondriacs notice and worry about them.) What about the psychological impact of not being taken seriously when your symptoms are debilitating?

There's a lot we don't understand about the interplay of psychological and physical health. Environmental illness offers us the chance to explore some of that uncharted territory.

CHATELAINE
NOVEMBER 1995

Some thing in the air

Between 1989 and 1993, 800 workers at Halifax's Camp Hill Medical Centre fell sick because of chemically contaminated air. More than 100 are still off work—and a fight is raging over the reasons why. Kim Pittaway explores the modern fears and slippery truths behind the environmental illness debate

73

Freelance writers know that making a good pitch is often the key to making a good sale. Kim Pittaway's proposal for a story on environmental illness, left, resulted in this article in *Chatelaine* magazine.

Keeping Track

All this suggests an approach in which you have a number of queries out for consideration at any given time, rather than depending on just one or two. That means keeping careful track of what's gone where. Kim Pittaway keeps a file for each magazine she's querying, with a recent copy of the publication, photocopies or tearsheets of the table of contents for the last year, and copies of all queries sent in, plus responses. ("That way, if an editor calls to discuss a query, I can grab the file quickly and sound a lot smarter than I feel.") Other writers use special software that allows them to call up from their computer system a list of all queries that remain unsold, so they can freshen them up and send them off again.

When your query is accepted, it's wise to get down on paper any oral agreements you and the editor have reached about story length, deadline, fees or expenses. Some editors send detailed assignment letters. Failing that, you should least to write to the editor, saying something like this:

> Thanks for your interest in my proposal for a profile on X. My understanding from our phone conversation is that you would like 1,500 words by February 21, plus a selection of at least five photos, and that you're willing to pay on approval $600, plus $50 for every photo to be used. Please let me know if I've misunderstood any of this.

Trying Again

If your proposal is turned down, of course, the professional approach is neither to attack the editor nor to toss the query in the drawer in a snit. You must think of another target publication and get the query in the mail again. And you must not assume the editor who turned you down is out to get you, or will automatically turn back your next query. Anyone who gives up after the first rejection is not really working at the task.

Novice writers sometimes wonder if editors will take advantage of them, using their idea without pay or acknowledgment. The short answer is that there's no guarantee against this, but to do so would be blatantly unethical, and most editors aren't. However, you can't expect to claim ownership of a story idea worded in a general way ("I'd like to do a story on the impact of acid rain on Canadian forests"). You must have a distinctive angle to make it your own.

MASTERING THE BASICS

While a number of books deal with the general problems of freelancing, some points are especially relevant for journalism students:

- If you're targeting newspapers, don't think first of the newspapers in the city where you're working. They're probably quite capable of getting the story you're offering with their own staff. Think instead of newspapers at the other end of the country (or in some other country) that may welcome a story they can't readily research with their own people. If you're stationed in Ottawa or Toronto, for instance, think of the material you can get on developments in business or government that have particular interest in the Maritimes or British Columbia. If you're stationed in the Maritimes, think of the business story, travel story or social issue story that might make an impact in Montreal or Toronto. (In this context, "business" news can cover everything from a new kind of baby's car seat to a surge in the sale of fur hats, while "governmental" news can include everything from patterns of AIDS testing to plans for new parks.)

- When you deal with magazines, take account of the problem of *lead time*. That is, assume as you write that your piece may not be published for months.

- Keep illustrations in mind — not just pictures but also line drawings, cartoons, graphs, maps, symbols. Smaller publications, especially, will welcome illustrations.

- Remember that most magazines have very clear target audiences, and this inevitably affects the way articles should be shaped. Some are directed at particular trades, religions or interest groups. Others are directed at one particular sex, or at people with particular demographic characteristics, such as English-speaking women with children at home and high disposable income.

- While accuracy is important to everyone in the business, in your first published work it's especially crucial *to you*. Given the tight links of Canada's journalistic community, you can't afford complaints about inaccuracy.

Some other, more general aspects of freelancing are well covered in a book called *Words for Sale* (Drobot and Tennant 1990). It not only offers sample query letters and outlines, but as well provides sound advice about development of story ideas, dealing with sources, writing and the nature of the freelancing life.

PROFESSIONAL ATTITUDE

While the key talents of the freelance writer are the same as those of any other journalist — the ability to get the material and write it well — veteran freelancers also stress that a professional attitude is crucial for newcomers. Above all, novices must produce clean and accurate copy, on deadline, and without fuss. If they're selling to the kind of magazine that's known to rewrite heavily (to "put everything in the Cuisinart," in Charlotte Gray's term), it makes little sense to throw a tantrum over damage done to your beautiful prose. Says Gray, "I know from having worked the other side of the fence that freelance writers whose names you see again and again are the ones who produce by deadline, and who understand that their work is going to be edited."

Gray also stresses the value of meeting editors face to face. Anyone who has a presentable portfolio and wants to make a serious move into freelancing, she says, should plan a trip to Toronto, where Canadian editors cluster, and arrange to meet some of them — first, of course, having read the target magazines carefully and having worked up a set of ideas. "Unless you're absolutely brilliant and have already established a rapport with Toronto or New York editors, it's tough to be a full-time magazine writer on the periphery," she says. In her own case, she was impressed by how welcoming editors were when she made that kind of approach. "I found that magazines have huge appetites — they need new writers and new ideas all the time, and everybody's a potential source. But it would be very hard to set up as a magazine writer if you were dealing only by long distance and didn't know anyone in the business."

While good contacts in the major centres are obviously critical, this doesn't mean you have to live in Toronto to make a living as a freelancer. Mark Zuehlke and Louise Donnelly, who work from British Columbia's Okanagan Valley, have published a book called *Magazine Writing From the Boonies* (1992) arguing that freelancers can successfully exploit the distinctive qualities of their areas.

FREELANCING AS A WAY OF LIFE

The lifestyle of a novice freelance writer may be an uncertain one, but some writers still prefer its chancy but engaging independence to the security and restrictions of standard office jobs. Kim Pittaway, for instance, says she can't imagine working any other way: she likes the feeling of control, the freedom to work in areas that interest her most, the variety that comes from keeping several projects in the air at once — and the freedom to shut down her computer when she wants to enjoy a perfect April afternoon. Some people see the life as financially insecure, she says, but it may actually be better in tough times to work for eight or nine editors than just one.

The drawbacks, Pittaway says, include the fact that you're "not following in someone else's footsteps" — there's not a standard route to advancement of the kind you can see in a corporate job. Freelancers thus sometimes feel isolated. They feel they're working in a vacuum, not knowing what editors are thinking or what other writers are doing. After years on her own, she welcomes an arrangement with *Chatelaine* whereby she edits two days a week for the magazine — one day at the office and the other by electronic connections from home. Pittaway feels that in the late 1990s, freelance markets are picking up after a period when young writers found it difficult to break in, as all the voices in magazines seemed to belong to the baby boom generation.

Pittaway adds, though, that young writers without earned reputations have a particularly difficult time in the long-running battle by freelancers to claim extra payment for re-publication. The problem is that publishers generally are moving toward contracts that cover ownership of articles for all future re-publications, either on the Internet or in sister publications. Freelancers and the Periodical Writers Association of Canada have fought, both in the courts and in contracts with publishers, to establish a principle of additional payment for re-publication. In practice, Pittaway says, senior writers can get higher rates if they sign away future rights, while new writers are at the mercy of the publishers who tell them they must either sign the contract as is or lose the work.

John Eberlee says his choice of freelancing was a matter of wanting to determine the kind of work he would do, and where he would do it. "I wanted to be a science writer, and if you're in mainstream media it's hard to get that slot. I didn't want to get on with a big newspaper and spend time covering beats I wasn't interested in. I didn't want to chase ambulances or cover city hall — I wanted to do science writing and I figured the easiest way to do that was to become a freelance writer and start selling stories."

The disadvantages Eberlee sees include the obvious ones: low financial return, at least at the start, lack of company-paid vacations, pensions and disability insurance. And he adds: "it can be lonely. You have to be self-disciplined. There's nobody looking over your shoulder to make sure you're not wasting time or goofing off, and that can be hard on some people. And you're not going to get the kind of social contact you get in a busy newsroom."

Gray agrees. She says she's sometimes jealous of people who go off to an office where they can enjoy the casual social lubrication of conversation around the water cooler. The freelance life can get very isolated: "you have to structure into your day some kind of human intercourse, whether it's just a telephone call or lunch with somebody — but some kind of social contact."

Selling Yourself

Pittaway says another built-in problem of freelancing is the need to sell not just your writing, but your ideas and yourself. That means extra effort to keep in touch with contacts, to network — to make efforts that have no immediate payoff but may bring returns somewhere down the road. Freelance writers are sometimes loners, more comfortable facing their computers than their editors or sources, and for these people, keeping in touch takes a constant effort of will. It makes sense to keep, in your computer or a notebook, a constantly growing list of contacts and their phone numbers, and to review it occasionally to see if you're losing touch and should therefore look for a reason to call or drop a note.

More important than keeping in touch with people, though, is freelance writers' need to keep in touch with the flow of information in their areas. They must keep up with specialized or foreign publications, with books, government reports, theses or commission studies.

Freelance writers, in fact, should take special note of two of Robert Fulford's guidelines spelled out in Chapter 1. Early in their working lives, he said, all journalists should find and immerse themselves in a subject that *matters* to them. And all good journalists must *read* far more than most people do.

Those are indeed the two primary guidelines. All the rest is secondary.

RECOMMENDED READING

Bazan, Judy, ed. (1998). *The Great Canadian Magazines Catalogue*. Toronto: Canadian Magazine Publishers Association.

Cassill, Kay. (1981). *The Complete Handbook for Freelance Writers*. Cincinnati, OH: Writer's Digest Books.

Drobot, Eve, and Hal Tennant, eds. (1990). *Words for Sale*. Toronto: The Periodical Writers Association of Canada and Macmillan of Canada.

Graham, Betsy P. (1980). *Magazine Article Writing*. New York: Holt Rinehart and Winston.

MacVoy, Sheila, ed. (1994). *Who Pays What, 1994–95: A Writer's Guide to Canadian Markets*. Toronto: Canadian Periodical Writers Association.

Neff, Glenda Tennant. (1991). *The Writer's Essential Desk Reference*. Chapter 6, "Writing and Selling in Canada." Cincinnati, OH: Writer's Digest Books.

Rivers, William L., and Alison R. Work. (1986). *Free-Lancer and Staff Writer*. 4th edition. Belmont, CA: Wadsworth Publishing Company.

Yudkin, Marcia. (1987). *Freelance Writing for Magazines and Newspapers*. New York: Harper & Row.

Zuehlke, Mark, and Louise Donnelly. (1992). *Magazine Writing From the Boonies*. Ottawa: Carleton University Press.

PART
five

ETHICS

Reporting is never a neutral activity. It takes place in complex webs of personal, professional and social codes. Part Five takes an introductory look at those codes, first reviewing the rich ethical tradition of western journalism, and then considering the development of a personal approach to ethical decisions.

To help define both the existing norms and the decision-making process, we include in Chapter 17 some ethics guidelines, a collection of short cases for discussion and a bibliography of current articles on ethical problems.

CHAPTER 17

Ethical Reporting

A ROUGH CONSENSUS EXISTS AMONG WESTERN journalists on ethical values and behavior. The makeup of this consensus is complex, fascinating — and dynamic. It has changed a great deal over the past hundred years, since the time when, for example, reporters saw nothing wrong in working quietly for a political party. And it continues to change, as each new generation of reporters and editors wrestles with the conflicts that inevitably arise in the course of their work.

In the late 20th century, the consensus is liberal, humanist and functional. This last idea derives from utilitarianism (the idea of doing the greatest good for the greatest number) but is shaped by modern professional and business values. In essence, it is the idea that in a smoothly operating society, certain vital functions must be performed. These include policing, teaching, doctoring — and disseminating information. Doctors betray their special function if they fail in their healing role. Police officers betray it if they fail to enforce the law. Journalists betray it if they fail to provide good-quality information, the kind people need to make intelligent choices about their lives.

While that general principle seems simple, putting it into practice means facing a variety of tough ethical choices. Like doctors or lawyers, journalists try to meet problems with responsible decisions that reflect the major values associated with their occupation. These values include such ideas as telling the truth as they see it, keeping an eye on public institutions and putting public interest above private gain. But again, these values are often easier to label than to use in particular instances.

For that reason, journalists have developed a system of working ethics, a body of standards based on experience, philosophical principles and "case law" that defines what is or is not acceptable behavior. These standards overlap in some areas with the legal system. Journalists should not assume, however, that what is ethical and what is legal are the same. Sometimes a legal act, such as sitting in on a meeting that was meant to be private, may be unethical. Sometimes an ethical act, such as staying with the story if a protest march trespasses on private property, may be illegal. And in many areas, the law simply doesn't address the question of ethics.

To a minor extent, ethical norms for journalists are set by official or non-official bodies — the broadcast regulatory agencies or press councils or trade organizations. To a much greater extent, they have grown through experience, through the actual response of media managers, commentators and reporters when conflicts arise on, say, the handling of a leaked budget or a reporter's participation in a demonstration. They cover things like conflict of interest (reporters working for a company or political organization they're also covering, for example), protection of sources, acceptance of favors and invasion of privacy.

Reporters learn these standards almost by osmosis. They are exposed to them through talking to their colleagues, journalism instructors and editors. They watch how other reporters behave. They may absorb them through reading cases studies in a reporting or ethics class. Finally, they learn them when they have to make decisions themselves. But there is a profound paradox — and a danger — in seeing the study of ethics as a matter of learning and accepting professional norms. There is, of course, a value in studying the ethical heritage of journalism and learning current standards. Yet this very process may lead to ethical standardization, to uniformity, or to a reliance on experts (professors, editors or publishers) to resolve dilemmas.

The challenge, then, is to examine ethics while holding one part of the mind aloof, recognizing that ethical norms may lead to conformity or to defensive, self-justifying thinking, and that the highest ethical duty may be to turn against group ethics. While journalism is very much a collective activity, the ethical decision is personal. That major qualification must be kept in mind in all discussions of ethics, along with these general points:

1. Professionals are not likely to act ethically unless they are convinced of the importance of what they do.

2. The subject of ethics in journalism is complicated by the commercial nature of the media in Canada and other western nations. The public interest is often in tension with the commercial interest — the need to make profits or sell advertising. To the extent that decisions are based on consideration of the public interest, they can be called ethical.

3. Because they get to tell the story, journalists tend to portray themselves as more righteous than the people they write about. This can lead to circular thinking — deciding that anything journalists do must be righteous because journalists are righteous. In invoking ethics, too, the greatest frauds are often the loudest. The most scabrous tabloid is as likely to wave ethical banners as the most serious journal.

With these general points in mind, this chapter takes a brief look at three areas, each of which might well be a text in itself:

• the origins of western journalistic values

• the process of ethical decision making

• the current norms and how they are changing

ORIGINS OF JOURNALISTIC VALUES

The western ethical consensus on journalism draws from a number of thinkers and schools of thought, but centres most firmly on the vision of free public discussion expressed by John Milton, John Stuart Mill and other liberal philosophers. When journalists are asked why they do what they do, when they are asked what broad principles govern their ethical decisions, they are likely to draw on the rhetoric of free speech, free discussion and the free marketplace of ideas. They believe in the *efficacy* of information — that exposing fraud and corruption and foolishness will force people to deal with it. They believe that society will be better if people know what is going on, and if those in charge know they are under scrutiny.

In addition, journalists believe that enlightened public opinion is likely to arise only from broad public discussion. They take it as an article of faith that this discussion ought to be wide enough to allow unpopular or irresponsible thoughts. They agree with Wilfrid Laurier that liberty exists not just for the friends of liberty, but for its enemies (*Hansard*, Mar. 28, 1889, 907). Like John Stuart Mill, they accept that irresponsible views must be tolerated because a wrong opinion may contain a grain of truth; because even a sound opinion will not be held on a rational basis unless it is tested; because opinions must be constantly tested or they will lose their vitality. More practically, they argue that censorship of any view implies an intolerable level of thought policing.

This liberal view is secular, in contrast to earlier codes of ethics that claimed direct descent from divine will, though it owes much (as do the general social values of the West) to Judeo-Christian values of honesty, compassion and so on.

The consensus also owes much to a number of thinkers and philosophers who have wrestled with questions on what constitutes the good society (freedom, equality, justice) or on what is to be expected of the good person (wisdom, compassion, temperance, courage). One strand of thought derives from Aristotle's idea of virtue ethics, focusing on the virtues of the individual as well as his or her actions. This philosophy is often presented in shorthand form as the "golden mean," the idea that the virtuous act lies between two extremes. For the journalist, for example, the golden mean might lie between trying to find out everything about the personal life of a new Liberal party leader and trying to find out nothing.

The ethical consensus also draws on the work of Immanuel Kant, particularly on the "categorical imperative" which says, in essence, that you should act in the way you think others should act. The test of a decision is whether it could be applied universally. If you feel, for example, you must tell a lie to get some information, you must accept that others facing the same circumstances should also lie. This view is particularly useful in reminding journalists that claiming a special privilege has its costs.

The consensus also draws on something of the utilitarian idea that public life must be shaped for the greatest good of the greatest number of people, and that the *consequences* of an action are important in deciding whether the action is ethical. In this view, a journalist could — indeed, should — expose the corruption of a public official. Though the act might harm the individual, it will benefit the larger whole.

Also significant is a widespread journalistic view that sees political/corporate elites as being in conflict with everyone else in society, including journalists. That view probably owes something to classic Marxist theory, which sees the political and corporate elites controlling not just the means of production but the flow of ideas. In this view, ethical behavior demands that journalists keep an eye on the elite controllers and side with the ordinary people. In recent decades journalists have often spoken of their "adversarial" role, meaning they must serve as critics of the elites, not simply as conduits for their statements and decisions.

The consensus also includes a professional dimension that might be called, at best, respect for the integrity of the craft (a phrase borrowed from Walter Lippman 1955, 46) and, at worst, a guild psychology in which members of a profession combine to resist both rivals and critics. These good and bad patterns show up in such groups as bar associations and medical associations that set limits on recruitment, devise standards of practice and set up committees to enforce them. Journalism has never achieved professional status of this kind, but in recent years it has moved in that direction. The establishment of professional organizations and training institutions, and media reviews or press councils that rule on the ethics of journalistic acts, contributes to a professional consciousness. At the same time, journalists have been extremely reluctant to seek any kind of exclusivity (through, for example, a licensing system) on the ground that it would limit press freedom. It is probably true to say, though, that in recent years journalists have developed a greater *sense of collective* — a sense of the shared values and responsibilities that detach them from politics and business, and from other sectors of society.

It is clear from this discussion that the ethical consensus is an intricate one, drawing on ideas and philosophies that are often seen as opposites — Marxism and classical liberalism, for example, or individualism and guild philosophy. (Indeed, this is what makes the study of ethics in journalism so fascinating.) Journalists may seldom pause to analyse it, but they manage to blend many of these concepts into a consensus focused on the idea of *function* — of disseminating "good" information of the kind people need to make "good" decisions. Generally, this is expressed as respect for the *public trust* or the *public interest*, a concept usefully defined by Lippmann to include not just the needs of the present public but also those of the future society (1955, 32–40). A statement of journalistic principles by the Canadian Daily Newspaper Association invokes this concept of public interest:

> The newspaper has responsibilities to its readers, its shareholders, its employees and its advertisers. But the operation of a newspaper is a public trust and its overriding responsibility is to the society it serves. (Statement of Principles, adopted by the Canadian Daily Newspaper Association, revised in 1995)

This statement, including the qualifications, could be replicated in the United States or almost any other western nation. This is not to say, however, that journalistic values are identical in all these countries, or even among reporters, editors and publishers in a single country. Canadian reporters disagree sharply on the idea of objectivity, for example, and on whether the role of the press is to report social change or to promote it. But they tend to accept greater limit on free speech than Americans, particularly in the realm of crime and court reporting. They may be more reluctant than employees of most Fleet Street

tabloids to pry into the bedrooms of the elites. Broadly speaking, however, the ethical blend in Canada, the United States, Britain and other
countries with similar media systems draws on the same ingredients,
though in different proportions.

ETHICAL DECISION MAKING

While journalists should understand their ethical heritage and the current
values of their trade, the toughest calls they have to make will, ultimately,
be lonely ones. The journalist will have to work through the problem and
make a decision that may not be popular with either colleagues or the
public.

Because of this, many journalism educators try to go beyond simply
teaching current ethical norms, concentrating instead on the personal
process of ethical decision making. Teachers use case studies to illustrate
general ethical principles but also to deal with dilemmas where it's possible to see conflicting "goods" — the "good" of public knowledge, for
example, as opposed to the "good" of protection of privacy. This
approach is designed not so much to define moral absolutes as to help
individuals find a way to analyse their own ethical priorities.

On one level this approach is useful in reminding you that ethical
considerations are usually more complex than they appear on first
glance. On another it helps you confront the essential challenge of ethical analysis. For instance:

- Where "goods" collide, how can a balance be struck? In a national
  tragedy like a mine disaster or an air crash, the whole society may be
  drawn together by painful television footage of the victims. But such
  footage is almost certain to invade the privacy of the people affected.
  Which "good" should prevail?

- Does the "good" or "evil" of an act dwell in the act itself, in the motivation behind it, or in its consequences? Lying is considered to be
  wrong. But what of the reporter who used deceit to gain entry to a
  mental hospital and exposed appalling conditions in it? What of the
  reporter who posed as a factory worker to reveal the exploitation and
  abuse of immigrant women in garment-district sweat-shops? Is lying
  sometimes virtuous, and if so, under what conditions? Which is more
  important — the rule ("I must be honest") or the consequences of
  breaking it? And how do you weigh a situation with more than one
  consequence ("If I am honest several people will suffer" or "If I pretend to be someone I'm not, the public may lose faith in the trust-
  worthiness of the information I gather")?

This photo gives dramatic insight into the work of firefighters — but it also raises questions about taste and invasion of privacy. When, and to what extent, should individual pain be exposed? *(Toronto Sun)*

Such discussions are seldom conclusive, but they are useful if they promote a habit of moral consideration, of internal moral argument, that examines pros and cons.

For instance, one of the ethical cases at the end of this chapter relates to the actual experience of a man who had been acquitted on a sex charge. The local newspaper prepared a story about the acquittal, in line with its policy of always covering the disposition of a case if it had published the original charge. The acquitted man, however, called the paper to urge that the story not be run, saying he had already been damaged enough and wanted no further mention of it.

In evaluating this case, students — and journalists — will probably think first of the individual, and decide there's no need to carry the story since the impulsion to do so is chiefly to clear the man's name. On reflection, though, most will see broader implications: community members have a legitimate interest in knowing how the case was disposed of, so they can evaluate the performance of the justice system. This discussion may lead to the bigger question of whether it's ethically necessary for the press to carry *any* names of those charged before disposition of the case. From the point of view of the larger society, what "good" is served by reporting the names of those charged but still deemed innocent until proven guilty? Is this merely a device through which the people in power (including the media) induce conformity? Or is it, as most journalists would insist, vital raw material for understanding how the police and courts are performing? This in turn leads to thoughts about the place of the press in the larger civic polity. Paradoxically, the press *is* part of the justice system — yet remains detached from it.

A similar broadening occurs in analysing the case of an embassy hostage-taking incident, drawn from a real occurrence in the mid-1980s. In this instance a wounded hostage escapes from the building and takes cover in bushes beside it, out of sight of the hostage-takers. The dilemma is: should broadcast reporters doing live reports mention this fact? On the one hand, it is obviously news — a major development in a hot story. On the other, a broadcast report might let the hostage-takers know where their victim is hiding.

Most people agree quickly that the reporters should not broadcast this escape until the hostage's safety is assured. But the discussion then moves to questions of when it is right for a reporter to suppress (or at least delay) news, or whether it is ever right to spread a false report, perhaps at police request, to save a life. One factor sure to emerge is the idea that any suppression or distortion has a cost to the public interest: if people develop the perception that reporters suppress and distort news, the quality of public discussion and, ultimately, public decision making may suffer.

In situations like these an overarching principle, such as respect for the informing function, is useful. Without it, the ethical decision making may descend to a level of pragmatics: What can I get away with? What is the opposition likely to do? Will I be criticized by my boss, or my friends in the newsroom, or the public, if I do this instead of that? Such questions always crowd in on ethical decisions, but they cannot replace ethical reasoning. In the latter, the questions are more likely to be something like this:

- What are my options, and what are the likely effects of each option?

- How (thinking of Immanuel Kant's rule) would I want other reporters to act if confronted with the same conditions I face?

- What (in line with the functional view of ethics) are the needs of my readers? Do they need to know now that a hostage has escaped, or can the development be suppressed for a time?

- Do any personal prejudices distort my decision? (For instance, journalists may be inclined to judge an act as ethical if it is done by a colleague or by someone they personally like, and inclined to consider it unethical if done by an individual or group they dislike.)

- If I do this instead of that, will I look back with satisfaction on the decision 10 years, or 50 years, from now?

All systems of moral reasoning contain some process of identifying issues and balancing values and principles. Some scholars in media ethics, led by Clifford Christians and his associates, use a model of moral reasoning called the Potter Box, devised by Dr. Ralph Potter (Christians et al. 1983, 1–23). Briefly, the box includes four stages of analysis:

1. **Defining facts.** This means assessing exactly what you know, and how much of it is relevant. Most people wrestling with an ethical decision want more facts than they have, in the belief that it will make the decision easier. This is not always the case. Often, too, arguments about ethics come down to arguments over the facts. (Was this document you received in a brown paper envelope leaked or stolen, and does that make a difference in what you do with it?)

2. **Defining values.** Ethics scholars Philip Patterson and Lee Wilkins point out that "values" is a much abused word: "people can value everything from their loved ones to making fashion statements" (Patterson and Wilkins 1991, 87). In ethics, they write, the word takes on a different meaning: if you value something it means you must be willing to give up something else for it. If, for example, you value truth above all things in your reporting, then you will be willing to give up the value of protecting the privacy of an individual caught up in a news story. It's important to be honest in identifying your values — the negative or self-serving ones as well as the positive — to allow a full consideration at this stage.

3. **Applying principles.** Here's where the philosophical precepts underlying the function of the journalist come into play. In their explanation of the Potter Box, Patterson and Wilkins use a story about the sexual assault of a mentally handicapped woman. They point out that utilitarian principles would suggest that the greatest good would be to run a story warning that the attacker is still at large. Aristotle's golden mean would suggest writing a report that

falls somewhere between reporting every detail (including those that might invade the victim's privacy) and none of the details. Kantian principles might argue that the maxim of protecting someone who can't protect herself could be made universal. In this case, the application of several principles leads to the same conclusion: it's best not to reveal the victim's identity (Patterson and Wilkins 1991, 86–88). In many other cases, however, the principles may collide. It's up to you as reporter to sort them out and to make a morally justifiable decision — you must be able to explain to your editor, or your readers if necessary, why you made the decision you did.

4. **Defining loyalties.** The question of sorting out loyalties is useful at any time, but it gains particular importance in ethical decisions. The reporter must determine how loyalty to a source, for example, balances with loyalty to the employer, or to the audience of readers, or to more abstract concepts like the public interest. Again, an honest assessment of these loyalties is crucial.

Finally, the Potter Box brings the analysis of loyalties around again, to help in a re-analysis of the definition and values. In effect, the process seeks to guarantee that each stage will be evaluated deliberately and that the connections will be weighed.

The Potter Box is by no means the only system of evaluation, of course. Lou Hodges, of Washington and Lee University in Virginia, has spoken of one that relies on an assessment of the range of possible actions and their consequences. Fairly quickly, reporters can eliminate the possible courses at the extreme ends of the range and focus on one or two likely actions and the likely consequences each would have. Many other writers, including Canadian journalist and scholar Nick Russell (1994), have tried to develop sets of reflex questions that will help a journalist test the ethics of a situation. Typical questions ask who will gain or lose by a story, what alternatives exist, and whether the harm of a story will outweigh the good it does.

Such systems are far from infallible. Any one of them can be used to justify the decision you *want to* reach. And the speed of journalism seldom allows for lengthy reflection.

But for reporters who have a capacity for self-critical analysis, the process may bring into view factors they were reluctant to confront, thus allowing them to distinguish moral reasoning from expediency. In practical terms, such reasoning must be done quickly — a matter of exposing the dilemma to quick tests on whether (for instance) extraneous issues are swaying your judgment, or personal loyalties and prejudices are getting in the way.

CHANGING STANDARDS

Most journalists would agree that ethical norms have tightened in recent decades in a number of areas, including fabrication and conflict of interest. Some older journalists delight in telling of times they made up news, stole photographs, cheerfully accepted major favors, casually invaded someone's privacy, or worked "on the side" for the same people they were covering. In part these tales may come from the simple pleasure of telling wicked stories; the old days may not really have been so bad. Still, the hostile reaction these tales invoke in many younger journalists shows a change in values.

Journalists now react with near-universal condemnation to cases where their colleagues passed off fictional anecdotes as real, or where they faked television footage. Conflicts of interest — when, for example, business writers do freelance public relations work for companies they're writing about — are viewed more seriously than in years past.

Similarly, gifts from sources (a basket of cheese and fruit at Christmas or an "honorarium" from a company whose product was featured) are no longer respectable. A few decades ago such gifts were commonplace: Robert Fulford once wrote that when he joined the *Globe and Mail* in the late 1950s, sports reporters and editors routinely accepted small fees to write press releases for promoters. On one occasion, he himself accepted a $100 "Christmas bonus" from Maple Leaf Gardens. Nowadays gifts sent to many newsrooms often end up at a local charity that can use them, or in the return mail to the gift giver.

On the other hand, some journalists in the 1990s, particularly those with a strong viewpoint on an issue, may not be as rigorous as they ought to be in ensuring that all sides in a controversy are heard. (Ironically, this problem may be greatest in those who are not aware of their own prejudices, or claim not to favor any viewpoint.) Others may be more aggressive in using technology to invade privacy. In classroom discussions at Carleton University, we find that many students see nothing unethical in taping a phone interview without advising the source (although, oddly, many of these same people say they would not wear a hidden microphone in a face-to-face interview). It is, of course, legal to tape a conversation in which you take part, as long as you don't broadcast it without the other person's permission. With that in mind, many journalists tape telephone conversations routinely, arguing that the process is no different from note-taking. Many interview subjects, on the other hand, feel deceived if they are not told that a tape recorder is running.

On another level, the close relationship between journalism and the entertainment industry is cause for concern. Critic John Haslett Cuff is one of many who have savaged that relationship: he writes of junkets in which journalists are wined, dined and allowed a five-minute brush with celebrity, and concludes, "media access to Hollywood comes only with compliance and docility" (*Globe and Mail*, July 27, 1991).

Similar concerns arise about alarmingly close relations between travel writers or sports reporters and the industries they cover. The worry is that these reporters often come to share the values and ideology of the people they are covering, losing sight of, or perhaps actively sacrificing, the values of journalism along the way.

The delicate coexistence between the newsroom and the advertising department is a continuing source of tension. While open dictation from the advertising department is now rare, many newspapers and radio and TV stations, particularly the smaller ones, are still often reluctant to take on stories that might offend advertisers. In the magazine world there is clearly great pressure to make editorial content support (or at least not hurt) the aims of advertisers.

More broadly, a continuing tension exists between journalists and business people who believe the media ought to be boosters of the companies and industries that supply their ads. The pattern is paralleled by government pressure exerted on reporters in times of crisis to turn into cheerleaders — to pull out all the stops in support of national unity efforts, for instance.

These are some areas where present concerns may change the ethical consensus over the next few years. In the meantime, a number of public issues have redefined the consensus in crucial areas. The fallout from Doug Small's broadcast of the leaked 1989–90 budget, for instance, solidified a clear consensus on journalistic duty in such cases. When Small, Ottawa bureau chief of Global Television, was told that an advance copy of budget papers could be obtained, he had a duty (as his colleagues saw it) to find out if this was really so and to publish the contents — both to demonstrate the government's mishandling of the material and to prevent anyone else who had a copy from profiteering from the information it contained. More broadly, the case reflected a strong journalistic willingness to resist official strictures, even at the risk of colliding with the law.

A more complex case occurred in 1990 when a journalist tapped a B.C. cabinet minister's cellular phone and discovered that another journalist had a personal relationship with the minister. The ensuing uproar strengthened concerns about surreptitious phone taps and about personal alliances between reporters and politicians.

SOLIDARITY? OR INTERFERENCE?

After the blockade by Mohawk Warriors at Oka, Quebec, in 1990, reporter Jeff Heinrich wrote of how he and other Montreal *Gazette* reporters had been excluded from the Warrior-controlled area. He told of how the rest of the press corps at the Warrior camp then walked out in protest, but returned the next day, while the *Gazette* was still excluded.

He wrote:

"So when do we stand up for each other and when don't we? Is it normal that in war zones the rules of the media game are different? I think so."

His question posed a tough ethical dilemma: should other journalists stick up for their colleagues in this kind of crunch, or go ahead with covering anything they're able to cover? (See Heinrich 1990.)

The Oka incident raised a number of other ethical dilemmas, including these:

• Should reporters accept, from a dissident group violently challenging authority, designation to a press "pool"? (A pool is an arrangement under which a single reporter or small group of reporters is given access, on condition they pass what they learn on to the rest of the press corps.) At Oka, most designated reporters agreed to take part in the pool, arguing that they couldn't properly cover the story unless they could get inside the barricades. Some critics said this

was like accepting accreditation from terrorists.

• Should television journalists, barred from close access to the scene of confrontation, accept video footage from police or the army?

• Is it acceptable for reporters to cover an event from all-news television and write as though from first-hand observation? Columnist Roy MacGregor wrote that in the Oka case, entire front-page stories were assembled by newspaper reporters watching television — the readers ending up with "news twice filtered." (See "War by scrum: TV becomes part of the news," Ottawa *Citizen*, Sept. 4, 1990.)

• Should reporters go along with a police request to help identify stone-throwers who assaulted women and children as they left the area? (See "Media asked to help identify rock throwers," *Globe and Mail*, Aug. 31, 1990.)

• If an official on one side of the dispute gives a "background" briefing and attacks the other side, should reporters honor their commitment not to identify the official? (See "Warriors 'criminal,' federal official says," *Globe and Mail*, July 24, 1990. In this case reporters did identify the official, a federal deputy minister who had called the protesters a criminal organization cloaking itself in the guise of Indian rights.)

In other areas standards are still evolving. How far should the media go, for instance, in publishing the misconduct allegations that are now endemic in political campaigns? What should you do when political enemies come up with seemingly authentic information that the candidate is a reformed alcoholic, or has been having an illicit affair? What should you do if rumors of this kind are published by your competitors or in the trashiest tabloids? No clear rules exist, but in recent years, as the supply of such material has expanded, many major media have become more rigorous in demanding evidence. In many newsrooms, the focus of the discussions is on whether the information is needed by readers, and on whether it's possible to prevent the sleaziest elements of journalism from setting the news agenda (see, for example, Reid 1992).

Another area of tension relates to co-operation with police and other authorities. Again, no clear rule exists for a spectrum of cases ranging from the robbery-with-hostages incident up to a major civil dis-

At times of civil disorder, reporters and photographers are caught in inevitable tension between officials who want them to stay in their designated "pens" and their need to go to the other side as well, to see the conflict from more than one perspective. (*Toronto Sun*)

order like the 1990 Oka crisis. In cases like the former, most reporters are willing to abide by police orders — taking care, for instance, not to broadcast live material that might endanger the hostages. In the latter, journalists with good conscience (and with added muscle arising from their own numbers and the public attention the case attracted) often resisted direction by the police and the military who were called in to handle the situation.

Also a constant problem are decisions relating to invasion of privacy: whether to use photographs of grieving parents of the family

REPORTERS AND AUTHORITY

By GEOFFREY YORK

Are there times when reporters ought to disobey civil authority? Reporter Geoffrey York of the Globe and Mail *argues that there are — that reporters must sometimes act as a check on official power. York covered the final weeks of the Oka crisis from inside the Warrior encampment and he is the author of* The Dispossessed: Life and Death in Native Canada *and the co-author of* People of the Pines: The Warriors and the Legacy of Oka.

In the darkness of a pine forest in southern Quebec, a small group of journalists huddled around a campfire, shivering in the autumn chill. Nothing in their careers had prepared them for this experience. The forest was surrounded by thousands of heavily armed soldiers, dozens of armored personnel carriers, searchlights, machine-gun nests, razor wire and sandbags. Military helicopters pounded in the sky overhead, while the shadowy figures of camouflaged Mohawk warriors slipped through the trees.

For weeks, this motley group of newspaper writers and freelance photographers had been the only source of eyewitness reporting from the inside of the Oka crisis of 1990.

Despite frigid rain and sleepless nights in a bleak basement room, despite bouts of boredom and discomfort and fear, the journalists had resisted pressure to leave.

Now, with the final act of the drama drawing near, the pressure was increasing. Politicians were complaining about them. Police officers were threatening to interrogate them. The army had refused to allow them to receive any supplies. Even some of their colleagues — newspaper columnists and television commentators — were criticizing their conduct.

On the afternoon of September 13, a high-ranking officer from the Fifth Mechanized Brigade had

(continued)

called them to deliver an ominous message: "for your own safety, we strongly advise you to leave by nightfall." Some of the journalists felt a brief spasm of fear. Was this the final warning before a military assault? Nobody could be certain.

But the journalists were determined to stay.

In the days that followed, there were more warnings and threats. Then the authorities switched to different tactics: court orders to cut off cellular phones of the reporters, electronic jamming of the airwaves, and platoons of public relations experts to control the outside media in a military compound. But when the siege finally ended, 10 journalists still remained inside the warrior compound.

Why did they stay? They stayed for the same principles that have always inspired journalists during conflicts with powerful authorities — the same instincts that motivated a CNN television crew to stay in Baghdad during the Gulf War of 1991, and the same beliefs that led the New York Times to publish the Pentagon Papers in 1971.

In each case, reporters were defying the intimidation and pressure tactics of their own governments. It was a kind of subversive journalism: a threat to the official version of authorized facts. And in each case, the defiance was necessary. Without the scrutiny of the media, the state is free to wield incredible power — including the crushing power of its military machinery.

Secrecy is a blank cheque for those who are tempted to abuse the instruments of power. When there are no witnesses, the victims are faceless and nameless, and governments can conceal the worst effects of their actions.

The role of the watchdog is crucial in times of national crisis, when the country is gripped by a fever of war or apprehended insurrection. The greatest threats to human rights can occur when the public mood has swung heavily against one group of dissidents — as it did in Quebec in the FLQ crisis of 1970 and again in the Oka crisis of 1990. This is the time when a society has its greatest need for witnesses, for newspaper reporters and television cameras. In the pine forest of Oka, the presence of the small band of journalists was vital in preventing bloodshed and thwarting official censorship. It ensured that the power of Canada's political and military authorities could not be exercised without accountability.

Finally, the reporters in the pine forest were simply following the basic principles of good journalism. They realized that they had to be at the centre of the story, watching the conflict with their own eyes, instead of relying on the authorized version at a military briefing. Ultimately they knew that their job was to provide an honest account of the conflict. The truth was more important than their comfort or their popularity.

whose home has burned down, or of the relatives of a serial killer. Each reporter or editor and each medium will answer these questions differently, though broad patterns will eventually emerge. An examination of case studies may help you understand where the lines are normally drawn in these areas. The process is dangerous, however, if it simply reinforces questionable standards of behavior. The case study approach is most useful if it signals where your views may be in conflict with mainstream thought, and where pressure can effectively be applied for change. It is also of benefit in helping you identify the overarching principles to bring to ethical decisions.

GUIDELINES

If indeed there is an ethical consensus among Canadian journalists, it should be an easy thing to draw up a list of principles that they all endorse. In fact, though, any such attempts immediately crash into controversy. It is not unusual, for instance, for journalists discussing ethical codes to disagree even on the statement that journalists should be truthful. Nevertheless, the following list — a de facto code of ethics, if you will — attempts to define standards that most journalists would endorse in the abstract, even though wide disagreement is likely on how each principle should be implemented:

- Admit error.
- Protect your sources.
- Don't in any circumstance distort, fabricate or plagiarize.
- Don't accept favors, or appear to accept favors.
- Don't let anybody else make your news judgments.
- Stay away from the pack as much as you can.
- Don't gratuitously harm people caught up on the fringes of events that are not of their own making.
- Don't harm *anyone* unless you feel you have to do so.
- Be reluctant to suppress news, even though there will be times when you'll find it essential to do so.
- Don't lie, steal or misrepresent yourself *except in extraordinary circumstances of a kind that would justify civil disobedience*. When you do lie or steal or misrepresent yourself, explain to your readers what you've

done and why — and then take your lumps, including going to jail if necessary.

• Where loyalty to your employer is concerned, be as faithful as you can without betraying the public trust.

NEWSROOM CODES

Many newspapers have their own sets of ethics guidelines. Below are excerpts from the guidelines of the Ottawa Citizen:

News Gathering

Using children as sources of news information should be done only with the utmost caution. A child's word should be corroborated before being published. Whenever possible, the child's street address and school will be omitted from the story or cutline.

Staff members should not induce people, including other staff members, to break the law or commit improper acts. ...

When pursuing news, staff should always be considerate of the privacy of others. Grief, for example, is not necessarily newsworthy in itself.

Monitoring conversations of a purely private and personal nature is improper and may, in some cases, be illegal. If the Citizen receives information about a private conversation, that information — as with any other information — is to be confirmed before publication. Information obtained from the public airwaves, police radio, cellular telephones or any similar source should be treated in the same manner. Quotes obtained from such sources should only be used in extreme circumstances and with approval of the executive news editor.

Conduct on the Job

Journalists may occasionally be asked to cover assignments or to edit material that conflicts or coincides with strongly held personal views. In such instances, journalists are expected to put aside personal beliefs and perform their duties in a professional manner.

Plagiarism is theft — a serious offence that undermines the profession and can bring dismissal. But the evidence must be conclusive, and the accused must have the opportunity to offer a defence. ...

Conduct off the Job

Newsroom employees should not publicly endorse products or businesses. ...

Reporters and editors who are directly involved with stories on specific companies on a regular basis (such as the high-technology beat) shall not own investments in such companies.

The investments of spouses of reporters and editors mentioned above must be disclosed to the employee's supervisor.

Staffers' off-the-job activities should not impair their journalistic credibility, or give the appearance of doing so. That will happen, for example, if reporters engage in off-the-job activities too close to their beat. ...

Legal Issues

All records relevant to the story, i.e. notes and tapes, should be kept for a minimum of eight weeks. ...

While the Citizen does not wish to obstruct or thwart the administration of justice, neither is it an investigative arm of the police, Crown or defence lawyers. Any requests for notes, tapes or photographs involving any legal matter — criminal or civil — should be refused. ...

- Don't lose your sense of humanity.

- Don't use your clout as a journalist to intimidate for personal ends.

- Live up to your commitments. (This may seem an obvious bit of ethical behavior that would apply to everyone, but it has a peculiar meaning for journalists, one comparable to the special self-discipline that makes a doctor turn out in the middle of the night, or an actor persist in seeing that the show goes on. Journalists deal with many people in many odd situations, and must carry about with them a reputation for reliability.)

- Provide in your reporting the widest possible forum for opposing views.

- Invade privacy only when you are certain it is in the public interest.

- Don't take on outside work or causes that would undermine your actual or perceived independence.

- Be careful to avoid doing careless or gratuitous harm to the least powerful sectors of society.

- Avoid smearing people by innuendo or implying guilt by association.

- Avoid thoughtless writing that reinforces racial, sexual or physical stereotypes. (In other words, think carefully about the meanings of the words you use and why you choose them.)

- Protect the right to a fair trial of everyone, even those you hold in the most contempt.

- Finally, respect the *informing function* — the obligation to supply people with the information you think they need to respond intelligently to their environment.

Such guidelines are by no means etched in stone. At best, they may provide you with a frame of reference from which to begin thinking about ethics. They must, however, be kept in the context of these two concluding thoughts:

1. While ethical principles may be abstract, the cases you will confront are real. In recent years Canadian newsrooms have been torn apart by, for example, the questions of whether a TV news anchor deserved to be suspended for a week without pay for protesting high property taxes at a public meeting (McMahen 1990) and whether an award-winning reporter had committed the sin of plagiarism by using material published in another newspaper (*Bulletin* 1991). These incidents show that the ethical process in newsrooms is dynamic, and rarely simply a matter of following a rule listed in some ethics code.

2. Most ethical acts imply a certain sacrifice. Some journalists risk their safety in Belfast or Bogota or the Balkans. Some of them do it out of bravado, or a yearning to be famous. Others do it because they consider it important, because they're fulfilling their professional function — just as police officers or doctors take risks. That is the most dramatic level of sacrifice. But other ethical decisions impose smaller costs: the loss of income because you refrain from accepting a freebie or a tempting public relations assignment that would create a conflict of interest; the sacrifice of refraining from using your journalistic clout in a private quarrel; the sacrifice of alienating a good source who wants you to twist the record; the pain of losing the friendship of colleagues through stories that show them in a poor light. Almost always, ethical acts come at some price.

When they deal with the touchiest social issues, like abortion, the mainstream media are usually careful to stay neutral, giving equal time to each side in a way that takes advantage of the drama while not offending people in either camp. More thorough reporting may demand that reporters take the risk of going beyond the public show to explore the underlying realities in the conflict. (Sheryl Nadler/Loyalist College)

ETHICS CASES

The following cases are designed to (a) help you consider in advance some of the ethical dilemmas reporters and editors face, and (b) help define the de facto code of ethics operating in Canadian journalism. (Some of these cases first appeared in Cumming 1988, 8–10.)

Read the cases and make a quick decision on how you would react. Keep the following considerations in mind:

- In most cases you'll probably wish you had more information before making the decision. Make the best choice you can with what's available.

- In each case, assume the decision is yours. (It's not an option to ask your editor what you ought to do.)

- In some cases there may be a legal dimension. Try to set that aside and make your decision on ethical considerations.

- This is in no sense a test. In most cases, perhaps all of them, there's no certain right or wrong. You may well change some decisions after discussing them.

Case 1: Your editor asks you to tape a phone interview without letting the source know, and you comply. Later, you arrange to do a face-to-face interview with the same source and your editor asks you to tape it secretly. Do you comply? If you're inclined to resist, how do you define the ethical difference?

Case 2: As a newspaper editor, you find your court reporter has taken part in an abortion rally at the Supreme Court. Do you censure the reporter?

Case 3: You're editor of a small newspaper and one of your reporters has come up with a story about a local politician's alleged sexual improprieties, ranging from rape to harassment. The story is supported by affidavits from eight victims, all of whom have spoken on condition they are not identified, although they're willing to testify if the politician sues. Do you run the story?

Case 4: You're news director for a radio station and notice in your local tabloid a line story, without evidence or citation, saying it has learned that a cabinet minister was guilty of an adulterous affair. You're unable to confirm the story. Do you run a story quoting the tab?

Case 5: You're a TV reporter covering a demonstration after police have shot a black youth during a holdup. You get dramatic footage of a man saying that the black community will execute the next officer who kills one of its members. It's not clear whether the man is an officer of any community organization. Do you use the tape?

Case 6: You're covering a hostage-taking incident for a radio station. One hostage manages to break out of the building, wounded, and hides where you and the police can see him, in the bushes beside the building. He's hidden from the hostage-takers and they apparently don't realize he's escaped. You're filing live to the station. Do you mention this incident?

Case 7: You're working for a small daily and are told you can, if you wish, take two working days to accept a trip to Detroit sponsored by an auto company to see the unveiling of their new cars, and write a story on it. The trip covers air fare, hotel and food for you and a guest. You'd like to go, but have some reservations about accepting hospitality. Do you accept?

Case 8: You're covering a national conference when a reporter for a newspaper in another city approaches you, says she's missed the whole day's proceedings and asks if you can give her a briefing on what's been happening. Do you do so?

Case 9: You and three other reporters have been interviewing a cabinet minister in a public lounge. After the minister leaves, you notice he's left a file behind on a couch. You're tempted to look through it to see if there's a story to be had. The other reporters have left. Do you look in the file or return it unopened?

Case 10: You're on the legislature beat and are told by a politician that a political opponent was convicted of armed robbery as a teenager, some 23 years ago, and served time in reformatory. He never told his constituents about his criminal past. You ask the accused politician if the story is true and he confirms it, but says you shouldn't print anything on it since he has paid his debt to society. Do you agree?

Case 11: You're covering medicine for a Toronto daily and get a call from the Canadian Medical Association asking if you will write a brief, anonymously, to be presented to the federal government. It's an area you know well, the money is good and you can do it in your spare time. Do you accept?

Case 12: You're reporting for a TV station and when you come back from an interview with a cabinet minister, your camera person says that in getting background shots she accidentally filmed a good deal of correspondence on the minister's desk. You read it and find some important material. Do you use it?

Case 13: You're told by a reliable source in the city water department that a neighboring township has allowed a serious water contamination problem to go unchecked. The source directs you to a person in the township's water department who confirms the account on condition you won't use her name. You write the story, pegged to unnamed sources. Two days later police visit you and say they want to lay charges but can't do so because they lack documentation, and therefore need to know the names of your sources. Do you comply?

Case 14: You're city editor of a daily newspaper and are called by the local exhibition association and asked to serve as public relations adviser for a fee of $2,000. You'll be required to attend one meeting and to be available in case your specialized experience is needed. Do you accept?

Case 15: Your photographer returns from the scene of a multiple slaying with a photo that was taken through a window and shows one of the victims clearly enough for identification, along with a police officer. Do you use the picture?

Case 16: You're working for a daily and are asked to go through the garbage bags in the yard of a printing company, just before provincial budget day, to see if they contain any of the budget material the company has been printing under contract. Do you accept the assignment without protest?

Case 17: You're covering an election campaign, flying with the prime minister, and late one evening he comes to the back of the plane to relax with a couple of drinks. No one specifies that it's off the record, but you realize everyone, including the prime minister, assumes it is. The prime minister makes an injudicious and very derogatory comment about another politician. Do you report it?

Case 18: You've been granted an interview by the leader of a revolutionary group, on condition you not reveal his identity or whereabouts. During the interview the leader says the group plans to blow up an airliner. You later tell police about the plan, and they insist on knowing who the source is and where he can be found. Do you reveal these things?

Case 19: You're a Washington correspondent for a Canadian paper, and you find out by accident that one of our embassies in an authoritarian country is secretly sheltering a number of people hostile to the regime. You want to write the story, but Canadian diplomats urge you to hold off, lest you endanger the people concerned. Do you do so?

Case 20: You're a Guild (union) representative on a newspaper, and are approached by the head of another union at the paper who says the paper is planning to run a disgusting picture of the international leader of her union. The picture shows the leader with her arm up, as though giving a Nazi salute. Your colleague says her union plans to walk out unless the picture is pulled, and asks your help. You agree the picture is grossly offensive. Do you agree to try to get your union behind the protest?

Case 21: You uncover a story on a planned downtown development and your publisher orders it killed on the ground that any premature release of the plan will inflate property prices in the area and perhaps prevent development. You confide your frustration to a friend on a local TV station, who asks that you give her the details for use on her station. Do you do so?

Case 22: You're covering a drug-trafficking case and testimony shows that the defendant was arrested leaving a party given by a well-known local actor. Do you use this?

Case 23: You're city editor of a daily and get a call from a man who has just been acquitted of a sex offence. He says he realizes your paper has a policy of always printing a cleanup story when it has printed original charges — but in this case he hopes you won't do so, because news of his acquittal would just damage him further. Do you agree to drop the story?

Case 24: The 19-year-old son of a nationally known columnist has been charged with trafficking in cocaine. Do you include the parent's name in the story?

Case 25: While working as a newspaper reporter, you pick up from a mother a picture of her son, who has been killed in a hostage-taking incident. As she's giving it to you she says it's her best picture and the only copy she has, and she would appreciate it if you would pass a copy to the local television station. You agree to do so. You tell this to your editor, who says a copy will indeed be passed on, but only after the paper is on the streets. Do you agree to this approach?

Case 26: You're covering city hall and, while going down a corridor, notice several reporters with tape recorders on and mikes pointed toward a partly opened door. Inside, the mayor is giving what presumably was meant to be an *in camera* briefing to councillors on an important new agency. Do you switch on your own tape recorder?

Case 27: You read a colleague's feature on scuba diving and notice that two paragraphs of it have been taken verbatim from an obscure hobby magazine you happen to read. Do you point this out to the editor?

Case 28: While covering the courts, you happen on a case in which two men are acquitted on charges arising from washroom sex. Afterward, the Crown attorney gives an angry news conference saying the law must be changed to close the loophole that allowed them to get off. Your paper didn't cover the original charges. Do you name the men in your story?

Case 29: While covering Parliament, you're approached by an old friend in the security service who asks if you'll help him out by keeping an eye on certain foreign correspondents in the press gallery. You refuse, and later mention the incident to your editor. She says you ought to write a story on it. Do you do so?

Case 30: You're covering a Senate committee on native policy. Just before it starts, a Newfoundland senator says jokingly to one of his western colleagues: "you people on the Prairies should have handled the native problem the way we did — we shot them all." Do you write a story on this?

Case 31: You're covering a national convention of the New Democratic Party. A secret caucus of disgruntled western delegates is in progress. You happen to find a delegate ID card and realize you could penetrate the caucus. Do you do so?

Case 32: You're covering in provincial court the case of a 20-year-old man identified as a schizophrenic, with past problems of drug and alcohol abuse, charged with assault on two women. He is also identified as a Mohawk from Point Sable, Ont. Do you include that last point in your story?

Case 33: You're the only reporter on duty at a radio station on Saturday afternoon. Police call you to say that a serious disturbance with racial overtones is developing in a particular immigrant community. They ask you to keep the news off the air for an hour, to avoid attracting more people to the disturbance. Do you comply?

Case 34: You're a Guild shop steward and learn a member of your union has been formally reprimanded by the managing editor because he used the threat of an exposure story to get a car repair bill lowered. The union member concedes he did make the threat, but insists it wasn't unethical because the size of the bill seemed to justify a story. He says you should support a union grievance. Do you do so?

Case 35: As a newspaper reporter, you're asked by your city editor to call a dating service, without identifying yourself as a journalist, to find out if it's legitimate or a prostitution service. Do you accept the assignment without protest?

Case 36: When you track down an anonymous donor who has put up $50,000 to send a small child abroad for special surgery, he pleads that his name not be published, on the ground that publication will bring on a flood of requests. Do you use the name?

Case 37: While covering a civil war that has driven many people from their homes, you encounter a number of refugees living in dangerous circumstances. When you're ordered home, you realize you could bring out a refugee child by adding her to your passport as your daughter. Do you do so?

Case 38: You're working for a radio station and are on duty alone when a hostage-taking is reported from a local company. It occurs to you that you might call the company number to see if you can get in touch with the hostage-takers. Do you do so?

RECOMMENDED READING

General Texts

Christians, Clifford G., Kim B. Rotzoll, and Mark Fackler. (1995). *Media Ethics: Cases and Moral Reasoning*. 4th edition. New York and London: Longman.

Christians, Clifford G., Kim B. Rotzoll, and Mark Fackler. (1983). *Media Ethics: Cases and Moral Reasoning*. New York and London: Longman.

Geyer, Georgie Anne. (1984). "Journalists: The New Targets, the New Diplomats, the New Intermediary People." In Robert Schmuhl, ed., *The Responsibilities of Journalism* (70–78). Notre Dame, IN: University of Notre Dame Press.

Goldstein, Tom. (1985). *The News at Any Cost*. New York: Simon & Shuster.

Hulteng, John L. (1985). *The Messenger's Motives*. 2nd edition. Englewood Cliffs, NJ: Prentice-Hall.

Lambeth, Edmund B. (1992). *Committed Journalism: An Ethic for the Profession*. 2nd edition. Bloomington, IN: Indiana University Press.

Patterson, Philip, and Lee Wilkins. (1994). *Media Ethics: Issues and Cases*. 2nd edition. Dubuque, IO: William C. Brown.

Rivers, William L., and Cleve Mathews. (1988). *Ethics for the Media*. Englewood Cliffs, NJ: Prentice-Hall.

Russell, Nicholas. (1994). *Morals and the Media: Ethics in Canadian Journalism*. Vancouver: UBC Press.

Specific Topics in Journalistic Ethics

Invasion of Privacy

Gitlin, Todd. (1992). "Media lemmings run amok!" *Washington Journalism Review*, April: 28–32.

Katz, Jon. (1992). "Note to the press: Mind your own business." *News Inc*, June: 34–40.

Leyne, Les. (1990). "Media ethics: The complicated case of Bud Smith." *Bulletin: Canadian Association of Journalists*, Fall: 17–18.

Madsen, Debbie. (1991). "Indecent exposure." *Ryerson Review of Journalism*, March: 10–16.

Reid, Cheryl. (1992). "Anonymous sources bring down a senator." *Washington Journalism Review*, April: 10.

Resisting Manipulation

Collier, Simone. (1991). "At war with the army." *Ryerson Review of Journalism*, April: 16–23.

Drolet, Daniel. (1990). "Mohawks and the media: Reporters attacked by police, crowds." Reprinted from the Ottawa *Citizen* in *Bulletin: Canadian Association of Journalists*, Fall: 7–9.

Mundy, Alicia. (1992). "Is the press any match for powerhouse P.R.?" *Columbia Journalism Review*, September-October: 27–34.

Pinsky, Mark I. (1990). "Cops and robbers — and a secrecy pledge." *Columbia Journalism Review*, September-October: 51.

Starr, Richard. (1992). "Where was the warning at Westray?" *content*, December: 10–13.

Weeks, Jennifer. (1992). "Patriot games: What did we see on Desert Storm TV?" *Columbia Journalism Review*, July-August: 13–14.

Conflict of Interest

Bindman, Stephen. (1991). "Conflict of interest and the Goldhawk case." *Bulletin: Canadian Association of Journalists*, Spring: 13.

Darling, Mark. (1991). "Conflict of interests." *Ryerson Review of Journalism*, April: 12–13.

Drainie, Bronwyn. (1989). "CBC policy makes waves in the wake of Goldhawk." Reprinted from the *Globe and Mail* in *Bulletin: Centre for Investigative Journalism*, Winter: 24.

Martin, Sandra E. (1992). "Horning in." *Ryerson Review of Journalism*, April: 32–37.

Shen, Anna. (1992). "Natasha's story: Judgment call in Sarajevo." *Columbia Journalism Review*, September-October: 22.

Tate, Cassandra. (1991). "Outside activities: When does a journalist's personal opinion become a public issue?" *Columbia Journalism Review*, March-April: 12–13.

Fabrication

Kaderlan, Alice. (1990). "TV reporter accused of staging a dogfight." *Washington Journalism Review*, November: 19.

Prendergast, Alan. (1991). "Wendy Bergen's exclusive hoax." *Washington Journalism Review*, October: 30–34.

Plagiarism

Bulletin: Canadian Association of Journalists. (1991). "Was it plagiarism or 'replication'?" Summer: 10–12.

Fine, Marlene. (1992). "Dubious distinction." *Ryerson Review of Journalism*, April: 52–57.

McGillivray, Don. (1989). "Plagiarism: Phrase filch or mental slip?" *Bulletin: Centre for Investigative Journalism*, Spring: 29–30.

McIntosh, Andrew. (1989). "The case of Ken Adachi." *Bulletin: Centre for Investigative Journalism*, Spring: 5–6.

Coverage of Suicide

McIntosh, Andrew. (1989). "The case of Ken Adachi." *Bulletin: Centre for Investigative Journalism*, Spring: 5–6.

Editorial Interference

Bolan, Kim R., and Mariken Van Nimwegen. (1989). Letter to the editor. *Bulletin: Centre for Investigative Journalism*, Spring: 2–6.

Negin, Elliott. (1991). "Washington Times writer quits over 'Update'." *Washington Journalism Review*, December: 12–13.

Schmitz, Christin. (1992). "Former ombudsman speaks out." *Bulletin: Canadian Association of Journalists*, Summer: 12–13.

Protection of Sources

Bindman, Stephen. (1989). "The legal beat." *Bulletin: Centre for Investigative Journalism*, Spring: 22–27.

Off Record/Background Material

Gessell, Paul. (1990). "Case history: How a not-so-anonymous source further soured Meech Lake debate." Ottawa *Citizen*, July 28.

Lee, Robert. (1990). "Government rules on dealing with the press are confusing, as Harry Swain found out this week." Ottawa *Citizen*, July 28.

Coverage of Race Relations

Bula, Frances. (1989). "Asian Money in B.C." *Bulletin: Centre for Investigative Journalism*, Spring: 9–13.

Identification of Victims

Arant, Morgan David, Jr. "Press identification of victims of sexual assault: Weighing privacy and constitutional concerns." *Journalism Quarterly*, 68:1 (Spring-Summer).

Use of Stolen Material

Kilgour, David. (1990). "No small affair." *Ryerson Review of Journalism*, Spring: 8–9.

APPENDIX A

Language

I've always told young writers that the best thing they could do would be to try to get a job on a newspaper because it would teach them to produce when they have to and not when they think the spirit moves them ... and to write tidily and concisely and without ambiguity.

— ROBERTSON DAVIES, QUOTED BY TREVOR LAUTENS, *VANCOUVER SUN*, SEPT. 24, 1988

To an outsider, the skill of "writing without ambiguity" may seem a minor one, a task of no great challenge. Those who make a living writing or editing know that it is a demanding, lifelong process. It is at least as exacting as an athlete's effort to stay in shape for professional sport.

If the skill develops best in journalism, that may be because the feedback is intense and regular. What do you *mean*, your editor asks, by this phrase? What's the connection between this thought and that one? Is that really the word you want? The same kinds of questions are sometimes raised of reports written in business or in government, but they are seldom asked in such a concentrated, continuing way.

That process may sometimes seem merely negative and critical (especially to the person taking the criticism) but there is as well a very positive side to language fascination. Journalism has more than its share of people who are, in Robert MacNeil's apt term, "wordstruck" — that is, absorbed by the sound of words and the subtlety of words. MacNeil symbolizes the pattern well when he writes of the many sources of his own love of language, and the pleasure he takes from it. But he tells as well in one revealing anecdote of the anger he felt when he was challenged (wrongly, he was certain) for using the word "envisage" rather than "envision" (1989, 218–219). Most people would find that anger puzzling; for the wordstruck it is entirely understandable. It is the other side of a two-sided fascination, the same sort of fury felt by a lover of flowers who finds a garden vandalized.

Unhappily, the side that often dominates in newsrooms is not the pleasure but the nit-picking, sometimes by editors who have mastered a number of grammatical rules and built a stockade of them, defending it to death. For novice journalists, the pleasure in language should of course be more important than the rulebook. Their feel for the weight and rhythm of language, their pleasure in discovering a new writer whose work shows them how to extend their own writing capacity, should be more important than grammar. But pleasure in language is consistent with a concern for precision and clarity. Every newsroom has at least one editor whose happiest hours are spent poring over Fowler's, or the big Oxford, examining a fine point of language. One colleague tells of being caught in the middle of an extended discussion between two editors, carried out in snatches over an entire editing shift, over a photograph caption. At issue was the difference between "twilight" and "dusk," and the point at which one becomes the other.

LANGUAGE: CONTESTED TERRAIN

Journalists rarely lead social change, but they are often among the first to recognize and be touched by it in their daily work. The words they use in writing the news have enormous power to create images in the minds of their readers and listeners. And as society changes, reporters constantly re-examine their own language and writing patterns to keep up.

Two principles guide the reporter's choice of language. The first is the need for *clarity*, for using words and images that are unambiguous, accurate and understandable to the broader public. Clarity rules out the use of fuzzy euphemisms, postmodern jargon or "politically correct" speech — a fad that, thankfully, seems to be fading. The second principle is a need for *sensitivity*, for recognizing that everyday words may reflect social conventions and attitudes that are already going out of style, and that people care about the words we use to describe them.

Journalistic style guides are good tools for tracking the state of the language. But it's important to see them as historical documents,

(continued)

reflecting the times in which they were published. What was acceptable in 1980 was different from what was acceptable in 1960. And by 2010, the language structures of the current style books may feel as outmoded as last year's dance craze.

That said, we look to two key references — the current editions of The Canadian Press's *CP Stylebook* and *The Globe and Mail Style Book* — for guidance on areas of language that have come under special scrutiny in recent years.

Age

Where age is relevant, it's best to go by the numbers. Many descriptive terms are imprecise — like teenager, middle-aged or youngster. Others are derogatory — like aged, elderly or oldster, which conjure up images of infirmity. Girls and boys are under 16 and considered children and may be referred to by their first name; after that, they're referred to by their last name, as are other adults.

Race

In the multi-ethnic Canada of the 1990s, news reports should draw on sources from many races, ethnic groups and national origins. However, unless race is relevant to the story, it is not mentioned. In stories where race is relevant, the general rule is to use terms that the source herself would use. (Ask, don't guess.) The style guides note that Canadian media tend to use "black" instead of African-American (or African-Canadian). And they tend to avoid hyphenated terms such as Polish-Canadian.

Some crime stories may require the use of racial identifiers. For example, a report on a suspect who has not been caught may include his race to aid the public in spotting him. Similarly, if an attack is racially motivated, the race of the people involved is probably relevant to the story. But in most crime stories, race is not relevant. Some media outlets appear to have developed a sort of "code" for conveying the race of people accused of crime — referring, for example, to "the dreadlocked teenager" as a way of saying the young person arrested at the scene is black. This ethically troubling practice should be avoided. If race matters, report it. If not, don't use gratuitous physical description to imply it.

A number of terms are used to describe native people in Canada — Aboriginal Peoples, original people, aboriginals, indigenous peoples, or First Nations. Many First Nations leaders prefer to use the word aboriginal rather than native. The word Indian is also problematic: it originated with European explorers, who mistakenly thought they had landed in India. Nonetheless, native people covered by treaties are known as status Indians, and many prefer that term. Because the indigenous peoples are not a homogeneous group, it's preferable to identify people by their band name or nation rather than using any of the generic terms.

(continued)

Disabilities and medical conditions

People with disabilities are people first, and they're not necessarily "suffering" from their disability, or the "victim" of a disease, or, unless they're under a doctor's care, a "patient." Don't write that a person who uses a wheelchair is "confined" to it. Wheelchairs are not prisons; indeed, they help people get out and about.

In addition, a disability may not be relevant to a story. For example, if you're doing a piece on shop keepers' reactions to a change in downtown parking regulations, the fact that a store owner uses a wheelchair is no more relevant than the fact that she is of Chinese origin. When it is relevant, avoid defining people by their disabilities.

If you are not certain about how to describe a disability, the best advice is to write in specific terms — refer to a child as having Down's syndrome rather than having a developmental disability, and avoid vague terms like intellectually challenged.

Gender

Journalists try to use gender-neutral language as much as possible. Gender-specific terms, like stewardess, fireman, policeman and mailman, are not only outmoded but may be inaccurate since both men and women may hold such jobs. It's preferable, therefore, to refer to flight attendants, fire fighters, police officers and mail carriers.

For the same reasons, it has become common practice to avoid using the masculine "he" as the generic pronoun. Rather than writing, "A student may enrol if he has finished Grade 12," reporters may opt for a plural construction: "Students may enrol if they have finished Grade 12." Sometimes the best choice is to avoid any pronouns at all — to write, "Most MPs eat lunch at the parliamentary restaurant," rather than "The average MP eats his lunch at the parliamentary restaurant."

Reporters should avoid stereotyping jobs or the division of labor in the home. They should also avoid adjectives or nuances that reinforce stereotypes in the home or workplace. If you interview two tough and frosty business executives, don't refer to the woman as "chilly" and her male counterpart as "cool and collected."

The style books are split on the use of the courtesy titles Mr., Mrs., Ms. and Miss: The Canadian Press doesn't use them; the *Globe and Mail* does. A few other newspapers use them too. These titles are troublesome to many women, since Miss and Mrs. refer to marital status as well as gender. In general, outlets that use honorifics follow the woman's preference, which means reporters must ask any woman they interview which title she prefers. Ms., which does not disclose marital status, has gained wide acceptance over the last 20 years and is used if the woman prefers it, or if her preference and marital status are not known.[1]

Still at issue in the battle over

(continued)

gender-neutral language are terms like chairperson and spokesperson. The style books continue to resist these words, preferring gender-specific terms like chairman or chairwoman. But as the gender-neutral variations become entrenched in the popular language, this preference is likely to change. *The Globe and Mail Style Book* opens the door a crack, saying it is permissible to use chairperson if the gender is not known, in a case such as "the party will elect a new chairperson next weekend."

Sexual orientation

The term gay appears to have emerged as the word of choice for describing homosexual men and women. Some gay women prefer lesbian, and reporters generally respect that preference. Some younger, or more militant, gay people use the term queer. Even within the gay community, however, this term is still widely viewed as derogatory. It should be used with great caution, even in quotations.

Style guides represent a consensus on appropriate language — and, when there is no consensus, a set of rules to follow. But in cases where there is neither consensus nor rule, journalists need to rely on their own judgment. The best way to make such judgments is to read as broadly as possible, and to think critically about the words in the report. Words carry the baggage of the culture in which they're used, and a reporter needs to be aware not only of dictionary definitions,

but of cultural ones as well.

One example should make this point: few Canadian reporters and editors would equate male circumcision with genital mutilation, and would probably react negatively to a report that referred to it as such. But what language would they use to refer to the practice in parts of Africa of removing the external genitalia of women? Is it a) female circumcision or b) female genital mutilation? Many Canadians would see it as mutilation, in part because it is a far more extreme procedure physically than male circumcision. Those who practise it, however, see it as a legitimate cultural convention. The term *you* choose is very much a reflection of your own cultural and ideological stance.

No matter how the conventional wisdom changes, problems of this kind will always confront reporters. The way they deal with them will in turn help determine how society deals with them too.

Source: *CP Stylebook: A Guide for Writers and Editors.* (1995). Peter Buckley, ed. Revised edition. Toronto: The Canadian Press; *The Globe and Mail Style Book.* (1996). J.A. McFarlane and Warren Clements, eds. Toronto: Penguin Books.

1. Ms. is a good example of how quickly — and how sharply — fashions in language use may change, as shown by this excerpt from a 1974 edition of The Canadian Press's CP *Stylebook:* "Certain militant members of the women's liberation movement wish to be known as Ms. ... Such use is not common in Canada. So use Ms. only when insistently requested. All stories using Ms. should mention the request and say whether the woman in question is married or single — not as a put-down but as a matter of news interest" (94).

No one expects newcomers to journalism to be this obsessive, to know all the rules of grammar or to be able to identify all their blind spots in syntax or diction. But just as artists, or even house painters, must gain intimate knowledge of color and paint before they can perform, new journalists must see the connection between the mechanics of language and the craft of writing. It is possible for all journalists-in-training to start building a systematic base for their own language interest. It's important to learn what a dangling modifier *looks* like, for example, as a step toward avoiding the error. It's important to be familiar with style guides, dictionaries, texts. All these should provide material for your personal language notebooks or computer files.

In the light of those needs, this appendix defines some of the most frequently recurring language problems, the ones that make editors swear. The list is by no means comprehensive; it is designed only to illustrate *types* of problems.

DISTINCTIONS

Computer spell-checkers are a boon to bad spellers, but these systems won't help you distinguish between "affect" and "effect," "principle" and "principal," or "it's" and "its." Nor will they warn you when you've improperly called someone a burglar who should be no more than a robber. So it's wise to keep your own list of key distinctions, perhaps including the following.

aid/aide
   Aid [help] ... *Aide* [an assistant]

allude/elude
   Allude [refer to] ... *Elude* [escape]

among/between
   Among [usually preferred for several items] ... *Between* [usually preferred for two items]

anxious/eager
   Anxious [implies concern] ... *Eager* [anticipating with enthusiasm]

burglary/robbery
   Burglary [implies breaking into a building to steal] ... *Robbery* [more inclusive term]

censor/censure
   Censor [to limit free speech] ... *Censure* [to criticize]

complement/compliment
   Complement [to fit with ... or a complete unit, as in "a full complement of waiters"] ... *Compliment* [commendation]

contagious /infectious

> *Contagious* [disease communicated by touch] ... *Infectious* [disease communicated by air or water]

continual/continuous

> *Continual* [repeated] ... *Continuous* [without interruption]

counsel/council

> *Counsel* [advice, or a legal adviser] ... *Council* [as in city council]

credible/credulous

> *Credible* [believable] ... *Credulous* [gullible]

defuse/diffuse

> *Defuse* [a bomb] ... *Diffuse* [spread widely]

discreet/discrete

> *Discreet* [circumspect] ... *Discrete* [separate, distinct]

disinterested/uninterested

> *Disinterested* [balanced, neutral] ... *Uninterested* [not interested]

THESAURUS VERSUS DICTIONARY

A new hazard of the computer age is the instant thesaurus, which throws up on to the computer screen a list of options when you're searching for the right word.

The problem is that it's all too easy to choose a word that *sounds* good, regardless of whether it carries the precise meaning. Is the mayor, for example, really facing a "dilemma" — a choice between equally unattractive alternatives — or merely a difficult choice?

Using a thesaurus to select for precise meaning is like using a lawn sprinkler to fill a glass of water. For example, a thesaurus listing of synonyms for the noun "discount" can include such wildly different words as deduction, kickback, allowance and rebate. Each has a substantially different meaning from the others, though there are points in common. So before substituting one word for another, you *must* check the precise meaning in the dictionary.

You may be particularly tempted to look for variations to the most commonly used verb in the news report, "to say," in the hope of livening up your report. However, the variations have their own shades of meaning.

The *CP Stylebook* explains: "**admit** implies confession, **affirm** states a fact, assert declares strongly, **claim** and **maintain** hint of doubt, **confide** implies a confidence, **declare** states explicitly, **disclose** and **reveal** presume prior concealment.

"Be especially wary of **explain, point out, claim** and **note**. They all imply that what is being said is fact" (1995, 141).

effect/affect

Effect [either "to bring about," as in "we can effect improvement," or "the result," as in "the effect is beneficial"] ... *Affect* [to change, as in "this affects our progress"]

enormousness/enormity

Enormousness [great size] ... *Enormity* [wickedness, heinousness — avoid using simply to mean great size]

ensure/insure

Ensure [to make sure] ... *Insure* [to buy insurance]

fewer/less

Fewer [for numbers, as in "fewer than 10 members"] ... *Less* [for quantity, as in "less than half full"]

flair/flare

Flair [an ability, as in "a flair for design"] ... *Flare* [a torch or flame, or a widening, as in "skirt flared from the hips"]

flout/flaunt

Flout [to defy] ... *Flaunt* [to show off]

forego/forgo

Forego [to go before] ... *Forgo* [to do without]

infer/imply

Infer [to take from what someone else says] ... *Imply* [to suggest by what you say]

its/it's

Its [possessive, as in "at its limit"] ... *It's* [contraction of "it is," as in "it's time to go"]

loathe/loath

Loathe [to hate, despise] ... *Loath* [to be reluctant]

persuade/convince

Persuade [preferred for influencing someone else, as in "I persuaded him to come"] ... *Convince* [preferred for belief arrived at without persuasion: "I am convinced he is the best candidate"]

principle/principal

Principle [standard, as in "he has sound principles." Also, fundamental truth or law, or basis, as in "the principles of Newtonian physics"] ... *Principal* [first, as in "he is the school principal," or "this is our principal aim"]

reject/refute

Reject [to turn back] ... *Refute* [to counter an argument successfully]

verbal/oral

> *Verbal* [covers all words, written and spoken] … *Oral* [referring to language, covers only the spoken word]

REDUNDANCIES

Redundancies are easy to spot in other people's writing but difficult to see in your own. Consider this sentence, for instance, and think about how it can be stripped down: "According to Jones, Waldorf students usually excel faster in math than those in other school systems."

Some other blatant redundancies:

advance planning
a forecast of future weather patterns
biography of the life of Churchill
by lunchtime at noon
circular in shape
close scrutiny
collaborating together
consensus of opinion
crisis situation
during the winter months
8 p.m. in the evening
emergency situation
excess verbiage
fatally strangled
former graduate
gathered together
general consensus
her first baby child
hibernate in winter
Jewish rabbi
legal jurisprudence
necessary prerequisite
new initiative
past history

PARALLEL CONSTRUCTION

The term "parallel construction" refers to using the same style or grammatical structure for each element in a list, or for sentence components on each side of a conjunction. The aim is simply to improve the rhythm of the sentence and thus make it easier to understand. Here's one example where the problem is fairly obvious:

The excess revenue is recovered in one of three ways:
- direct taxation of the worker
- take it directly from the company
- companies deduct excess at source

Putting these elements "in parallel" gives a clearer picture:

The excess revenue is recovered in one of three ways:
- direct taxation of the worker
- direct payment by the company
- deduction of the excess at source

The following sentences are gross instances of out-of-sync construction. It's easy to spot the problem and easy to imagine how a rewrite would improve clarity — but again, this is the kind of pattern that's sometimes hard to spot in your own work.

A surplus of negative ions is credited with making people more lively, improve productivity, boost morale, spread healing and increase resistance to infection.

A committee of professional people, farmers and industry met today.

Jones outlined a three-point plan to create more jobs, open more industries, manpower retraining schools.

He wants to get a job, an apartment, and keep better care of his appearance.

The next examples are a little more subtle — cases where the grammatical constructions on each side of a linking word like "and," "but," "also" aren't quite the same:

Awkward: He spends all his time watching television and on the phone.
Better: He spends all his time watching television and talking on the phone.

Awkward: They want an increase of 10 per cent and to improve the dental plan.
Better: They want an increase of 10 per cent and improvements in the dental plan.

Awkward: It was both a long lecture and very tedious.
Better: It was both a long lecture and a very tedious one. (*Or:* It was a long and tedious lecture.)

Sometimes parallel problems simply arise from comparing apples and oranges. For instance:

Unlike many provinces [*substitute:* premiers], Tobin favors another meeting.

THE RULE OF OPPOSITES

Former prime minister Pierre Trudeau once said that the only constant in his thinking was opposition to accepted opinions. Reporters often show the same tendency to doubt and challenge. For instance, veteran instructor Mack Laing, of the University of Western Ontario Graduate School of Journalism, shows it in his language "rule of opposites," which goes like this:

Most news-writers know copy should not be loaded with adjectives. The rule of opposites underlines this. It states: if the adjective (or adverb) *opposite* in meaning to the one being tested makes the phrase ridiculous, it's likely that the adjective being tested should be dropped.

For instance, Laing says, if you're tempted to write of a *brutal* murder, test the phrase by considering the opposite: a *gentle* murder. Since this is ridiculous, you realize that "brutal" is also unnecessary. All murders are brutal: the noun already contains the meaning of the adjective.

Other examples: a *brave* hero becomes a *cowardly* hero; a *solid* wall of resistance becomes a *mushy, liquid* wall of resistance. In each case the test of opposites shows you don't need the original adjective. Adjectives often weaken a strong noun — as in a "terrible" holocaust, or a "dreadful" obscenity.

Harvey Schachter, former editor of the Kingston *Whig-Standard*, suggests the same kind of rule can be applied to test politicians' platitudes.

When a political candidate says something like "I believe in keeping taxes down, providing good municipal services and meeting the needs of the community," journalists can apply the test by imagining the opposite point of view. If that view is untenable or absurd ("I believe in keeping taxes high, providing poor municipal services and ignoring the needs of the community") then reporters need to probe deeper.

Schachter says applying the rule of opposites leads reporters to substantive questions. How serious is the candidate's commitment to low taxes? What kinds of compromises is the candidate willing to make on services to keep taxes down? Which services does the candidate see as untouchable? Which could be cut? If the candidate is advocating expansion *and* low taxes, how will that work out at budget time?

In a sense, then, the rule of opposites is a reminder to reporters to look critically at language and ideas, rather than accepting uncritically what they read or hear.

... but the suicide rate in Sweden is well above Canada [*substitute:* Canada's].

Mitchell claims many times it is the parents' lack of patience rather than the pharmacist [*substitute:* the pharmacist's carelessness] that is responsible for poisoning.

"Fat" Words

All editors have a personal hit list of words and phrases they find bloated, pretentious, overdone — in short, language that some word experts describe as "fat." The following sentences take the pattern to its most absurd limits, to illustrate the point:

In terms of the dynamics of social interaction, children currently need viable role models.

The committee is working on an open-ended time frame but hopes to finalize its input in the foreseeable future.

I cannot conceive of any scenario in which that would eventuate.

The new bill allows provinces to discontinue their involvement in the program.

Although those are extreme examples, they suggest some of the words that editors like to hate. These are some of the fat words and phrases that show up on most lists:

a function of at
at an early date [soon]
at this point in time [now]
currently [now]
declare, state, assert [say]
dichotomy
facilitate [make possible?]
fruitful interaction
initiated [started]
interface [link?]
in terms of
in the field of [in]
is indicative of [indicates; or shows]
It is not impossible that...
It may be observed that ...
meaningful dialogue
non-productive expenditures [waste?]

ongoing
paradigm [model, pattern]
parameters [characteristics?]
presently [ambiguous — can mean "now" or "soon"]
priorize ... prioritize ... make priority determinations [set priorities]
prior to [before]
proactive
relating to [about?]
relevant
resource allocation [spending]
scenarios [plans]
societal
substantive
terminal objectives [goals?]
urban complex [city]
utilized [used]
viable [means "capable of independent existence" so shouldn't be
    used simply as a synonym for "good"]
with regard to ... [about?]

METAPHORS

Fresh metaphors and similes make reading a delight; mixed, mangled or
tired images make it a chore. (The difference between a metaphor and
simile is the difference between saying someone *is* a tiger and saying he *acts
like* a tiger; the first is a metaphorical statement, not to be taken literally.)

For journalists, the greatest danger comes from using thoughtlessly in
print the tired or weak figures of speech so often used in conversation. A
good, though perhaps overly strict, guideline is George Orwell's much-
quoted advice: "never use a metaphor, simile or other figure of speech
which you are used to seeing in print" (1968, 139). The guideline is
intended to help writers discipline themselves to note the images they're
using and consider whether they contribute anything. Tired metaphors, in
which the image is obvious but overused ("His work *bogged down*"), should
be avoided, although sometimes they provide a useful way of making a
point quickly. Overworked metaphors used without thought lead to
clumsy mixed metaphors ("He got *bogged down* in *red tape*"). Dead
metaphors are not as much of a problem because neither the speaker nor
the hearer is aware of the metaphorical meaning. (When someone says
that phone solicitors are the *bane* of his existence, for instance, it's doubtful if speaker or hearers think of the word's original meaning: poison.)

The following is a list of metaphors by category.

Tired metaphors
> turned thumbs down
> riveted the audience
> cloaked in secrecy
> ill-fated expedition
> head in the clouds
> got their act together
> [and thousands more]

Dead metaphors
> on the hustings [election platform]
> got short shrift [The culprit was shriven — granted absolution — quickly before execution.]
> scapegoat [goat sacrificed to expiate sins]
> bell-wether [sheep with bell that leads flock]
> shambles [slaughter-house]

PRISONERS OR HOSTAGES

In time of war, if truth is the first casualty, the second is language precision:

- *Their side has terrorists; ours has freedom-fighters.*

- *Their side takes hostages; ours takes prisoners.*

- *Their side bombs women and children; ours inflicts collateral damage.*

These examples are blatant ones. On more subtle levels, we all constantly use language that says more about *the images already fixed in our minds* than about the world outside them.

If we write of "socialized medicine," we probably reflect a different internal reality than if we write a phrase like "universal medical care."

If we write of union "demands" we display a different mental map than if we write of union "proposals."

Is it possible to escape these language traps created by our own beliefs, or by the beliefs and values of our sources?

Not entirely. But it helps if you can develop an intense interest in language — in the meanings of words and the messages they convey. It also helps to develop a critical sensibility to how words and phrases can be manipulated to reinforce stereotypes or to promote ideas.

Mixed metaphors

We must hitch our wagon to the explosion of knowledge if we are to reach the stars.

Fraser is eager to see these regulations cast in parchment.

Ministers are working soundlessly in overdrive beneath the crust of government in preparation for Act II.

Once you've bitten the bullet you can no longer sweep it under the rug.

I don't want to go out on a limb. If you spread yourself too thin, you can go down in flames.

He ignited a blood-bath.

The proposal marks a seminal sea-change in our thinking.

Mangled metaphors

missed by a hare's breath [hair's breadth]

students were told to tow the line [toe]

gave free reign to his emotions [rein]

to be on tenderhooks [tenterhooks — hooks on a frame for stretching newly woven cloth]

she is very straight-laced [strait-laced — i.e., tightly laced]

he decided to take another tact [tack — as in sailing]

waited with baited breath [bated — hushed, held back]

now in its death throws [throes]

Bad metaphors

They are attempting to weed out [select?] the best-qualified people.

Her career plans are not unravelling [unfolding?] as she hoped.

He has unleashed [provoked?] a sharp protest from his workers by cutting their pay.

Horse and buggy age metaphors, still wheezing

runaway inflation

rode herd on

kicked over the traces

giving a leg up

feeling his oats

hobbled

jockeyed for position

kept on a short tether

spurred to greater effort

rode roughshod

blinkered view

saddled with the problem

[and many more]

Baseball metaphors

> two strikes against him
> pinch-hitter
> caught off base
> in the right ballpark
> touch base

Sailing metaphors

> took the wind out of her sails
> on an even keel
> got back on course
> fired a broadside

Great metaphors (or similes)

> Turning anxiously on the spit of his own ego, John Updike has developed the habit of seeing everything in his life as powerfully symbolic (Robert Fulford, Ottawa *Citizen*, Aug. 19, 1989).

> The book is drenched in Jungian fantasies she has dreamed, or dreamed that she dreamed, and her choice of setting is about as commercially safe as a hand-knit parachute (June Callwood, *Globe and Mail*, Aug. 31, 1984).

> Human language is like a cracked kettle on which we beat out tunes for bears to dance to, when all the time we are longing to move the stars to pity (Gustave Flaubert, *Madame Bovary* [London: Oxford University Press, 1959], 253).

GRAMMAR

Books on grammar can form a useful part of any beginning journalist's desk equipment (some are listed at the end of Appendix A). What follows is by no means a full grammar reference, but only a glance at problems editors frequently encounter.

Dangling Modifiers

In the following list, the initial phrase or clause is said to dangle because the noun or pronoun it is supposed to modify is missing. In effect, there is no sentence subject controlling the action of the first part of the sentence (see Gowers 1973, 147–149).

1. Referred from one person to another, the chase became boring. [Referred from one person to another, *we found* the chase boring.]

2. After passing through the first set of doors, the second set opened soundlessly, extending a spooky invitation to the unknown. [After *I passed* through…]

3. To re-establish control, the underlying problem must be addressed. [To re-establish control, *you must address* the underlying problem.]

Note that some short "absolute constructions," grammatically unconnected with the rest of the sentence, do not require a modifier. These include constructions like "*Generally speaking,* I don't work on Fridays," or "*Given the danger,* it's not surprising she doesn't go out at night." Theodore Bernstein (1977) offers two rules to distinguish these exceptions: does the reader expect a noun that the phrase modifies? Is the phrase common enough to be considered an idiom?

Misplaced Modifiers

Modifiers should be as close as possible to the words they modify. Note the difference in meaning in these two sentences:

She watches TV only in the evening.
She only watches TV in the evening.

And in these:

He spoke at McGill University on the increase in racist language.
He spoke on the increase in racist language at McGill University.

Make sure clauses starting with "who" or "what" are as close as possible to the word or phrase they modify. Avoid constructions like this one:

The books were written by two French academics between 1960 and 1980 who found earlier texts inadequate.

Run-on Sentences

Note that in each of the following cases, the two clauses should be separated by a full stop (a period or at least a semi-colon).

The plan seems to be collapsing, negotiators are still seeking a common ground.

"That is deplorable," she said, "pharmacists just aren't taking the time they should when dealing with safety measures."

"The child is exposed to a lot more people," she says, "that can help language development and even social development."

Agreement of Verbs/Nouns

Watch out especially for the following three traps.

Pattern 1, in which writers tend to use the plural form, wrongly, because they've just typed a plural noun:

> Air Canada, together with other airlines, has [not "have"] been losing money.
>
> Smith, along with many other teachers, faces [not "face"] dismissal.

Pattern 2, in which writers use the plural form after a singular collective noun:

> Bell Canada has decided to raise its [not "their"] international profile.
>
> The committee issued a report which it hopes [not "they hope"] will be adopted.

But since it's hard to imagine *a committee* hoping, it's better to say committee *members* hope. And if the group is not acting as a unit, a plural pronoun is correct: "the team put on *their* uniforms."

Pattern 3, in which confusion arises when you're writing of one among many. For instance:

> Leclerc is one of the few players who have [not "has"] scored 50 points.

To test this one, invert the sentence:

> Of the few players who have scored 50 points, Leclerc is one.

Who/Whom

The standard rule is: use *who* as subject of a clause, *whom* as object. The most common error occurs in sentences like these:

> His friend, who he said would arrive tonight … ["Who" is correct, as subject of the clause "who would arrive."]
>
> His friend, whom we all admire, is … ["Whom" is object of "admire."]
>
> To whom are you referring? ["Whom" is object of the preposition "to."]
>
> Whom have they chosen? ["Whom" is proper for formal language, but "who" is acceptable in informal usage.]
>
> Give the job to whoever types best. ["Whoever" is the subject of the clause "whoever types best," and the whole clause is object of the preposition "to."]

Which/That

A tricky one for many writers, but the basic rules are simple.

- Use "that" when the clause is *essential* in explaining or defining the noun.

    Example: The car *that I drove to work today* is blue.
    [The clause defines or "restricts" the subject.]

- Use "which" for clauses *introducing a new element* in the sentence.

    Example: My car, *which I left at home today*, is black.

Note: "That" clauses usually don't need commas; "which" clauses usually do.

Like

Most editors resist the use of "like" with a verb ["She looked like she knew what she was doing"]. It is usual for "like" to modify a noun ["She looked like an athlete"].

Misuse of Semi-colon

Except in lists, the material after a semi-colon must be an independent clause, with characteristics of a complete sentence.

> *Incorrect:* Smithfield's other two children are enrolled as well; Willie in Grade 6 and Mary in kindergarten.

> *Correct:* Smithfield's other two children are enrolled as well; Willie is in Grade 6 and Mary in kindergarten.

> *Also correct:* Smithfield's other two children are enrolled as well. Willie in Grade 6 and Mary in kindergarten.

MISCELLANEOUS LANGUAGE POINTS

Avoid Passive Voice

> *Poor:* Smith *was defeated by* Jones on a vote of 5–3.
> *Better:* Smith *lost* to Jones. Or: Jones *defeated* Smith.

> *Poor:* The renovations are behind schedule because some supplies *were delayed* and *there were minor changes made* to the original plans.
> *Better:* Minor changes in the original plans and delay in the arrival of supplies *put* the renovations behind schedule.

Don't Combine Active and Passive

Poor: As he rode into the paddock, cheering was heard.
Better: As he rode into the paddock, the crowd cheered.

Avoid Superfluous "Involves"

Poor: It is a six-month program *that involves educating* residents about drug abuse.
Better: It is a six-month program *to educate* residents about drug abuse.

Poor: The people involved in the QNI project believe it will end soon.
Better: The QNI *researchers* believe their project will end soon.

Poor: So far, the research *has involved interviewing* Liberal politicians.
Better: So far the researchers *have interviewed* Liberal politicians.

Avoid Acronyms

A sentence like this is a stopper, even if the acronyms have been previously identified:

The CBIE report says Tanzania is actually one of the luckier LDCs, with more than 100 ODA-sponsored students.

Avoid Fragment Quotes

Poor: Stewart says Canada offers "a better quality of education."

Use fragment quotes only when it's important to show this was the exact language used.

Avoid Non Sequiturs

A native of New Brunswick, Mr. Singh has strong views on deficit financing.

Watch Out for "Sound-Alikes"

He said safety considerations will be tantamount [paramount?].
Racist factions perpetuated [perpetrated?] brutal outrages against ethnic minorities.
The course focused on the tenants [tenets?] of various theorists.
Her career has now been interminably [irretrievably?] damaged.
He offered a peon [paean?] of praise.

Use Terms Precisely

- unique [Don't qualify the word by calling something extremely unique, or rather unique — the thing either is or is not unique]

- a voting bloc [not block]

- only [Avoid "one of the only." Make it "one of the few."]

- ad nauseam [not ad nauseum]

- ad hominem [not ad homimum]

- vis-à-vis [Means "face-to-face." Don't use as equivalent to "in," or "in connection with."]

- He was led [not lead] down the path.

- hopefully [Means "in a hopeful manner," not a synonym for "I hope" or "it is to be hoped."]

- literally [Often misused in place of figuratively, as in "I literally exploded."]

- a lot [Often erroneously written as "alot."]

- everyday [An adjective, often misused when "every day" is intended.]

Avoid Adjectival Pileup

Especially in broadcast writing, don't put a cumbersome string of adjectives before the noun.

Poor: Maplebrook-Howard United Church Minister Rev. James Johnson said he is not worried.

Better: Rev. James Johnson of Maplebrook-Howard United Church said he is not worried.

Or (for broadcast): Rev. James Johnson, who is pastor of Maplebrook-Howard United Church, said …

Avoid Weak Forms of "To Be"

Some forms of the verb "to be" — such as "it is" and "there are" — can often be replaced by stronger verbs, especially at the start of a sentence.

Poor: There are several new approaches being tried.

Better: Several new approaches are being tried.

Poor: McRae said there is now a membership of 15 in the group.

Better: McRae said the group now has 15 members.

Use Hyphens Carefully

Adjectival phrases before the noun are usually hyphenated [up-to-the-minute fashion]; avoid the temptation to hyphenate similar word groups after the noun [an increase of five per cent].

Some adjectival phrases before the noun are not hyphenated if the words customarily go together and therefore do not need a link [a Grade 3 class, a high school building].

Most editors prefer not to hyphenate adverbial phrases ending in *-ly* since that ending is thought to link naturally with the next word [a slowly moving train, a widely known author].

Use Contractions Properly

An awkward form coming into common use is a contraction followed by a bracketed reference.

Poor: He's (Robert) the lead actor in the play.

Better: He (Robert) is the lead actor in the play.

Avoid Loose Antecedents

Poor: Mary told Leila she had won the prize. [Antecedent of "she" is unclear.]

Poor: Jones says she is sure that if they had taken Joey to a big city hospital for the spinal surgery they would not have taken him. [Second "they" is ambiguous, presumably referring to "hospital."]

Poor: He was one of three politicians criticized by the columnist when he had been drinking heavily. [Who did the drinking?]

Poor: Bruce McArthur scored three touchdowns and led his team to a 58–17 victory over Danforth yesterday. It was one of the highest-scoring games of the year. ["It" has no antecedent, so make it: "*The game* was one of …]

Capitalize Trade Names

Kleenex, Xerox, Aspirin, Spandex, Band-Aid, Coke, Jeep, Vaseline and Mace are among many trade names that are sometimes accidentally used as generic terms. Capitalize them, or reword to avoid the problem (use "tissue" instead of Kleenex, for instance, or "photocopy" instead of Xerox).

ORWELL'S RULES

George Orwell's six basic writing rules (1968, 139) have been often quoted —
and deserve to be quoted again:

1. Never use a metaphor, simile or other figure of speech which you are used to seeing in print.

2. Never use a long word where a short one will do.

3. If it's possible to cut a word out, always cut it out.

4. Never use the passive where you can use the active.

5. Never use a foreign phrase, a scientific word or a jargon word if you can think of an everyday English equivalent.

6. Break any of these rules sooner than say anything outright barbarous.

RECOMMENDED READING

Bates, Jefferson D. (1985). *Writing With Precision*. Revised edition. Washington, DC: Acropolis Books.

Bates, Jem. (1996). *The Canadian Writer's Market*. 12th revised edition. Toronto: McClelland & Stewart.

Bernstein, Theodore M. (1977). *The Careful Writer: A Modern Guide to English Usage*. New York: Atheneum.

Buckley, Joanne. (1991). *Fit to Print: The Canadian Student's Guide to Essay Writing*. 2nd edition. Toronto: Harcourt Brace Jovanovich.

Burchfield, R.W. (1996). *The New Fowler's Modern English Usage*. Oxford: Clarendon Press.

CP Stylebook: A Guide for Writers and Editors. (1995). Peter Buckley, ed. Revised edition. Toronto: The Canadian Press.

Freelance Editors' Association of Canada. (1987). *Editing Canadian English*. Vancouver: Douglas and McIntyre.

Gowers, Sir Ernest. (1986). *The Complete Plain Words*. 3rd edition. Rev. Ed. by Sidney Greenbaum and Janet Whitcut. London: Her Majesty's Stationery Office.

Hodges, John C., Mary E. Whitten, Judy Brown, and Jane Flick. (1994). *Harbrace College Handbook for Canadian Writers*. 4th edition. Toronto: Harcourt Brace.

Kessler, Lauren, and Duncan McDonald. (1996). *When Words Collide: A Media Writer's Guide to Grammar and Style*. 4th edition. Belmont, CA: Wadsworth.

MacNeil, Robert. (1989). *Wordstruck*. New York: Viking.

Strunk, William, Jr., and E.B. White. (1979). *The Elements of Style*. 3rd edition. New York: Macmillan.

APPENDIX B

Libel

Sooner or later — and the odds are it will happen sooner rather than later — every reporter comes across information about someone that, if published or broadcast, could lead to a libel suit. One of your sources for a story about sexual abuse of psychiatric patients gives you the name of the doctor who made a pass at her. A local police officer you count among your best contacts tells you, over coffee, a hilarious tale about a city councillor's drunken antics at the Canada Day parade. An angry city resident calls the newsroom urging a story on a garage operator who, the caller is convinced, is keeping crooked books.

Some of the tales a reporter hears in the workday are mere gossip — not worth repeating, much less publishing. Others demand serious attention. They are natural story ideas, or seemingly natural elements of a story you are already working on. But if you want to use this information, you need to be aware of the risk of libel actions — and what you can do to prevent a suit or to defend against one.

Libel law in Canada is complex and confusing. The discussion that follows will not necessarily equip you to make decisions on libel-sensitive stories, but it is designed to try to make you libel-conscious. It is meant to help you spot problems that should be referred to an editor or lawyer.

The most important advice is this: good digging is the best protection against a libel action. If you are going to write a story that someone may consider defamatory, make sure you have the hard evidence to back up the allegation. That's because, under Canadian law, it's up to you to prove in court that the story is true, and not up to the person suing you to prove it is false.

You should also know that it's not going to do you any good to show in court that you were simply quoting accurately what one of your sources said to you. Accuracy is fundamental to good reporting. But the issue in a libel case may centre on whether the story was true, not whether it was an accurate account of a source's comments. To put it another way, your job as reporter is not simply to record what sources say to you, but to try to establish the truth of what the sources say. Under the law, *repeating* a libel is as dangerous as originating one.

DEFAMATION DEFINED

Because the civil law on libel is the one that is of most pressing concern to Canadian journalists, this discussion will concentrate on it and leave aside the question of criminal libel.

Under civil law, you *defame* someone when you say or write something about an individual that lowers the individual's reputation in the eyes of the community. Statements that a particular athlete cheats, that the owner of a car repair shop is crooked, or that a Canadian history professor doesn't know when the War of 1812 began, for example, could be defamatory. In general, *libel* is the written or broadcast version of a defamatory statement, and therefore is the chief concern of the news media. *Slander* is the conversational form of defamation.

Libel is considered to be a *tort* — a wrong that causes injury or loss. Each province has its own libel and slander act or defamation act, with local variations on the Canadian common law of defamation. In Quebec, with its Civil Code tradition, libel law has a few unique wrinkles. (For a discussion of Quebec law see Flaherty 1984, 31–33.)

The general rule across the country is that individuals may sue for libel if they believe their reputation has been damaged. The person suing — known as the plaintiff — must prove only three things about the story in question:

1. The statements are defamatory.
2. The statements were published or broadcast.
3. The statements refer to the plaintiff, who is living and identifiable.

This last point needs some explanation. First, Canadian libel law applies only to the living: it is not possible to libel the dead. Also, libel is said to be a personal action — an individual sues because his individual reputation has been attacked. Because of the personal nature of the action, individuals in large groups cannot necessarily sue just because they feel the group has been defamed. They must prove that the libel refers to them personally.

If, for example, a newspaper ran a story saying "university professors are so poorly educated that they couldn't pass a high school history test," no individual professor could sue successfully. That's because the group is so broad that no individual professor is identifiable. If, on the other hand, the story said, "Canadian history professors at Carnation College are so poorly educated they couldn't pass a high school history test," any one of the people who teach Canadian history at that school might sue for defamation, even though their names were not published. That's because the statement could be seen as referring to each of them, individually. Of course, if the statement said, "Professor Louise Brown of Carnation College is so poorly educated she couldn't pass a high school history test," only Prof. Brown could claim defamation.

Sometimes reporters think that if they use a made-up name to avoid referring to a particular individual they can avoid a libel action. This offers little protection. If a plaintiff can prove at trial that a reasonable reader who knew the facts would conclude that the plaintiff was the individual behind the made-up name, the plaintiff might win her suit.

The law also recognizes the value of a reputation to an organization like a corporation or a law firm. These also may sue for libel, though they are limited to claiming that damage was done to the organization.

The law presumes that the plaintiff who proves all three points (identification, defamation, publication) has suffered *damage*. Plaintiffs may be paid compensatory damages for the loss or injury. They may also seek punitive damages — payments aimed at punishing the people who spread the libel, or at deterring others from doing the same.

The amount of compensation ranges from a minimal payment to settlements in the hundreds of thousands of dollars. Settlements often require that the losing party pay the other's legal costs — which can add up to a considerable expense. Compared with those in the United States, however, Canadian libel awards tend to be modest.

Many cases never get to the trial stage. Instead, they are settled out of court, through negotiations between the plaintiff and defendant. The terms of such settlements vary tremendously, and often include a requirement that the newspaper or magazine publish an apology and retraction. In most cases, the wording of these apologies is worked out with the plaintiff.

Defending Against Libel

Journalists have two main defences against libel — truth and fair comment — and a number of less common ones, including consent and qualified privilege.

The defence of truth, also known as justification, is probably the best-known one among reporters. It is a complete defence in all provinces but Quebec, where you must also prove that the defamatory statement was published without malice, in the public interest.

If, for example, you write that a city councillor was drunk at the Canada Day parade and made rude remarks about the mayor, the city councillor may threaten legal action, claiming that the statement is defamatory. If you can prove that the story was true, he cannot win his suit.

The burden of proving the truth may be a heavy one, however. You may know beyond a shadow of doubt that something happened, but the depth of your personal conviction is irrelevant. To *prove* that it happened, you usually need a reliable witness who can give first-hand evidence. ("I saw the councillor put away three doubles before the parade," or "I heard him refer to the mayor as a 'boob' and as 'a tin-pot dictator.'") Evidence at a libel trial may also include unedited tapes of interviews, public records, letters, diaries, pictures and so on. All may help you establish the truth of the report.

Second-hand evidence ("My buddy was on patrol at the parade and he told me the councillor was really smashed") is considered unreliable and therefore inadmissible in court.

Sometimes, people who were reliable sources when the story was written back off at the prospect of having to appear in court. In addition, if you promised confidentiality to a source at the time you wrote the story, you are ethically obligated to keep that promise. In parts of the United States, so-called shield laws sometimes allow reporters to keep the identity of sources confidential. Canada has no such laws, which means that in some circumstances, a court can compel you to reveal the identity of a source.

Clearly, therefore, it's best not to rely too much on a single source, especially a single, confidential source. Clearly, too, the best protection against a libel action is to make sure you have your facts right in the first place. (Indeed, accurate reporting of true stories is the best way to pre-empt libel actions.)

The defence of fair comment is based on the idea that everyone in society, including the media, has a right to express an honest opinion on issues of public concern. What is a fair comment? Basically, it must be clearly recognizable as a comment — not a statement of fact — on a matter of public interest. It must be based on true facts, and it must be an honest opinion.

Media lawyer Stuart Robertson, in his useful handbook on the law, offers a simple example of the difference between a statement of fact and a comment — and a good lesson in how knowing the difference can help you avoid trouble.

Example 1: "Sam Sly pays most of his debts, but *not* the little ones. He is a collection risk." Robertson says the first sentence is a statement of fact. The second sentence is a comment on the facts in the first sentence.

Example 2: "Sam Sly is a collection risk." Without any background facts, what was clearly a comment in the first example has been turned into a statement of fact. Robertson notes that if Sly sues, it might be difficult for the writer to prove that Sly is a collection risk if he pays most of his debts, and always the large ones. "Therefore, you should always include in your publication enough relevant and true facts to fairly and reasonably support a comment published by you, whether it is your own comment or someone else's" (1983, 70).

Two other defences are worth examining: consent and qualified privilege. The former may apply if the person agrees to talk with you about a defamatory allegation, knowing that you intend to publish it. That person may be seen to have "consented" to the publication. (If the person simply denies the allegation, there is no consent.) In cases where consent may become the defence, Robertson says, it's a good idea to record the interview, or at least have a witness present who can testify that consent was given (1983, 68–69).

The defence of qualified privilege is based on the idea that in some circumstances, the free exchange of ideas and information is more important to society than the private rights of an individual to protect against defamation. The best-known examples of this are courts of law, provincial legislatures and the House of Commons, where people have an "absolute privilege" to speak without fear of a civil suit. The reporter covering these situations is granted by law the privilege to report what happened.

For example, a witness at a murder trial can testify about the accused's history of violent behavior without fear of being sued for defamation. The reporter covering the trial may report this testimony, also without fear of civil action. There are some limits on the reporter's privilege, however. The report must be fair, accurate, written without comment and published contemporaneously with the trial.

Reporters have a qualified privilege to report on the proceedings of city councils, legislative committees, royal commissions, administrative bodies created by governments and so on, and to report on the documents these organizations prepare for public information, including press releases (Robertson 1983, 72). Reporters also may report on the findings of groups like medical associations, which discipline their members. Again, such reports must be fair and accurate, and done without malice.

You must be aware that the condition of absolute privilege usually applies to the *locale*, not to the individual. In other words, if you write a fair and accurate report on a member of Parliament standing up in the House of Commons and saying, "Jones is a crook," Jones can't sue you or the MP successfully. But if instead the same MP makes the comment to you in an interview at lunch and you publish it, Jones could sue you both.

Avoiding Libel

Lawyer Julian Porter, in a handbook published by the Canadian Book Publishers' Council, points out that a writer's statements may be libellous even if there was no intention to do harm. He warns that avoiding libel is more difficult than many people think, and lists a number of examples of tactics that *won't* work, such as the following:

- Just because the same thing has been said before and the person about whom it was said did not sue does not mean that he or she can't sue this time. (The prior libels cannot be referred to in court except in very special and rare circumstances.)

- Something that was said as a joke might be libellous if it is taken out of context and published as a serious statement.

- You cannot avoid libel by saying, "*It is alleged* that Jones is a thief," or "*Rumor has it* that Jones is a thief." If you say, write or publish it, you are responsible for having made the statement.

- Slang and colloquial or esoteric expressions cannot be used to avoid libel. Some words may carry an innuendo, a meaning known to some people. For example, "McDougall is a schnorrer" [a mooch]; John was a Leporello [a procurer] to his friends"; "Like Brutus [who conspired to kill Julius Caesar], he is a trustworthy man."

- It is not a defence to say that words were meant in jest if they don't read that way (Porter 1987, 14–15).

RETRACTIONS AND APOLOGIES

If you make a mistake — if you publish a defamatory story and have no defences — you may want to consider publishing a retraction of the story, and apologizing for the incident. An apology is not a defence against a libel suit, but the fact that you retracted (or offered to retract) the original story may be taken into account in the decision about how much the plaintiff should receive in damages.

Sometimes, however, a retraction and apology can actually make things worse. Lawyer Gerald Flaherty writes, "To be of any benefit to a defendant, an apology must be genuine in its withdrawal of the defamatory imputation, and in expressing regret for having published it" (Flaherty 1984, 61). Also, if you eventually plan to use the defence of truth, issuing an apology could appear to be inconsistent and perhaps insincere, which might damage your case. A half-hearted apology can be worse than no apology at all. Flaherty notes that an apology that repeats the original defamation may aggravate damages, "and could even support an action for republication of the libel" (62).

If you must apologize, it's usually a good idea to have a libel lawyer work with you on crafting an appropriate statement.

COMPARISONS WITH U.S. LAW

Libel laws in Canada and the United States both draw on the same British roots, but sharp differences have developed. Canadian journalists familiar with well-known U.S. cases may be at hazard if they assume that the U.S. standards, set through a number of Supreme Court decisions, also apply here.

In the United States, for example, public figures — the term may include politicians, army generals, film or TV stars or less glamorous figures such as officials from county government — can successfully sue a journalist or newspaper for libel *only* if they can prove that the journalist or the newspaper acted out of malice. In other words, they have to show that the journalist went with the story knowing it was false, or without caring whether it was false.

The idea behind this approach, in its simplest rendering, is that public figures, because of their position, should expect more scrutiny and criticism than private people.

Many Canadian reporters look with some envy at the libel situation south of the border. In Canada, the question of whether the person filing the suit is a public figure is irrelevant to the law. The leader of a federal political party, therefore, has only to prove the same three points (identification, defamation and publication) as a private individual, despite the fact that the federal leader lives very much in the public eye.

In practice, few Canadian political leaders ever sue for libel. Like American politicians, they expect that hostility from some members of the media simply comes with the job. When one does sue — as when former defence minister Robert Coates sued the Ottawa *Citizen* in the mid-1980s — the suit tends to attract substantial attention from the rest of the media, including calls for the libel laws to move closer to the U.S. model.

THE DEBATE OVER LIBEL CHILL

In recent years some of the largest and most publicized libel suits have come from Canada's corporate elite, from families or individuals who are able to marshal columns of lawyers to fight a case. For a mid-size magazine, or even for a giant daily, the prospect of fighting a lawsuit against one of these people is daunting. The legal costs will be staggering. If you lose, your side will probably have to pay the other side's bills, as well as damages.

The big question is, how will this knowledge affect your work? Will you soften a story in hopes of making it libel-proof? Will you back off from investigating someone who is known to be suit-happy? Will your editor or publisher cut out the muscle from a story, worrying more about whether the subject of the story will sue than about what the story says? Will the editor decide not to pursue a good lead, for fear that going ahead with it might prompt a libel suit? The phrase used to describe this kind of thinking is "libel chill," the idea that the strict libel laws have a chilling effect on the exercise of freedom of the press.

The concept of libel chill is a matter of sharp debate in the journalism community. Some argue that if reporters and editors do their jobs properly — in other words, if they work hard at gathering proof to back up what they write — they have little to fear from libel laws. (See, for example, Martin 1991b, 757–770, and Cohen and Pohle 1992, 14–15.) Others, including a group of prominent writers calling for reform of Ontario's libel laws, say the law has been turned into a tool to muzzle journalists (see, for example, Herrington 1991, 8–9).

One of the central issues in the debate turns on the question of *who* has to prove *what*. The plaintiff has to prove only identification, defamation and publication. The defendant has the far more difficult task of proving that the statements at issue are true, or represent a fair comment. Some call this "reverse onus" — the idea that the *defendant* bears the burden of proof rather than the plaintiff. They argue that if the plaintiff has a beef with the newspaper, the plaintiff should have to prove that the newspaper was wrong.

Others argue that since the newspaper took the first shot by publishing something that the plaintiff says is defamatory, it's the newspaper's responsibility to prove the truth of what it published. They say it doesn't matter who the plaintiff is or who the defendant is; what's important is who is the *accuser*. And there would be no case if the newspaper hadn't made an accusation against the person who later sues.

One final point on libel: a great deal of Canadian libel law is derived from case law. This means lawyers and judges look to similar cases for guidance on how to proceed in any particular case. For reporters, this has two consequences. First, it means that you can't carry around a precise summary of the law — as you can with the Criminal Code, for example. Second, it means that the finer points of libel law are subject to change, as each decision adds to the body of case law.

RECOMMENDED READING

Crawford, Michael G. (1996). *The Journalist's Legal Guide*. 3rd edition. Toronto: Carswell.

Flaherty, Gerald A. (1984). *Defamation Law in Canada*. Ottawa: The Canadian Bar Foundation.

Freelance Editors' Association of Canada. (1987). *Editing Canadian English*. Vancouver: Douglas and McIntyre. See especially Chapter 11 (145–155), "Editors and the Law."

Martin, Robert. (1997). *Media Law*. Toronto: Irwin Law.

Martin, Robert, and G. Stuart Adam. (1991). *A Sourcebook of Canadian Media Law*. Revised edition (new case material). Ottawa: Carleton University Press. See especially Chapter 5 (539–822), "Legal Limitations Arising From Private Rights."

Porter, Julian. (1987). *Libel: A Handbook for Canadian Publishers, Editors and Writers*. Toronto: Canadian Book Publishers' Council.

Robertson, Stuart M. (1983). *Media Law Handbook*. Vancouver: International Self-Counsel Press.

Williams, Jeremy S. (1988). *The Law of Libel and Slander in Canada*. 2nd edition. Toronto: Butterworths.

For further information on the debate over libel chill, we recommend:

Bain, George. (1991). "The Fourth Estate and libel chill." *Maclean's*, May 27: 58.

Cohen, Lynne, and Klaus Pohle. (1992). "Libel chill fever misguided." *content*, March-April: 14–15.

Crawford, Michael G. (1992). "The big chill." *Canadian Lawyer*, April: 14–20.

Fraser, John. (1991). "The great 'libel chill' clash." *Saturday Night*, May: 10–13.

Herrington, Doug. (1991). "Libel chill issue heats up." *content*, May-June: 8–9.

Noble, Kimberley. (1992). *Bound and Gagged: Libel Chill and the Right to Publish*. Toronto: HarperCollins. (This is one of the *Point of View* series of pamphlets.)

Wells, Jennifer. (1990). "Where writers fear to tread: The cost of libel chill." *Financial Times of Canada*, November 19: 1, 3.

APPENDIX C

Glossary

Agence France-Presse International news agency, French-owned.

American Journalism Review National U.S. Magazine analysing journalism practices. (Formerly *Washington Journalism Review*.)

Asia Pacific Fellowship Program Sponsors up to six journalists for two months in a country in the Asia Pacific region.

Associated Press International news agency, based in the United States.

Atkinson Fellowship Fellowship open to all print and broadcast journalists sponsoring a year of research and writing on a series of in-depth articles.

Background Statements made "on background" with a reporter's agreement may be used but not attributed. (See "off the record.")

Broadcast News The broadcast subsidiary of The Canadian Press; it provides news summaries and newscasts to radio and television outlets.

Bullets The large dots at the start of paragraphs written in point form.

Canadian Association of Broadcasters Trade association representing private broadcasters.

Canadian Association of Journalists National professional organization, formerly the Centre for Investigative Journalism, publisher of *Media*, sponsor of CAJ Awards for investigative reporting.

Canadian Broadcasting Corporation Publicly owned national broadcasting corporation, controlling CBC radio and TV networks, including Radio-Canada.

Canadian Broadcast Standards Council Independent body set up in 1989 by private broadcasters to deal with public complaints relating to codes and standards of the Canadian Association of Broadcasters.

Canadian Cable Television Association Trade association representing cable TV broadcasters.

Canadian Press National news agency set up by the daily newspapers of Canada to exchange news among themselves and with international news agencies.

Canadian Radio-television and Telecommunications Commission Regulatory body responsible for broadcasting and telecommunications.

CanWest Global System Group of autonomous television stations in Ontario and Western Canada.

Columbia Journalism Review Major U.S. publication for analysis and criticism of journalism.

Computer-assisted reporting Term used to refer to news gathering through the use of databases and Internet sources, or to reporting based on statistical analysis of raw data.

content Canadian magazine for journalists that merged with Canadian Association of Journalists' *Bulletin*, becoming *Media* magazine in 1994.

Desktop publishing Computerized publishing systems integrating text and graphics.

Dummy Page plan or mockup used in page makeup.

Fédération professionnelle des journalistes du Québec Professional association of Quebec journalists.

Follow A followup to an earlier story, leading with the latest development.

FYI For your information.

Hollinger International Headed by Conrad Black, the largest daily newspaper publisher in Canada, controlling 60 newspapers, including those published by the Southam and Sterling chains.

InfoGlobe Electronic information service that provides indexed access to *Globe and Mail* stories, plus a range of other databases. (See Chapter 3, "Research Sources.")

Infomart Electronic information service originally covering Southam papers and the *Toronto Star*, later expanded to include many other databases. (See Chapter 3, "Research Sources.")

Irving Group New Brunswick-based newspaper and broadcasting group founded by K. C. Irving.

Literary journalism Genre that combines writing techniques drawn from fiction with immersion research by the reporter. Also known as creative non-fiction.

Maclean Hunter group Diversified media company controlling magazines, broadcasting outlets and newspapers.

Matthews Media Directory Reference listing current media executives in Canada.

Magazine Markets and Fees Biannual directory listing rates of payment for more than 300 Canadian periodicals.

Media Canadian magazine for journalists, founded by Canadian Association of Journalists in 1994.

Michener Award Given annually to a Canadian media organization for outstanding public service.

Michener Fellowships Two fellowships of $20,000 each, provided, when warranted, to allow journalists four months of out-of-office study.

Morgue Newsroom library.

National Newspaper Awards Premier Canadian competition for best newspaper journalism.

Newspaper Guild Major journalistic union in English Canada. Merged with Washington-based Communications Workers of America in 1995. Some breakaway Canadian units have merged with Communications, Energy and Paperworkers union.

Obit Obituary article. In the case of prominent people it is often written in advance and held for release on their death.

Off the record Statements made "off the record" with a reporter's agreement are not to be published, even without attribution.

Ombudsman Semi-autonomous newspaper employee whose role is to evaluate complaints against the paper and assess the paper's performance.

Parliamentary Press Gallery Organization linking journalists assigned to cover Parliament and government.

Periodical Writers Association of Canada Professional organization open to those earning "a significant portion of their income" from freelance writing. It sponsors a number of craft publications.

Pix Short for pictures.

Precision journalism Reporting that uses social science survey and content analysis methods to measure patterns or opinions.

Press Councils Public bodies set up to hear and assess complaints against newspapers.

Privilege Legal concept that entitles reporters to a measure of protection in reporting contentious public affairs.

Quebecor Quebec-based newspaper group, including *Le Journal de Montréal* and *Le Journal de Québec*.

Query Letter or phone call designed to interest an editor in a story idea.

Reuters Major international news agency, based in Britain. (Spelled without the *s* when bracketed in placelines.)

Royal Commission on Newspapers (Kent Commission) Body headed by Tom Kent which in 1980–81 studied the Canadian newspaper industry, especially group ownership, after the closing of Southam Newspapers' *Winnipeg Tribune* and Thomson Newspapers' *Ottawa Journal*.

Ryerson Review of Journalism Magazine devoted to journalism practice, published by Ryerson School of Journalism, Toronto.

Sidebar Secondary story associated with a main story.

Slot Editor who organizes copy flow.

Slug Story designation — usually one or two words.

Southam Fellowships Fellowships sponsored by Southam Newspapers, open to journalists with five years' experience, for a year's study at the University of Toronto.

Southam Inc. Major Canadian newspaper group, including dailies in Montreal, Ottawa, Calgary, Edmonton and Vancouver. Controlled by Hollinger International.

Special Senate Committee on Mass Media (Davey Committee) Committee headed by Senator Keith Davey which inquired into ownership and control of Canadian mass media in 1969–70.

Task Force on Broadcasting Policy Group headed by Gerald Caplan and Florian Sauvageau which studied the Canadian broadcasting system in 1985–86.

Thomson Newspapers Major Canadian and international newspaper chain, including the *Globe and Mail* of Toronto and the *Winnipeg Free Press*, founded by Roy Thomson (later Lord Thomson of Fleet).

BIBLIOGRAPHY

Adam, G. Stuart. (1993). *Notes Toward a Definition of Journalism*. The Poynter Papers, No. 2. St. Petersburg: The Poynter Institute for Media Studies.

Adam, G. Stuart. (1988). "Thinking journalism. ..." *content*, July-August: 4–11.

Adam, G. Stuart. (1976). *Journalism, Communication and the Law*. Scarborough, ON: Prentice-Hall.

Alia, Valerie, Brian Brennan, and Barry Hoffmaster. (1996). *Deadlines and Diversity: Journalism Ethics in a Changing World*. Halifax: Ferwood Publishing.

Allen, Ralph. (1967). *The Man From Oxbow: The Best of Ralph Allen*. Toronto: McClelland & Stewart.

Bain, George. (1991). "The Fourth Estate and libel chill." *Maclean's*, May 27: 58.

Bainbridge, Roger, ed. (1989). *Quiet Voices: Diverse Essays and Stories From the Whig-Standard Magazine*. Kingston, ON: Quarry Press and the *Whig-Standard*.

Bart, John T., ed. (1987). *Canadian Investors Manual: The Handbook for Learn-by-Doing Investing*. Windsor, ON: Canadian Shareowners Association.

Barzun, Jacques. (1986). *On Writing, Editing, and Publishing*. 2nd edition. Chicago: University of Chicago Press.

Bates, Jefferson D. (1985). *Writing With Precision*. Revised edition. Washington, DC: Acropolis Books.

Bates, Jem. (1996). *The Canadian Writer's Market*. 12th revised edition. Toronto: McClelland & Stewart.

Bazan, Judy, ed. (1998). *The Great Canadian Magazines Catalogue*. Toronto: Canadian Magazine Publishers Association.

Berger, John. (1972). *Ways of Seeing*. London: BBC.

Bernstein, Theodore M. (1977). *The Careful Writer: A Modern Guide to English Usage*. New York: Atheneum.

Biagi, Shirley. (1992). *Interviews That Work: A Practical Guide for Journalists*. Belmont, CA: Wadsworth Publishing Company.

Bird, Roger. (1997). *The End of News*. Toronto: Irwin.

Black, Edwin R. (1982). *Politics and the News*. Toronto: Butterworths.

Blundell, William E. (1988). *The Art and Craft of Feature Writing*. New York: Plume/Penguin.

Bourque, Pierre. (1996). *Government On-Line in Canada*. Toronto: Stoddart.

Brady, John. (1977). *The Craft of Interviewing*. New York: Vintage Books.

Bruser, Robert S., and Brian MacLeod Rogers. (1985). *Journalists and the Law: How to Get the Story Without Getting Sued or Put in Jail*. Ottawa: The Canadian Bar Foundation.

Buckley, Joanne. (1995). *Fit to Print: The Canadian Student's Guide to Essay Writing*. 3rd edition. Toronto: Harcourt Brace Canada.

Bulletin: The Canadian Association of Journalists. (1991). "Was it plagiarism or 'replication'?" Summer: 10–12.

Burchfield, R.W. (1996). *The New Fowler's Modern English Usage*. Oxford: Clarendon Press.

Bywater, Tim, and Thomas Sobchack. (1989). *Introduction to Film Criticism: Major Critical Approaches to Narrative Film*. New York: Longman.

Callwood, June. (1989). "Innermost echoes of the soul are heard in the human voice." *Globe and Mail*, August 30.

Cameron, Stevie. (1989). *Ottawa Inside Out*. Toronto: HarperCollins.

Canadian Advertising Rates and Data. (1997). *Publication Profiles*. Toronto: Maclean-Hunter.

Canadian Figure Skating Association. (1990). *Skating: An Inside Look*. Ottawa: The Canadian Figure Skating Association.

Canadian Labor Congress. *Notes on Unions*. This series of handouts produced by the leading labor federation includes a useful glossary of labor terms.

Carey, John, ed. (1987). *The Faber Book of Reportage*. London: Faber and Faber.

Carroll, Jim, and Rick Broadhead. (1996). *Canadian Internet Handbook*. 3rd edition. Scarborough, ON: Prentice-Hall.

Cassill, Kay. (1981). *The Complete Handbook for Freelance Writers.* Cincinnatti, OH: Writer's Digest Books.

Charity, Arthur. (1995). *Doing Public Journalism.* New York and London: The Guilford Press.

Cheveldayoff, Wayne. (1978). *The Business Page: How to Read It for Profit, Politics and Peace of Mind.* Ottawa: Deneau and Greenberg.

Christians, Clifford G., Kim B. Rotzoll, and Mark Fackler. (1995). *Media Ethics: Cases and Moral Reasoning.* 4th edition. New York and London: Longman.

Christians, Clifford G., Kim B. Rotzoll, and Mark Fackler. (1983). *Media Ethics: Cases and Moral Reasoning.* New York and London: Longman.

Clark, Roy Peter, and Don Fry. (1992). *Coaching Writers: Editors and Reporters Working Together.* New York: St. Martin's Press.

Cohen, Lynne, and Klaus Pohle. (1992). "Libel chill fever misguided." *content,* March-April: 14–15.

Copple, Neale. (1964). *Depth Reporting: An Approach to Journalism.* Englewood Cliffs, NJ: Prentice-Hall.

CP Stylebook: A Guide for Writers and Editors. (1995). Peter Buckley, ed. Revised edition. Toronto: The Canadian Press.

Crane, David. (1993). *The Canadian Dictionary of Business and Economics.* Toronto: Stoddart.

Crawford, Michael G. (1996). *The Journalist's Legal Guide.* 3rd edition. Toronto: Carswell.

Creighton, Donald. (1948). "Sir John Macdonald and Canadian historians." *Canadian Historical Review,* 29 (1) March: 1–13.

Cumming, Carman. (1988). "Ethics: No easy answers." *content,* May-June: 8–10.

Daintith, John, et al. (1988). *Who Said What When.* London: Bloomsbury.

Demers, David Pearce, and Suzanne Nichols. (1987). *Precision Journalism: A Practical Guide.* Newbury Park, CA: Sage Publications.

Desbarats, Peter. (1996). *Guide to Canadian News Media.* 2nd edition. Toronto: Harcourt Brace Canada.

Didion, Joan. (1968). *Slouching Towards Bethlehem.* New York: Farrar, Straus & Giroux.

Dolan, Rob. (1994). *A Reporter's Guide to Municipal Government.* Toronto: Association of Municipalities of Ontario.

Drobot, Eve, and Hal Tennant, eds. (1990). *Words for Sale.* Toronto: The Periodical Writers Association of Canada and Macmillan of Canada.

Eaman, Ross A. (1987). *The Media Society: Basic Issues and Controversies.* Toronto: Butterworths.

Ericson, Richard V. (1982). *Reproducing Order: A Study of Police Patrol Work.* Toronto: University of Toronto Press.

Ericson, Richard V. (1981). *Making Crime: A Study of Detective Work.* Scarborough, ON: Butterworths.

Fensch, Thomas. (1989). *Writing Solutions: Beginnings, Middles, & Endings.* Hillsdale, NJ: Lawrence Erlbaum Associates.

Ferguson, Jock, and Dawn King. (1988). "Behind the boom: The story of York region." Reprinted in *The Eye-Opener* (1989). Centre for Investigative Journalism.

Ferguson, Jock, and Paul Taylor. (1987). "High rise corridor engulfs Bay Street." *Globe and Mail*, December 12, 1987. Reprinted in *The Eye-Opener* (1988). Centre for Investigative Journalism.

Flaherty, Gerald A. (1984). *Defamation Law in Canada.* Ottawa: The Canadian Bar Foundation.

Franklin, Jon. (1986). *Writing for Story.* New York: Plume/Penguin.

Fraser, John. (1991). "The great 'libel chill' clash." *Saturday Night*, May: 10–13.

Frayne, Trent, ed. (1996). *Trent Frayne's Allstars: An Anthology of Canada's Best Sportswriting.* Toronto: Doubleday.

Frayne, Trent. (1990). *The Tales of an Athletic Supporter.* Toronto: McClelland & Stewart.

Freelance Editors' Association of Canada. (1987). *Editing Canadian English.* Vancouver: Douglas and McIntyre.

Frizzell, Alan, Jon H. Pammett, and Anthony Westell. (1994). *The Canadian General Election of 1993.* Ottawa: Carleton University Press.

Fulford, Robert, et al. (1981). *The Journalists.* Vol. 2, Research Publications, Royal Commission on Newspapers. Ottawa: Minister of Supply and Services.

Gerbner, George. (1981). "Ideological perspectives and political tendencies in news reporting." *Journalism Quarterly* 41(3): 495–508.

The Globe and Mail Style Book. (1996). J.A. McFarlane and Warren Clements, eds. Toronto: Penguin Books.

Goldberg, Kim. (1996). "Taking on Newspaper Chains." *Media*, Fall. This issue includes related articles on freelancers' copyright claims.

Goldstein, Tom. (1985). *The News at Any Cost.* New York: Simon & Schuster.

Gowers, Sir Ernest. (1986). *The Complete Plain Words.* 3rd edition. Revised by Sidney Greenbaum and Janet Whitcut. London: Her Majesty's Stationery Office.

Graham, Betsy P. (1980). *Magazine Article Writing.* New York: Holt Rinehart and Winston.

Gray, Charlotte. (1990). "Massaging the beast." *Saturday Night*, January-February.

Greenspon, Edward, and Anthony Wilson-Smith. (1996). *Double Vision: The Inside Story of the Liberals in Power.* Toronto: Doubleday.

Griffiths, Curt T., and Simon N. Verdun-Jones. (1994). *Canadian Criminal Justice.* 2nd edition. Toronto: Harcourt Brace.

Hayakawa, S.I., and Alan R. Hayakawa. (1990). *Language in Thought and Action.* 5th edition. New York: Harcourt Brace Jovanovich.

Hayes, David. (1992). *Power and Influence: The* Globe and Mail *and the News Revolution.* Toronto: Key Porter.

Heinrich, Jeff. (1990). "Media solidarity? Not when there's a good story to be had." *content*, September-October: 14.

Heron, Craig. (1996). *The Canadian Labor Movement: A Short History.* 2nd edition. Toronto: Lorimer.

Herrington, Doug. (1991). "Libel chill issue heats up." *content*, May-June: 8–9.

Higgins, Donald J.H. (1986). *Local and Urban Politics in Canada.* Toronto: Gage.

Hodges, John C., Mary E. Whitten, Judy Brown, and Jane Flick. (1994). *Harbrace College Handbook for Canadian Writers.* 4th edition. Toronto: Harcourt Brace.

Hohenberg, John. (1973). The *Professional Journalist.* 3rd edition. New York: Holt Rinehart and Winston.

Horowitz, Lois. (1984). *Knowing Where to Look: The Ultimate Guide to Research*. Cincinnati: Writer's Digest Books.

Hulteng, John L. (1985). *The Messenger's Motives*. 2nd edition. Englewood Cliffs, NJ: Prentice-Hall.

Hyatt, Laurel. (1994). "Silenced: Does private radio news have a future?" *Media*, October: 20–22.

Jackson, Robert J. and Doreen Jackson. (1996). *Canadian Government in Transition: Disruption and Continuity*. Scarborough, ON: Prentice-Hall.

Jackson, Robert J. and Doreen Jackson. (1994). *Politics in Canada: Culture, Institutions, Behaviour and Public Policy*. 3rd edition. Scarborough, ON: Prentice-Hall.

Justman, Stewart. (1983). "Orwell's plain style." *University of Toronto Quarterly* 53(2), Winter 1983–84: 195–203.

Keith, W.J., and Ben-Zion Shek. (1980). *The Arts in Canada: The Last Fifty Years*. Toronto: University of Toronto Press.

Kessler, Lauren, and Duncan McDonald. (1996). *When Words Collide: A Journalist's Guide to Grammar and Style*. 4th edition. Belmont, CA: Wadsworth.

Kluge, Pamela Hollie, ed. (1991). *The Columbia Knight-Bagehot Guide to Business and Economics Journalism*. New York: Columbia University Press.

Koestler, Arthur. (1964). *The Act of Creation*. New York: Macmillan.

Lambeth, Edmund B. (1992). *Committed Journalism: An Ethic for the Profession*. 2nd edition. Bloomington, IN: Indiana University Press.

Landes, Ronald G. (1991). *The Canadian Polity: A Comparative Introduction*. 3rd edition. Scarborough, ON: Prentice-Hall.

Levy, Harold J. (1986). *A Reporter's Guide to Canada's Criminal Justice System*. Ottawa: The Canadian Bar Foundation.

Lippmann, Walter. (1955). *The Public Philosophy*. Boston: Little Brown.

Lorimer, Rowland, and Jean McNulty. (1996). *Mass Communication in Canada*. 3rd edition. Toronto and New York: Oxford University Press.

MacNeil, Robert. (1989). *Wordstruck*. New York: Viking.

MacVoy, Sheila, ed. (1994). *Who Pays What, 1994–95: A Writer's Guide to Canadian Markets*. Toronto: Canadian Periodical Writers Association.

Martin, Robert. (1997). *Media Law*. Toronto: Irwin Law.

Martin, Robert. (1991a). "Criticizing the judges." 28 *McGill Law Journal* 1: 13–20. Reprinted in Robert Martin and G. Stuart Adam, *A Sourcebook of Canadian Media Law* (274–276). Revised edition (new case material). Ottawa: Carleton University Press.

Martin, Robert. (1991b). "Does libel have a 'chilling effect' in Canada?" In Robert Martin and G. Stuart Adam, *A Sourcebook of Canadian Media Law* (757–770). Revised edition (new case material). Ottawa: Carleton University Press.

Martin, Robert, and G. Stuart Adam. (1991). *A Sourcebook of Canadian Media Law*. Revised edition (new case material). Ottawa: Carleton University Press.

McCartney, James. (1997). "News lite," *American Journalism Review*, June: 19–25.

McGuire, Mary, Linda Stilborne, Melinda McAdams, and Laurel Hyatt. (1997). *The Internet Handbook for Writers, Researchers and Journalists*. Toronto: Trifolium Books.

McLaughlin, Paul. (1990). *How to Interview: The Art of the Media Interview*. Vancouver and Toronto: International Self-Counsel Press.

McNaught, Carlton. (1940). *Canada Gets the News*. Toronto: Ryerson.

Metzler, Ken. (1977). *Creative Interviewing*. Englewood Cliffs, NJ: Prentice-Hall.

Meyer, Philip. (1979). *Precision Journalism*. 2nd edition. Bloomington, IN, and London: Indiana University Press.

Miller, John. (1990). "Rethinking old methods." *content*, September-October: 23–25.

Morton, Desmond. (1990). *Working People: An Illustrated History of the Canadian Labour Movement*. Revised and updated. Toronto: Summerhill Press.

Neff, Glenda Tennant. (1991). *The Writer's Essential Desk Reference*. Cincinnati, OH: Writer's Digest Books.

Nichols, Ralph G. (1948). "Factors accounting for differences in comprehension of materials presented orally in the classroom." Cited in Frank R. DiSilvestro (1989), *Effective Listening in the Classroom*. Bloomington, IN: Indiana University Office for Learning Resources. March.

Noble, Kimberley. (1992). *Bound and Gagged: Libel Chill and the Right to Publish*. From the *Point of View* series. Toronto: HarperCollins.

Orwell, George. (1968). "Politics and the English language." In Sonia Orwell and Ian Angus, eds., *The Collected Essays, Journalism & Letters of George Orwell* (127–140). London: Secker & Warburg.

Osborn, Alex F. (1963). *Applied Imagination: Principles and Procedures of Creative Problem-Solving*. 3rd revised edition. New York: Charles Scribner's Sons.

Overbury, Stephen. (1989). *Finding Canadian Facts Fast*. Revised edition. Toronto: McGraw-Hill Ryerson.

Patterson, Philip, and Lee Wilkins. (1994). *Media Ethics: Issues and Cases*. 2nd edition. Dubuque, IO: William C. Brown.

Pavlik, John V. (1997). "The Future of Online Journalism." *Columbia Journalism Review*, July-August: 30–36.

Porter, Julian. (1987). *Libel: A Handbook for Canadian Publishers, Editors and Writers*. Toronto: Canadian Book Publishers' Council.

Prosser, David. (1989). "What are reviewers for?" In Roger Bainbridge, ed., *Quiet Voices: Diverse Essays and Stories from the Whig-Standard Magazine*. Kingston, ON: Quarry Press and the *Whig-Standard*.

Reid, Cheryl. (1992). "Anonymous sources bring down a senator." *Washington Journalism Review*, April: 10.

Richman, Alan. (1991). "The death of sportswriting." GQ, September: 254–261, 334–337.

Rivers, William L., and Cleve Mathews. (1988). *Ethics for the Media*. Englewood Cliffs, NJ: Prentice-Hall.

Rivers, William L., and Alison R. Work. (1986). *Free-Lancer and Staff Writer*. 4th edition. Belmont, CA: Wadsworth Publishing Company.

Robertson, Stuart M. (1983). *Media Law Handbook*. Vancouver: International Self-Counsel Press.

Royal Commission on Newspapers. (1981). *Report*. Ottawa: Supply and Services Canada.

Rudolph, Barbara. (1995). "Skirting the issue." *Time*, June 5: 44–48.

Russell, Nicholas. (1994). *Morals and the Media: Ethics in Canadian Journalism*. Vancouver: UBC Press.

Saunders, Eileen. (1992). "Mass media and the reproduction of marginalization." In Frederick J. Fletcher, ed., *Reporting the Campaign: Election Coverage in Canada*. Vol. 22, Research Studies, Royal Commission on Electoral Reform and Party Financing. Toronto: Dundurn Press.

Sawatsky, John. (1991). *Mulroney: The Politics of Ambition*. Toronto: Macfarlane, Walter and Ross.

Schiller, Dan. (1981). *Objectivity and the News: The Public and the Rise of Commercial Journalism*. Philadelphia: University of Pennsylvania Press.

Sewell, John. (1985). *Police: Urban Policing in Canada*. Toronto: Lorimer.

Singer, Benjamin D. (1995). *Communications in Canadian Society*. 4th edition. Toronto: Nelson Canada.

Slinger, John H. (1985). *No Axe Too Small to Grind: The Best of Joey Slinger*. Toronto: McClelland & Stewart.

Steel, Ronald. (1980). *Walter Lippmann and the American Century*. Boston: Atlantic Monthly Press/Little Brown and Company.

Stein, David Lewis. (1993). *Going Downtown: Reflections on Urban Progress*. Ottawa: Oberon.

Stein, David Lewis. (1972). *Toronto for Sale*. Toronto: New Press.

Stephens, Mitchell. (1997). *A History of News*. 2nd edition. Fort Worth: Harcourt Brace.

Stroud, Carsten. (1985). *The Blue Wall: Street Cops in Canada*. Toronto: McClelland & Stewart.

Strunk, William, Jr., and E.B. White. (1979). *The Elements of Style*. 3rd edition. New York: Macmillan.

Talese, Gay. (1966). *The Kingdom and the Power*. New York: World Publishing.

Taras, David. (1990). *The Newsmakers: The Media's Influence on Canadian Politics*. Scarborough, ON: Nelson Canada.

Tasini, Jonathan. (1990). "Lost in the margins: Labour and the media." *Extra!*, Fairness and Accuracy in Reporting newsletter, Vol. 3, No. 7, Summer.

Tindal, C.R., and S. Nobes Tindal. (1995). *Local Government in Canada*. 4th edition. Toronto: McGraw-Hill Ryerson.

Tuchman, Barbara. (1982). *Practicing History*. New York: Ballantine.

Van Loon, Richard J., and Michael S. Whittington. (1996). *The Canadian Political System: Environment, Structure and Process*. 6th edition. Toronto: McGraw-Hill Ryerson.

Verma, Anil. (1990). "The lonely seven: Full-time reporters — an endangered species." *content*, May-June: 10–11.

Vipond, Mary. (1992). *The Mass Media in Canada*. 2nd edition. Toronto: Lorimer.

Ward, Jean, and Kathleen A. Hansen. (1997). *Search Strategies in Mass Communication*. 3rd edition. New York and London: Longman.

Webb, Eugene J., and Terry R. Salancik. (1966). "The interview, or The only wheel in town." In Bruce H. Westley, ed., *Journalism Monographs*, No. 2, November.

Westell, Anthony. (1976). "Reporting the nation's business." In G. Stuart Adam, ed., *Journalism, Communication and the Law*. Scarborough, ON: Prentice-Hall.

Wilhoit, G. Cleveland, and David H. Weaver. (1990). *Newsroom Guide to Polls & Surveys*. Bloomington: Indiana University Press.

Williams, Jeremy S. (1988). *The Law of Libel and Slander in Canada*. 2nd edition. Toronto: Butterworths.

Winter, James. (1997). *Democracy's Oxygen: How Corporations Control the News*. Montreal: Black Rose Books.

Yudkin, Marcia. (1987). *Freelance Writing for Magazines and Newspapers*. New York: Harper & Row.

Zinsser, William. (1994). *On Writing Well*. 5th edition. New York: Harper & Row.

Zuber, Thomas G. (1974). *Introduction to Canadian Criminal Law*. Toronto: McGraw-Hill Ryerson.

Zuehlke, Mark, and Louise Donnelly. (1992). *Magazine Writing From the Boonies*. Ottawa: Carleton University Press.

INDEX

READER REPLY CARD

We are interested in your reaction to *The Canadian Reporter, Second Edition* by Catherine McKercher and Carman Cumming. You can help us to improve this book in future editions by completing this questionnaire.

1. What was your reason for using this book?
   ☐ university course   ☐ college course   ☐ continuing education course
   ☐ professional   ☐ personal   ☐ other _____
       development   interest   _____

2. If you are a student, please identify your school and the course in which you used this book.

3. Which chapters or parts of this book did you use? Which did you omit?

4. What did you like best about this book?

5. What did you like least about this book?

6. Please identify any topics you think should be added to future editions.

7. Please add any comments or suggestions.

8. May we contact you for further information?

Name: _____

Address: _____

_____

Phone: _____

(fold here and tape shut)

0116870399-M8Z4X6-BR01

Larry Gillevet
Director of Product Development
HARCOURT CANADA
55 HORNER AVENUE
TORONTO, ONTARIO
M8Z 9Z9